1

A Companion to the BIBLE

A Companion to the BIBLE

by

MIRIAM WARD, R.S.M.
Editor

ALBA · HOUSE NEW · YORK

SOCIETY OF ST. PAUL, 2187 VICTORY BLVD., STATEN ISLAND, NEW YORK 10314

Library of Congress Cataloging in Publication Data

Main entry under title:

A Companion to the Bible.

  Includes bibliographies.
  1. Bible—Criticism, interpretation, etc.—Addresses,
essays, lectures. I. Ward, Miriam.
BS511.2.C65   1985   220.6   85-15817
ISBN 0-8189-0487-9

Designed, printed and bound in the United States of
America by the Fathers and Brothers of the
Society of St. Paul, 2187 Victory Boulevard,
Staten Island, New York 10314, as part of their
communications apostolate.

1 2 3 4 5 6 7 8 9 (Current Printing: first digit)

FOREWORD

REV. JOSEPH A. MIRRO
Institute Coordinator

The story of the Bible has always been about people. From its origins among the people of ancient Israel, to its global influence today, the Bible has been bringing people together to tell and retell the story of God. Whether your knowledge of Scripture is limited or extensive, I think you will find this volume helpful as this story continues to unfold in your own life and study. But first, a word about the people involved in this book.

A very recent chapter in the long and rich history of the Bible has been unfolding these twenty years in the mountains of Vermont. In November, 1965, the Second Vatican Council of the Roman Catholic Church promulgated the *Dogmatic Constitution on Divine Revelation.* Inspired by this document and the deep current of ecumenism that was running through Christianity, the first annual Trinity College Biblical Institute took place the following June in Burlington. Every spring since then teachers and students of the Bible have been gathering on the campus on Colchester Avenue.

The teachers are members of a particularly distinguished group of Catholic, Protestant and Jewish scholars from Europe, America and the Near East. Their work is on the cutting edge of contemporary biblical studies. The students, now numbering over 4,000, have come from all over the United States, Canada, and eight other nations.

However, scholarship alone does not accurately characterize this institute. Together with Rev. Thomas

Aquinas Collins, O.P., who served as associate director until 1977, Sister Miriam Ward, R.S.M. founded it and has made it a reality every year. Through her effort the spirit of communal faith and ecumenism which first inspired the institute has never faded. It is the experience of truly biblical faith, love and hope that keeps faculty and participants coming back year after year.

While the printed word can never have the life and impact of the spoken, I think you will find that this book captures both the scholarship and spirit of the institute. In the editing, Sister Miriam has just as carefully selected the authors from among the institute's excellent faculty members as she has carefully provided the faculty each spring. The authors themselves have responded to this project with the same eagerness and warmth that they have brought to the annual gathering. Many of the articles have been presented at Trinity College. All of them reflect the institute's scholarship.

Incidently, this is not the first time the research of the institute has taken form in print. In 1975, on the occasion of the tenth anniversary, Sister Miriam edited a similar volume entitled *Biblical Studies in Contemporary Thought,* including articles by Raymond Brown, Peter Duncker, T.A. Collins, Eugene Borowitz, Peter Ellis, Eugene Maly and George Ernest Wright among others. In 1980, Reginald H. Fuller and Pheme Perkins collaborated on a series of lectures on Christology which resulted in the book entitled *Who Is This Christ?* (Philadelphia: Fortress Press, 1983). M. Lucetta Mowry's series of lectures, *Paul At Corinth: His Message To A Divided Church* will appear in 1985 in book form. Many other lectures have appeared in various books and periodicals over the years.

In the twenty years since that first institute there has been many a revolutionary breakthrough in biblical studies.

From the impact of new methods from the science of language to the application of the high technology of the age of computers, the story of the Bible has entered the twenty-first century. Keeping track of these developments however, has become increasingly difficult. Scholars have become more and more specialized, and for the beginner or the general reader, comprehension of the field has become almost impossible.

This book then, is of great value to both the general reader and the specialized student. The articles, covering topics from current trends to the future of biblical studies, encompass a large portion of the spectrum of recent developments. So, whether your interest is in one particular area or in an overview of the story of the Bible in the '80s, I think you will find this work a real *Companion to the Bible*.

PREFACE

MIRIAM WARD, R.S.M.

This book is a celebration of life — life at its deepest
level: faith. It commemorates on the one hand twenty years
of implementing the call to renewal made by Vatican
Council II as witnessed in the annual Biblical Institute at
Trinity College. At the same time it commemorates the
great strides made in the field of biblical studies. But its
purpose is greater than simply marking a milestone on the
way. It is my firm hope that this book will serve to inspire
others to further renewal in their search for meaning in and
through the Scriptures.

Vatican Council II did for Roman Catholics what
Luther accomplished for Protestants: put the Bible into the
hands of the ordinary person on the street. So the saying
goes. But it might be more accurate to say "attempted" to
bring the Scriptures into the center of the average person's
life. The directives of Vatican II clearly indicate the concern
for reviving the liturgy and daily life of the people through a
deeper understanding of the Bible. But how to accomplish
this revival? One response has been through the annual
Biblical Institute with its roster of scholars at the forefront of
the modern biblical movement.

In comparing the past 50 years with the previous mil-

lennium, perhaps there is no field of study which has made
such revolutionary gains as that of biblical studies. The
resulting wealth of knowledge among biblical scholars has
created a need to translate and transmit the results of their
study to the non-specialist. Uppermost in the planning of
each Trinity College Biblical Institute has been the quality
of the faculty: excellence has been and is the basis of selection. The rationale is simple: at the heart of real renewal
must be a sound foundation. The authors whose essays are
represented in this book demonstrate both their scholarly
competence and ability to convey their scholarship to those
who have not had the leisure or inclination to pursue such
studies on their own, and at the same time to enrich those
whose ministerial function demands an on-going personal
formation for the good of their respective congregations.
Roman Catholic scholars are fulfilling the mandate of Vatican Council II to be the instruments in bringing about this
renewal at the grassroots level. Representation of Protestant
and Jewish contributors to this volume characterizes the
ecumenical atmosphere in which the Trinity Institutes have
been conducted. Long before ecumenism became a household word among the faithful, it was practiced among biblical scholars. Happily it now lends a liberating effect in the
common search for deeper meaning in the Scriptures.

Profound scholarship and the ability to transmit the
resulting knowledge to the non-specialist must have an audience. The thirst for a deeper spirituality and more mature
faith, a desire to look to the Bible as a challenge rather than a
support for one's preconceived answers, have characterized
those who have attended the Biblical Institute through the
years. This response on the part of Roman Catholics —
priests as well as the laity — to the charge of Vatican Council
II to read the Bible critically has been very heartening.
Likewise, the presence of Protestants and Jews at the Insti-

tute has been gratifying. However, much remains to be done. We have hardly scratched the surface: the gap between the high level of biblical scholarship and the ecumenical atmosphere in which this work is conducted on the one hand, and the acquisition of this knowledge for a less fundamentalistic approach to the Bible is enormous. We have just begun to close this gap. Indeed, it is the very raison d'etre of this book and the Biblical Institute from which it results. Renewal is a long and difficult, sometimes painful, process. Our hope is that through touching the lives of the thousands of persons who have attended our Institute in these two decades, they in turn will have brought about within their sphere of activity some incentives for renewal of life in faith. The aim of this book is to lead others to study the exciting and inspiring new approaches to the Bible. For the student who is just starting to get acquainted with the Bible and for the interested, educated non-specialist this book will provide insights and perspectives from some of the best representatives in the field.

Through the years I have been deeply impressed by a common characteristic of the biblical scholars who have comprised our faculty: humilty, a deep faith, and love for the Scriptures. Their commitment to the often tedious work of scholarship and their efforts to transmit this to "the folks in the pews" leave me with a feeling of gratitude. The image of scholars playing intellectual games is shattered through contact with these men and women. In the introductions to each section of this book, therefore, I shall focus more on the person behind the essay, and let each article speak for itself. In so doing I think I shall fulfill a responsibility incumbent upon a teacher to introduce to a class the eminent scholars in the field, in this case, the area of biblical studies.

I would be remiss if I did not mention a word of thanks to the faculty members whose articles are not included in this book. The explanation is fairly simple: the faculty now numbers 56, and they have been a prolific group. Because we were limited to one volume, selection of articles had to be restricted. The omission of some articles in no way reflects on the scholarship of those authors.

In planning the first Biblical Institute in 1966, I was encouraged by the immediate and enthusiastic response of Dr. James B. Pritchard who gave at that Institute the first public lecture ever delivered on Tel es-Saidiyeh. That first biblical faculty has a special place in my heart: James Pritchard, Peter Ellis, and Rev. Thomas Aquinas Collins, O.P., who served as associate director until 1975.

To Lucetta Mowry, consultant, contributor, and friend, I give my heartfelt thanks for her unwavering support.

For our faithful staff who have created the spirit of real community for each Institute, words are inadequate. Father Joe Mirro, Bill Greenwood, Sisters Jeanne Gonyom, O.C.D., Rita Hammond, R.S.M., Rose Rowan, R.S.M., Saint Jerome Gribbon, C.S.J., I thank you.

From the inception of the Institute a book display has been an integral part of the program, and my gratitude is due to Thom Wombwell, formerly of Episcopal Theological Bookstore, Cambridge, MA, and to Bill and Roddy Cleary of Hopkins Bookshop, Burlington, VT for helping us to promote good literature on the Word of God.

ACKNOWLEDGMENTS

Grateful acknowledgment is made to the following authors and publishers for permission to use material under their copyright:

"The Bible As A Classic and the Bible As Holy Scripture" by Krister Stendahl. Reprinted from *The Journal of Biblical Literature*, Vol. 103, No. 1 (1984), pp. 3-10. Reprinted with permission of the Editors.

"Biblical Studies Since 1950" by John L. McKenzie. Reprinted from *Cross Currents*, Vol. 31 (Winter, 1981-82), pp. 400-406. Reprinted with permission of the Editors.

"What Is Happening In New Testament Studies?" by Reginald H. Fuller. Reprinted from *St. Luke's Journal of Theology*, Vol. 23, No. 2 (1980), pp. 90-100. Reprinted with permission of the Editors.

"The Meaning of the Bible" by Raymond E. Brown. Reprinted from *The Critical Meaning of the Bible* (New York: Paulist Press, 1981), Chapter Two, pp. 23-44. Reprinted with permission of the Publishers.

"The Dilemma of a Translator" by M. Lucetta Mowry. Lectures given at the 18th Biblical Institute, Trinity College, Burlington, Vermont, June 20-25, 1982. Printed with permission of the author.

"The Revised Standard Version" by Bruce M. Metzger. Reprinted from *Duke Divinity School Review*, Vol. 44 (1979), pp. 71-87. Reprinted with permission of the Editors.

"Inspired Texts: The Dilemma of a Feminist Believer" by Carolyn Osiek. Reprinted from *Spirituality Today*, Vol. 32 (1980), pp. 138-147. Reprinted with permission of the Editors.

"The Contributions of Archaeology to Biblical Studies" by Philip J. King. Reprinted from *The Catholic Biblical Quarterly*, Vol. 45, No. 1 (Jan., 1983), pp. 1-16. Reprinted with permission of the Editors.

"The International God *Elohim/Ntr*" by Cyrus H. Gordon. Reprinted from *Hebrew Studies*, Vol. 23 (1982), pp. 33-35. Reprinted with permission of the Editors.

"Corinthian Bronze" by Jerome Murphy - O'Connor. Reprinted from *Revue Biblique*, Vol. 90, No. 1 (1983), pp. 80-93. Reprinted with permission of the Editors.

"Tradition and Scripture in the Community of Faith" by Bernhard W. Anderson. Reprinted from *The Journal of Biblical Literature*, Vol. 100, No. 1, (Jan., 1981), pp. 5-21. Reprinted with permission of the Editors.

"The Artful Dialogue: Some Thoughts on the Relation of Biblical Studies and Homiletics" by Elizabeth Achtemeier. Reprinted from *Interpretation*, Vol. 35, No. 1, (Jan., 1981), pp. 18-31. Reprinted with permission of the Editors.

"The God of the Hebrew Scriptures" by Bruce Vawter. Reprinted from *The Biblical Theology Bulletin*, Vol. 12, (1982), pp. 3-7. Reprinted with permission of the Editors.

"The Prophetic Combat For Peace" by Carroll Stuhlmueller. Reprinted from *The Way*, Vol. 22, (1982), pp. 79-87. Reprinted with permission of the Editors.

"The Theological Contributions of Israel's Wisdom Literature" by Roland E. Murphy. Reprinted from *Listening*, Vol. 19, No. 1, (Winter, 1984), pp. 30-40. Reprinted with permission of the Editors.

"An Apocalyptic Shift in Early Christian Tradition: Reflections on Some Canonical Evidence" by Paul J. Achtemeier. Reprinted from *The Catholic Biblical Quarterly*, Vol. 45, No. 2, (April, 1983), pp. 231-248. Reprinted with permission of the Editors.

"The Eucharist in Mark" by Donald Senior. Reprinted from *The Biblical Theology Bulletin*, Vol. 12, No. 3, (1982). Reprinted with permission of the Editors.

"Christ's Resurrection as Mystery of Love"by Gerald O'Collins. Reprinted from *Heythrop Journal*, Vol. 25, (1984), pp. 39-50. Reprinted with permission of the Editors.

"Idealism and Realism in Paul" by David M. Stanley. Reprinted from *The Way*, Vol. 21, (1981), pp. 34-46. Reprinted with permission of the Editors.

"Dissent Within A Religious Community: Romans 9-11" by James A. Fischer. Reprinted from *The Biblical Theology Bulletin*, Vol. 10, (1980), pp. 105-110. Reprinted with permission of the Editors.

"New Patches On An Old Garment: The Book of Revelation" by Archbishop John F. Whealon. Reprinted from *The Biblical Theology Bulletin*, Vol. 11, (1981), pp. 54-59. Reprinted with permission of the Editors.

I am very grateful to Mrs. Erica Randall for her tireless assistance in preparing the manuscript.

CONTENTS

NEW TESTAMENT THEMES

THE FUTURE OF BIBLICAL STUDIES

A Companion to the BIBLE

ABBREVIATIONS

Old Testament

Genesis	Gn	Proverbs	Pr
Exodus	Ex	Ecclesiastes	Ec
Leviticus	Lv	Songs of Songs	Sg
Numbers	Nb	Wisdom	Ws
Deuteronomy	Dt	Sirach	Si
Joshua	Jos	Isaiah	Is
Judges	Jg	Jeremiah	Jr
Ruth	Rt	Lamentations	Lm
1 Samuel	1 S	Baruch	Ba
2 Samuel	2 S	Ezekiel	Ezk
1 Kings	1 K	Daniel	Dn
2 Kings	2 K	Hosea	Ho
1 Chronicles	1 Ch	Joel	Jl
2 Chronicles	2 Ch	Amos	Am
Ezra	Ezr	Obadiah	Ob
Nehemiah	Ne	Jonah	Jon
Tobit	Tb	Micah	Mi
Judith	Jdt	Nahum	Na
Esther	Est	Habakkuk	Hab
1 Maccabees	1 M	Zephaniah	Zp
2 Maccabees	2 M	Haggai	Hg
Job	Jb	Malachi	Ml
Psalms	Ps	Zechariah	Zc

New Testament

Matthew	Mt	1 Timothy	1 Tm
Mark	Mk	2 Timothy	2 Tm
Luke	Lk	Titus	Tt
John	Jn	Philemon	Phm
Acts	Ac	Hebrews	Heb
Romans	Rm	James	Jm
1 Corinthians	1 Cor	1 Peter	1 P
2 Corinthians	2 Cor	2 Peter	2 P
Galatians	Gal	1 John	1 Jn
Ephesians	Ep	2 John	2 Jn
Philippians	Ph	3 John	3 Jn
Colossians	Col	Jude	Jude
1 Thessalonians	1 Th	Revelation	Rv
2 Thessalonians	2 Th		

CURRENT TRENDS IN BIBLICAL STUDIES

Introduction

MIRIAM WARD, R.S.M.
Trinity College,
Burlington, VT 05401

In his keynote address to the first annual Biblical Institute at Trinity College in 1966, T.A. Collins, O.P. presented the topic "Biblical Studies Today." In that talk Father Collins surveyed the tremendous strides that had been made in the field of biblical studies, particularly among Catholic exegetes since the publication of *Divino Afflante Spiritu* in 1943. He noted the accomplishments, but at the same time the problems confronting scholars, and pointed to the vast potential as well as the limitations of biblical studies. All in all he charted a very promising future.

As we move into the latter part of this 20th century I think it appropriate to reflect once again on the current trends in biblical studies, and to assess the state of the discipline. In the articles that follow various perspectives will be represented: that of a Swedish Lutheran, a Roman Catholic and an Anglican. One will readily be impressed by the common ground that seems to obtain. The potential impact for ecumenical dialogue is immeasurable.

Krister Stendahl, until recently the Dean of Harvard Divinity School, and now the Bishop of the Swedish Lutheran Church in Stockholm, is one of the most distinguished interpreters of the New Testament, particularly the letters of Paul. In the lead article for this volume, Bishop Stendahl points to the shift from history to story in its literary and philosophical aspects that has taken place in recent biblical scholarship. He concludes with an insistence that the normative dimension is an irreducible part of Scripture and therefore demands "the services of the descriptive biblical scholars." The Bible is a classic precisely because it is regarded as the Holy Scriptures. To attempt to consider the Bible as simply a classic is to force a dichotomy which at best is contrived, artificial. Sound biblical criticism, therefore, must bear this in mind.

One of the most prolific, widely read, and highly regarded biblical scholars of our time, John L. McKenzie can indeed say, "You may say that I was there." For many of us it was his *The Two-Edged Sword,* published in 1956, that introduced us to the modern biblical movement.

A Jesuit with the critical training so valued in biblical studies, Father McKenzie not only has been "there," but "tells it like it is," even from "retirement." His forthright presentation of the trends in biblical studies by Roman Catholic scholars is placed in the context of liberation from the restrictions placed upon Catholic scholars by the pontifical magisterium. He spells out what scholars have been liberated *from* over the past thirty years, but challenges scholars and biblical students to discover more precisely what they were liberated *for.*

Although Reginald H. Fuller had been writing for a decade prior to the publication of *A Critical Introduction to the New Testament* in 1966, it was this book that introduced him to the United States as one of the most critical thinkers whose succeeding years of teaching and writing would carry a profound influence upon American biblical scholarship. An ordained priest in the Anglican communion, Reginald Fuller explores in the third article of this section the current state of New Testament studies, in a sense up-dating his 1962 *The New Testament in Current Study*. His reflections on the historical situation expand while complementing those made by John L. McKenzie. He sets forth a problem for biblical scholars on how to make the message of Scripture "heard" by the community of faith today. He presents here his response to the charge that biblical exegesis in some of its forms is bankrupt. At the same time he challenges biblical scholars to relate their work of theological exegesis of the NT within the contexts of (a) the NT canon as a whole, (b) the OT canon, as well as (c) the on-going tradition of creeds and confessions "in dialogue with dogmatic and systematic theology."

The more precise delineation of hermeneutical problems alluded to in this first section on the "state of the discipline" will be found in the next section of this book.

The Bible As A Classic And The Bible As Holy Scripture*

KRISTER STENDAHL
Harvard Divinity School
Cambridge, MA 02138

Thirty years ago there was hardly any attention to an alternative like the Bible as a classic and the Bible as Holy Scripture. Then the proper discussion was about the Bible as history and the Bible as Holy Scripture. And the battle was about *geschichtlich und historisch,* historic and historical, about historicity and myth, the historical Jesus and the kerygmatic Christ, history of salvation and just plain history.

Now there has been a shift from history to story: the Bible as story, theology as story.[1] For both philosophical and literary reasons the focus on language and on forms of literary criticism demand the center stage. The odd idea of a "language event" strikes me as a hybrid in the transition from the one perspective to the other.

It is tempting to speculate about deeper cultural forces at work in this shift. Could it be that preoccupation with history comes natural when one is part of a culture which feels happy and hopeful about the historical process? Hegel's pan-historic philosophy belongs, after all, to the ascendancy of western imperialism — it was even said that other parts of the world were lifted "into history" when conquered, colonized, or converted by the West. Now the western world is not so sure or so optimistic about where history — that is, "our" history — is going. So the glamour, the glory, the Shekinah has moved away from history.

There is a striking analogy to such a move from history to story and wisdom. I think of the major move of rabbinic Judaism after the fall of Jerusalem and the Bar Kokhba catastrophe. Rabbinic Judaism — a child of the very tradition which is often credited with having given "the idea of history" to the world — cut loose from the frantic attempts at finding meaning in and through history. At Jamnia and through the Mishnah the center of religious existence was placed in Halakah, i.e., in the lifestyle and wisdom of Torah. To be sure, the historical consciousness remained strong in Judaism, but not any more as the center of attention. It becomes exactly "story," Haggadah, with far less binding authority. To be sure, the Mishnah and the Talmud are not the sum total of Judaism. There are the prayers and the memories, but the center, the equivalent to what Christians came to call theology, is in Torah as Halakah. Those Jewish writings that struggled with meaning in and through history, writings like 4 Ezra and 2 Baruch, have survived through Christian transmission.[2] They were not part of the living tradition of Judaism. It was the Christians, new on the block, who inherited and renewed the historical mode. To them history was not mute, for now "in these last days God has spoken to us by a Son" (Heb 1:2). With continuity and with fulfillment, history worked well — or what turned out to be a very long time — a time which now may come to an end in western theology.

Whatever the value and truth of such rather wild speculations, the shift in contemporary biblical and theological work from history to story is obvious and well substantiated by a perusal of the program for the annual meeting of our Society of Biblical Literature and of our sister, the American Academy of Religion.

Thus it has become natural to think in the pattern of the Bible as a classic and the Bible as Holy Scripture. The shift is appealing for a very simple additional reason. It expresses so much better the way in which the Bible actually exists within our western culture, and sometimes even beyond its confines: as a classic with often undefined distinctions on a sliding scale of holiness and respect.

By "classic" I mean any work that is considered worth attention beyond its time, and sometimes also beyond its space — although I doubt there is any truly global classic — across all cultures. It would be western myopia to claim such recognition for Homer or for Shakespeare, or even for the Bible. For it is its recognition that makes a classic a classic, not its inner qualities. Hence I try to avoid the more romantic terminology in which modern studies abound, such as "excess of meaning" or "the power of disclosure." Such terminology tends to obscure the societal dimension of a classic. It is common recognition by a wide constituency of a society that makes a certain work into a classic. No inner quality suffices unless widely so recognized.

Thus I limit myself to western culture and its classics. There is the Bible, Dante, Milton, Cervantes' *Don Quixote,* and Shaw's *Pygmalion* — becoming even more of a classic by dropping the Greek name for the English title *My Fair Lady.* And there are the classics of philosophy and science: Plato, Aristotle, Kant's *Critiques,* and Darwin's *Origin of Species.* There are classics of law and classics of medicine. There is even Kierkegaard, who wrote a novel with the title *Fear and Trembling* — he did call it a novel.

Furthermore, as the West broadens its perspective

there are ways in which the Quran and the Gita become
classics in our eyes. We read the holy texts of other communities as classics, mostly without consciousness of their
being "only" classics. Readers find that such classics speak to
them, often in undefined ways.

So there are many types of classics, and they come in
many shapes and forms, in various styles and genres. And
awareness of the genre is part of their being a classic for the
reader. To speak of the Bible as a classic is therefore not the
same as speaking of it as a literary classic. The issue is rather
how to assess what kind of a classic we are dealing with.
Scholars are of course free to pronounce it — or its various
parts — a literary classic, or a classic of language, or a classic
of history, or a classic of philosophy, or whatever. But as a
living classic in western culture the perceptions of common
discourse on a more democratic basis are decisive. And it is
my contention that such perceptions include an irreducible
awareness of the Bible as Holy Writ in church and/or
synagogue.

What then about Holy Scripture? That designation is
not innocent of culture and theology. It is our language.
After all, Quran means "recitation," not "scripture," and the
Hebrew Bible knows not only the *kĕtîb* but also the *qĕrê* —
Jesus presumably never used the *kĕtîb* Yahweh.

It is as Holy Scripture, Holy Writ, that the Bible has
become a classic in the West. Personally, I prefer the plural
form, Holy Scriptures. I do so not primarily in recognition
of the fascinating and often elusive ways in which the
Hebrew Bible is common to Jews and Christians — the same
text word for word, and yet so different when it becomes the
Old Testament of the Christian Bible. I speak rather of
"Holy Scriptures," plural, in order to highlight the diversity
of style and genre within the scriptures. In various ways such
diversity becomes important for those to whom the

scriptures function as the bearer of revelation.[3] When the Bible functions as a classic in culture, such distinctions play no significant role, but for theological and philosophical reflection it is crucial. In the scriptures we have the oracles, the laws, the prophets, the dreams, the interpreters of dreams, the wisdom, the history, the stories, the psalms, the letters, and so on. To be sure, it is a whole library. Bible means after all, "the little books."

Nevertheless, what makes the Bible the Bible is the canon. Here is where the Bible as a classic and as Holy Scripture meet: the canonical books, bound together by those complex historical acts of recognition in the communities of faith which we can trace as the history of canonization. For it is as Bible that the biblical material has become a classic of the western world, and whatever part of the Bible is in focus — be it Job or Leviticus, the Christmas story or the Sermon on the Mount — it functions as a classic by being part of the Bible. It is perceived and received as a classic by being part of the Bible.

The Bible as a classic exists in western culture with an often undefined but never absent recognition of its being the Holy Scriptures of the church and/or the synagogue. I have my doubts that it — or substantial parts of it, at least — would have ever become a classic were it not for its status as Holy Scripture. Perhaps not even Job, the literary favorite; certainly not Leviticus, except as a legal classic. And Arthur Darby Nock used to say that the Gospel of John did not become beautiful as literature until 1611, when the King James Version gave it a beauty far beyond what the Greeks perceived.[4]

It is as Holy Scripture that the Bible is a classic in our culture. Therefore there is something artificial in the idea of "the Bible as literature." Or rather, it can be artificial and contrary to the perception of both most believers and most unbelievers, as artificial as "the Bible as history" or "the Bible as a textbook in geology or biology" or — the Bible as anything but Bible.

Most readers know, in often undefined ways, that the Bible is Holy Scripture, and it is a classic exactly as that special kind of classic. I wonder if some of our attempts at literary analysis — be it structuralism or not so new "new criticism" — are not, when all is said and done, a form of apologetics, sophisticated to a degree which obfuscates the apologetic intention even to its practitioners.

I do not consider apologetics to be a sin, provided that the apologetic intention is conscious and not obscured by having it masquerade as something else or offered as an alternative to a traditional apologetic of theological and doctrinal special pleadings. About such apologetics Northrop Frye says: "Such systems of faith, however impressive and useful still, can hardly be definitive for us now, because they are so heavily conditioned by the phases of language ascendant in their time, whether metonymic or descriptive." Then he continues:

> A reconsideration of the Bible can take place only along with, and as part of, a reconsideration of language, and of all structures, including the literary ones, that language produces. One would hope that in this context the aim of such a reconsideration would be a more tentative one, directed not to a terminus of belief but to the open community of vision, and to the charity that is the informing principle of a still greater community than faith (*The Great Code*, p. 227.)

It seems rather obvious to me that Frye's program of reconsideration in all its humble tentativeness is an apologetic attempt with its own theology, appealing to charity over against the outdated "systems of faith," and addressing "a still greater community than faith." In short, here is an attempt at cutting loose from the moorings of Holy Writ. It is an attempt at allowing the text to speak as literature freed from the very claims which made the Bible a classic in the first place.

That can be done, and with great effect, not least in the hands of masters of exposition like the Auerbachs and the Fryes of literary criticism. In Frye's case the very fact that the Bible is already in itself a continuum of interpretation and reinterpretation, then becomes a glorified manifestation of a "capacity of self-re-creation," and that "to an extent to which I can think of no parallel elsewhere." (p. 225)

Such an approach yields significant insights and opens the senses that have been numbed by overly familiar ways of reading, greedily hunting proof texts for cherished doctrines. Titles like *Mimesis* and *The Great Code* help our mental liberation.

Or to shift to Ricoeur's proposal of a "non-heteronomous dependence of conscious reflection on external testimonies," a literary approach allows new space for the imagination. He suggests that we "too often and too quickly think of a will that submits and not enough of an imagination that opens itself . . . For what are the poem of the Exodus and the poem of the resurrection addressed to if not our imagination rather than our obedience?" Thus there is the non-heteronomous possibility of encountering revelation "no longer as an unacceptable pretension, but a nonviolent appeal."[5]

Frye and Ricoeur both address the imagination, but while Frye looks away apologetically from the revelatory dimension of Scripture, Ricoeur defines a way in which revelation can be revelation in a "nonviolent" manner. But Ricoeur is driven toward a dichotomy between imagination and will or obedience. Yet in speaking of an appeal, be it nonviolent, it seems that the issue for him is not will versus imagination, but rather *how* the Scriptures affect the readers, in their full persons, imagination as well as will and action.

This attention to revelation, will, obedience, and action is important for our discussion, and it would seem that any culture-apologetics that circumvents those dimensions of Scripture misjudge the ways in which the Bible is actually perceived as a classic by the common reader in western culture. For such readers do recognize the Bible as a classic just in its belonging to the genre of Holy Scripture. Thereby there is a recognition of the normative nature of the Bible. That is an irreducible component in the kind of classic that the Bible is. In this it is different from Shakespeare or from the way one now reads Homer.[6]

How one relates to that normativeness is a very different question. The spectrum here is wide indeed, both within and outside the communities of faith, all the way from rejection of that claim to the most minute literal obedience. But that does not change the fact that the normative claim is recognized as intrinsic to the Bible.

It may be worth noting that the more recent preoccupation with "story" tends to obscure exactly the normative dimension. Following upon the history-kerygma preoccupation — via the "language event" — we come to story. It should be remembered, however, that even much of biblical story was preserved and shaped by the halakic needs of the communities of faith, rather than by the kerygmatic urge of communication. What was told or remembered was shaped by the need for guidance in the life of the communities; hence the normative nature of the texts as they are given to us.

It is this element of the normative which makes the

Bible into a peculiar kind of classic. This is of course true in an intensive sense within the Christian community (and what a sliding scale of intensity there is). But I find it important to remember that the normative character is present also in the minds of most people who read the Bible "only as a classic."

When biblical scholarship has become greatly enriched by learning methods of literary criticism, it seems that this sense of the "normative expectation" has been lost or overlooked, for the literary models have been non-normative genres. To ask poets (or artists) what they actually meant or intended with a piece of art is often an insult, and they are apt to answer: "It is for you to answer what it means to you." That is fair enough. The more meanings the merrier.

The normative nature of the Bible requires, however, a serious attention to original intentions of texts. The intention of the original sayings, or stories, or commandments can hardly be irrelevant, as they might well be in other genres of literature. Let me give only one example, the "lex talionis" (Ex 21:22-25; Lv 24:20): ". . . eye for eye, tooth for tooth, hand for hand . . .," words that must strike most contemporary readers as ferocious. Self-serving Christians even quote it as an example of that spirit of vengeance which is supposed to characterize Judaism as compared with Christianity, the religion of love and forgiveness.[7] But attention to "what it meant," to the intention of the legislation, to descriptive historical exegesis, all make it abundantly clear that the point made was the quantum jump from "a *life* for a tooth." Thus it was a critique of vengeance, not a sanction for vengeance. Such example could be multiplied seventy times seven — and more.

All of this leads me to the conclusion that it is exactly the Bible as a classic *and* as Holy Scripture which requires the services of the descriptive biblical scholars and their simple reminder "that from the beginning it was not so," as Jesus said. That is as true about the commandments as it is about the theological constructs or the human self-under-standings of the Bible.

Actually, the more intensive the expectation of norma-tive guidance and the more exacting the claims for the holiness of the Scriptures, the more obvious should be the need for full attention to what it meant in the time of its conception and what the intention of the authors might have been.[8] But also where the Bible is enjoyed in a far more relaxed mood as a classic, people do like to find its support or sanction for their thoughts and actions. The low intensity of the normativeness often makes such use of Scripture less careful. Many even think they give honor to God and Chris-tianity by such use of the Bible. Not least on such situations, the call to historical honesty by access to what it meant is necessary and salutary, lest vague biblical authority become self-serving, trivializing or even harmful.

In conclusion: we are a Society of Biblical Literature. The word "biblical" includes both the Bible as a classic and the Bible as Holy Scripture, and I have tried to argue that in both respects the normative dimension is an irreducible part of biblical literature. Hence our responsibilities include the task of giving the readers of our time free and clear access to the original intentions which constitute the baseline of any interpretation. This task is both one of critique and of mak-ing available those options which got lost in the process. For true criticism is also the starting point for new possibilities, hidden by the glories and by the shame of a long history under the sway of the Bible.

FOOTNOTES

*The Presidential Address delivered 18 December 1983 at the annual meeting of the Society of Biblical Literature held at the Loews Anatole Hotel, Dallas, TX.

1. This shift has many facets. There is the literary dimension as found in Northrop Frye, *The Great Code: The Bible and Literature* (New York/London: Harcourt, Brace, Jovanovich, 1982). There is the movement represented by the Society of Biblical Literature journal *Semeia* (1974-), edited by J. Dominic Crossan and foreshadowed by the pioneering work of Amos N. Wilder (see *Semeia* 12-13, 1978). The depth of the philosophical and theological shifts are perhaps best expressed in David Tracy, *The Analogical Imagination: Christian Theology and the Culture of Pluralism* (New York: Crossroad, 1981). Tracy significantly uses as one of his main categories "The Classic." For a theological critique see the review by Peter Manchester, *Cross Currents* 31 (1981/82) 480-84. See also Patrick A. Kiefert, "Mind Reader and Maestro: Models for Understanding Biblical Interpreters," *Word and World* 1 (1980/81) 153-68; and in the same issue (entitled "The Bible as Scripture") Karlfried Froehlich, "Biblical Hermeneutics on the Move," 140-52.

2. See now Jacob Neusner, *Ancient Israel After Catastrophe: The Religious World View of the Mishnah* (Charlottesville, VA: University Press of Virginia, 1983). Note also Neusner's observation about the revelatory style of 4 Ezra and Baruch in contrast to the Mishnah (p. 26).

3. See Paul Ricoeur's Dudleian Lecture at Harvard Divinity School. "Toward a Hermeneutic of the Idea of Revelation," *Harvard Theological Review* 70 (1977) 1-37. Here Ricoeur differentiates Prophetic Discourse, Narrative Discourse, Prescriptive Discourse, Wisdom Discourse. The first constitutes to him the "basis axis of inquiry" concerning revelation. Indeed, this is the discourse which declares itself to be "pronounced in the name of [God]," p. 3. Cf. the Book of Revelation — the only NT book which claims such authority.

4. For a penetrating understanding of the glories of the King James Version see J.L. Lowes, "The Noblest Monument of English Prose," *Essays in Appreciation* (1936), 3-31.

5. *Harvard Theological Review* 70 (1977) 37.

6. There was, of course, a time when Homer served as a "sacred" text which became the object for religious and philosophical interpretation. The Stoics are famous for this approach, and such commentaries on Homer came to serve as prototypes for both Jewish and Christian commentators on the Bible in the Hellenistic and Graeco-Roman world. See Rudolf Pfeiffer, *History of Classical Scholarship: From the Beginnings to the End of the Hellenistic Age* (Oxford: Clarendon, 1968) 237ff.

7. On the Jewish interpretation of the *lex talionis*, see W. Gunther Plaut, et al., *The Torah: A Modern Commentary* (New York: Union of American Hebrew Congregations, 1981) 568, 571-75; and Jakob J. Petuchowski, *Wie unsere Meister die Schrift erklaren* (Freiburg: Herder, 1982) 58-64.

8. Since I have placed so much emphasis on the Bible as canon, it is important to stress this point. Contemporary stress on the Bible in its canonical wholeness is often coupled with disregard for the intention of the various strata and theologies within the Bible. I would argue rather that exactly the normative quality of scripture necessitates the attention to original intentions; see my discussion with Brevard Childs in the introductory essay in my forthcoming book *Meanings* (Philadelphia: Fortress, 1984) and also the essay on "One Canon is Enough" in that volume.

Biblical Studies Since 1950

JOHN L. McKENZIE, S.J.
De Paul University Emeritus
Chicago, IL 60604

The thirty years which my topic covers have not been the most eventful thirty years in the history of biblical studies, but they have been exciting enough. There have been advances and there have been setbacks; it is not a story of unimpeded progress, and I suppose the story of biblical studies has never been that. Let me mention a few examples of what I found were advances and what I found were setbacks. Most of those thirty years coincided with my teaching career, which began in 1942 and ended with retirement in 1978. I may say that I was there.

In 1943 occurred the event which has since been regarded as the great dividing line, the encyclical *Divino Afflante Spiritu* of Pius XII, intended to liberate Catholic biblical studies. I would say that not until 1950 did it become clear what they were being liberated from; in the ensuing thirty years we are still discovering more in detail what this means. We have not yet found out what they were liberated *for*.

The thirty-year period which I cover opens with what I suppose was the blackest day in my memory as a biblical student, the publication of the encyclical *Humani Generis* of Pius XII. I remember my first reading of this document very distinctly. When the text arrived, I tore through it rather rapidly and said to my colleagues in the seminary where I was teaching, "There goes *Divino Afflante Spiritu,* and there goes biblical scholarship — down the drain." It appeared that Pius XII did his best to reverse the entire proceedings of *Divino Afflante Spiritu;* and it soon became clear that this was not only what it appeared to be, but what it was intended to be. The Pope had been reached by those who had no part in the composition of *Divino Afflante Spiritu,* who did not believe in it, and who finally extorted from him, by means which I do not know, a statement which put a negative in front of the encyclical of 1943. That something was different, however, was clear from the reaction of world Catholic scholarship to this encyclical. It was not afraid, it did not panic, and it did not change its course; it just lay back and waited. And in a few years it was as if *Humani Generis* had never been written. The current that had been set in motion by *Divino Afflante Spiritu* was in full course and could not be reversed.

I would like to say that the relations of Catholic biblical scholarship and the Roman hierarchy were closed with this episode, and that further discussion of my topic could ignore this factor; but it is not true. The roots of *Humani Generis* go back before the period I am discussing. If one were to attempt to treat the history of Catholic biblical scholarship from 1900 to 1950, it could be written very briefly and almost entirely in terms of the relations of biblical scholarship to the pontifical magisterium. The attitude expressed in numerous statements of the magisterium before 1943 could be expressed in a saying attributed to a Jesuit superior of many years ago, somewhat celebrated in the Middle West: "If any of Ours would do anything, let him not do it." (Jesuit official documents usually refer to the members as Ours.) Scholars read the message from the Holy See as saying: If scholars would say anything, let them not say it. Let them not even think it. I do not know that the intention of the pontifical hierarchy during these years was to suppress, even to kill biblical scholarship, but that was what its policy meant. During these thirty years that has been put behind us, and it can be taken as certain that that sort of thing will not happen again. Biblical scholarship is now more or less free to do its work without much thought for anything except the principles of scholarly integrity which should govern it. In other fields of learning this has to be enough. In biblical scholarship the church in modern times has not thought that it was enough. Instead of trusting scholars to do their work, it has asked us to regard them as untrustworthy and irresponsible, and to put our trust in prelates who are responsible. I would like to think that this body of men is more responsible than my colleagues (who are not heroes to me), but they are not. They are no more responsible than the scholars I know, no more worthy of confidence in their integrity. We are dealing with a church which is run by human beings. It is quite true that ultimately you must put your trust in scholarship or in the government. But there remain reservations which keep that trust from being total. Either one can lead you astray.

Let us illustrate from the field of medicine. At my age I have had more experience with doctors than I once thought I would have, or than I ever wanted to have. Without them I probably would not be alive; without them I also would have been spared a deal of needless pain. I will continue to consult them because there is no other place to go. I trust them because I have to. There is a scientific consensus of medicine concerned with what is good and bad for our health and survival; I trust them with an attitude not dissimilar to that with which the American Indian trusted his medicine man. I have my reservations, but I have nobody else to trust.

Must you trust biblical scholars? The issues are not as vital. If you do not trust biblical scholars, you can do your own thinking. You cannot do that about your health because you will die. If you do your own thinking about the Bible, your mind will die, but nobody will notice it. And if you let your thinking about the Bible be done by others who have never studied the Bible, your mind will die just as surely.

What progress have biblical scholars made in the last thirty years? There have been clear signs of liberation from the Holy See. About 1965 (I cannot check the dates where I now write) there was a response from the Pontifical Biblical Commission which said in effect that all the responses issued by this Sacred Commission up to 1920 can be safely ignored. These responses included statements about the authorship of the books of Moses, the book of Isaiah, the book of Psalms, and the historical character of certain parts of the Bible, which were completely at variance with the consensus of modern scholarship. All these may be safely ignored, as Catholic scholars had long been ignoring them. Scholars may now rest assured that the hierarchy is not expressly opposed to what they are doing. This does nothing for a list of men as long as your arm — I do not exaggerate — who were deprived of their jobs, their reputation, and in some cases of their membership in the Catholic Church because of these decrees, which are now confessed to be in error. Since most of them are now long dead, nothing can be done. But one would think that decency demands that care be taken not to do the same wrongs again.

When I read about my friend Hans Kung, I see that things have not entirely changed. I know him as a devout Roman Catholic priest — which is more than I know about his accusers — and when I hear someone say he is not, it angers me. When I hear it said quite publicly that he is not worthy to teach as a Catholic, and when I hear no reasons given, I answer (but no one has asked me): "Look, specify your objections. If you can't specify, shut up." That is slander: and if the Holy See needs slander to get its work done, it can do it without my help, which it does not need anyway. These tactics are not Catholic, they are not Christian, they are not even ethical. We must get rid of that sort of thing. I should say, giving every one his due, that my friend Hans Kung is at times quite abrasive. Since I believe that the same word is used about me, I find it easy to forgive. In any case, abrasion is one thing, heresy is another. If the Roman See finds Hans Kung offensive, let them respond in kind, but let them not say things about him which they cannot prove. My only encounter with the Holy See arose from something I wrote which was flippant, irreverent and disrespectful. It did not show proper submission. That is probably the worst sin Hans Kung has committed. It has nothing to do with scholarship, does it?

I have no time to recite the accomplishment of the scholarship of the last thirty years. No one should misinterpret my brief remarks as meaning that I do not even recognize them, since I do; my critical remarks are those of an old uncle who loves the children even when their noise gets on his nerves. He should be more tolerant and sympathetic. When I read the journals, I find in every issue things taken for granted which, if published in a Catholic journal forty years ago, would have cost the author his job. These things are taken for granted for the good reason that the evidence for their truth or at least for that kind of conviction scholarship can reach is overwhelming. Among my unpublished works is an essay which casts doubt on the historical reality of a man and a woman named Adam and Eve. These things are now easily said because you cannot reasonably say anything else. In biblical studies we now allow ourselves to be led by the evidence rather than what someone tells us who has not looked at the evidence or who has looked only at what has always been said. Why should one be forced to wonder whether this is the approach scholars are encouraged to take?

The two volumes of Schillebeeckx, *Jesus* and *Christ* have recently been submitted to an examination by the Holy See, announced with many allegations from more or less prominent churchmen about the suspicious character of the books and their author. The books drew attention because of more than their size. First of all, the author is pre-eminent among theologians. In taking him on the Holy See knew what it was doing; one might as well go for the big ones and frighten the little ones. Secondly — and this is unrelated to scholarship — Schillebeeckx was supported by all but three of the Dutch bishops. This episcopal body has been less than duly submissive to the Holy See, as the Holy See understands due submission; through Schillebeeckx the bishops were attacked. Thirdly, Schillebeeckx in these two books did put together in a remarkable way almost all of contemporary Christology, of which they are a kind of *Summa*. Through suspicion cast on these books suspicion was cast on most contemporary theologians and theology. To the surprise of nearly everyone, Schillebeeckx and his books were cleared. But before the process was finished, the author was publicly smeared. Many people heard and read about the smear. How many heard or read about the vindication? How much spilled milk is the Holy See expected to pick up? A small child who spilled a bottle of milk with the same carelessness which the Holy See exhibited would, if I had the care of that small child, wipe up every drop with its own little hands.

We are now through with the hierarchy, for which no one will be sorry. Let us resume the thread of our discourse if we can find it. You have learned that historical criticism is now at home in Catholic scholarship. Form criticism, once treated as a heresy by people who did not even know what it was, is a routine tool of study, and that is all it is meant to be; it is not a theory, not a doctrine, but a tool. Like all tools, it can be well or poorly used. We do not worry about the authorship of the books of Moses or even of the Gospels. We are not alarmed by the fact that the Gospels were not written by eyewitnesses; we accept them for what they are, collections of anecdotal memories, originally completely unarranged, and therefore in most cases impossible of historical verification. We are aware that the Catholicism of the New Testament writers and of the first century church was not the Catholicism which we know, nor that of the Council of Trent or the Council of Nicaea. We know that Paul would not recognize much of what is now taught as Catholic doctrine. I suppose for some that would make him less a Catholic. Now we are faced with a vast and still unfinished task. We have done much in the last thirty years; and I think we have suffered a case of what I may call the bends. Protestantism was largely spared this affliction because the Protestant adjustment to modern learning was spread out over a much longer time, although many Protestant churches suffered from the bends in the nineteenth century. Certain fundamentalist churches are where the Catholic Church was in 1905. They have opted out. The world of scholarship is not going to spoil their faith; they have decided that you cannot combine the two, and they want none of it. I think that there are a few Catholics, no longer able to make much noise, who feel that way too. Occasionally they write letters, sometimes anonymous, to some of us.

I would project on the present probabilities in 1981, even under the present Holy See, continued slow progress in the same direction. I did see in an academic journal last year (and I am unable now to verify the reference) a report that some Catholic educators are very much alarmed at the prospect of the reformed Canon Law. They fear because the reformed code contains a provision not found in the present code that anyone who teaches theology anywhere in a Catholic institution such as Holy Cross may do so only in virtue of a canonical mandate. Unless the reformed code makes other changes, such a mandate may not be held by women. If that were to happen, theology would no longer be taught in departments of theology. That is the way we would deal with that, now that we have learned; no trouble, no fuss. That is really the only threat I see, and we do not know that the reformed Canon Law will be instituted in these terms. Nor do I believe that it would have serious effects, even if that did happen. Therefore I forecast continued slow progress in the same direction.

I wish to address a few words about this progress to my colleagues, and I am embarrassed by the probability that I shall find the wrong words. Biblical scholars have long sought and have achieved a certain degree of freedom from ecclesiastical harassment. This they should have to do their work; it is the same freedom which other scholars have to do their work, no more and no less. No more should be sought and no less should be given. But there is something about biblical and theological scholarship which we must remember, and that is, its concerns touch a large public, almost as large as the public which shares the concerns of medicine. In both of these fields premature discussion of rash conjectures is regarded as irresponsible. It is not irresponsible to make them — I have a few of my own — and the judgment of responsible conduct should be made by one's peers in the profession. If they are not responsible, it does no good if someone else is. The hierarchy has always regarded itself as the custodian of the consciences of that public whose concern is touched by biblical scholarship. We have considered how the hierarchy has responded to that charge. It has not been well done. There can hardly be any greater danger involved in letting biblical scholars do their work than there has been proved to be in the kind of suppression which the church has known for the last eighty years. I do not suggest that scholars take up the office of custodian of the conscience of the faithful; we need no more moral imperialism. I do suggest that they owe the faithful some thought on how they sound. At the risk of being offensive, I will say that my colleagues sometimes look like small boys writing dirty words on the walls of public buildings, showing off their newly-discovered knowledge.

There are serious questions. I am not sure I like the way we are attacking some of them. And I have to trust my colleagues to find a better way; I will not set the dogs on them. Let me give you an example, admitting that it is vague. As I read the journals, I observe that they speak less and less about Jesus and more and more about what Matthew, Mark, Luke and John thought. Perhaps it is a matter of method and will lead to something — but to what? A better understanding of Mark? I am not sure I want that, or need it. I thought that Matthew, Mark, Luke and John, or whoever is designated by those names, had established themselves quite on the evidence they left in their writings as third-rate minds. They are of interest only because of their subject; and nobody was ever less well served by his biographers than Jesus of Nazareth. They are means to knowing him, but they are also obstacles to knowing him.

Modern studies sometimes seem to hesitate between a fear of looking at Jesus more closely and a despair of ever seeing him better. Jesus has the reality of figures from *Idylls of the King,* or Homer, Shakespeare or Dickens. We study the authors of the Gospels because they are all we can touch; but they are not our primary interest. The quest for the historical Jesus was a false quest which should never have been pursued; but Jesus should not have been relegated to the mists inhabited by the likes of King Arthur, Achilles, Hamlet and Sydney Carton. Hans Kung has said as well as any contemporary what it means to be a Christian. It means, to borrow a phrase from the late Vince Lombardi, that Jesus is not just the most important thing, he is the only thing. Rudolf Bultmann said that Jesus is important and stays important because he realized better than anyone else who ever lived the complete possibilities of human existence — the quotation retains the sense but is not verbal.

The words attributed to Jesus are generally quite clear. They are addressed to an audience of the mental age of twelve, and that may be what gives scholars trouble. When Jesus says forgive your enemies or give what you have to the poor, it is playing games to ask what it means; it may be hard to do, but it is very easy to understand. What we can gather from the words of Jesus about how people should live together is more radically revolutionary than any other statements ever made by anyone. There is much to be done, and we can do it. When the journals come across my desk and I see what my colleagues are discussing, I realize that my next book must contain a chapter on contemporary biblical studies entitled, "On Re-arranging Deck Chairs." Who else will deal with the modern delusion that jet travel or computers or nuclear weapons have altered human nature or the nature of sin, and rendered Jesus archaic and quaint? There is a right way of using freedom. I would like to think, but I dare not hope, that I will live long enough to see my colleagues find it.

What Is Happening In New Testament Studies?

REGINALD H. FULLER
Virginia Theological Seminary
Alexandria, VA 22304

Historical Reflections

For a church which accepts the primacy and supremacy of Scripture as the Anglican churches have professed to do, and which therefore regards Scripture as the source and norm of its preaching and doctrine, the teaching of the New Testament is perforce a central activity in the curriculum of its seminaries. Building upon the work of the Old Testament studies, the New Testament discipline assembles the results of exegesis in order to pass them on to the systematic theologian, the ethicist, and the homiletics department to fashion them into contemporary doctrine and ethics, and into contemporary proclamation (the church historian contributing to the process by demonstrating how Scripture has been interpreted and the scriptural message lived out in the past), and to the pastoral department to inform contemporary practice of ministry.

As a discipline, New Testament study has been traditionally divided into three parts: introduction, exegesis, and New Testament theology. Introduction uses the various critical methods that have evolved in the past two centuries, and seeks to establish the original *Sitz im Leben* of the New Testament texts, so that the exegete in turn may interpret what the text originally said and how it was understood by the original hearers.

New Testament theology has always been a step-child in the NT discipline. Its exact nature and role have been debated ever since its origin in pietism and continue to be debated today. It has been held to be a biblical *substitute* for dogmatic and systematic theology,[1] a purely historical discipline,[2] and a theological discipline feeding into dogmatic and systematic theology.[3]

The period from 1920-1950, during which NT scholars of the present writer's generation were trained, marked the heyday of the revival of "biblical theology."[4] This movement replaced the purely historical approach to the Bible (the exclusive study of what it meant) with a renewed appreciation of the biblical message precisely in its strangeness as the word of God for the contemporary church. Biblical theology sought to combine the critical methods of the liberal period that immediately preceded it with this renewed appreciation of the biblical message. It focused its attention upon the Bible as the record of the mighty acts of God in history.

The mid-sixties saw what was widely trumpeted as the demise of biblical theology.[5] Several factors contributed to this alleged demise. First, there was the ascendancy of Rudolph Bultmann after World War II, replacing the pre-war preeminence of Karl Barth.[6] Bultmann has been described as a "very complex phenomenon." As a dialectical theologian he belonged to the biblical theology camp with a strong sense of the Word. But there were other elements in his thought which undermined the commonly accepted positions of biblical theology. To begin with, although — as we have noted — biblical theology professed to retain the historical critical method, its critical positions tended to be moderate to rather conservative,[7] whereas Bultmann accepted the rather more radical positions of Heinrich Holtzmann.[8] Bultmann was also a pupil of the History of Religions school.[9] In addition he had imbibed a good deal of existentialist philosophy from his Marburg colleague, Martin Heidegger, particularly in his earlier phase represented by his work, *Sein und Zeit* (1927). The result of this mix in Bultmann can be seen in his *Theology of the New Testament*.[10] Here he treats major strata in the New Testament (Jesus, the church, Palestinian and Hellenistic Christianity aside from Paul) as mere past history, irrelevant for contemporary faith. Only Paul and John (suitably reduced[11]) are the bearers of a viable message for today, albeit in a "demythologized" or existentialist interpretation. Bultmann retained the concept of the Christ event as the eschatological act of God, but this act seemed to occur more in the act of preaching than in the event of "1-30 AD." Even where the influence of Bultmann's theology was not immediately apparent, the whole theological atmosphere changed in the sixties. Biblical theology as a viable source of proclamation for the contemporary church was seriously called into question.[12] The alleged mighty acts of God seemed to vanish on critical examination, like grasping a bubble. The exodus turned out to be nothing more than a few reeds by the seashore and a shift of wind. Jesus of Nazareth was no more than an eschatological prophet, his resurrection the hallucinations of his disciples, and the empty tomb a late legend. None of these tenuous reports could provide an adequate basis for the two central "mighty" acts of God, the exodus and the Christ event.

    Where, then, was a viable message to be found? For a

time, some American NT scholars looked to the "new hermeneutic" emanating from Germany and the Bultmann school. The organ of this movement was the *Journal for Theology and the Church*.[13] It substituted for the mighty acts of God the (later) Heideggerian concept of the "language event" — the power of language to change self-understanding. This "new hermeneutic" seemed for a while to offer a possibility to use the NT as a source for contemporary proclamation. But the concept of language event was too recherche, too German-Lutheran, to find wide-spread acceptance in the English-speaking world. The Germans wanted to play their game by themselves, anyhow, and the much heralded German-American co-operation fizzled out with the demise of the short lived *Journal for Theology and the Church*.

Some of those concerned with the hermeneutical problem then turned to France, to the French structuralists and especially to the work of Paul Ricouer.[14] The real, thoroughgoing, structuralism of the French school (they call it "deep" structuralism) theorizes that human language vibrates with psychological impulses and seeks to discover these vibrations in literature, and to set them in motion in the reader.

Having listened to some examples of this sort of interpretation at the Paris meeting of the SNTS (the International New Testament Society) by French scholars in 1978, I can only say that their interpretations seemed so "deep" as to be purely speculative when applied to biblical texts and of little help for the hermeneutic task. On a simpler level, however, the study of literary structures has proved a valuable tool in the interpretation of the parables, especially in the hands of J.D. Crossan.[15] He studies the way a parable is loaded. For example in the Parable of the Good Samaritan the reactions of the priest and levite are passed over briefly while the loving care of the Good Samaritan is described in meticulous detail. The result is to engage the hearer, to get him involved at the weighted points, in this case the Samaritan and his actions. This engagement or involvement in the story produces a response from the hearer, a judgment upon himself and a decision for a new course of behavior.

The failure of the German new hermeneutic and of French structuralism to provide an overall solution to the hermeneutic task has caused some radical New Testament scholars to abandon the whole effort. The most extreme example is Dennis Nineham,[16] whose recent resignation as Warden of Keble to become head of the Department of Religion in Bristol University (a secular institution) seems an act of prophetic symbolism. Nineham believes that the gulf between the present and the past, especially the biblical past, is now unbridgeable. The Bible in its message as well as in its form is so irretrievably time-conditioned, that it defies being "translated" in order to become a living address to modern men and women. Hence the whole enterprise must be abandoned. The study of the New Testament must be relegated to antiquity and present preaching conducted without reference to the NT text. Mr. Nineham recommends that the preacher simply read the newspaper, pray about it and study the Christian mystics!

A somewhat similar attitude dominates some academic centers in this country. It is significant that the great work on the Nag Hammadi documents is being done at "The Institute for Antiquity and Christianity" — the name suggesting that the study of Christian origins has the same kind of a faith claim as the study of Homer and other classical literature. A conscious expression of this position was articulated in an address delivered by Robert W. Funk to the SNTS at the 1976 annual meeting, held at Duke University, Durham, North Carolina. Funk's thesis was that the center of NT studies had shifted from the great interdenominational

seminaries like Harvard, Yale and Union to the new departments of religion in the secular universities. The significance of this shift, Funk argued, was threefold. First, the
churches were clearly saying that they no longer considered
NT scholarship sufficiently important to justify their support. Second, it marked the emergence of truly American
NT scholarship, no longer dependent upon Europe as Yale,
Harvard, and Union had been. Third, it marked the
emancipation of NT scholarship from the shackles of confessional control and its freedom to operate in a secular-
humanist context. The evidence Funk offered was not very
convincing, however. For instance he cited the University of
Chicago as a lively center of NT studies. But at the time the
British scholar Norman Perrin was the leading light there,
and that institution has a confessional origin. And since his
untimely death Perrin has been succeeded by the German,
Hans Dieter Betz. Funk also praised the study of the epistolary genre being conducted under the inspiration of Prof.
Niels Dahl — but Dahl is Norwegian and he is at Yale. There
was strong criticism of Funk's humanism as the proper
ideological context for NT studies — particularly from
those Europeans who had lived through the German
Church Struggle. Europeans did not want to consign NT
exegesis to the department of antiquities, and most wanted
to understand it as a service to the church. The sociological
study of the early Christian communities advocated by
Wayne Meeks of Yale at the SNTS meeting in Paris (1977)
similarly brought down upon his head the wrath of Ernst
Kasemann.

Current Issues

It is undeniable, however, that not all is well in the
relation between NT studies and the church. The malaise

has been voiced impressively by Walter Wink in his book, *The Bible in Human Transformation.* [17] Wink was so dissatisfied with the "NT guild" that he deliberately cancelled plans to spend a sabbatical in a German university and went instead to San Francisco to study under Elizabeth Boyden Howes at the Guild for Psychological Studies. The result was this book. Wink is convinced of the bankruptcy of a purely historical-critical approach to the NT. It results in the yawning gap between the study of the Bible and our religious experience. One can sympathize with this: Ph.D. theses, and articles in learned journals, and works published by NT scholars, are preoccupied more and more with atomizing the text, and assigning the fragments to various levels of tradition. This phrase goes back to the historical Jesus, another phrase was added by the Aramaic speaking church, another by the Hellenistic community, and finally we have the evangelist's redaction. [18]

Again, it seems to be a real sign of originality and intelligence to deny the authenticity of something everyone has previously accepted. A recent work for instance has propounded the view that all the great Lucan parables (Good Samaritan, prodigal son, rich man and Lazarus) are Lucan compositions. [19] Similarly, the view that the parable of the ten maidens in Matthew 25:1-13 is an allegory constructed by the evangelist, rather than a parable of Jesus allegorically interpreted, has been revived. [20] That a saying or a pericope is a creation of the evangelist is a conclusion we should resort to only where all other possibilities fail. It is more reasonable to assume that the process of traditioning involves the constant *reapplication* of older traditions to new situations. Such a view certainly does not mean that we reject redaction criticism. Rather, it means that we are applying it in a cautious, less speculative way.

Since, however, this is not being done, at least in the

most influential scholarly circles today, we are compelled to agree to a large extent with Walter Wink's claim that the historical-critical approach to the Bible is bankrupt. Nor is Wink's the only expression of this malaise. In Germany, from the very midst of the historical-critical school, two biblical scholars have voiced similar concerns, namely, Ferdinand Hahn and Peter Stuhlmacher,[21] pupils respectively of Bornkamm and Kasemann. Stuhlmacher echoes Wink's complaint about the "distancing and objectifying" of texts that so often happens in historical-critical exegesis. That is the consequence of being excessively analytical, and concentrating exclusively on what the text meant, as opposed to what it means now.

Future Directions

How is this bankruptcy to be overcome? First, we must take seriously (far more seriously than the guild has done so far; the guild has tended rather to reject Wink's book as anti-intellectual) the need for historical-critical study to be constantly receiving feedback from the believing community. Seminary professors of NT might take seriously the possibility of spending at least part of their sabbaticals working in parishes (as is now beginning to happen at Virginia Theological Seminary) instead of going off to Heidelberg or Oxbridge. This does not mean the abandonment of the historical-critical method. Since the biblical texts come down to us from the past, it is only the historical method that can help us to recover what those texts meant to the original writers and to those for whom they wrote. That meaning, at least for the Reformation churches, has to control what the texts mean for the believing community today. It would indeed be ironical if mainline Protestant and Anglican scriptural scholarship were to turn its back to the historical-critical method just at a time when Roman Catholics[22] and more recently conservative evangelicals[23] have been using these methods in ways which, far from causing them to abandon, are leading to an enrichment of their respective faith commitments. But it does mean that we must rediscover that the historical-critical study of the Scriptures is a service which it is our vocation to perform for the faith-community rather than merely for our scholarly peers.

Now this means also that historical-critical exegesis is not enough. We must discover how to move beyond historical-critical to theological exegesis. What does this mean? Historical criticism means, as defined by Ernst Troeltsch, operating with the principles of analogy and correlation. To these principles Stuhlmacher proposes to add a third: "We must again learn to ask what claim or truth about man, his world, and transcendence we hear from these texts." How are we to do this? The answer is not yet fully clear. But as Stuhlmacher suggests, we can begin by re-establishing the connection between the Old Testament and the New. It is remarkable that the most significant advances in New Testament studies have been pioneered in the Old Testament field; one thinks of source criticism, form criticism, redaction criticism, and tradition-historical criticism. At the present time, the Old Testament scholars are leading the way in what they call "canon criticism."[24] It is their conviction that biblical texts have an ongoing life of their own. Their meaning does not come to rest until the texts have found their way into the canonical books where we find them today, and then, as the canon is formed, in the OT canon as a whole. More than that, these texts were then taken up into its two-canon Scripture by the Christian community. So the exegesis must be done by relating texts to their total place in the two-Testament canon.[25]

Such a canonical-theological exegesis should help us to

recover the sense of unity of the Scriptures. For some time NT scholars have been emphasizing the pluralism of the NT message, but that has now become largely an intellectual game. The unity of the two-Testament canon is ultimately (i.e., after historical-critical analysis) to be found in its witness to the saving act of God in Christ. It is in recognition of that witness that we must reaffirm the inspiration of Scripture and, may I dare say it, its infallibility in the sense that the Scriptures will not deceive us about Christ as our salvation.[26]

If this scriptural message is to be heard by the believing community today, then the work of theological exegesis of the NT must be related forward (as it is related backward to the OT) to dogmatics.[27] This will mean recovering the importance of the Creeds and Confessions for our exegetical work (N.B.: this just at the time when our liturgists have consigned the Athanasian Creed, the Chalcedonian formula and the Thirty-nine Articles to the waste-basket of past history!). As a Reformation church, Anglicanism asserts, or is meant to assert, the supremacy and sufficiency of Scripture. That means that the Creed and Confessions cannot dictate the results of exegesis. But it can and should mean that exegesis and dogmatics should enter into a critical dialogue with each other, to the fructifying of each.

It is time to call a moratorium on much of our historical-critical work, the proliferation of which is getting us nowhere. Can we do this, given the current pluralism in critical positions? Perhaps there are grounds for some degree of optimism here. The much-heralded return to the Griesbach solution of the synoptic problem has turned out to make very little real difference to redactional presentations of the theologies of Matthew, Mark and Luke.[28] If we do our exegesis at the canonical level, it may turn out that our differing views about the pre-canonical history of the text are not all that significant.

Further, there are signs that critical and conservative scholars are moving closer together in their interpretation of Johannine theology. While holding to the traditional authorship of the gospel by the Beloved Disciple, the conservatives are coming to recognize a heavy ingredient of the evangelist's style and thought in the composition of the discourses,[29] while the critical scholars are coming to recognize that there is a much earlier, perhaps authentic Jesus tradition not only in the narrative portions, but even in the discourses of the Fourth Gospel. Yet at the same time these discourses are given full authority as proclamations of the truth about Jesus by appeal to the role of the Paraclete in developing Johannine theology (John 16:12-15).[30]

Acts remains an area of crucial difference between conservatives and critical scholars.[31] Coupled with this are the differences over the disputed letters in the Pauline corpus. It makes a difference to the theological as well as to historical exegesis whether Ephesians and the pastorals are included among the authentic letters of Paul or accounted as Deutero-Pauline. It also makes a difference if the so-called catholic epistles are treated as pseudonymous and late. Those who take the critical stance in these areas are more likely to allow for a stratum in the NT which they designate as early (or emergent) catholicism. Such a recognition is wholly lacking in the NT theology of a conservative scholar like G.E. Ladd.

In view of the foregoing circumstances we propose that critical scholars, at least those who understand their vocation as a service to the church, should impose upon themselves the self-denying ordinance of a moratorium on historical-critical analysis of the Gospel and the Pauline homologoumena and concentrate upon their theological exegesis, relating that exegesis first to the NT canon as a whole, then backward to the OT canon and forward to the Creeds and Confessions in dialogue with dogmatic and systematic theology. As for Acts, the Pauline antilegomena and the catholic epistles, NT scholars of churchly orientation should enter into dialogue with the conservative evangelical scholars and explore the possibility of convergence or of eventually agreeing to differ over historical-critical questions, while moving if possible toward a consensus on theological exegesis at the canonical level.

What the possibilities are, it is difficult to say. But if the charge of bankruptcy, as voiced differently by such scholars as Walter Wink, Robert W.Funk and Dennis Nineham, is correct, the handwriting is on the wall: "Set your house in order; for you shall die, you shall not recover" (2 Kings 20:1).

FOOTNOTES

1. "The beginnings of NT Theology as a distinctive discipline lie in Pietism and the Enlightenment. Each sought to evolve a biblical theology which would serve as a substitute for the current orthodox theology of Protestant scholasticism." see R. Bultmann, *Theology of the New Testament* (New York: Scribners, 1955) II:242-44.

2. Most notably by William Wrede in his classic treatment, *Uber Aufgabe und Methode der sogenannten neutestamentlichen Theologie* (Gottingen: Vandenhoeck & Ruprecht, 1897), ET in Robert Morgan, *The Nature of New Testament Theology* (SBT 2-25; London SCM, 1973).

3. So Adolp Schlatter, *Theologie des Neuen Testaments* (Stuttgart: Calwer Vereinsbuchhandlung, 1909-10), a work which was followed by a *Dogmatik* (1911). Schlatter discussed the relationship between NT Theology and Dogmatics in a programmatic essay, *Die Theologie des Neuen Testaments und die Dogmatik* (Stuttgart: Calwer Vereinsbuchhandlung, 1909).

4. See, e.g., E.C. Hoskyns and N. Davey, *The Riddle of the New Testament* (London: Faber, 1931) and C.H. Dodd, *The Apostolic Preaching and its Developments* (London: Hodder & Stoughton, 1936). In this country biblical theology was pioneered by Old Testament scholars, especially by W.F. Albright and G. Ernest Wright. See the latter's *God Who Acts: Biblical Theology as Recital* (SBT 1-8; London: SCM, 1952).

5. Langdon Gilkey, "Cosmology, Ontology and the Travail of Biblical Language," *JR* (1961) 41:194-205; Brevard S. Childs, *Biblical Theology in Crisis* (Philadelphia: Westminster Press, 1970); James W. Barr, *The Bible in the Modern World* (London: SCM, 1973).

6. The decisive shift from Barth to Bultmann occurred after the latter launched his demythologizing program. See H.W. Bartsch, *Kerygma and Myth* (2 vols.; London: SPCK, 1953-62).

7. As were Vincent Taylor, T.W. Manson, W. Manson, and C.H. Dodd. Dodd for instance accepted the authenticity of Ephesians. Hoskyns was open to rather more radical views on critical questions; see pp. 265-88 of *Riddle* (n. 4).

8. H.J. Holtzmann, *Lehrbuch der historisch-kritischen Einleitung in das Neue Testament* (Tubingen: Mohr, 1885).

9. See R. Bultmann, *Theology of the New Testament*, II:245-47. Bultmann was a pupil of W. Heitmuller and succeeded him at Gottingen.

10. See the review of Bultmann's *Theologie* by N.A. Dahl, first written in 1954 and published in ET in *The Crucified Messiah and Other Essays* (Minneapolis: Augsburg, 1974) 90-128.

11. Bultmann eliminated references to future eschatology and the sacraments from the Fourth Gospel as interpolations of an ecclesiastical redactor. Cf. R. Bultmann, *The Gospel of John: A Commentary* (Philadelphia: Westminster, 1971), p. 11.

12. See note 5.

13. The first five volumes (1964-1968) were edited by Robert W. Funk in association with Gerhard Ebeling and published jointly by Mohr of Tubingen and Harper of New York; the sixth and seventh volumes were published by Herder (1969).

14. On structuralism see *Interpretation* (1974) 28:131-270. Also helpful, especially on the parables, is Norman Perrin, *Jesus and the Language of the Kingdom* (Philadelphia: Fortress, 1976).

15. John Dominic Crossan, *In Parables; The Challenge of the Historical Jesus* (New York: Harper & Row, 1973).

16. D.E. Nineham, *The Use and Abuse of the Bible* (London: Macmillan, 1976).

17. *The Bible in Human Transformation: Toward a New Paradigm for Biblical Study* (Pheladelphia: Fortress, 1973).

18. The most egregious example of this atomizing analysis I have come across is a study, by a German Catholic scholar, Dieter Zeller, of the wisdom tradition in the sayings of Jesus, *Die weisheitlichen Mahnspruche bei den Synoptikern* (FzB 17; Wurzburg, 1977). He leaves very few such logia to the historical Jesus, assigning them to different levels of the tradition.

19. John Drury, *Tradition and Design in Luke's Gospel: A Study in Early Christian Historiography* (Atlanta: Knox, 1976). Drury was a pupil of Austin Farrer and follows his teacher's synoptic theory (Mark-Matthew-Luke, dispensing with Q). Most of the material in Luke which is not taken from Mark and Matthew Drury attributes to Lucan creativity, using the LXX.

42   A COMPANION TO THE BIBLE

20. Karl Donfried, "The Allegory of the Ten Virgins (Mt 25:1-13) as a Summary of Matthean Theology," *JBL* (1974) 93:415-28. Donfried reverts to Bornkamm's view, which had been refuted, to my mind convincingly, by J. Jeremias.

21. F. Hahn, "Probleme historischer Kritik," *ZNW* (1972) 63:1-17; also his essay "Die neutestamentliche Wissenschaft" in *Wissenschaftliche Theologie im Uberblick* (ed. W. Lohff and F. Hahn [Gottingen: Vandenhoeck & Ruprecht] 20-38 [not accessible to me]); P. Stuhlmacher, *Historical Criticism and Theological Interpretation of Scripture* (Philadelphia: Fortress, 1977). I am greatly indebted to Stuhlmacher's suggestions for the future course of biblical exegesis in the section on "Future Directions".

22. See particularly Raymond E. Brown's two most recent books, *The Birth of the Messiah* (Garden City, NY: Doubleday, 1977) and *The Community of the Beloved Disciple* (New York: Paulist, 1979).

23. See, e.g., *New Testament Interpretation* (ed., I. Howard Marshall; Grand Rapids, MI: Eerdmans, 1977). In this country the faculty of Fuller Theological Seminary has led the way in breaking with the scholastic fundamentalism of the older Princeton school, thus freeing conservative evangelicalism for the use of the historical-critical method. See *Scripture, Tradition and Interpretation* (ed., W. Ward Gasque and William LaSor; E.F. Harrison Festschrift; Grand Rapids, MI: Eerdmans, 1978).

24. See the various recent writings by James A. Sanders, especially his *Torah and Canon* (Philadelphia: Fortress, 1972); also Brevard S. Childs, *Biblical Theology* (n. 5), pp. 99-114.

25. A recent example of such a commentary is Brevard S. Childs, *The Book of Exodus: A Critical, Theological Commentary* (Philadelphia: Westminster, 1974).

26. For the conservative evangelical recognition that Scripture's purpose is to proclaim the message of salvation in Christ, not to convey factual information on matters of science and history, see Jack B. Rogers, *Confessions of a Conservative Evangelical* (Philadelphia: Westminster, 1974); Jack B. Rogers and Donald K. McKim, *The Authority and Interpretation of Scripture: An Historical Approach* (New York: Harper & Row, 1979); on the question of unity behind the pluralism see James D.G. Dunn, *Unity and Diversity in the New Testament* (Philadelphia: Westminster, 1977). Apart from its anti-sacramental bias, this is an excellent and most important work.

27. See Stuhlmacher, *Historical Criticism* (n. 20) pp. 76-91.

28. At a conference on "The Gospel Tradition and the Owen-Griesbach Hypothesis," held at Pembroke College, Cambridge 13-18 August 1979, three papers were produced on the redactional theology of Matthew, Mark, and Luke assuming the Griesbachian hypothesis. The theology of the three synoptists did not appear to be essentially different from the redactional studies which assumed the usual two-source theory. In fact, Jack D. Kingsbury's paper on Matthew suggested that redactional studies on any of the

Gospels could be conducted without presuming any particular theory of synoptic relationships, simply by internal study.

29. See Eldon Ladd, *A Theology of the New Testament* (Grand Rapids, MI: Eerdmans, 1974), pp. 213-308.
30. The critical shift began with the discovery of the Dead Sea Scrolls, and with C.H. Dodd, *Historical Tradition in the Fourth Gospel* (Cambridge, University Press, 1963) and has been continued in Raymond E. Brown, *The Gospel According to John* (AB 29 and 29a; Garden City, NY: Doubleday, 1966-70).
31. See W. Ward Gasque, *A History of the Criticism of the Acts of the Apostles* (Grand Rapids. MI: Eerdmans, 1975).

HERMENEUTICAL PERSPECTIVES

Introduction

MIRIAM WARD, R.S.M.
Trinity College
Burlington, VT 05401

To Hermes, the divine messenger, was attributed the invention of those things which serve to communicate, especially language and writing. Thus we derive the meaning of the term "hermeneutics" from the Greek *hermeneuein*, to express, to explain, to translate, to interpret. By no means then is the problem of hermeneutics a modern phenomenon. The ancient Greeks, preoccupied with probing the meaning of their myths and poetical works, dedicated themselves to the interpretation of these texts through the trilogy of grammar, rhetoric, and poetics.

Hermeneutics, regardless of how it has been recognized or expressed as applied to the Bible, is an existential problem. Judaism encountered this in having to interpret and reinterpret the Law for ever-new situations. The Christ-event furthered the need for interpretation of the text in the light of history. Although subsequent periods of church history did not ignore the hermeneutical problem, it is relatively recent times that have focused on it as a key issue in theological and biblical studies.

The articles that follow examine various aspects of modern concern for discovering the meaning of the Bible and the words which will best convey that meaning to persons faced with quite a different set of problems from those of biblical times.

Raymond E. Brown, Auburn Professor of Biblical Studies at Union Theological Seminary in New York, is recognized world-wide for his biblical scholarship and ecumenical endeavors. His earned doctorate from Johns Hopkins University has been crowned with over a dozen honorary degrees, among which is one from the prestigious Uppsala University in Sweden. His two-volume commentary on the Fourth Gospel has been highly acclaimed as has his recent book *The Birth of the Messiah*. His work on the Passion of Jesus is to be published this year.

In "The Meaning of the Bible," Father Brown raises a basic hermeneutical problem: of relating the meaning of the Bible as intended by the author — a meaning historically conditioned and limited in outlook — to the normative dimension of reinterpreting that meaning in the on-going life of the believing community. He defends the use of the historical-critical method as essential for discovering the literal sense intended by the author. He also describes the role of church authority in discovering the meaning of Scripture, and examines aspects of the tensions that have developed in speaking of what the Bible *meant* (for the author) and of *what it has come to mean* (in subsequent church history).

Few people are as well qualified as Lucetta Mowry to speak on "The Dilemma of a Translator." Having lived in Korea for much of her young life, and having spent several Sabbaticals in India, she is very much aware of the interplay between culture and language. This realization was under-scored upon her return to the United States for higher education. To the general culture shock experienced in taking up life in the United States was added the challenge of entering Yale Divinity School as one of the first women to brave that male bastion. Her subsequent biblical studies took her into field archaeology at Jericho and Dhibon, and especially relevant here is her work on the late Professor Kenneth Clark's four-person team over a two-year period in Jerusalem. From the thousands of rare ancient manuscripts found at St. Catherine's Monastery in the Sinai they com-piled a new set of variant readings for the Greek New Testament. These are available on microfilm for study in the Library of Congress. Currently she is the only woman serving on the Committee of the Revised Standard Version. She is presently completing a book, *Paul at Corinth: His Message to a Divided Church.*

In her article "The Dilemma of a Translator," Professor Mowry discusses the two principal matters that concern members of the RSV Committee in the work of translating the Bible: (1) "the reliability of the ancient texts," and (2) "the four-fold mandate given by the Division of Education and Ministry of the National Council of Churches." In con-sidering all aspects of finding a modern idiom while remain-ing faithful to the text she describes the nagging question always at the back of the translator's mind: "Have I been a traitor?"

Bruce M. Metzger is without reservation the acknowl-edged expert on the text of the New Testament in the United States and throughout the world today. Professor Metzger is chairman of the RSV Committee. Among his many publications, *A Textual Commentary on the Greek New Testament* has become a standard reference book. A number of his works have been translated into Chinese, Korean, Japanese, and German.

I daresay few people are aware of the time, talent and dedication behind a given translation of the Bible. In "The Revised Standard Version" Professor Metzger gives the genesis of not only the Revised Standard Version, but includes in the historical background earlier revisions of the King James Version and the Revised Version in England and the American Standard Version. He describes the work of the RSV Committee and also identifies certain problems in the translating process.

The increased number of women in the field of biblical studies is heartening. Among the young women scholars is Carolyn Osiek, member of the Society of the Sacred Heart. Having earned a doctorate in New Testament and Christian Origins from Harvard, she is currently Associate Professor of New Testament at the Catholic Theological Union in Chicago. She has already proven herself a thoughtful and prolific writer, and an effective speaker. Sister Osiek is an associate editor of *The Bible Today* and *Scripture in Church*. Students of the Bible will do well to keep abreast of her work in the future.

In the final selection in this section of our book, Sister Osiek confronts a serious problem that modern feminists, specifically feminist believers, have in dealing with the Judeo-Christian tradition, especially as witnessed in the Scriptures. The presence of misogynism in the Bible is comparable to the problem of anti-Semitism in the New Testament. She suggests that this misogynism must be approached on the hermeneutical, historical, theological, and ecclesiological levels, and that one must revise one's thinking and speaking of God.

The Meaning of the Bible[1]

RAYMOND E. BROWN, S.S.
Union Theological Seminary
New York, NY 10027

We have now seen that *word* of God (since God does not really speak in words) means a divine communication in human words spoken and written by people who had limited knowledge and restricted worldview and were facing specific problems. Granted such limitation, how does the meaning they intended relate to the normative role of the Bible in the Church? The answer to this question involves a consideration both of hermeneutical (or meaning) issues and of the role of church authority in discerning the meaning of Scripture. I shall devote half of a chapter to each of these two considerations; but before I begin, let me recall official Catholic statements on both issues. In *Divino Afflante Spiritu* (DBS 3826) Pope Pius XII affirmed clearly the primacy of the literal sense: "The foremost and greatest endeavor of the interpreters should be to discern and define that sense of the biblical words which is called literal . . . so that the mind of the author may be made abundantly clear." And *Dei verbum* (10) of Vatican Council II states, "The task of authentically interpreting the word of God, whether written or handed on, has been entrusted exclusively to the living teaching office of the church, where authority is exercised in the name of Jesus Christ."

What the Bible Meant

The above-cited equation of the literal sense with what the author intended may be too narrow, as will be discussed below. But certainly the author's intent is a major factor in a literal sense that is detected by the historical-critical method developed in the last one hundred years. The pope's insistence that such a meaning and such a method constitute "the foremost and greatest endeavor of interpreters" is not universally accepted. Indeed, some would regard it as a very dubious endeavor. Let me survey the different scholarly or religious reasons that lead people to an unappreciative attitude toward the literal meaning of the Bible as diagnosed by the historical-critical method:

(1) Some liberals regard the quest for the literal sense as the correct approach to the Bible, but not very important, simply because the Bible is not very important. In their judgment the Bible represents a phase in the history of religion, and some modern theological factor may be far more important in determining a correct stance than is an antiquated voice from the past.

(2) From an opposite viewpoint, some who regard the Bible as their complete source of spirituality or religion find sterility in the historical-critical quest for the literal sense. The meaning thus uncovered is often not particularly elevating or spiritual, and sometimes it has little apparent applicability to modern needs. With qualifications I would place in this category Walter Wink's famous charge that the historical-critical method is bankrupt.[2] This charge has been taken up by Reginald Fuller[3] who states that the bankruptcy

of the historical-critical method should be overcome by feedback received from the believing community. However, George Landes[4] has perceptively challenged Wink's assertion: "What is bankrupt is not the method itself, but the attempt to make it serve purposes it was not intended to serve." And rhetorically I would wish to ask Fuller what is there in the nature of the historical-critical method that should ever have prevented its practitioners from being members of the believing community, and is he not blaming a method for the prejudices of some who employ it. It is true that, as a child of the post-Enlightenment, biblical criticism has tended to be almost doctrinaire in its skepticism about the transcendent, e.g., in ruling out of court any evidence that Jesus worked miracles. There has also been a tendency to regard as unscientific any interest in what the texts meant religiously to the people who wrote them. But it is time that we identify such prejudices as regrettable accretions rather than as intrinsic principles of the method.

(3) Some object to the historical-critical quest as too pretentious, uncovering a sense of the Bible but not the most important meaning. They appreciate more the spiritual sense, or canonical sense, or theological sense or literary sense. I shall discuss this approach in detail below; for the moment I simply remark that in evaluating it, one must pay close attention to whether it makes the literal sense a major or minor factor in a larger picture.

(4) Some reject the historical-critical method as theologically dangerous. We may distinguish here two different attitudes. (a) One theological objection (encountered among conservative circles, both Protestant and Catholic) is that the quest for what the human author intended treats the Bible as if it were not the word *of God*. When the historical-critical method uncovers the limitations and shortcomings in the author's religious views, that is seen

as a blasphemous denial of the claim that God has spoken. Chapter One was dedicated precisely to the rejection of such an approach which really denies that the Bible is the *word* of God. (b) Another theological objection (most often encountered among Catholic conservatives) flows from the fact that the literal sense uncovered by the historical-critical method often does not agree with the way in which the church has interpreted a passage. Since they accept the church's interpretation, they reject the exegetical method as false and dangerous. The second half of this chapter will be devoted to that issue.

But before I move away from this catalogue of disparagements of the historical-critical method, let me comment on two attitudes that I find among some Roman Catholics. Too often one hears the glib assertion that the church and Christians read the Bible without the historical-critical method for 1700 years and therefore it cannot be an essential method. The rejection of the necessity of employing new intellectual tools on the grounds that one's predecessors did not have them has been encountered over and over again in Christian history, e.g., in the early centuries the resistance to the introduction of formal philosophy into Christian theology; in the Middle Ages the condemnation of Aquinas' attempts to import Aristotelianism into theology; in modern times the resistance to information derived from natural sciences, psychology, and sociology. It is one thing not to use a method when it has not been discovered and no one else is using it. But to refuse the historical-critical method now when it has become part of the modern approach to all other literature is tantamount to a theological statement denying the human element in the word of God. It removes the biblical authors from the world of ordinary experience with its limitations. The decision *against* the historical-critical method, even under the guise of a sophisticated appreciation of the history of exegesis, is a form of theological fundamentalism.[5]

A second attitude among some Roman Catholics is that historical-critical exegesis is being overused and abused by their fellow-religionists. Extreme caution is required here. There are a number of scholars particularly among the French, who distinguished themselves in the difficult days before Vatican II by adopting a mildly critical approach to the Bible and by using that to construct a biblical theology, the very richness of which served as an apologetic for a more open stance by the church toward biblical criticism. But when after Vatican II another generation of scholars pursued the critical issues in a much more "hard-nosed" way, the hitherto appreciated work of the older generation now began to be criticized as uncritical and not "up-to-date." Such criticisms left their wound, and famous "names" of the early 1960s have sometimes aligned themselves with ultraconservative positions and with expressions of fear about the future. Alas, it is often a case of there being none more conservative than the old liberal whose time has passed and who thought that he knew exactly how far progress would go. But while one can understand this human drama, firmness is required in pointing out that some of the Catholic scholars most vociferous in their attacks on biblical criticism and Catholic critics are people whose own work has been judged as quite inadequate.

Let me give as an example a contemporary assailant on the American scene who has been quite blunt. Manuel Miguens has devoted much of his writing career in these last years to attacking fellow Catholic scholars for the dangers he sees in their application of biblical criticism to early Christian ecclesiology, christology, and mariology. In a recent issue of *Communio* (7 [1980] 24-54) he was severe on such biblical criticism as a threat to the Gospel; but in evaluating this attitude, judgments upon Miguen's own ability to understand and practice biblical criticism should be remembered. His book *Church Ministries in New Testament Times* (Arlington, VA: Christian Culture Press, 1976) was reviewed in the *Catholic Biblical Quarterly* (40 [1978] 130-31) by J.H. Elliot of the University of San Francisco: "I cannot in good conscience recommend this work . . . It reflects an awareness neither of the current *status quaestionis* of this complex issue nor of the main research involved. The historicity of texts and the unbiasedness of the biblical authors are accepted with uncritical credulity. Exegetical and historical problems are dismissed as fabrications produced by 'modern fashions and moods in scholarship.' " Another book by Miguens, *The Virgin Birth: An Evaluation of Scriptural Evidence* (Westminster, MD: Christian Classics Inc., 1975) was reviewed by the Lutheran scholar Karl Donfried of Smith College in *Theological Studies* (38 [1977] 160-62): "While at points raising significant questions and suggesting viable exegetical possibilities, this is, on the whole, a very uncautious book which is bound to mislead many naive readers. Under cover of academic biblical respectability, it abounds in incomplete and inaccurate exegesis and unwarranted generalizations. The real methodology employed is not that of exegesis but of eisegesis." A Catholic scholar's judgment on the same book of Miguens was recorded by Stanley Marrow of Weston School of Theology in the *Catholic Biblical Quarterly* (38 [1976] 576-77): "The literary genre of this monograph can best be described as polemical exegesis. But to the present reviewer, the exegesis is faulty and the polemic wide of the mark." Marrow warns, "What militates most against the proper evaluation of the Scriptural evidence, however, is the fact that the exegesis is not *voraussetzungslos* (without presuppositions), in that it presupposes its own outcome from the start."

By way of personal comment let me state firmly that I regard as ridiculous the charge that biblical criticism is now being overused in Roman Catholicism. Catholic scholars have been permitted to use criticism for no more than one-third of a century, and indeed its implications are only now being appropriated.[6] We have produced full-scale commentaries on very few books of the Bible. We are still struggling with giving our people even an elementary knowledge of the Bible as it is understood in scholarship. Critical biblical thought has had relatively little impact on some leading theologians whose scriptural views were shaped in the Catholicism of a pre-critical period. There has been no evidence of a major impact of critical biblical thought upon Roman statements. To Catholics who express fears about biblical criticism, one may well reply in the crude argot of the street: "Don't knock it till you've tried it."[7] And I would add to that maxim, " — tried it and been judged by your fellow-scholars as knowing what you are doing." In my judgment the use of the historical-critical method is not simply an option but a necessity because, when practiced by believers, it involves a fundamental theological statement about the *word* of God as always conditioned by time and place and circumstance, and yet truly "of God." Despite their different agenda, ultraliberals and ultraconservatives can agree that the historical-critical method leads to denying the "of God" in favor of the human "word" element, but that may well be because neither group can accept an incarnational theology of the fully divine in the fully human.

Various Biblical Senses

I have made this point strongly so that my further remarks about the inadequacy of the quest for the literal sense cannot be understood as denigrating the importance of that quest. In suggesting that what is grasped through the historical-critical method is not the whole meaning of the Bible, I am in good company among exegetes and theologians today.[8] However, I am not jumping upon any bandwagon; for such an approach has marked my own academic career from the very beginning, as illustrated in my interest in the *sensus plenior* of Scripture.[9] I have returned to that interest from time to time,[10] although I recognized quickly that formulated in terms of the *sensus plenior,* the hermeneutic stress that I advocated was too narrowly scholastic and tied into the principle of single authorship for a biblical book.[11] Moreover, in the 1950s and 1960s it was not the *sensus plenior* that needed emphasis in Roman Catholicism but the primacy of the literal sense, lest the challenge of the biblical authors be relativized and not bring about the appropriate change in Catholic attitudes.

Before going beyond the literal sense, let me first comment that the equation of the literal sense with what the (final) human author intended is too narrow. A quest conducted by the historical-critical method employs form criticism, source criticism, redaction criticism, audience criticism, etc. Applying these to the Gospels, for instance, one would investigate what Jesus meant when he did or said something (if recoverable); how that was shaped in the apostolic preaching and pre-canonical source (both as to meaning and form); what Mark meant when he incorporated this earlier tradition into his Gospel and used it to answer religious problems in the community he addressed; and further (if applicable) what Matthew and Luke meant when they rewrote the Marcan tradition, at times correcting the Marcan emphasis. Under the rubric of the literal sense one would also have to include the intentions of the redactor. For instance, the fourth evangelist, responsible for most of John, had his own meaning; but sometimes that was modified by additions of passages representing the work of a redactor — the literal sense would involve both meanings. An even more dramatic example is found in the Book of Isaiah where one must take into account not simply what Proto-Isaiah meant but how his work was modified through the additions of Deutero-Isaiah and Trito-Isaiah. A commentator must never fail to give attention to the sense a passage has in a book taken as a whole.[12]

In my judgment we go beyond the literal sense when we move from the meaning of the book in itself to the meaning that the book has when it is joined to other books in the canon of Scripture. For the books of the Hebrew Scriptures (so far as Christians are concerned), incorporation into a canon would have a double perspective: when they became part of the collection we call the Old Testament, and when that collection was modified through the addition of the New Testament. Let me illustrate this "canonical sense" of Scripture. The joining of Deutero-Pauline works (the Pastorals, Ephesians, perhaps Colossians and 2 Thessalonians) to the indisputably genuine Pauline writings means that we have a larger view of how the Pauline theology developed and was adapted. (This was not necessarily a smooth and harmonious adaptation; at times it involved correction, albeit benevolent, of what were seen by the end of the 1st century to be Pauline lacunae or even exaggerations.) In Chapter One I pointed out how the rejection of an afterlife by Job is modified when Job is included in an OT canon that contains affirmations of resurrection or other forms of afterlife (Isaiah 26; Daniel; Wisdom; 2 Maccabees) and is modified even more when joined to a NT that is unanimous in its affirmation of an afterlife. Some of the adaptations caused by the presence of a book in a canon are more subtle. NT interpreters can scarcely avoid thinking of Luke as a Gospel and comparing it to Mark and Matthew; in part that is because in the canonical process Luke was separated from Acts and placed in the midst of three other "Gospels." But this may represent a serious qualification of Luke's intention. The man we call "Luke" not only modified Mark in composing the work we call "Luke"; he also accompanied the story of Jesus with a story of the church called "Acts." Presumably that was because he did not feel that one could do justice to God's revelation and plan simply by telling the story of Jesus without an explicit account of what the Spirit and the apostles did. The canonical process has, in a sense, undone his intent.

Let me show the implication of the canonical sense for a specific theological point. A work done jointly by Roman Catholics and Protestants, *Mary in the New Testament*,[13] acknowledged that it is extremely difficult to be sure that a Mary/Eve parallelism was the literal sense (author's intent) in the accounts of the mother of Jesus in John 2 and 19 and of the woman who gives birth to the messianic child in Revelation 12. But the *Mary* volume continued, "When John and Revelation are put in the same canon, a catalytic action may occur so that the two women are brought together and the parallelism to Eve becomes more probable." In *Theological Studies* (40 [1979] 539) Neil J. McEleney, a Catholic scholar, criticized this approach strongly: "The book concedes too much to 'canonical criticism.' Unless one allows biblical inspiration to the act of assembling the NT canon, any 'catalytic action' [?] would not result in a biblical meaning inherent in the text but would be eisegesis or, in a kinder view, theologizing upon the text." If one lays aside the issue of inspiration which is a dubious distraction in relation to this question,[14] McEleney is denying that a meaning that surfaces *after* books are placed in the canonical collection is a "biblical meaning" — for him it is an imposed meaning. Yet if one thinks of terminology, the shoe is on the other foot: Is the meaning that a book has *before* it is placed in the Bible a biblical meaning? Despite the meaning they have in themselves, the individual books of the Bible are not normative taken alone. (Indeed, a good case can be made that any major book of the Bible taken by itself and pressed to its logical conclusion will lead to heretical distortions.) These books did not come down to us separately but as a part of a collection,[15] and they were not accepted as authoritative by the Jewish and Christian communities in isolation but as a normative collection. How then can one deny the designation "biblical meaning" to the meaning they have as part of the Bible?

The real issue, with which I have more sympathy, is the relationship between the literal sense which a book has when it has left the pen of the author (and/or redactor) and the canonical sense which it has when seen in the context of its Testament or of the whole Bible, especially when the change of meaning is substantial. In part, this may be an issue treated in literary and philosophical studies; for in both fields it is often affirmed that a writing, once composed, has a life of its own, and so the literal sense of the author's intent cannot absolutely control meaning.[16] While I agree with that, I would still lend a preponderant importance to the literal sense in exegetical investigation.[17] Even when the quest of a larger sense has uncovered spiritual and theological possibilities that go beyond the literal sense and those possibilities have been accepted in Christian thought, the literal sense (which did not include those possibilities) remains a conscience and a control. Some use the word "criterion"; but that may imply that developments not justified by the literal sense are wrong,[18] and that is too absolute. It is rather a control toward which one must be responsible, even if responsibility is exercised by recognizing the inadequacy of the literal sense. Granted the difficulty of historical-critical research and the alien character of a book completed 2000 to 3000 years ago, there will always be an innate tendency to skip over lightly the quest for the literal sense — especially on the part of beginners and on the part of those whose primary interest is elsewhere (theologians, philosophers, literati). To start off students with a preponderant emphasis on the canonical sense (or any other larger sense), or to begin theological discussions with the broader applicabilities of Scripture may be a wrong pedagogy. Although one must grant the legitimacy of the more-than-literal meaning, it is an essential discipline to struggle for the literal meaning, so that one may be aware of how far one has gone beyond it.

What the Bible Means

Many modern scholars would be content to stop with the canonical sense of Scripture, i.e., with the meaning that a book has as part of the biblical collection. B.S. Childs states (*Introduction*, 83): "A canonical Introduction is not the end, but only the beginning of exegesis." I would carry that statement farther by insisting that the canonical sense which the biblical books were seen to have when they were placed in the canon in a past century (the 4th century served much of Christianity as the terminus for the canon-forming process) marked only a stage in the unfolding of the meaning of the Bible. The very existence of the Bible understood as a normative collection of books supposes an ongoing community willing to shape itself by responding to that norm. Childs (*Introduction*, 80-82) would surely admit that, but he is not lucidly clear as to whether such an ongoing process is only a matter of "receiving and transmitting the authoritative Word" or is actually formative of biblical meaning. I would contend that the way the church in its life, liturgy, and theology comes to understand the Bible[19] is constitutive of "biblical meaning" because it is chiefly in such a context that this collection is serving as the Bible for believers. We are not dealing merely in such an instance with application, accommodation, or eisegesis; we are dealing with the issue of what a biblical book *means*, as distinct from what it *meant*, either when it was written (literal sense) or when it became a part of a canonical collection (canonical sense[20]).

Having affirmed this, I would argue that we need to be precise on how "what it meant" and "what it means" can be related in Roman Catholicism, especially in light of the Vatican II principle enunciated above which gives "the task of authentically interpreting the word of God . . . to the living teaching office of the church." The following observations are meant to aid that precision.

(1) *It is crucial that we be aware that the church interpretation of a passage and the literal sense of that passage may be quite different.* Let me give some practical examples of the way in which I have encountered the failure to understand that difference. Recently I reported on how different priesthoods are described in the Bible . . . D.J. Unger, a priest who in times past has written on the Bible, composed an indignant letter to the *Pittsburgh Catholic Newspaper* (May 2, 1980) complaining about the distinction I made between the priesthood of Jesus Christ described in Hebrews (the unique priesthood of the Divine Son) and the cultic priesthood associated with the eucharist by the church of the 2nd century as an heir to the Levitical priesthood of Israel — a priesthood not described in the NT. Unger wrote that the cultic priesthood is a "function of Christ's priesthood as the Popes have said repeatedly," and he urged the readers of the newspaper to ignore me and to read John Paul II's Holy Thursday message for the Catholic teaching about the priesthood. I accept the teaching of the popes as much as

Father Unger does, but that teaching in no way shows what was in the mind of the author of Hebrews whose words about the uniqueness of Christ's priesthood and the once-for-all character of his sacrifice would be very hard to understand if he thought there were Christian cultic priests and the eucharist was a sacrifice. In associating the Christian form of the Levitical priesthood with the priesthood according to the order of Melchizedek, the church has clearly gone beyond the NT and, indeed, in a direction that might have made some of its authors unhappy. Knowing clearly the 1st-century situation need not lead one to deny the validity of subsequent development; but it makes intelligible why other Christians reject the notion of a Christian cultic priesthood, and it warns (as I indicate in Chapter Six) against allowing the cultic priesthood an exclusive domination in Roman Catholic thought about priesthood.

I can illustrate the failure to distinguish between church interpretation and the literal sense in another way. In my *Birth of the Messiah* (Garden City: Doubleday, 1979) p. 9, I wrote: "I see no reason why a Catholic's understanding of what Matthew and Luke meant in their infancy narratives should be different from a Protestant's." Manuel Miguens[21] asks, "Does Brown mean that Protestants are generally right and Catholics generally wrong?" (After seeing such exegesis of my statement, I can understand why those who have reviewed Miguen's books, as reported above, do not value highly the objectivity of his attempts to interpret Scripture.) My statement has no such deprecatory intent. What "Matthew and Luke meant" is the literal sense of their Gospels; and critical scholars, whether Catholic or Protestant, have to use the same methods in determining that sense. But perhaps what is behind such a polemical attitude toward my statement is better understood from the work of another writer who misinterprets me. J.T. O'Connor[22] cites my statement correctly but then goes on to refute it by changing its wording: "A Catholic's understanding of what Matthew and Luke *mean* in their infancy narratives cannot be the same as a Protestant's" to the extent that Catholic tradition informs the Catholic's understanding of the written word of God. I have italicized the present tense of the verb to show how he has misrepresented my view.[23] Of course, it is precisely in the area of what the infancy narratives *mean* to the Christian community that I would expect a difference between Catholics and Protestants (e.g., in terms of mariology), but not in terms of what the infancy narratives meant to Matthew and Luke.

(2) *The role of church authority in interpreting the Bible has been more properly in the area of what Scripture means than in the area of what Scripture meant.* For me the principle that the teaching office of the church can authentically interpret the Bible is more important now than ever before, granted the diversity and contrariety among biblical authors uncovered by historical criticism. Cardinal Baum[24] has spoken eloquently of the situation: "The 'evidence' of Scripture — both to the scholar and even to the believer . . . — is *of itself* inconclusive in determining the meaning of the most fundamental tenets of the Christian faith: The identity of Jesus, the meaning of his life and death, the nature of his triumph, the obligations imposed on his followers, the consequences of his life for us, etc." In that situation church guidance is supremely important, but it does *not* aid the cause of church authority if we inflate into unreality the area of its authority. We must be clear as to just where in the search for biblical meaning church authority plays its role.

Certainly it is unrealistic to expect the church to settle questions of biblical composition, authorship, dating, etc. Confusion has arisen on that score from the decrees of the Roman Pontifical Biblical Commission in the period 1905-

1915 which gave precise directions on such questions, setting as Catholic policy the unicity of Isaiah, the apostolic authorship of Matthew and John, the genuinely Pauline character of Hebrews and the Pauline authorship of the Pastorals, Mary's responsibility for the *Magnificat*, etc. The church was not simply taking a cautionary position, warning against the possible dangers of "new" views; it was invoking authority to bind scholars to internal obedience on such questions. Some may want to debate whether the church can do that, but the history of the episode warns at least that the church *should* not do that. Within less than 50 years the secretary of the same Pontifical Biblical Commission (JBC, art. 72, #25) found himself giving Catholics "full freedom" with regard to the previous decrees; and certainly today it would be hard to find a majority of Catholic scholars taking even one of the positions inculcated in 1905-1915. In Catholic belief the authorities of the church are guided by the Holy Spirit in matters of faith and morals, but scarcely in matters of date and authorship; and so one may ask by what authority the church could decide such issues. It is quite indefensible to claim that such issues are inextricably intertwined with matters of faith and morals, since no doctrine of the church depends on who wrote a book and at what time, so long as one allows that the book is inspired. Nor is an appeal to tradition satisfactory, for in questions of authorship the church writers simply copied each other (or expanded what they received with legendary additions). Most of the time the "tradition" about such an issue, however unanimous, has little more value than the credibility of the first attestation.

Limitations also affect the ability of church authorities to settle questions of historical fact, very few of which are intrinsic to doctrine. Outside the general acceptance that Jesus lived and was crucified, the only facts of his career that have become part of specific doctrines seem to be that he was conceived without a human father, that his body did not corrupt in the grave, and that at a supper before he died he related bread and wine to his own flesh and blood. Other doctrines are scarcely pinned down to the historicity of a specific incident.[25] The church has defined Mary's continued virginity in such a way that the "brothers" of Jesus mentioned in the NT cannot have been Mary's children (a position I accept as a Catholic) but by what authority can the church tell us positively who they were? One may reply that there was a virtually unanimous tradition in the West that they were Jesus' *cousins,* based on Jerome's rejection of an earlier tradition that they were his stepbrothers as children of Joseph by a previous marriage. To my mind the existence of such a tradition in a matter that is not of faith and morals (exact identity of relatives) does not of itself establish truth. Did Jerome have special historical information on this question not available to others? Is Jerome's exegesis of the pertinent texts convincing? Is Jerome's theological interest in the virginity of Joseph compelling? Those are the questions that decide the validity of a tradition that cannot authenticate itself simply by being tradition. The necessity of caution about tradition is no hypothetical problem. On pp. 38f. of the article discussed above, J.T. O'Connor criticizes my exegesis of the infancy narratives: "Brown will not use the Catholic tradition as an objective element aiding his exegesis of the text." He assumes that there has "always" been a community tradition that family testimony supports the virginal conception. I would respond that the virginal conception is doctrine; the idea that a family testimony is our source of information is not doctrine, and any tradition to that effect must be judged not on the basis of the Holy Spirit guiding the church but on the basis of the evidence that supports such a tradition. In point of fact there is no

1st-century claim to such testimony; it appears later in the apocryphal *Protevangelium of James*, thus named because it is supposed to be a work by a stepbrother of Jesus. The facts narrated by the *Protevangelium* are demonstrably fictitious. What really gave rise to the tradition that Joseph and Mary respectively were the sources of the infancy narratives of Matthew and Luke was the observation that Joseph was the main character in Matthew's story and Mary the main character in Luke's story. The fact that this tradition was accepted for centuries means nothing if its basis is shown by historical criticism to be implausible. The church is the ultimate judge of faith and morals; historical criticism is the criterion of history — confused transfer in either direction can have disastrous results.

Limited too is the ability of church authorities to determine the literal sense of a passage of Scripture. In Scripture interpretation the reason for turning to church authority guided by the Holy Spirit is that such interpretation affects the way people believe and live. What a passage *means* to Christians is the issue for the church — not the semi-historical issue of what it *meant* to the person who wrote it. We see this from the fact that normal Roman Catholic Church intervention into exegesis has been to *reject* an interpretation that represents an intolerable challenge to its life, e.g., the rejection of Reformation attempts to prove from Scripture that there should be only two or three sacraments. To the best of my knowledge the Roman Catholic Church has never defined the literal sense of a single passage of the Bible.[26]

It needs to be underlined that the use of Scripture in doctrinal statements composed by church authorities in a pre-critical period may *not* be read as the answer to historical-critical problems raised subsequently. It has been affirmed by the Roman Doctrinal Congregation[27] that doctrines enunciated by the magisterium solve only certain questions and are sometimes phrased in the changeable conceptions of a given epoch. That must be remembered when we relate such doctrines to modern biblical questions. Tridentine statements that Christ instituted seven sacraments (DBS 1601) and that by the words "Do this in commemoration of me" Christ ordained the apostles priests (DBS 1752) represent an interpretation of the general thrust of the whole NT for the life of the church. They do not and will not answer historical-critical questions such as: Did the historical Jesus have a clear idea of sacrament? In his earthly life how many of what we call sacraments did he consciously envision? Before his death did Jesus actually utter the words "Do this in commemoration of me" (missing in Matthew and Mark's account of the Last Supper), or is that a post-resurrectional interpretation of the implication of his Last Supper based upon the eucharistic practice of the primitive churches known to Luke (22:19) and Paul (1 Cor 11:25)? Did the Jesus of the earthly ministry think of any of his followers as cultic priests and did he think of the eucharist as a sacrifice? These questions are best answered, not by citing church doctrine phrased by people who were neither asking nor answering them, but by studying the Gospels historically and seeking to pierce behind the professions of early faith to the circumstances of Jesus' ministry and his world view. Even if many of them are answered in the negative, however, this does not mean that the subsequent Roman Catholic Church was wrong at Trent in insisting that its doctrines of seven sacraments, eucharistic sacrifice, and priestly ordination were a valid interpretation of Scripture — an interpretation of what by symbiosis Scripture had come to mean in church life, but not necessarily an interpretation of what it meant in the mind of those who wrote the pertinent passages.

(3) *Tension is not an improper relationship between what the Scripture meant to its authors and what it has come to mean in the church.* Other theories would stress absolute harmony, or contradiction, or development that is always congruous; but there are difficulties in each of those suggestions. Obviously the literal sense of a biblical passage and the church usage of that passage will often be harmonious, but my point (1) above insists that the two senses can be different. Yet personally I would not accept the opposite extreme which allows the literal meaning and the church interpretation to be contradictory in the strict sense. If one takes an example from the few doctrines that I have mentioned above as including or presupposing specific historical facts, some would not be disturbed by a situation in which historical criticism would make it virtually certain that Jesus was conceived normally, even though church doctrine speaks of a virginal conception. Yet that is modernism in the classic sense whereby doctrines are pure symbols that do not need to be correlated at all with the facts of which they speak. On the other hand, just as problematic is the contention that an exegete who accepts the church doctrine of virginal conception must establish by critical investigation that Jesus had no human father. In fact, most often in such instances historical investigation will leave an ambiguity, so that church doctrine will be neither in clear harmony nor in sharp contradiction with the results, but will need its own theological basis.

A more sophisticated Catholic thesis would seek to trace a congruous development from the literal sense of Scripture to the church interpretation of Scripture (or church doctrine based on Scripture). Careful historical study, however, does not always support such a benevolent picture. The church position may follow directly from some trends in Scripture but not from others. For instance, the episcopal-presbyteral structure is a prolongation of the direction incipient in the Pauline Pastorals, but is quite alien to some Johannine sensitivities. A developed mariology lies on a trajectory that begins with Luke's picture of Mary as the first Christian but finds little support in the Marcan judgment that Mary did not understand Jesus. Granted a tension, then, between church positions and some strains of Scripture, is that tension harmful? Must it always be relativized by Catholics in absolute favor of the doctrine, so that the literal sense of the contrary biblical passage is explained (away) as a partial insight of an imperfect past? Joseph Ratzinger,[28] now a very influential cardinal, faulted Vatican II for stressing only the harmony of Scripture and tradition and not recognizing the critical use of one to adjudicate the other. If the tension I have described is seen as an opportunity rather than as a threat, its critical impact may be helpful in many ways to a church that lives by tradition as well as by Scripture.

For instance, some church doctrines vocalize a theological insight in historical phraseology, and a knowledge of the biblical picture may help to distinguish what is really important in that combination. It is Catholic doctrine that the bishops have been placed by the Spirit as successors of the apostles (DBS 1768, 3061), and often that dogma has been identified with the thesis that the apostles themselves chose and ordained bishops who in turn ordained their successors . . . This understanding finds its first attestation in Clement of Rome (42:4) at the end of the 1st century (but there without the claim that *all* bishops were appointed by apostles). It is challenged by a work of equal antiquity, the *Didache* (15:1), which tells a community that seemingly does not yet have such officials: "Appoint [ordain] for yourselves bishops and deacons." The NT gives evidence that apostles like Paul may have appointed bishops (or presbyters) in some of the churches, but no evidence that this was a common apostolic practice. One should not polemically relativize the silence and negative evidence in favor of succession through linear ordination; one should rather recognize that apostolic succession did not require linear, tactile ordination in the first centuries and that a later practice has been too simply equated with the doctrine. That does not mean that the church cannot insist on linear episcopal ordination now, but it makes intelligible why other Christians may not see the need of such ordination and makes less unthinkable an occasional exception allowed to achieve Christian unity, were that advisable.

Besides clarifying doctrine, the tension between church interpretation and the meaning of Scripture discovered through historical criticism may result in the modification of exaggerations. Positions taken by the church represent a partial grasp of truth and a choice made at a price; and opposing voices from the Bible may help to preserve what would otherwise be lost. I have mentioned that Job and Sirach denied an afterlife. To a church that has opted for Jesus' positive attitude toward an afterlife the voice of Job still has something important to say. Anticipation of an afterlife often leads people to neglect the importance of encountering God in this life — a neglect challenged by Job who could take God so seriously even though he thought that there was only this life with all its misery.

I shall not prolong this chapter by examples of how this tension can benefit the church. Harmony between the church's stance and the views of the biblical authors helps to assure the church of its apostolic continuity; occasional lack of harmony can remind the church of the vicissitudes of history and of human limitations. The literal sense of Scripture uncovered through historical-critical research may challenge the church; it is incumbent on scholars to present that challenge not hostilely but by way of invitation. The challenge should not be feared or neutralized by the generalization that the scholarship behind it is uncertain and never unanimous — that has always been so, but that does not free the church from the obligation of using the best scholarship available. Scripture would not be the word of God if it always confirmed Christians or the church, for the God who inspired the Scriptures is a God whose thoughts are not our thoughts. Jesus is not heard if at times he is not reminding God's people that we are capable of transgressing the commandments of God for the sake of our own traditions (Mt 15:3). A Bible at times in tension with the church can serve as the conscience of the church reminding it that it is not yet what it should be.

FOOTNOTES

1. Raymond E. Brown, *The Critical Meaning of the Bible* (New York: Paulist Press, 1981), Chapter Two; Originally printed in *Theology Digest* 28 (Winter 1980), pp. 305-19.
2. *The Bible in Human Transformation* (Philadelphia: Fortress, 1973) I.
3. "What Is Happening in New Testament Studies?" *St. Luke's Journal of Theology* 23 (1980) 96. (Reprinted in this anniversary volume. ed.)
4. *Journal for the Study of the Old Testament* 16 (1980) 33.
5. I have no objection to the contention that the historical-critical approach is not the whole of exegesis, but only to those who substantially reject the literal sense. See the discussion by D.C. Steinmetz, "The Superiority of Pre-Critical Exegesis," *Theology Today* 37 (1980) 27-28.
6. Cf. Raymond E. Brown, op cit., Chapter Four, in which he examines the slowness of the impact of NT scholarship on the Church. (ed.)
7. See my warning on this in *The Jerome Biblical Commentary*, art. 77, #24.
8. J.A. Sanders, *Torah and Canon* (Philadelphia: Fortress, 1972); H. Frei, *The Eclipse of Biblical Narrative* (New Haven: Yale, 1974); G.T. Sheppard, "Canon Criticism: The Proposal of Brevard Childs and an Assessment for Evangelical Hermeneutics," *Studia Biblica et Theologica* 4 (1974) 3-17; also his *Wisdom as a Hermeneutical Construct* (BZAW 151; Berlin: de Gruyter, 1980) on "canon conscious redactions"; B.S. Childs, *Biblical Theology in Crisis* (Philadelphia: Westminster, 1970); also his *Introduction to the Old Testament as Scripture*

(Philadelphia: Fortress, 1979) esp. 72ff.; P. Stuhlmacher, *Historical Criticism and Theological Interpretation* (Philadelphia: Fortress, 1977).

9. *Catholic Biblical Quarterly* 15 (1953) 141-62; also *The Sensus Plenior of Sacred Scripture* (Baltimore: St. Mary's Univ., 1955).

10. *Catholic Biblical Quarterly* 25 (1963) 262-85; *Ephemerides Theologicae Lovanienses* 43 (1967) 460-69; *The Jerome Biblical Commentary*, art. 71, esp. ##56-70.

11. Perceptively J.M. Robinson, *Catholic Biblical Quarterly* 27 (1965) 6-27, saw beneath the scholastic dress and related the quest for the *sensus plenior* to the problems of the new hermeneutic.

12. I should caution here that some would already speak of this as "canonical criticism." I object strongly to removing the sense of a whole book from the literal sense, because that would reduce the literal sense to the meaning of non-existent sources. No matter how certain our conclusions, Proto-, Deutero-, and Trito-Isaiah are reconstructions; the only extant literature is the *book* of Isaiah, and the literal sense is the sense of that book. On the borderline between the literal and the canonical senses are additions made by a final redactor in order to harmonize a book with other sacred books. This resembles Sheppard's "canon conscious redactions."

13. Edited by R.E. Brown et al. (New York: Paulist 1978), pp. 30-31.

14. I am not certain with what theory of inspiration McEleney is working but the theory advanced by Pope Leo XIII in *Providentissimus Deus*, which virtually presupposes a single author for a book, is not adequate to deal with many of the hermeneutic problems that we face today — it does not cover the developmental process I have described above under a broader approach to the "literal sense." Moreover, respectable Catholic scholars extend the inspiration/inerrancy discussion precisely to the canonical process, e.g., P. Benoit, "The Inspiration of the Septuagint," in *Jesus and the Gospel* (New York: Herder and Herder, 1973), pp. 1-10; N. Lohfink, "The Inerrancy and the Unity of Scripture," *Theology Digest* 13 (1965) 185-92.

15. At times there were partial collections, e.g., the (five books of the) Law, or the Prophets, or the Pauline Letters; and canons varied for groups within Judaism and for churches of different regions.

16. See P. Ricoeur, *Interpretation Theory: Discourse and the Surplus of Meaning* (Fort Worth: Texas Univ., 1976); H.-G. Gadamer, *Truth and Method* (New York: Seabury, 1975). In American Catholic thought, Sandra M. Schneiders has sought to apply the principles of Ricoeur and Gadamer to the Bible.

17. It is not clear to me to what extent those who emphasize "canonical context" or "canonical criticism" give preponderance to the meaning derived from historical criticism. Very interesting is the critique of B.S. Child's views by J.A. Sanders, "Canonical Context and Canonical Criticism," *Horizons in Biblical Theology*, on pages 173-97 in vol. II (1980), Sect. 2. In Sanders' view canonical criticism is a subdiscipline of biblical criticism; but what percentage of effort should be devoted to it as compared to another subdiscipline, historical criticism? I am not asking for an exact mathematical response, but an indica-

tion of where the various canonical critics stand on the issue. The same needs to be asked of those interested in the approach described in the previous footnote.

18. A. Dulles, "Ecumenism and Theological Method," *Journal of Ecumenical Studies* 17 (1980-81) 40-48, esp. 43, criticizes H. Kung's attempt to make the criterion of all theology "the original Christian message itself . . . analyzed by historical critical analysis." I agree with this criticism if criterion is understood as described above (a norm to which all must conform), but such a message is *a* criterion in the sense of something which enters importantly into the evaluation of all Christian theology. One may never ignore the literal sense of Scripture, and Christians must be aware of and justify instances in which they seriously differ from it.

19. This process has continued from the moment of canon formation until the present moment, and a thorough study of the hermeneutical issue would involve the interrelation of various stages of church interpretation, which are not always harmonious among themselves. Here I shall concentrate upon what a passage means to the contemporary church; and even then I cannot deal with the problem that a passage may not mean the same thing in all sections of the church, or even the same thing in liturgy and theology. Obviously I am approaching the question from a Christian viewpoint; a Jewish scholar might be concerned with what the Hebrew Scriptures came to mean in the rabbinic academies and the synagogues.

20. Paradoxically, then, "canonical sense" does not mean for me the sense that is once and for all times normative. Those who wrote the biblical books and gave to them what we call the literal sense had a partial insight into truth; so did those who formed the canon and thus gave to the books their canonical sense; the church has another partial insight when it finds a meaning for those books in its own life. The quest for meaning is open-ended, and the interaction of these various senses provides the excitement and wealth of exegesis. It is a challenge to do this exegesis constructively and yet not blandly.

21. *Communio* 7 (1980) 52.

22. "Mary, Mother of God and Contemporary Challenges," *Marian Studies* 29 (1978) 26-43, specifically 36-37.

23. It would please me if this misrepresentation was indeliberate. I note, however, that later O'Connor (p. 42) cites me as holding what he regards as a dangerous view, namely, that, were (contrary-to-fact) Joseph the human father of Jesus, this would not have excluded the fatherhood of God, which is an ontological not a biological concept. In so doing, O'Connor conveniently neglects to tell his readers how I emphasized that Cardinal Ratzinger, one of the most respected conservative theologians in Roman Catholicism, holds the same view (see my *Virginal Conception and Bodily Resurrection of Jesus* [New York: Paulist, 1973] 42); also *Theological Studies* 33 (1972) 16.

24. *The Washington Star*, Sunday Jan. 27, 1980, section G.

25. The affirmation that in order for a particular doctrine to be true a particular

fact must be historical needs to be proved in every case. Our history from Galileo on is filled with the wrong identification between doctrines and a customary but not necessarily accurate articulation of that doctrine in terms of historical facts.

26. See *The Jerome Biblical Commentary*, art. 71, #87, which gives attention to what is sometimes (but dubiously) presented as an exception, i.e., Vatican I's use of Mt 16:17-19.

27. For the pertinent passage of *Mysterium Ecclesiae* (1973), see my *Biblical Reflections on Crises Facing the Church* (New York: Paulist, 1975) 116-18.

28. In *Commentary on the Documents of Vatican II*, ed. H. Vorgrimler (5 vols.; New York: Herder and Herder, 1969) 3. 193.

The Dilemma Of A Translator*

M. LUCETTA MOWRY
Wellesley College Emerita
Wellesley, MA 02181

Recently, as I was reading an English translation of a contemporary German play, I was reminded of the Italian proverb: "The translator is a traitor," (*traduttore traditore*). How well the Italian understood the translator's dilemma. For months the translator of that play, "Dark River" by Lasker-Schuler, puzzled over the problem of rendering into English the local dialect of characters portraying persons living in Wuppertal during the 18th century. Should one follow the standards of modern English usage or select a regional American dialect? In either case the German idiom would not be well represented. To give the equivalent effect of the German the translator had decided to create a dialect which would be recognized as such but would avoid being associated with an identifiable American locale. This translator had worked imaginatively and faithfully to reflect the thought, intent, and style of the author, but there remained for her the nagging question: Have I been a traitor?

During the first century of the printing of the Bible in English vernacular, from Tyndale's New Testament of 1526 to the King James or Authorized Version of 1611, the work of translators was so closely associated with the religious and political turmoil of that period that some translators, regarded as traitors and heretics, had to leave their native land and even to forfeit their lives. In his prefatory address to the reader Tyndale defended his translation of the New Testament by saying, "I am sure and my conscience beareth me record that of a pure intent, simply and faithful, I have interpreted it as far forth as God gave me the gift of knowledge and understanding." His aim had been to make available a dignified yet simply worded English rendition of the Greek text. Dissatisfied with his first translation of some biblical passages, he rephrased them with greater stylistic grace. For example, his translation of Mt 1:23 in his first edition, "Emmanuel which is as much to say by interpretation, God with us," became in the 1534 edition "Emmanuel, which is by interpretation, God with us." Adversaries bitterly opposed his efforts by declaring his translation to be dishonest and heretical, and "in truth the food of death, the fuel of sin, the veil of malice, the pretext of false liberty, the protection of disobedience, the corruption of discipline, the depravity of morals, the termination of concord, the death of honesty, the well-spring of vices, the disease of virtue, the instigation of rebellion, the milk of pride, the nourishment of contempt, the death of peace, the destruction of charity, the enemy of unity, the murderer of truth." The translators of the KJV, who incorporated about 90% of Tyndale's New Testament in their work, did not escape harsh criticism even though they had been given royal authority for their version and took great pains in the preface to the reader to explain that the purpose of their translation was not to "make a bad one a good one . . . but to make a good one better." Nevertheless they were accused of being theologically unsound, ecclesiastically biased, of catering to a king's belief in witchcraft, of being blasphemous and intolerably deceitful, and of producing a vile imposter. During this period the translator's traitorous dilemma was not a casual matter.

Members of the RSV Bible Committee have worked since the 1930s and are still working with comparable dedication to make a good translation better. Opposition to its work, however, has not been as strident as that to the Tyndale and King James versions and has been expressed in critical pamphlets, an occasional examination of the theological record of its members, and in such colorful episodes as that of an American preacher who declared, as he burned a copy of the RSV with a blow torch in his pulpit, that like the devil it was hard to burn. The major problems of translation for the Committee concern matters of the reliability of ancient texts and the four-fold mandate given by the Division of Education and Ministry of the National Council of Churches. Since I am a member of the New Testament section of the Committee, I will discuss each of the two issues as it has been dealing with them, although it should be understood that the views I am expressing here are not necessarily those of all members of the Committee.

During the last hundred years textual critics have made great progress in establishing the authenticity of the Greek text of the New Testament documents. It has been noted that by modern standards of textual criticism the translators of the KJV (1611) used "a handful of late and haphazardly collected minuscule manuscripts, and in a dozen passages its reading is supported by no known Greek witness." By the end of the 19th century translators of the Revised Version were able to base their work on a Greek text which relied heavily on two uncial manuscripts of the fourth century, Codex Sinaiticus and Codex Vaticanus. This noteworthy advance in scholarly achievement had its detractors. The leader of the opposition was John W. Burgon who denounced the newly edited Greek text and the translation based on it by saying that "the systematic depravations of the underlying Greek is nothing else but a poison of the River of Life and its sacred source" and that "our revisors, with the best and purest of intention, no doubt, stand committed of having deliberately rejected the words of Inspiration in every page." Burgon believed that if the words of scripture had been dictated by the inspiration of the Holy Spirit, God would have providentially prevented them from being seriously corrupted during the course of their transmission. While translators agree that God in his providence does wondrous things, they need the aid of textual critics for the establishment of the most reliable Greek text; for they realize that the copying of manuscripts has been done by fallible persons who have problems with eyesight, hearing, wanderings of mind, judgment, spelling, grammar, interest in harmonizing conflicting scriptural passages, and the like.

Further discoveries of ancient manuscripts have magnified the work of textual critics during this century. After a careful examination of about 5,000 manuscripts and parts of manuscripts the United Bible Society, an international and interdenominational committee of textual scholars, has prepared a text now used by translators throughout the world. According to this committee, four special features of its Greek text are: "(1) a critical apparatus restricted for the most part to variant readings significant for translators or necessary for the establishing of the text; (2) an indication of the relative degree of certainty for each variant adopted as the text; (3) a full citation of representative evidence for each variant selected; and (4) a second apparatus giving meaningful differences of punctuation." The Committee has also published a supplementary volume, *A Textual Commentary on the Greek Text* (3rd ed., 1971) which summarizes its reasons for adopting one or another variant reading. An authoritative discussion of textual issues and the principles followed by textual critics in preparing the Greek text for translators is *The Text of the New Testament* (1968) by Bruce Metzger, a member of the UBS Committee and Chairman of the RSV Bible Committee.

While the UBS Greek text of the New Testament provides translators with a reliable basis for their translation, they still need to weigh the evidence of significant variant readings and to work out a translation which most accurately reflects the author's thought and is intelligible to the reader. The text of John 1:18 is "No one has ever seen God; the only Son, who is in the bosom of the Father, he has made him known" (RSV of 1946). In the textual apparatus the Committee noted that there are four variant textual traditions for "the only Son" (KJV and RSV): (1) "only God," (2) "only Son," (3) "only Son of God," and (4) "the only." The majority of the UBS Committee gave the first variant, "only God," a 'B' rating: that is, it accepted this with some degree of doubt. In its *Commentary* the Committee explains this by saying that "only God," a more difficult reading than "only Son," appears in two early papyri fragments (about A.D. 200 and early third century), that it does not seem to have been "the result of scribal assimilation to Jn 3:16, 18; 1 Jn 4:9," and that the use of "God" without the article seems to be more primitive. While the textual evidence for "only God" is sufficiently compelling to warrant making a change in the English version, how can a translator do this in a way that would be intelligible to the reader? It would be baffling to read "only God who is in the bosom of the Father." The context of the passage suggests that the author's thought is not misrepresented by saying, "God the only Son who is . . . ."

The second problem for the RSV Bible Committee is to make a translation of biblical texts which follows the fourfold mandate given by the Division of Education and

Ministry of the National Council of Churches: to make "revision involving necessary (1) changes in paragraph structure and punctuation, (2) elimination of archaisms while retaining the flavor of the Tyndale-King James tradition, (3) changes in the interest of accuracy, clarity and/or euphony of English expression, and (4) the elimination of masculine-oriented language so far as this can be done without altering passages that reflect the historical situation of ancient patriarchal culture and a masculine-oriented society." The dilemma for translators begins with the injunction to make only necessary changes and concludes with the difficult request to use inclusive language in translating the words of authors who lived during periods far removed from the feminist movement. In this situation it would have been remarkable for those authors to have given women their just due. We turn now to each of the four directives to show how the Committee is attempting to follow these guidelines as it works on the new revision.

In the first directive the Committee has been given the charge to make only necessary changes in paragraph structure and punctuation. Since editors of Greek editions of the text, including that of the UBS, differ in their judgment about the breaks for paragraphs, translators are not bound by their analysis of the major structural units of an author's thought. The editors of the UBS text, for example, regard Jn 3:1-21 to be a section in which the Johannine author reports Jesus' conversation with Nicodemus, and they suggest by their paragraphing two major conceptual developments in that conversation: 3:1-15 and 3:16-21. An examination of this section, however, reveals peculiarities which justify other possibilities. One notes in 3:11, after the typical Johannine formula "I tell you truly," that the author shifts to the first person plural for the speaker and to the second person plural for the persons addressed. While this is not the only shift in 3:11-16, its first appearance indicates that Jesus' conversation with Nicodemus has been concluded in 3:10, that the Christian community is now adding the testimony of its experience to Jesus' words, and that it is addressing persons of an unbelieving world. Its testimony comes to a climax in the statement that God in a selfless act of supreme love gave his Son for the whole world so that those who accept Christ in faith might have eternal life, that is, an existence in a new type of being which is spiritual and not limited by death (3:16). In the verses that follow (3:17-21) the author turns to the implications of that statement. If this is a correct understanding of the structure of the author's thought, the paragraphing of the text should be changed to that of three paragraphs: 3:1-10, 11-16, and 17-21.

The second part of the first directive concerns necessary changes in punctuation. An examination and analysis made by the editors of the UBS text of about six hundred variations of punctuation symbols indicated that it was necessary "to evaluate punctuation symbols and to determine their function and 'weight' in each set of meaningful variants." In suggesting changes of punctuation marks, therefore, translators are aided by notations about these symbols but are not bound by those which appear in the UBS text. For example, the English reader needs to have the long, involved, and complex sentences of the Greek text of Ephesians divided into shorter sense units. We note that after the salutation of that letter (Ep 1:1-2) the first chapter consists of two sentences, 1:3-14 and 1:15-23. The translators of the KJV followed that sentence structure, and by quoting only a part of the first sentence it is obvious that shorter sentences would be helpful in comprehending its meaning:

. . . in whom (Jesus Christ) we have redemption
through his blood, the forgiveness of sins, according to
the riches of his grace; wherein he hath abounded
toward us in all wisdom and prudence; having made
known unto us the mystery of his will, according to his
good pleasure which he hath purposed in himself: that
in the dispensation of the fulness of time he might
gather together in one all things in Christ, both which
are in heaven, and which are on earth; even in him: in
whom also we have obtained inheritance, being predestined according to the purpose of him who worketh
all things after the counsel of his own will; that we
should be to the praise of his glory, who first trusted in
Christ . . . (Ep 1:7-12).

Translators using the UBS text for John 1:3b, c, 4a with
its variants must wrestle with a complicated and difficult
problem of punctuation, one which did not exist for the
translators of the KJV who had before them a Greek text
with only one position for the period, at the end of verse 3.
On the basis of that text their translation reads: "and without him (the Word) was not anything made that was made.
In him was life;". If translators follow the punctuation of the
UBS text, however, they need to consider revising the translation to deal with a sentence which ends with the words
"anything made" and begin the next sentence with the
words "that was made." In previous editions of the RSV the
committee resolved the problem by retaining the punctuation of the KJV and by adding a footnote which translated
the UBS text "was not anything. That which has been made
was life in him." There were reasons for the decision not to
incorporate this reading in the text itself. Of the three
textual variants for the position of the period the UBS
Committee had given the variant selected for its Greek text a

'C' rating, that is, a rating which indicates a considerable degree of doubt about its reliability. Also, in its *Commentary* the Committee questioned a translation reading "that which has been made in him was life" by remarking, "whatever that may be supposed to mean."

There are, however, compelling reasons for translators to reconsider a translation which follows the punctuation of the UBS text and to resolve the difficulties still present in translations which follow the KJ tradition. There are four difficulties with that text. First, the final clause of verse 3 (1:3c) seems superfluous to the rest of the verse. Second, the consensus of orthodox and heretical ante-Nicene writers associated that clause, "that which has been made," with what follows in verse 4, a fact that persuaded the UBS Committee of the superiority of this variant. Third, the period after the final clause of verse 3 creates a break in the sequence of thought. In verse 4 we note that the thought returns to the Word instead of continuing with the creation of the world (1:3a-b) to say something that is true about the world (1:3c-4a) and to serve as a transitional statement about people (1:4b). Finally, the period after the final clause of verse 3 destroys the homogeneity of the poetical line and the anaphoric pattern observable in this section of the prologue (1:1-5). As many have noted, this section differs in diction and expression from the material immediately following. The former contains pronouncements or short statements which are tied together by the association of words and is concerned with a reality, metaphysical or theological in character, and the way that reality impinges upon the world and human life. But the latter are prose statements which speak of events in the mundane sphere.

As we consider revising the translation of John 1:3-4 we have three options: (1) we can decide to make no change by hanging on to the safe and time-honored rendering of the KJV, (2) we can accept the so-called unsatisfactory translation of the RSV footnote on 1:4a, or (3) we can follow the UBS text by suggesting a translation which may prove to be more satisfactory than that of the footnote. The decision depends in part on an understanding of the Johannine significance of the word "life" which appears here for the first of frequent times in the Fourth Gospel and 1 John.

As we look at a few of the references to "life," we find that "life" is something which God has and gives to the Son to have (5:26), that Christ himself is the way, the truth, and the life (14:6), and that Christ comes to give people life (10:10, 28). These passages indicate that "life" does not mean animate existence or even pre-existence. Hence we cannot accept the second option: "That which has been made was life in him" (1:3c-4a). As people come to know life, according to the evangelist, it is that kind of existence or power to exist in the full sense of the term; for "life" is that which people obtain from Christ through his words (6:68 and 63) and through eating his flesh and drinking his blood (6:54) and is that which all his believers have (3:16, 6:47). The significance of the term "life" is to be found, then, in the fact (a fact in the author's opinion) that Christ is the one who has the power to give life. Hence the Johannine term "life" is an active principle causing people to live, for Christ is indeed the way, the truth, and the life, terms which have directive significance. This means that the first option is possible as a simple statement about the Word as the kind of being who has continually in his power the ability to give life to people. But this translation does not resolve the problem of the four difficulties mentioned above.

For a new attempt to translate the UBS text of 1:3b-c, 4a one may take the clause "that which has been made" as an accusative of reference rather than as a nominative. This does not solve the problem of translation, however, for the

Greek sentence may be translated in four ways: "As for what
has been made in it (or, him) there (or, he) was life." The
first possibility is to translate the sentence to read: "As for
what has been made in *it there* was life." In a speculative line
of thought which declares something to be true about the
world in the physical sense the translation is permissible, but
it is not an appropriate transitional link with the thought of
life as being the light of all people. The second possibility is
"As for what has been made in *him he* was life," but the
translation makes no sense after the reference to "what has
been made." The third, "As for what has been made in *him
there* was life," is acceptable because the translation asserts
that there was continuously present in the Word the power
for obtaining life. However, the final possible translation,
"As for what has been made in *it he* was life," seems preferable for two reasons: (1) it maintains the continuity of what
has been made by declaring that in it the Word was and is
continuously present as that power which gives life,
and   (2) it makes the Word the subject of this sentence as it
is for this section of the prologue. In this section, which is
inspired by the statement in Genesis that God gave the
breath of life to people, the Johannine writer declares that
the Word, having created the world, is present in it as life,
namely as that power which continuously makes it possible
for people to receive through him the only existence that
deserves the term "life," existence in God. In 1:3-4 the
author, then, has subsumed cosmogony under soteriology
as earlier in 1:1-2 he subsumed ontology under soteriology.

This translation seems to resolve two of the four main
problems mentioned above: the superfluous character of
1:3c and the placing of the period in the ante-Nicene writings. It also appears to deal adequately with the other two
problems; the break in the sequence of thought and the
destruction of the homogeneity of poetical line with its

anaphoric pattern. This may be shown by printing the text
as follows:

> In the beginning was the *Word*
> and the *Word* was with *God,*
> and *God* was the *Word.*
> *He* was in the beginning with God.
>
> All things were made *through him,*
> and *without him* was not *anything made.*
> As for *what was made* in it he was *life,*
> and the *life* was the *light* of all people.
> The *light* shines in the *darkness,*
> and the *darkness* has not overcome it. (Jn 1:1-5)

I have chosen to discuss this first mandate about making only necessary changes in punctuation and paragraphing at some length to demonstrate the difficulties encountered by a translator who attempts to give an accurate
rendering of passages some of which have considerable
theological significance. We can now turn to the second
directive which concerns the elimination of archaisms while
at the same time retaining the flavor of the Tyndale-King
James tradition.

The Tyndale-King James tradition is noted and re-
vered for its simplicity and dignity of expression and for its
rhythmic cadences and resonances. Its "Bible English,"
which was not an accidental development of literary style, is
so loved that some want only the archaic "thee's" and
"thou's" changed. For them "Bible English" has given the
translation an aura of holiness, and they concur with the
judgment about the merits of old and new wine: "No one
after drinking old wine desires new; for he says, 'the old is
good.' " The mellowing of the old was a process that lasted
almost ninety years. During this time intensive work on

English versions of the Bible produced some outstanding translations: the Tyndale New Testament of 1526, the Coverdale Bible of 1535, the Matthew Bible of 1536, the Great Bible of 1539, the Geneva Bible of 1560, the Bishop's Bible of 1568, and the King James Version of 1611. This process, according to Mary Ellen Chase, brought about a fine "winnowing of words," which she illustrates by quoting translations of Job 38:7:

> When the morning stars gave me praise, and when all the angels of God rejoiced (The Coverdale of 1535)
> When the stars praised me together, and all the children of God rejoiced triumphantly (The Geneva Bible of 1560)
> When the morning stars sang together, and all the sons of God shouted for joy (KJV of 1611)

A factor contributing to the mellowing process was the extraordinary development in English language and literature during the Elizabethan era when persons like Spenser, Sidney, Hooker, Marlowe, and Shakespeare created a fine sense of literary style and raised the standards of literary taste. As today's translators work on the mandate to eliminate archaisms of the Tyndale-King James tradition, they would benefit by a comparable development.

It is instructive for the modern translator to review a few trends in translation which substitute expressions for the archaisms of the Tyndale-King James tradition. One trend was intended "to clothe the ideas of the Apostles with propriety and perspicuity" and to replace the "bald and barbarous language of the old vulgar version with the elegance of modern English." The reference to the barbarous translation is to the KJV. To illustrate the difference between the barbarous and the elegant translations I have selected a passage from Luke's Magnificat (Lk 1:46-48). The KJV reads: "My soul doth magnify the Lord, and my spirit hath rejoiced in God my Saviour. For he hath regarded the low estate of his handmaiden; for behold, from henceforth all generations call me blessed." The more elegant translation reads: "My soul with reverence adores my Creator, and all my faculties with transport join in celebrating the goodness of God my Saviour, who hath in so signal a manner condescended to regard my poor and humble station.Transcendent goodness! Every future age will now conjoin in celebrating my happiness!" Other examples include: "A city set on a hill cannot be hid" became "A city situate on a mountain must be conspicuous," and "whosoever shall kill shall be in danger of the judgment" became "whosoever commits murder shall be obnoxious to the judge." Other trends in modernizing English translations were the use of idiomatic English and colloquial paraphrases. Representative of the former are the commendable translations of James Moffatt and Edgar Goodspeed. The colloquial paraphrases of biblical texts, however, seem at times to make the authors' thoughts trivial and even banal. For example, Ferrar Fenton in his translation, *The Bible in Modern English* (1903) translated Psalm 100:1 to read:

"Hurrah to the Lord, all the Earth;
Serve the Lord with delight."

The Lord seems to be regarded as the captain of the local cricket team and the worshipers spectators cheering him on to victory. J.B. Phillips has modernized the archaism of "the holy kiss" of Rm 16:16 (KJV) — "Salute one another with a holy kiss. The churches of Christ salute you" — by the paraphrase "Give one another a hearty handshake all around for my sake."

In the American Bible Society's publication of the New Testament in today's English, *Good News for Modern Man* (1966), we find interpretative paraphrases. The translators begin their translation of the Gospel according to John with the sentence "Before the world was created, the Word already existed: he was with God, and he was the same as God." Interestingly, they have not used a paraphrastic expression for "Word" (Greek, *logos*) and have followed the long tradition of translating the Latin *verbum* of the Vulgate. Of all the many nuances of the Greek *logos* one of the few it never had was "word." Erasmus was one of a very few who tried to be more precise, and for changing *verbum* to *sermo* in his 1519 edition of the Latin text, he was accused of demeaning the incarnation. The translators of the *Good News* prudently retained "word" for *logos*, but paraphrased the rest of the sentence by altering three Greek terms: "before the world was created," "already existed," and "the same as God." Have they aided or misled the reader? One cannot be certain about the author's meaning for two of the terms, "in the beginning" and "was the same as God." Is "beginning" to be taken in the absolute or relative sense, that is, eternity out of which time emerged or the moment when time began and the process of coming into being began to begin? Does the declaration that the Word "was the same as God" mean that this sameness is to be understood as being essentially same in nature, as having comparable attributes, or as having functional similarity in actions? Finally, to translate the imperfect tense of the Greek verb "to be" by the words "already existed" does not convey the idea of continuous state of existence, that is, when the beginning began to begin the Word already was and still is in a continuous state of existence. When translators run into such problems, it seems wiser not to resolve them by interpretative paraphrases but to make the translation as literally faithful to the Greek text as possible and to leave interpretation to commentators.

As translators try to avoid colloquial and interpretative paraphrases, they also need to beware of being so literal in rendering the Greek text that they fall into the trap of producing a "schoolmaster's" version. At the end of the 19th century the translators of the first authorized revision of the KJV endeavored with consistent honesty to make a word-for-word translation of the Greek text, one which even followed the word order of Greek sentences. They changed, for example, the translation of Lk 9:17 of the KJV which reads: "and they did eat, and were all filled; and there was taken up of the fragments that remained to them twelve baskets" to "And they ate, and were filled: and there was taken up that which remained even to them of broken pieces, twelve baskets." A literal translation, though useful for the "schoolboy" beginning his study of New Testament Greek, is frequently alien to current idiomatic English usage, lacks graceful literary style, and at times is incomprehensible.

Since the Tyndale-King James tradition has been so successful and the dilemma so great, does a translator need to struggle with the problem of eliminating archaisms? Some say, "no"; others say, "only the thee's and thou's"; and others want a thorough revision of archaisms. Among the last was Noah Webster, the lexicographer. Though he had a high regard for the KJV, he tried his hand at making a translation of the Bible because he felt compelled to correct wrong and misleading words and phrases. In his opinion "a version of the Scripture for popular use should consist of words expressing the sense which is most common in popular usage so that the first ideas suggested to the reader would be the true meaning of words according to the original language." An example of the use of words from the

Elizabethan period which have lost their meaning may be found in the Markan story of the woman who wished to be healed by touching Jesus' garment. In the KJV of Mk 5:30 we find the words "press" and "virtue" used with a significance no longer given to them. The KJV reads: "And Jesus immediately knowing in himself that virtue had gone out of him, turned him about in the press, and said, Who touched my clothes." There are other archaisms familiar to you such as "whosoever," "lest haply," "if perchance," and "children of Israel," a phrase which evoked the comment: "It makes the Hebrews on their way through the wilderness to the promised land appear like babes in the woods." Let me use these expressions in a fictitious news item: "And it came to pass on the second day of the meeting of the Biblical Institute at Trinity College in Burlington, Vermont that a messenger came from McAuley Hall to bring to Sister Miriam Ward tidings of great commotions around Delehanty Hall; and lo, Sister Miriam was sore afraid lest haply the children of Hunt Hall be smitten by the sons of Sichel Hall if perchance they be scattered abroad. She saith, Whosoever killeth one of these little ones shall be slain by the sword."

According to the Division of Education and Ministry of the National Council of Churches, archaisms are to be eliminated while the flavor of the Tyndale-King James tradition is retained. This judicious mandate means preserving the simplicity and dignity of that tradition while using such current idiomatic expressions as make the thought of biblical authors contemporary and relevant. The resolution of the dilemma is not to be found in paraphrases or literal translations but in English versions which give the equivalent meaning of the author's words and the equivalent effect of his literary style and processes of thought.

The third charge given to the RSV Bible Committee

concerns changes in the interest of accuracy, clarity, and euphony. In the discussion of the first two directives we have noted that translators need to keep this third charge constantly in mind. Here we need to mention only a few examples. For more accurate wording, "the book of genealogy" (Mt 1:1) may be changed to "an account of the origin," "clamor" (Ep 4:31) to "wrangling," and "uncleanness" (1 Th 4:5) to "immorality." For greater clarity, the petitional section of the prayer in Ephesians 3:14-19, a single sentence in the Greek text, may be more clearly understood by introducing each of the three petitions by the phrase "I pray that" at the beginning of verses 16 and 18 and of the second half of verse 19. And for greater euphony, the Lukan statement about John the Baptist in 1:15 may be changed from reading "and he will be filled with the Holy Spirit, even from his mother's womb" to "even before his birth he will be filled with the Holy Spirit." Similarly, to change the exhortation in 1 Th 3:13 which reads "establish your hearts unblamable in holiness before our God and Father" to "strengthen your hearts in holiness to be blameless before our God and Father" seems to give a more polished rendition of the Greek.

The fourth and final charge of the Division of Education and Ministry presents the dilemma of eliminating masculine-oriented language so far as this can be done without altering passages that reflect the historical situation of ancient patriarchal culture and a masculine-oriented society. Bruce Metzger, chairperson of the RSV Bible Committee, in a memo to its members stated clearly and concisely the basic nature of the dilemma: "The main problem is where to draw a line between   (1) re-writing passages that reflect a historical situation of an ancient patriarchal and masculine-oriented society, and   (2) eliminating masculine expressions some of which have been introduced during the translation process. The latter can usually be eliminated without producing cumbersome and unnatural English; the former cannot be eliminated without committing violence to the text."

The RSV Bible Committee has few problems with optional masculine expressions, especially the word "man" in the generic sense, a significance no longer acceptable in feminist circles. In passages where this word does not even appear in the original text translators may replace "any man" with "anyone," etc.; and they can change "insolent men" to "the insolent." In John 2:10 it is possible to change the translation from "every man serves the good wine first; and when men have drunk freely, then the poor wine" to "everyone serves the good wine first, and then the inferior after the guests have become drunk." For "men" in the collective sense one can use "human beings," "people," etc. However, if the original text specifically refers to persons of the masculine sex as in Mk 6:44 and Jn 1:13, the words "man" or "men" must be retained.

The news media brought the dilemma of the use of inclusive language to public attention at the end of 1980 when reporters revealed the recommendations of a Task Force appointed by the Division of Education and Ministry to examine biblical translations. The Task Force chose to concentrate its attention on the use of inclusive language and frankly admitted that it was also faced with a dilemma. On the one hand, it recognized that, since the KJV, the RSV had become the most used standard English text, especially in scholarly and ecclesiastical circles, and that extensive use of inclusive language for a new revision of the KJV would so change original biblical expressions that the original conceptuality of the Bible would be lost. On the other hand, a process of paraphrasing for the sake of using inclusive language, including the terms for God and Christ, would have the advantage of making "half of humanity" feel enfranchised.

The public response to the report on the proposals of the Task Force was not unanimous applause. The Task Force had specifically recommended: (1) that the RSV Bible Committee move more boldly in changing the language about persons, e.g. the replacement of male terms by "humankind," "siblings," and the like, and the inclusion of the names of wives with those of their spouse (Abraham and Sarah, Adam and Eve); (2) that it retain the Greek neuter when referring to the Spirit, or in the Old Testament the Hebrew feminine; (3) that with reference to Jesus Christ it use language which does away with maleness of the incarnate one who by becoming flesh became human; and (4) that it realize that connotations for God such as Lord, Father, or He are accidents of the limitations of human language. On the last point the Task Force notes that these accidents occurred at the time of ancient Israel's rejection of a pagan pantheon with its male and female deities, and it sees no need to retain the language of an ancient theological victory in an era when all segments of God's vast human family need assurance of God's concern and love. Some members of that vast family responded quickly to the recommendations of the Task Force with sarcastic fury. In letters to editors of newspapers and journals one read: "Now the Bowdlerized Bible . . . with all the filthy language scrubbed out"; "Do they really think that Jesus meant for us to be baptized in the name of the Parent, the Sibling, and the Holy It"; and "Rumor has it, the translation is being executed by a team of eunuchs."

While translators are sympathetic to the Task Force's concern for the feminist cause, they also need to remember that ancient biblical literature was permeated by the views and vocabulary of a patriarchal culture. In a reflective mood one wonders about the reaction of biblical authors to the entrance of Eve and Sarah into their texts. Would their reaction be one of mild irritation (Does the modern translator not realize that I meant what I wrote in speaking of Adam and Abraham without mentioning their wives?); one of amused resignation (I ought to have known that some day a translator would let women crash the stag-party.); or one of grateful relief (Hurrah to God, all the Earth, for the translator has at last granted Eve and Sarah freedom from male domination, an impossible dream in my day!)? How far can honest translators rewrite an author's text?

The Task Force gave as a model to be followed a rendition of Rm 8:28-29: "We know that in everything God works for good with those who love God, who are called according to God's purpose. For those whom God foreknew, God also predestined to be conformed to the image of God's child in order that it might be the firstborn among many children." To eliminate the use of the masculine pronoun by repeating the word "God" and to substitute "child" for the Greek "son" seems to be a very contrived paraphrastic way to translate the text.

Much can be done legitimately in changing the language with reference to persons and possibly some with reference to God, but the boldness of feminist paraphrases urged by the Task Force removes the translator as far from the original text as do paraphrases for ideological or other purposes. One can think of other reasons for not moving with unwarranted boldness. Concentration on the use of inclusive language raises the question about the basic message of the Bible. According to one commentator, those who urge us to paraphrase its message for such purposes seem to be following the "guidelines set down by the Equal Employment Opportunities Commission," and he states further that they "care more about new ideas than true ideas and live in blind idolatry of the future rather than in simple gratitude to the past." While biblical authors were deeply committed to society's realization of its full potentiality and the creation of a better world, they were primarily concerned about calling people to obey God's will. Their social message was a by-product of this central, all-encompassing theme. Regard for the Bible as an instrument for specific social changes in contemporary society gives it an anachronistic character. Its authors were not interested in portraying Adam and Abraham as champions of the women's cause. And the procedure of injecting new ideas into an ancient text actually minimizes the achievements of today's feminist movement by suggesting that it had its origin in past millennia.

The RSV Bible Committee, following the King James tradition which did not permit marginal notes of sectarian nature, produced in 1977 an ecumenical version of the Bible used by Protestants, Roman Catholics, and Greek Orthodox. Translations which attempt to eliminate references to "sexism," and in due course other social issues such as racism, classism, scientism, and anti-semitism would represent the opposite trend and result in what was known in Jesus' day as Targums, that is, paraphrastic versions rendering Hebrew texts into Aramaic with the freedom of adapting those texts to satisfy the sensibilities of synagogue congregations. If translators made a Targum to satisfy the sensibilities of scientism, would they substitute scientific terminology for the mythical and legendary language of the biblical accounts of creation and Jesus' nativity?

This kind of boldness would be not only a divisive factor in the church but also too violent a reaction to the problem of resolving the translator's dilemma. We note that in all religious traditions, including the Christian tradition, a distinction is made between the ultimate basis upon which we build our personal faith and the expression of that faith by others before us. We accept the biblical expressions as traditional, and to remove ourselves from that tradition seems to be an unnecessary loss; for we live not to ourselves alone but by the increment of all that persons of every age have held to be true and sacred.

Confronted with the dilemma of meeting the requests of groups with specific interests and of avoiding a distortion of an author's views, translators find their satisfaction in resolving it by trying to understand and express the meaning of authors' words and the organization of their ideas. This gives translators the opportunity to enter the processes of their thought, their hopes and fears, and their affirmations of faith. Translators will have succeeded if the reader finds that language has not been a barrier for understanding them.

FOOTNOTES

*We are grateful to Prof. Mowry for summarizing in this article the two lectures entitled *The Dilemma of a Translator* presented at the 18th Biblical Institute held at Trinity College, Burlington, Vermont, June 20-25, 1982. Because the material was originally given in the form of lectures, she has omitted footnotes. (Ed.)

The Revised Standard Version

BRUCE M. METZGER
Princeton Theological Seminary
Princeton, NJ 08540

The New Testament of the Revised Standard Version
(RSV) was published in 1946; the Old Testament in 1952;
the books of the Apocrypha in 1957; the second edition of
the New Testament in 1971; and the expanded edition with
the Apocrypha in 1977. The Revised Standard Version is, in
fact, still in the making, for the RSV Bible Committee is an
on-going committee, and its annual meetings are devoted to
taking into account the discovery and publication of still
more ancient manuscripts of the Old and New Testaments
as well as the refining of the English expressions chosen to
render the original text. At the moment the Committee is
also giving attention to the presence of masculine-oriented
phraseology imposed in the Bible by earlier translators (See
below, "The Next Stages", Ed.). The most noteworthy new
development was the publication in 1977 of the first truly
ecumenical edition of the Bible in English, suited for use by
members of all three principal branches of the Christian
Church — Protestant, Roman Catholic, and Eastern Orthodox (See below, "The First Truly Ecumenical Bible",
Ed.).

In what follows attention is given to the historical background of the RSV Bible, including earlier revisions of the King James Version culminating in the American Standard Version (1901) and the subsequent formation of the RSV Bible Committee. This is followed by consideration of certain problems, old and new, in Bible translating, and the on-going work of the RSV Committee in preparation of the forth-coming revision of the RSV text.

Earlier Revisions of the King James Version

When King James I of England assembled about fifty scholars in the early seventeenth century, it was not to make an entirely new translation of the Bible, but to revise the English version of 1568 called the Bishops' Bible. Let it be said with all due emphasis that these learned men produced, from a purely literary point of view, a classic rendering of the Scriptures, and the 1611 Bible has deserved the acclaim that it eventually won for itself.

Despite the wide acceptance which the 1611 Bible eventually attained, in subsequent generations occasional proposals were voiced as to the desirability of introducing here and there various corrections and other alterations of phraseology. During the eighteenth and nineteenth centuries several dozen private ventures in Bible translating were undertaken in England and in America. Some of these were merely revisions of the King James Version; others were more independent paraphrases. An example of the former type was John Wesley's revised edition of the Authorized Version of the New Testament, published in 1768 with some 12,000 alterations in all, but none of them, the reader is assured, for altering's sake. The same year saw the publication of a quite paraphrastic rendering in the stilted, verbose style of eighteenth-century English popular in the time of Samuel Johnson. Made by the bibliographer Edward Harwood, an ordained Presbyterian minister, its style can be seen from the grandiose manner in which Harwood renders Jesus' Parable of the Prodigal Son:

> A Gentleman of a splendid family and opulent fortune had two sons. One day the younger approached his father, and begged him in the most importunate and soothing terms to make a partition of his effects betwixt himself and his elder brother — The indulgent father, overcome by his blandishments, immediately divided all his fortunes betwixt them, etc. (Luke 15:11ff.)

Harwood's elaboration of the familiar text of John 3:16 is as follows:

> For the supreme God was affected with such immense compassion and love for the human race, that he deputed his son from heaven to instruct them — in order that everyone who embraces and obeys his religion might not finally perish, but secure everlasting happiness.

In America Noah Webster, the lexicographer, prepared a revision of the King James Version which was published in New Haven in 1833. A Congregational layman who had been admitted to the bar, Webster's purpose was, as he says, to remove obsolete phrases, to remove grammatical infelicities,[1] and to correct mistranslations. To this he added one thing more, which he considered of very grave importance. In his own words:

> To these may be added many words and phrases very offensive to delicacy, and even to decency. In the opin-

ion of all persons with whom I have conversed on the subject, such words and phrases ought not to be retained in the version. Language which cannot be uttered in company without a violation of decorum, or the rules of good breeding, exposes the Scriptures to the scoffs of unbelievers, impairs their authority, and multiplies or confirms the enemies of our holy religion. (Preface to Webster's Bible)

Another American production, similar to Harwood's British monstrosity, was *A New and Corrected Version of the New Testament,* prepared by Rodolphus Dickinson, an Episcopalian rector, and published in Boston in 1833. The preface to this volume is an astonishing exhibition of conceit. The author condemns the "quaint monotony and affected solemnity" of the King James Version, with its "frequently rude and occasional barbarous attire," and he declares his purpose to adorn the Scriptures with "a splendid and sweetly flowing diction" suited to the use of "accomplished and refined persons." Here are Mr. Dickinson's renderings of three well-known passages:

And it happened, that when Elizabeth heard the salutation of Mary, the embryo was joyfully agitated (Luke 1:41).

His master said to him, Well-done, good and provident servant! you was[2] faithful in a limited sphere, I will give you a more extensive superintendence: participate in the happiness of your master (Matthew 25:21).

Festus declared with a loud voice, Paul, you are insane! Multiplied research drives you to distraction (Acts 26:24).

One of the curiosities in the history of the English Bible is the translation of the Scriptures made by Julia E. Smith, the Women's Suffragist of the past century. Published in 1876 at Hartford at her own expense, this version is excessively wooden, using throughout the same English word for the same Hebrew or Greek word. She thought that, as she says in the Preface, this would give "much clearer understanding of the text." The end result, however, of such a policy of mechanical translation was much nonsense and, in some passages, almost complete mistranslation. In historical narratives she rendered Hebrew verbs in the future tense, giving the reader the impression that everything in those narratives, including the acts of creation in Genesis, chapter 1, was yet to happen. The extent of the obscurity is suggested by Jr 22:23, presented as a complete sentence and reading: "Thou dwelling in Lebanon, building a nest in the cedars, how being compassionated in pangs coming to thee the pain as of her bringing forth."

Miss Smith illustrates dramatically a fact which some persons do not appreciate, namely, that most words have more than one meaning, and in translation the more specific meaning of a word in a particular context has to be determined from that context. Perhaps her initial mistake was to seek no help or advice in her venture, as she naively discloses to the reader: "It may be thought by the public in general that I have great confidence in myself in not conferring with the learned in so great a work, but as there is but one book in the Hebrew tongue, and I have defined it word for word, I do not see how anybody can know more about it than I do"!

The Revised Version in England and the
Standard Version in America

As time went on, an ever greater need was felt for a thorough revision of the 1611 Bible to be made by a committee comprising representatives of diverse ecclesiastical affiliations. In 1870 both Houses of Convocation of the Anglican Church in England adopted a recommendation which led to the preparation of an "official" revision. A committee of British scholars and divines, numbering at various times twenty-four to twenty-eight, labored for ten and a half years to produce the Revised Version of the New Testament and fourteen years to produce the Old Testament. Soon after work on the revision had begun, an invitation was extended to American scholars to co-operate with the British in this work of common interest. Thereupon an American committee, comprising about thirty members (of which only about twenty members were active), was appointed from nine different denominations, with the eminent church historian Philip Schaff acting as chairman.

The Revised Version of the Bible was published and copyrighted by the University Presses of Cambridge and Oxford, the New Testament appearing in 1881, the Old Testament in 1885, and the Apocrypha in 1895. Readings which the American Committee preferred but which the British Committee rejected were printed in an Appendix (for example, the Americans preferred "Jehovah" to represent the Hebrew divine name [tetragrammaton] instead of the traditional word "Lord" printed with a capital and small capitals).[3] The agreement was that after fourteen years the Americans would be allowed to publish an edition of the Revised Version that incorporated into the text itself the several preferences previously listed in the Appendix. Accordingly, in 1901 the American Committee issued through Thomas Nelson and Sons the Standard American Edition of the Revised Version of the Bible (the Apocryphal books were not included). In order to protect the integrity of the version, which came to be called the American Standard Version, its text was copyrighted by the publisher.

The fate of the Revised Version in Great Britain was disappointing. Complaints about its English style began to be made as soon as it appeared. Charles Hadden Spurgeon, the great English preacher at the close of the nineteenth century, put it tersely when he remarked that the Revised New Testament was "strong in Greek, weak in English." The Revisers were often woodenly literal, inverting the natural order of words in English to represent the Greek order; and they carried the translation of the article, and of the tenses, beyond their legitimate limits. An example of rather tortuous order in English in the Revision is Luke 9:17, "And they did eat, and were all filled; and there was taken up that which remained over to them of broken pieces, twelve baskets." These criticisms apply as well to the American Standard Version.

In the United States the work of the Revisers was somewhat more widely adopted than in Britain. But in both countries the Revision failed to supplant the King James Version in popular favor. Furthermore, proponents of other versions in a more modern idiom deprecated the Revisers' continued use of archaic speech.

The need, then, for a generally acceptable revision continued, and was accentuated during the twentieth century by the discovery of new evidence for the text and its meaning. Many private translations appeared, representing various interests and emphases. Three widely used modern speech renderings were those of R.F. Weymouth, James Moffatt,[4] and E.J. Goodspeed. More idiosyncratic were the "immersionist" Bible, which uses "immerse" in place of "baptize," and the Jehovah's Witnesses' *New World Translation*, which introduces the word "Jehovah" 237 times into the New Testament.

The Revised Standard Version

Steps to produce a suitable revision of the American Standard Version were undertaken in 1928 when the copyright of that version was acquired by the International Council of Religious Education. In the same year the American Standard Bible Committee was appointed, with an original membership of fifteen scholars, to have charge of the text of the American Standard Version and to make further revision of the text should it be deemed necessary. The chairman of the Committee was Luther A. Weigle, Dean of Yale Divinity School and Chairman of the Federal Council of Churches of Christ.

For two years the Committee wrestled with the question whether or not a revision should be undertaken; and if so, what should be its nature and extent. At one extreme stood James Hardy Ropes of Harvard, who held that the revisions of the King James Version published in 1881 and 1901 ought not to have been made, and opposed any further revision.[5] At the other extreme was Edgar J. Goodspeed of Chicago, who advocated a new version in present-day colloquial English. Finally, after revisions of representative chapters of the Bible had been made and discussed, a majority of the Committee decided that there should be a thorough revision of the American Standard Version of 1901, which would stay as close to the King James tradition as it could in the light of present knowledge of the Greek text and its meaning on the one hand, and present usage of English on the other.

In 1930 the nation and the churches were going through a serious economic depression and it was not until 1936 that funds could be secured and the work of revision could begin in earnest. A contract was negotiated with Thomas Nelson and Sons, publishers of the American

Standard Version, to finance the work of revision by advance royalties, in return for which Nelson was granted the exlusive right to publish the Revised Standard Version for a period of ten years. Thereafter it was to be open to other publishers under specific conditions.

With the financial undergirding thus provided, it was possible to schedule regular sessions of both the Old Testament and the New Testament Sections. Travel expenses and lodging and meals for the members were provided. No stipends or honoraria, however, have been given to RSV Committee members, who contribute their time and energies for the good of the cause.

After serious work had begun, a hope was expressed that co-operation of British scholars might be obtained, thus making the version an international translation. The war years of 1939-1945, however, made such collaboration impossible. In the summer of 1946, after the war was over, an effort was made to secure at least a token of international collaboration in the work on the Old Testament, the RSV New Testament having been published in February, 1946. Such partial collaboration was not to be forthcoming, for in that same year delegates of several Protestant Churches in Britian decided that they should begin work on a wholly new translation, one which made no attempt to stand within the tradition of the 1611 Bible. The outcome of this effort was the New English Bible published in 1970.

Meanwhile, work continued on the RSV Old Testament. After 81 separate meetings, totalling 450 days of work, the complete Bible was published September 30, 1952, the festival day, appropriately enough, of St. Jerome.[6] The new version was launched with an unprecedented publicity campaign. On the evening of the day of publication, in the United States, in Canada, and in many other places,

3418 community observances were held with over one and a half million persons attending.

The fanfare, however, did not protect the version from adverse criticism. Pamphlets appeared bearing such titles as *The Bible of Antichrist, The New Blasphemous Bible,* and *Whose Unclean Fingers Have Been Tampering with the Holy Bible, God's Pure, Infallible, Verbally Inspired Word?* The last named pamphlet opens with the sentence: "Every informed and intelligent person knows that our government is crawling with communists, or those who sanction and encourage communism" — which indicates the line along which the version was attacked. In fact, those who were looking for an opportunity to calumniate the National Council of Churches, under whose auspices the RSV had been produced, managed to influence Senator Joseph McCarthy's investigative committee to bring insidious and absurd charges against several members of the RSV Committee, to the effect that they were either communists or were hospitable to communist ideas — allegations that were eventually printed, of all places, in the United States Air Force Training Manual! As the result of a thorough investigation conducted by non-partisan authorities, this entirely unsupported charge was rebutted on the floor of the House of Representatives in Washington.[7]

Despite these and other criticisms during succeeding years, the RSV made its way in the United States and in other countries where the English language is used. It is a testimony to its qualities that in Great Britain, where it has not enjoyed the intensive "promotion" which it was given in North America, it has made steady headway on the ground of its intrinsic merit.

The Revised Standard Version, Catholic Edition

A new and unexpected development came in the autumn of 1953 when the Chairman of the Standard Bible Committee received a letter from the Catholic Biblical Association of Great Britain, asking whether there would be any disposition to confer with them about certain emendations in the RSV which they had in mind, with an eye to the possibility of issuing an adaptation for Roman Catholic readers. After consultation with members of the RSV Committee, Dean Wiegle and Dr. Gerald E. Knoff, who was then the General Secretary of the Division of Christian Education of the National Council of Churches, began conversations with representatives of the Catholic Biblical Association. By 1956 most of the desired New Testament changes were reviewed, a draft of a Foreword was discussed, and the exact wording on the title page was approved. All seemed to be going well — but the uncertainties of human life interposed a delay. Cardinal Griffin of London, who had written a Foreword for the RSV New Testament, Catholic Edition, died suddenly.

The promoters of the edition in England were faced with a quandary. Did the Cardinal's authorization for the edition still hold? And if technically legal, was it wise and prudent to proceed? As it turned out, Cardinal Griffin's successor, Archbishop William Godfrey, declared in 1958 that he could not sanction the venture, that it would cause a scandal to the faithful to receive a translation of the New Testament that had been made originally by a committee of Protestant scholars.

In the course of time, however, in view of the new climate that began to pervade the Roman Catholic Church after Vatican Council II, negotiations were resumed, and finally in the spring of 1965 the Catholic Edition of the RSV New Testament was published by the two branches of Thomas Nelson and Sons, in Edinburgh and in New York.

An appendix in the volume lists the 93 verses involving 67 slight changes in the wording required by the Catholic biblical scholars. (The list includes also the original RSV wording.)

The next stage began when consideration was given to a Catholic Edition of the RSV Old Testament. As is generally known, the Old Testament in Catholic Bibles includes more than the thirty-nine books of the Hebrew Scriptures. These additional books and parts of books, accepted as Deuterocanonical by Catholics, are regarded by Protestants (with several other books) as Apocryphal. The Apocrypha, originally included in the King James Bible of 1611, were translated by a panel of the RSV Committee (working from 1953 to 1956) and published by Nelson in 1957.

Surprisingly enough, the scholars of the Catholic Biblical Association decided to ask for no changes whatever in the RSV Old Testament (including even the rendering of Isaiah 7:14, "Behold, a young woman shall conceive and bear a son . . ."), or in the RSV Deuterocanonical books, which were placed throughout the Old Testament in accord with their position in the Latin Vulgate Bible. In 1966 the RSV Catholic Edition of the entire Bible was published, with a brief Foreword by Cardinal Heenan in the British edition and one by Cardinal Cushing in the American printing. Catholic notes, as at that time required, were included, but Protestant nomenclature in the titles of the biblical books was adopted.

The Catholic Edition of the RSV was just that — a special edition of the RSV text adapted for Roman Catholic readers. The notes as well as the expanded form of the Old Testament made it unsuited as a common or ecumenical Bible. The steps which led to making such an edition, however, were taken during the following decade.

The First Truly Ecumenical Bible

The first step in the production of a truly ecumenical Bible was taken in 1966 when Richard Cardinal Cushing, Archbishop of Boston, gave his imprimatur to *The Oxford Annotated Bible, with the Apocrypha.* This edition, prepared by Herbert G. May and Bruce M. Metzger, contained the original RSV text, not the text modified for the Catholic Edition. The books of the Apocrypha were segregated and stood after the New Testament.

The next step was in 1971 when the second edition of the RSV New Testament was issued.[8] This incorporated a number of changes that reflect the Greek text as adopted for the third edition of the United Bible Societies' *Greek New Testament,* which serves throughout the world as a standard text for translations and revisions made by Protestants and Catholics alike. Among such changes was the transfer of the ending of the Gospel of Mark and of the *pericope de adultera* (Jn 7:53-8:12) from the RSV footnotes into the text, though the passages continue to be separated from the context by a blank space to show that they were not part of the original text.

Soon afterward a significant step was taken by scholars of the Catholic Biblical Association of Great Britain. Under the leadership of Dom Bernard Orchard, O.S.B., and Dr. Reginald C. Fuller, a plan was evolved to divide the books of the Apocrypha into two sections, those which the Catholic Church regards as Deuterocanonical and those which are not so regarded. In an edition issued by Collins Press in 1973 these two sections were bound separately between the Old and New Testaments. The volume, therefore, had four sections: the thirty-nine books of the Old Testament; the twelve Deuterocanonical books; the First and Second Books of Esdras and the Prayer of Manasseh (three books which are part of the traditional Apocrypha but are not included among the Deuterocanonical books); and the twenty-seven books of the New Testament. No Catholic notes were included, since this Bible was to be "common," for use by Roman Catholics and Protestants alike.

It should be noted that in such an arrangement Catholics made a significant departure from the accepted practice of their long history. The separation of the Deuterocanonical books from their places throughout the Old Testament is essentially an accommodation to the Protestant arrangement of the books of the Bible.

In May of 1973 a specially bound copy of the Collins RSV "Common Bible" was presented to Pope Paul. In a private audience granted to a small group comprising the Greek Orthodox Archbishop Athenagoras of London, Lady Priscilla and Sir William Collins, Herbert G. May, and the present writer, Pope Paul accepted the copy as a significant step in furthering ecumenical relations among the churches.

Worthy as the "Common Bible" is, however, it fails to live up to its name, for it lacks the full canon of books recognized as authoritative by Eastern Orthodox Churches. The Greek, the Russian, the Ukrainian, the Bulgarian, the Serbian, the Armenian, and other Eastern Churches accept not only the traditional Deuterocanonical books received by the Roman Catholic Church, but also the Third Book of Maccabees. Furthermore, in Greek Bibles Psalm 151 stands at the close of the Psalter, and the Fourth Book of Maccabees is printed as an Appendix to the Old Testament. Inasmuch as these texts were lacking in the "Common Bible" presented to Pope Paul, on that occasion Archbishop Athenagoras expressed to the present writer the hope that steps might be taken to produce a truly ecumenical edition of the Holy Scriptures.

Actually, in 1972 a subcommittee of the RSV Bible Committee had already been commissioned to prepare a translation of III and IV Maccabees and Psalm 151. The members of the subcommittee were Demetrios J. Constantelos, Sherman E. Johnson, Robert A. Kraft, Allen Wikgren, and the writer. In 1976 the completed translation of the three additional texts was made available to the five publishers licensed to issue the RSV Bible. Oxford University Press took steps immediately to produce an expanded form of *The New Oxford Annotated Bible, with the Apocrypha,* the edition of the RSV which had earlier received the imprimatur of Cardinal Cushing.

This expanded edition[9] was published by the Oxford University Press on May 19, 1977. A special pre-publication copy was presented by the present writer to His All Holiness Demetrios I, the Ecumenical Patriarch of Constantinople and titular head of the several Orthodox Churches. In accepting the gift, the Ecumenical Patriarch expressed satisfaction at the availability of an edition of the sacred Scriptures which English readers in all branches of the Christian Church can use.

Thus, the story of the making of the Revised Standard Version of the Bible with the expanded Apocrypha is an account of the slow but steady triumph of ecumenical concern over more limited sectarian interests. For the first time since the Reformation one edition of the Bible has the blessings of leaders of the Protestant, Roman Catholic, and Eastern Orthodox Churches alike.

The Next Stages

As was mentioned earlier, the RSV Bible Committee is an on-going committee that meets annually. Like Luther, who in repeated revisions continually sought to refine and polish his German translation of the Scriptures, the RSV Committee has not hesitated "to bring backe to the anuill [anvil] that which we had already hammered" — to quote an expression used in the preface of the King James Bible.

By the mid-1980s it is expected that the second edition of the RSV Old Testament will be finished. A certain number of changes will also be introduced into the current second edition of the New Testament. Among significant changes will be the dropping of the archaic second person singular pronouns from the Psalms and other prayers in the Bible. In the sixteenth and seventeenth centuries it was customary to use "thou," "thee," and "thine" in ordinary speech. Twenty-five years ago the RSV Committee abandoned this usage except for the Psalms and other prayers in the Bible. Today the archaic pronouns are being used less and less frequently in contemporary liturgy and public prayers, and the Committee has decided that future editions of the RSV will employ the same forms in addressing the Deity as are used for individuals. Such a step will, in fact, reproduce more accurately the usage of the Hebrew and Greek texts themselves; which make no linguistic differentiation between address to God and to a person.

In another area of English usage the RSV Bible Committee has become sensitive to what is termed masculine-oriented language. Increasing numbers of persons are becoming dissatisfied with the generic use of the word "man" or "men," which traditionally has referred to both men and women. In fact, for some persons such language has become highly offensive, and during the past several years a wide variety of steps have been taken to introduce what is called "inclusive" language. Instead of saying, for example, "The West was settled by the pioneers who with their wives and children, overcame many difficulties," it is obviously fairer to phrase the statement, "The West was settled by pioneer families, who overcame many difficulties." Several major publishers (including Ginn; Holt, Rinehart and Winston; Houghton Mifflin; McGraw-Hill; Macmillan; Random House; Scott, Foresman and Co.)[10] have prepared guidelines concerning the use of inclusive language for authors who plan to submit manuscripts for consideration. The State of Connecticut has revised its constitution to make equal reference to men and women. Several Protestant denominations, as well as groups within Roman Catholic orders and within Reformed Judaism, have undertaken to rephrase their psalter, liturgy, hymns, and a variety of church standards and constitutional documents.

Now, in earlier versions of the Bible, one finds that translators more than once inserted the word "man" where it is lacking in the original text. In many other passages where the original text permits the rendering "any one" or "no one" the King James translators chose to say "any man" or "no man." This practice limits many statements unduly, and results in occasional infelicities. For example, the original printing of the King James Version of Mark 10:18 read: "And Jesus said unto him, Why callest thou me good? There is no man good, but one, *that is* God." Since this implies that God is a man, the unfortunate rendering was soon altered to read, "there is none good but one, *that is* God." Rv 3:20 in the King James Version reads, "Behold I stand at the door, and knock: if any man hear my voice, and open the door I will come in to him, and sup with him, and he with me." Here the Greek text has no word for "man" and in 1946 the RSV correctly rendered it, ". . . if any one hears my voice . . ." In Luke 17:34 the King James translators inserted the word "men," contrary to the Greek text, so as to read, "I tell you, in that night there shall be two *men* in one bed; the one shall be taken, and the other shall be left." In the second edition of the RSV (1971) the Committee, for obvious reasons, removed the intrusive word, thus returning more closely to the Greek and, incidentally, to all English translations of the verse in pre-1611 Bibles.

At its annual meetings in recent years the RSV Committee has been giving attention to instances where the traditional English rendering has inserted "man" or "men" without support from the Hebrew or the Greek. For example, in Psalm 54:3 "insolent men" and "ruthless men" will become "the insolent" and "the ruthless"; Psalm 66:6 "men passed through the river on foot" will become "they passed through . . ."; and similarly in 106:16; 119:136; 141:5; 142:4; 143:2.

In John 2:10, the Committee has proposed to change "Every man serves the good wine first; and when men have drunk freely, then the poor wine" to "Everyone serves the good wine first, and then the inferior wine after the guests have become drunk"; in Rm 1:17, "He who through faith is righteous . . ." to "The one who . . ."; and in Rm 2:6, "He will render to every man according to his works" to "He will repay according to each one's works."

Besides passages such as these where earlier translators have inserted the word "man" or "men," though it is lacking in the original text, the RSV Committee is giving attention to instances where it may be possible without producing contrived English, to render the Hebrew word 'ish and the Greek word anthropos in an inclusive sense. For example, in the first Psalm, the Committee, taking 'ish as a collective term, has replaced "Blessed is the man who walks not in the counsel of the wicked," with "Blessed are those who do not walk . . ." The frequently occurring expression "children of men" or "sons of men" (Psalm 11:4; 12:1, 8; 14:2; 21:10; 31:14; 33:13; 36:7; etc.) has been replaced by a variety of expressions, including "all people," "everyone," and "humankind."

In the Letter to the Romans the RSV Committee has

proposed to make the following changes: "wickedness of men who . . . suppress the truth" to "wickedness of people who . . ." (1:18); "exchanged the glory of the immortal God for images resembling mortal man" to ". . . glory of the imperishable God for images resembling perishable humanity" (1:32); "God judges the secrets of men" to ". . . secrets of human beings" (2:16); "His praise is not from men but from God" to ". . . from human beings . . ." (2:29)

Much more perplexing is the problem of what should be done and what can be done with passages that use the third person singular pronoun "he," "him," and "his." The RSV Committee is not prepared to use contrived English or such expressions as "he/she" or "s/he." In its deliberations consideration has been given to the possibility of replacing the third person imperative with the second person imperative; for example, changing "He who has an ear let him hear what the Spirit says to the churches": (Rv 3:22) to "If you have an ear, listen to what . . ." Similarly, in Rv 3:20, to which reference was made earlier, it is currently proposed to read, "Listen! I am standing at the door and knocking; if any of you hear my voice and open the door, I will come in to you and sup with you."

Revision after Revision

If, as Qoheleth says, "of making many books there is no end" (Ec12:12), one can also add, nor is there an end of making revisions and new translations of the Scriptures. Some of these seek to attain still greater accuracy and felicity of expression; others are prepared for special groups of readers. Among the latter are a rendering of the Gospels, by Frank Shaw (a customs officer) and the Reverend Dick Williams, in "Scouse," the dialect used by dock-workers in

Liverpool, and Dr. Kenneth Jordan's Cotton-Patch Version in the idiom current among laborers in rural Georgia.

While an individual's free-lance translation of the Bible is entirely legitimate — in spite of a phrase in the New Testament itself about "private interpretation" — there are precedents and reasons for having successive revisions undertaken by a committee. The compromises which the individual makes unconsciously when working alone become more conscious when committee members differ in opinion and votes. There is some safety in numbers, since in a discussion more aspects of a problem are presented than any individual would have considered. The substantial unanimity resulting in most cases is reassuring to the translators, though not easily or accurately transmitted to the public. The latter may not understand that every word has to be weighed, even if it is left just as it was translated before, and that the easy flowing wording of a single verse represents at times long and repeated debate, sometimes ending in unity and sometimes in a well-justified difference of judgment. These less-favored alternatives constitute the bulk of a few marginal notes which modern revisers have allowed themselves.

Whatever the scholarly advantages of translations by groups of workers, the process involved provides many pleasant social compensations to those who are thus engaged. Intimate and prolonged sessions of discussion, held annually over a period of years, are conducive to a spirit of camaraderie among the members of the committee. Indeed, the sense of fellowship extends in each generation back over the years to earlier revisers and to the many scholars in many lands.

Other men and women have labored, and we have entered into their labors. This process cannot stop in 1611 or in 1952 or in 1979. Slowly, not spectacularly, knowledge of Hebrew and Greek text and language may be expected to grow, and the English language to change. At some future date a new set of revisers will again echo the words in the Preface to the King James Bible of 1611:

> . . . as nothing is begun and perfited at the same time, and the later thoughts are thought to be the wiser: so, if we building upon their foundation that went before us, and being holpen by their labours, doe endeuour to make that better which they left so good: no man, we are sure, hath cause to mislike us; they, we perswade our selues, if they were aliue, would thanke us.

FOOTNOTES

1. The King James Version contains more bad grammar than is commonly realized. Much of it is failure to observe agreement in singular and plural number, the rule for which was very loosely observed in the sixteenth and seventeenth centuries. In Luke 9:17 we read that "there was taken up . . . twelve baskets." Peter was astonished at the miraculous draught of fish "and so was also James and John" (Luke 5:10). Jesus is reported as saying, "This is an evil generation; they seek a sign, and there shall no sign be given it" (Luke 11:29). Likewise "Whom do men say that I am?" (Mt 16:13) should be "who."
2. The use of "was" with the second person singular pronoun occurs occasionally in authors of earlier centuries.
3. An example of a much less important difference between the two committees is the following. The King James reading of Gn 22:23, "These eight Milkah did bear to Nahor," was changed by the English Revisers to "these eight did Milkah bear to Nahor," despite the Americans' objections that, when read aloud, this sounded like "did milk a bear"!
4. This was Moffatt's second translation of the New Testament. In 1901 he had issued a modern speech version with the books arranged in the sequence in which many scholars think they had been written.
5. Professor Ropes resigned from the Committee in 1932.
6. At the time of publication of the RSV Old Testament a limited number of changes were introduced into the RSV New Testament. For example, because of euphony the translation of Acts 17:28 "In him we live and move and are" was changed back to the King James phraseology "we live and move and have our being." Of more consequence was the restoration of the words "sanctify"

and "sanctification" to certain passages, in order to preclude mistaken inferences that had been drawn from their replacement by "consecrate" and
"consecration" and to agree with the Committee's retention of the term
"sanctify" in the Old Testament.

In 1959 the Committee authorized a number of changes, chiefly in connection with matters of punctuation, capitalization, and footnotes. Some examples of such changes are "without" changed to "from," Job 19:26; "loaf" to
"bread," Mt 7:9 and I Cor 10:17; "be he" to "is he," Mt 21:9 and parallels; "the
son" to "the Son," Mt 27:54 and Mk 15:39; "married only once" to "the
husband of one wife," I Tm 3:2, 12; 5:9 and Tt 1:6.

7. See the *Congressional Record*, vol. 106, part 6 (April 19, 1960), pp.8247-8284.
8. The third edition, prepared in 1969 by K. Aland, M. Black, C.M. Martini, S.J.,
    B.M. Metzger, and A. Wikgren, was finally published in 1975, but the changes
    from previous editions were known in 1971 through the publication of
    Metzger's *A Textual Commentary on the Greek New Testament* (London, 1971).
9. Herbert G. May and Bruce M. Metzger, editors, *The New Oxford Annotated
    Bible, with the Apocrypha*, Expanded Edition, Revised Standard Version (New
    York: Oxford University Press, 1977).
10. See Ginn and Company, "Treatment of Minority Groups and Women"; Holt,
    Rinehart and Winston, "Guidelines for the Development of Elementary and
    Secondary Institutional Materials: The Treatment of Sex Roles"; Houghton
    Mifflin Co., "Avoiding Stereotypes"; McGraw-Hill Book Co., "Guidelines for
    Equal Treatment of Sexes in McGraw-Hill Book Company Publications";
    Macmillan Publishing Co., "Guidelines for Creating Positive Sexual and
    Racial Images in Educational Materials"; Random House, "Guidelines for
    Muti-Ethnic/Nonsexist Survey"; and Scott, Foresman and Co., "Guidelines
    for Improving the Image of Women in Textbooks."

One can also call attention to *Sexism and Language*, by Alleen P. Nilsen, Haig
Bosmajian, H. Lee Gershuny, and Julia P. Stanley, and published by the
National Council of Teachers of English, Urbana, Illinois, 1977.

Inspired Texts: The Dilemma Of A Feminist Believer

CAROLYN OSIEK, R.S.C.J.
Catholic Theological Union
Chicago, IL 60615

As woman, believer, feminist, and biblical scholar, I find that my work with biblical texts cannot be simply an intellectual exercise. I cannot only look at texts and exegete them as a scholar. While doing that, I also find myself caught up in what those texts mean to me personally. Obviously, then, I come at this task as a believer with a dilemma. What do I do when the primal image of God in my religious tradition, that of Father, is one to which I cannot relate? I come as a believer with this further dilemma — what do I do when I realize that a considerable portion of my faith tradition, even parts of its sacred texts, are permeated with contempt for who and what I am as a woman?

This misogynism, to call it what it is, can be compared to the problem of anti-Semitism in the New Testament and ongoing Christian tradition. It is often said that misogynism in the Scriptures is simply a cultural phenomenon. Is Christian anti-Semitism only cultural? Recent studies have raised the issue and made us aware that a deeper theological problem is involved: built into the very theology of the New Testament may be, at one level, a rejection of Jews along with their religious claim.[1] We have to face that possibility honestly. Today a change of mind and change of heart are required of us in response to a new understanding of the data.

It seems to me that we have to do something analogous when we attempt to face the problem of mysogynism and biblical texts of our Judeo-Christian tradition: we have to undergo a change of heart. In spite of many formal attempts, we have not yet arrived. We have not yet come to serious terms with misogynism in our society and in our churches. The proof for me is the fact that sexist jokes are still acceptable in some situations where racist jokes are not. Many (including churchmen) still tell sexist jokes in the *presence* of women, but they do not tell racist jokes even in the *absence* of those against whom they are directed, because it would be considered bad taste. In church contexts, the same people who seriously advance sexist arguments on theological or psychosociological grounds, would not dare offer similar racist theological or psychological arguments, because they know that the time for that sort of thing is gone. Women find themselves today in this credibility gap in the church, not yet being taken with full seriousness.

I approach this problem as one who stands in the Roman Catholic tradition, a tradition that can be crippling at times, especially when dealing with the problem of authority. Its good side, however, is its sense of tradition which, if properly understood and honestly accepted, allows the fullness of revelation in Jesus Christ to take concrete form in history, so that we are not dealing only with what happened in the first century. This concept of tradition can be very helpful and very supportive — as long as tradition is not understood as that beyond which we cannot go (that is, "it has never been done, so we cannot do it now"), but rather as the living of the Christian faith left as a legacy to us by those who have gone before.

One of the key questions we have to assess in regard to this tradition is: Did the church liberate or enslave women? That is a good question with no perfect answer. Some say, for instance, that Paul is the greatest misogynist in the Bible, and others say that Paul is the great Christian liberator of women. I do not think either is true. Rather, I think that the church both liberates and enslaves. Some original impulses in Christianity, as in the beginnings of any charismatic movement, were extremely liberating. A reading of Paul's First Letter to the Corinthians reveals such an impulse. But almost any religion is basically conservative to the extent that it is oriented to the past. Religion must hang onto something; it will, therefore, be conservative, both in the original sense of preserving and in the derived sense of closing in on itself. A religion with a sacred text is even more inclined to be conservative, for it must safeguard that sacred text. This basic conservative tendency is often experienced as enslaving because it means resistance to change, to newness, especially to insights that come from outside. But no religion is a self-contained unit. No culture is. No person is. Nor is Christianity! Conflicts, therefore, perpetually arise in the church between outside sources of inspiration and inside tendencies to preserve stability.

Christianity, obviously, does not exist in a "pure state" anywhere. In regard to women, Christianity adopted a mind-set according to which, in the symbolic realm, man images rationality and spirit, and woman images materiality and earth. Biblical authors both reflected and perpetuated this dichotomy, but they did not invent it; they simply absorbed it from the world in which they lived in the same way that they accepted compliance with slavery, another feature in the New Testament. A cyclic movement is at work here. At times it becomes a vicious circle: culture influences Christianity, which influences culture, which influences later generations' understanding and practice of Christian faith.

Rosemary Ruether claims that the greatest misogynism springs from this soul-body, male-female dualism.[2] It prevents man and woman from relating to one another as subject to subject. It defines woman as a relative being, existing only in relation to the male, who alone has autonomous being. This mind-set is reflected in much of the biblical material. In modern psychological terms, it prevents intersubjectivity, person relating to person with each one's total being.

Most people these days have done enough reading to be aware that there are texts in both the Jewish Scriptures and the New Testament that exalt the dignity of woman, but these texts usually confine her to a rather restricted role. On the other hand, some texts express what I could only call contempt.[3] There is, of course, the famous Galatians 3:28: "In Christ there is no longer male and female" (the literal translation). This statement may not be the great emancipatory declaration that some would have it be. In view of its context, it appears to be a quotation from a baptismal liturgy.[4] Paul seems to have been borrowing from a formula which probably means that the new life, the new creation in Christ, is one which symbolically restores the primeval unity of man as he came forth from the hand of the Creator, as narrated in the first creation account in Genesis (1:26-27).

Against the background of 1 Corinthians 11:2-16 and 14:34-35, Paul obviously did not intend Galatians 3:28 to mean that no distinctions should prevail in the role and behavior of women in the Christian community. What he definitely did intend — and this is a nearly constant element in Christian tradition after him — is that women as well as men have equal access to salvation in Christ. That affirmation does not translate into a cultural revolution for Paul or for anyone who came after him, though it did translate ultimately into mutual dependence of man and woman on one another, and their equal dependence on God (see 1 Cor 11:12). The First Letter to the Corinthians goes on to say, however, that it is shameful for a woman to speak in church (14:34).[5] The Pastoral Epistles go on to prohibit women from being allowed to have any kind of authority over men (1 Tm 2:12). Today this is usually understood as limited to the religious sphere; but a young man once told me that if he found himself in a job in which his immediate boss was a woman, he could not continue in that job because of the authority of the biblical text. When a text goes that deeply into a person's life and attitude toward half of the human race, I think there are some serious hermeneutical problems to be solved.

Challenging Questions

What do I do when my faith and the church that mean so much to me are the very instruments of suffering and, in some cases, of real oppression? What do I do when the sacred texts upon which our religious faith is based contain the very elements upon which that oppression builds?

Several answers are inadequate. The first of these I would call the "sons-and-brothers" syndrome. "We are all sons and brothers of the Father; and, of course, women are included, so what's the problem?" Don't believe it. Take the example of Psalm 1: "Blessed is the man who does not walk in the counsel of the wicked." "Blessed is the man" is *ashre ha ish* in Hebrew, *makarios ho aner* in the Greek Septuagint, *beatus vir* in the Latin Vulgate. In all three cases, the male term for male, not the generic human term, is used. Was this a deliberate attempt to exclude women? I think not. In that male-oriented world, it would never have seemed necessary to formulate such a statement so as consciously to include women. The generic and the male terms simply became interchangeable in many instances because only male experience was considered worth articulating. Do not believe that women are always included in the supposedly generic term.

The second inadequate answer is dismisal: "The problem is not worthy of consideration, so let's get on with more important things." This response is expressed in the case of religious misogynism by: "Oh, all that stuff about women being silent in the churches is cultural conditioning, an antiquated mind-set, so don't worry about it."

The third inadequate approach is pseudo-dialogue: "Maybe if they think I'm listening, they'll get what they want and go away." In regard to religious misogynism, this approach is expressed in such words as: "Well, we've said we're in favor of eliminating sexist language, so why aren't they satisfied?"

The problem of misogynism in the Judeo-Christian tradition *does* exist. It must be faced. It is serious. It will not go away with dialogue and understanding, and it will not be remedied by changing *chairman* to *chairperson*. So what do we do with it?

The Bible is not just a curious piece of history. It is our story and a major bridge between us and God. It contains both history and revelation. Saying that misogynism in the Bible is only a question of cultural conditioning risks rejecting, or at least downplaying, Scripture's revelatory element. Saying, on the other hand, that everything in the Bible is revelation leads to fundamentalism and the rejection of history as a significant human reality. But we cannot live without history; we cannot afford to reject it. A biblical scholar may distinguish between Pauline and deutero-Pauline writings. That distinction may exonerate Paul, but where does it leave us? It does not solve the problem, because the deutero-Pauline texts are still Scripture. Likewise, a biblical scholar may distinguish between Old and New Testaments, layers of tradition, oral tradition, written tradition, redaction of inherited texts, and so forth. But all these distinctions do not change the fact that we must deal with the biblical text as we have it. The heart of the problem is that history and revelation are so inextricably intertwined in the Bible that it is extremely difficult, perhaps impossible, to separate them completely in every case.

If some answers to the dilemma have been tried and found inadequate, others merit more serious consideration. The first is to realize that the problem is fourfold and has to be tackled on four fronts at once. It is a *hermeneutical* problem because it involves such questions as what kind of meaning is conveyed by the author of the text and by the mind-set of interpreters, translators, theologians, and commentators throughout the history of Christian tradition. The problem is *historical* because it makes us ask what forces were brought to bear on the author and on the interpreters throughout the tradition — not only what was their mind-set but also what were the factors that influenced that mind-set? With this question the aspect of culture conditioning enters the scene. But the problem also involves a very serious *theological* question: whether and how Scripture is to be norm or source. Is it the limit beyond which we do not go, or is it the beginning from which we proceed? Finally, the problem has an *ecclesiological* aspect because it involves the crucial question of whether the church is a static institution or an organic one. Is it something which has its definitive and irrevocable structure from the beginning, or is it something which evolves and develops throughout history?

If at least some kind of agreement on these basic issues does not exist, dialogue is nearly impossible on a secondary level, where the interpretation of particular texts is the question. If the people in dialogue do not agree in some measure on questions like what is the nature of the church or how Scripture functions in the church, not much meeting of minds will take place about less substantial problems. Because of the lack of agreement on fundamentals, questions of women in ministry or the ordination of women are threatening to many. Such questions undermine one whole way of understanding the church and Scripture. All the basic questions about the formation, development, and value of tradition are thrown open, and many are not prepared for the consequences.

God As Feminine

A second response to the dilemma that deserves attention is to think and speak of God as female. Certainly the feminine face of God is glimpsed, however obscurely, in the Bible and in early Christian tradition. God gave Israel birth (Dt 32:18); God carried Israel from the womb, cares for and comforts Israel as a child (Is 46:3-4; 49:15; 66:13; Ho 11:1-9). The prophets used this kind of language frequently, but always on the plane of metaphor; when they spoke directly of God, the masculine gender was always used.

Clement of Alexandria, a most unlikely early church father to be a feminist, had a deep appreciation of the feminine aspect of God. He says, for instance, that the unspoken part of God is father, but the part that feels toward us is mother; by loving, the Father has become like a woman, and the great sign of this is what he brought forth from himself, for what was born of love is love.[6] That is one of the boldest attributions of feminine characteristics to God in orthodox early Christian literature. There is a saying in a noncanonical gospel, known to Origen and Jerome, in which Jesus calls the Holy Spirit his mother. In it Jesus says, "My mother, the Holy Spirit, took me by the hair of my head and brought me to the holy mountain Tabor."[7] The Odes of Solomon, a collection of early Christian mystical poems, speak of the "full breasts" of the Father, the Spirit, or Christ. The male and female sides of Christ were expressed in Gnostic literature; and it was characteristic of many groups in early Christianity which later came to be labeled heretical that, because of their openness to the feminine as well as the masculine aspect of God, they were more open to allowing women to take leadership roles.

This kind of theology and praxis reminds us that most feminine religious symbolism we have inherited derives immediately from relationship to the male: virgin, bride, wife, mother, and whore are the most familiar examples. The feminine figure of wisdom is a rare exception that can stand alone. Male religious images, on the other hand, independent of direct reference to the female (such as creator, redeemer, warrior, and judge), abound. But why was the kind of theology and praxis which favored feminine religious symbolism suppressed in that line of Christianity which we have inherited?

It was suppressed because it inevitably became identified with fertility, with earth, and therefore with flesh and sensuality; and the "male" rational principle, spirit, shied away from all that. Again we have returned to the male-female duality symbolism. The Jewish-Christian God has usually been conceived of as a sky-god, that is, one whose residence is in the sky and whose worship is oriented in the same direction. Hence, he could not tolerate fertility cults, at least those centered on women or earth, for they stood in opposition to what the sky-god represents in human experience.

I believe, however, that we are now in an earth-god phase of Christianity, due mostly to outside forces: a new appreciation of the body, of sexuality, of earth, of matter, and of scientific method. I wonder what Christianity is going to do with this. It is going to have to change to some extent. The Christianity of the near future will have to bear the stamp of this new affirmation of the material that has been developing. This opens the possibility of developing feminine imagery for God. But is the reintroduction of feminine imagery for God really a solution to our dilemma, or does it merely lead us deeper into a mistaken anthropomorphism?

We have arrived at a point of paradox, which is the third and probably the best response to the dilemma. Paradox is, after all, the heart of Christianity. Jesus is human and yet he is divine. He died and yet he lives. His kingdom is in this world and yet not of it. It is in giving that we receive. It is in losing life that we find it. These phrases have a familiar ring; they are all biblical. I am by no means advocating a return to a passive servant image for women. Contemporary consciousness of personhood came from modern psychology, not from Christianity. Our consciousness of personhood and sense of justice and the lack of it are new levels of awareness that make return impossible. Yet with Elisabeth Moltmann-Wendel, I still believe in the value of self-surrender once there is a self to surrender, a self that can be discovered only through self-assertion.[8] Again, the paradox. I must wrestle with it, unless I choose to take the simplistic attitude of rejecting part of the tradition — and to me that would be a cop-out. As a result, I must realize that what gives me spiritual life, what nourishes me, and what I love, also has the potential to hurt and destroy and it will undoubtedly do so again. In time, a new consensus will break through into Christian consciousness, as it did in other times about issues like slavery and anti-Semitism. In the meantime, the pain seems unavoidable.

I offer no clear, logical, consistent solutions. Even if I did, I probably would not be believed. But I submit that to walk out of the conflict is no solution at all. To take that step would cut me off from history, and I believe I cannot afford to do that.

Galatians 3:28 may yet hold a piece of the solution. The position I have taken is that troublesome texts cannot simply be dismissed but must be carefully weighed. If this is true of 1 Timothy 2:11-16 with its oppressiveness, it is equally true of Galatians 3:28 with its promise. Its meaning is not limited to the confines of the first-century Mediterranean world. Its living message bears for us a glimpse of a new vision, just as it did in its own time for Jews and Greeks, and centuries later for slaves: the liberation brought by the Lord Jesus.

What is the role of Jesus in a feminist Christianity? This important question needs further investigation. In light of the above considerations, his role may be to serve as a sign of contradiction or, to put it in Christian theological terms, a sign of the cross, that which stands as both obstacle and the way through and onward.

Where do I go? Anger is a good feeling to have, but it is no final resting place. Anger must be recognized eventually for what it is, not so much anger, but pain. Anger is the reaction to pain, and pain is not something to be circumvented and avoided. Pain is what must be passed through. I cannot go around the pain of being a woman in the Judeo-Christian tradition and say that I will not deal with the conflict of being both Christian and feminist, but, rather, I will choose one and reject the other. No, I must go directly into that conflict and through it. Only in this way can I move toward a creative solution. That is the simple human process in both its psychological and spiritual dimensions: the movement from conflict into creativity. In other words, I must learn how to define myself as Christian, as woman, as what I am, *within* my own tradition. If at least some of us can succeed in doing that, we will have immeasurably enriched that very tradition for those who will come after us.

FOOTNOTES

1. See, for instance, Rosemary Ruether, *Faith and Fratricide: the Theological Roots of Anti-Semitism* (New York: Seabury, 1974).
2. *Liberation Theology* (New York: Paulist Press, 1972), p. 100.
3. E.g., Pr 21:19; 27:15; Si 25:12-25; 26: 5-12.
4. See Robin Scroggs, "Paul and the Eschatological Woman," *Journal of the American Academy of Religion* 40 (1972): 283-303, especially 291-93.
5. The way that 1 Cor 14:34-35 seems to break into its context and the textual uncertainty of a few manuscripts lead to the possible conclusion that the two verses are an interpolation in the text by a later editor.
6. *Who is the Rich Man Who Can Be Saved* 3, 7.
7. *Gospel of the Hebrews,* cited in Origen, *Commentary on John,* 2:12 (*Sources Chretiennes,* no. 120, p. 262). The same passage is quoted also in Origen's *Homily on Jeremiah* 15:4 and Jerome's commentaries on Micah, Isaiah, and Ezekiel. See H. Hennecke, *New Testament Apocrypha,* ed. W. Schneemelcher and, in English translation, R. McL. Wilson, vol. 1 (Philadelphia: Westminster Press, 1963), p. 164.
8. *Liberty, Equality and Sisterhood: On the Emancipation of Women in Church and Society,* trans. Ruth C. Gritsch (Philadelphia: Fortress Press, 1978), pp. 69-87.

ARCHAEOLOGY AND THE BIBLE

Introduction

MIRIAM WARD, R.S.M.
Trinity College
Burlington, VT 05401

Each age has had its questions and methods in approaching the Bible. For the early Church Fathers allegory was used extensively; in the Middle Ages commentaries and grammars were popular; with the invention of printing which made the Bible more accessible, textual criticism was pursued; the introduction of historical criticism and later the comparative study of religion brought their own set of questions; the scientific impact of evolutionary theory and the documentary hypothesis raised questions unasked in previous centuries. Past ages have formulated their questions and arrived at methods of approaching the Scriptures. For the present age, archaeology is one of the principal means used to study the Bible. This, in summary, is the thought expressed by Dr. James B. Pritchard in a lecture presented at the first Trinity Biblical Institute in June, 1966.

Following the directive of *Divino Afflante Spiritu* which urged biblical scholars to take into account the findings of archaeology for a better understanding of the context of the Scriptures, and thereby to a more certain knowledge of what the authors intended to convey, the Trinity Biblical Institutes have included almost annually talks on the relation and impact of archaeology on the Bible. Until his death in 1974 George Ernest Wright, then Dean of American archaeologists, was a strong supporter of the Trinity College Biblical Institute as was Nancy Lapp who has preserved and carried on the work of her late husband, Paul Lapp, as well as making her own contribution to the field.

A relatively new discipline, archaeology has progressed beyond the dreams of the pioneers in the field. For an evaluation of the current state and trends in biblical archaeology Philip J. King, priest, professor and field archaeologist offers "The Contribution of Archaeology to Biblical Studies." As field archaeologist on digs in Jordan, Israel, Turkey, and North Yemen, and as President of the American Schools of Oriental Research from 1976-1982, Father King brings to his topic invaluable first-hand experience complemented by his work in the classroom at Boston College where he is professor of Old Testament and Director of the Institute of Religious Education and Pastoral Ministry. In addition to his publications in archaeological journals, he has published in the area of Old Testament studies.

After giving a brief historical introduction, Father King's article points up some of the shifts that have taken place in the field, notably towards an interdisciplinary approach, now standard practice in the Mideast. By citing specific examples of archaeological excavations, Father King illustrates that often archaeology raises questions concerning traditional theories of chronology, for example at Jericho and Lachish, rather than furnishing answers. While listing the positive contributions of archaeology which "prevent the Bible from being mythologized by keeping it in the realm of history," he nevertheless cautions against a too facile expectation for historical reconstruction through archaeology.

I strongly urge the reader to have a Bible Atlas open as you read Father King's article, but as one who succumbed long ago I give fair notice: the archaeology-bug is contagious.

Biblical archaeology involves many steps after the material remains have been uncovered. One such task is the deciphering of ancient texts or inscriptions and extracting meaning from them, and in some cases relating them to the biblical text.

By and large biblical archaeology situates Israel within the international community, conditioned by the cultural, political, economic, religious, and literary trends within the world of their time.

The bibliography and biography of Cyrus H. Gordon suggest that here is a scholar who can speak to both these concerns (the deciphering of texts and the international situation): The former lists some 400 articles and books, and an expanse of archaeological subjects from ancient Minoan civilization to the modern Near East, as well as writings on art, law, sociology, literature, religion, but always within the panorama of history. He is especially known for his expertise in Ugaritic and work on the texts found at ancient Ugarit, as well as the more recent finds at Ebla.

Professor Gordon's article included in this volume will challenge the reader to reconsider any alleged relationship between the Egyptian solar-monotheism and the monotheism of Israel when confronted by the fact that the Egyptian equivalent of the Hebrew "Elohim" was not "Ra" but "Ntr", and he illustrates one facet of making textual comparisons of ancient extra-biblical documents with the biblical text, in this instance the concept of the "International God." Further reflection might challenge the reader to reflect on one's own God-construct.

A native of Cork, Ireland, Jerome Murphy-O'Connor, O.P., studied in Dublin, Jerusalem, Rome, Fribourg, Heidelberg, and under Ernst Kasemann in Tubingen. He is Professor of New Testament and Intertestamental Literature at the Ecole Biblique in Jerusalem. As is fitting for one whose education has a global reach, Father Murphy-O'Connor is the official United Nations guide to archaeological sites in Israel. As the thousand people who have studied under him at the 1972, 74, 76, 78, and 1984 Trinity College Biblical Institutes will testify, Father Murphy-O'Connor's expertise in Pauline studies marks him as one of the most perceptive scholars of our time.

To illustrate another facet of archaeology as described in Father King's article, we have included "Corinthian Bronze" by Jerome Murphy-O'Connor, O.P. He considers the wider sociological and cultural contexts in which Corinth of biblical times was known for its bronzeware. Because Corinthian bronze was a collector's item, Father Murphy-O'Connor examines the pertinent texts of such writers as Pliny the Elder, Plutarch, Petronius, and Pausanias among others, and for the special interest of those with a classical bent, provides the Latin text or the transliterated Greek text. Readers who would like more of this type of analysis might read *St. Paul's Corinth* by Father Murphy-O'Connor.

The Contribution of Archaeology to Biblical Studies[1]

PHILIP J. KING
Boston College
Chestnut Hill, MA 02167

In a 1963 article entitled "Palestine: Known But Mostly Unknown" Paul Lapp wrote, "Palestinian archaeology may be past infancy but has hardly gotten beyond childhood."[2] In the two decades since that article appeared the archaeology of Palestine has developed enormously but certainly has not reached its maturity. Palestinian archaeology was born in 1890 when Flinders Petrie traveled from Egypt to Palestine to dig Tel el Hesi in the southern coastal plain on the assumption he was excavating biblical Lachish. Petrie was among the first to recognize the structure of Near Eastern tells. The explorer Edward Robinson assumed they were natural formations; the surveyor Claude Conder thought they were ancient brick factories. With a correct understanding of tells and aware of the importance of pottery for chronology, Petrie laid the foundations at Tel el Hesi for the stratigraphy and ceramic typology of Palestine.

The American School in Jerusalem was established in 1900, principally on the initiative of biblical scholars, to provide the opportunity for firsthand contact with the Bible lands. Most of the School's directors before World War I were biblical scholars. Although none conducted his own dig, all were keenly interested in the major excavations in progress at Gezer, Megiddo, Samaria, Taanach, and Jericho. With the exception of George Reisner's work at Samaria, by contemporary standards the techniques of digging in those days were primitive; nonetheless some of the results were significant.

The period between the World Wars has been described as the "golden age" of Palestinian archaeology. The marked improvement in field technique and the greater accuracy in dating helped to make archaeology a systematic discipline. William Albright was the leading figure in this era. With Tel Beit Mirsim in southern Judah as his field laboratory Albright refined the ceramic index for Palestine. His outstanding student was Nelson Glueck; trained at Tel Beit Mirsim, Glueck became an explorer in the tradition of Edward Robinson. His surface surveys in Transjordan and the Negev opened a whole new world to archaeology; only recently have they been matched in Jordan and Israel.

The period between the wars witnessed intense field activity in archaeology. The large-scale projects included the American digs at Megiddo and Beth-shan and the British excavations at Jericho and Samaria. The excavations of this era, whose basic approach was architectural, shed light on the political history of Palestine and placed the country on the map of the ancient Near Eastern world.

After World War II Palestinian archaeology developed quickly and began to come of age; Kathleen Kenyon and Ernest Wright fostered this growth. Kenyon's dig at Jericho was a landmark in method; her stratigraphic technique with its meticulous attention to soil layers influenced nearly every subsequent dig in Palestine. The most important American undertaking was Wright's excavation at Shechem, where he trained a whole generation of younger archaeologists. Following the Kenyon method, Wright supplemented it with close attention to pottery typology in keeping with the Albright tradition.

One of the most promising students of Albright and Wright was Lapp, who directed seven excavations, including Taanach and Bab edh-Dhra. As he was about to take his place among the leading archaeologists of Palestine, he died at the age of 39. William Dever, another of Wright's prominent students, succeeded Wright as director of the Gezer excavations. Gezer was the pioneer American dig in initiating the interdisciplinary approach to archaeology; Hesi, Hesban, and subsequent digs advanced the process by emphasizing environmental and anthropological studies. Today interdisciplinary archaeology is standard practice in the Mideast.

Yigael Yadin gave Israeli archaeology a great impetus by undertaking the excavation of Hazor, one the largest sites in the country. The members of his team have become the leading archaeologists in Israel. Hazor served as the field school of a new generation of Israelis; today Israeli archaeologists number over 200.

Palestinian archaeology came to maturity during the 1970s, a period of dramatic development in the scientific and technical tools of archaeology, which are providing much greater precision in the recovery, recording, and processing of material evidence. The natural and social sciences are responsible for much of this progress in Near Eastern archaeology. For a long time the archaeology of Palestine focused almost exclusively on political history; the major concern was the names of kings and the battles they fought. As archaeology moves away from a narrow historical perspective, it is increasingly interested in the social and cultural reconstruction of early Israel.

Israel and Jordan are bustling today with field activities of all kinds: excavations, soundings, salvage, and surveys. Surveys of geographically limited zones have become an integral part of field archaeology. The regional approach coupled with excavations provides a more comprehensive view, allowing the archaeologist to ask many new questions that cannot be answered by digging isolated tells.

Until now there has been a heavy concentration on the great urban centers to the exclusion of the neighboring village sites. These rural towns can provide information about the daily life of people, social change, economics, population shifts, and similar issues. Evidence of this kind can assist sociologists and other social scientists in formulating answers about the socio-economic organization of village life in rural Israel.

Even with its new sophistication archaeology has inherent limitations, as two leading practitioners of the discipline pointed out a decade ago. After a lifetime in archaeology Roland de Vaux[3] and Ernest Wright[4] cautioned against expecting too much from archaeology in the way of historical reconstruction; they also warned against the tendentious use of archaeological evidence. Despite the fact that Palestine, including modern Israel and the occupied West Bank, is perhaps the most excavated land in the world, only a small portion of the material data has been retrieved; much more remains to be done. Fragmentary evidence and a paucity of epigraphic finds constrict archaeology in reconstructing the history and culture of the ancient Near East. Both de Vaux and Wright advised that when actual texts are available, "Archaeology does not confirm the text, which is what it is, it can only confirm the interpretation which we give it."[5]

Despite archaeology's innate limitations the discipline does make a meaningful contribution to biblical studies. Archaeology prevents the Bible from being mythologized by keeping it in the realm of history. Archaeology provides the geographical and chronological context of biblical people and events. Archaeology recovers the empirical evidence necessary for clarifying the biblical text. Archaeology illustrates the daily life of biblical people by recovering their pottery, utensils, weapons, seals, ostraca, and architecture. As Palestinian archaeology lengthens its geographical horizon to the Arabian peninsula and expands its chronological perspective to the prehistoric period, it is possible to understand the Bible in a much larger context.

The nature of the Israelite settlement in Canaan is a perennial and perplexing problem in biblical history and archaeology; few issues in biblical research have generated so many hypotheses. In 1912, at the annual meeting of the Society of Biblical Literature and Exegesis Lewis Paton chose as the topic of his presidential address "Israel's Conquest of Canaan."[6] Seventy years later it is still a timely topic, but now there is much more archaeological evidence to be considered. Today there are three dominant models for the settlement: conquest, immigration, and revolt; each admits of modification and refinement. The contradictory accounts in Joshua and Judges prepared the way for this maelstrom of conflicting interpretations about biblical Israel's origins.

Accepting the basic historicity of the biblical account, Albright[7] championed the conquest model, the decisive military assault on the Canaanite cities. Yadin, Wright, Malamat, and other scholars follow Albright. The evidence at Hazor is convincing; the Late Bronze Age city was destroyed and replaced by a small Iron Age I settlement. Hazor accounts in part for Yadin's adherence to the conquest model, but Hazor is the exception. To be sure, Yadin acknowledges, as did Albright, the problems raised by the discrepancies between the archaeological evidence and the biblical data at Jericho, Ai, amd Gibeon.

The German school of Albrecht Alt,[8] Martin Noth,[9] and Manfred Weippert[10] formulated the immigration model. On the basis of literary analysis and ethnographic observation of the Bedouin they have understood the settlement as a slow, peaceful infiltration into the hill country unoccupied by the Canaanites; later some military campaigns took place. Sheep-goat pastoralists who had been living in the desert steppe gradually penetrated into the wooded highlands. From a seminomadic way of life they adopted an agricultural economy. Among Israeli scholars Aharoni was the leading defender of this model; Anson Rainey, Aharon Kempinski, and others share this interpretation. De Vaux's view was closer to the German school than to the Albright school; rejecting the view of the invasion as a military conquest, de Vaux considered the settlement an extended process, combining peaceful penetration and military operations, two concurrent aspects of settlement.

The conquest and immigration models of settlement are founded on the hypothesis that the early Israelites were pastoral nomads who came from the steppes that lay to the south and east of Canaan. Sociology and cultural anthropology simply do not support such an hypothesis. In his study of transhumant pastoralism Norman Gottwald,[11] using the sociological method, has demolished the pastoral nomadic hypothesis. According to him, Israel was essentially an agricultural society, not a nomadic and pastoral society. Gottwald maintains that the conflict in social organization at the time of Israel's appearance in Canaan was between the city and the countryside, between urban and rural life.

George Mendenhall[12] was the first to propose the

model of social revolution in Late Bronze Age Canaan; it is known as a "peasants' revolt" in the form of a new religious ideology. Reliance on Yahwism provided the impetus for the social change. John Bright abandoned the conquest model in favor of Mendenhall's hypothesis; John McKenzie and others also support Mendenhall. Gottwald in his sociological study of early Israelite religion considers the revolt model the most satisfactory explanation of events in Canaan at the end of the Late Bronze Age, but he has his own version. He understands the revolt in socio-economic terms. According to Gottwald, there was no invasion or immigration from outside; in his words, it was "an inside job," an indigenous revolutionary social movement; Israel derived from the inborn Canaanite society. Mendenhall, too, emphasizes the indigenous nature of the uprising against the city-states.

Archaeology is producing new evidence useful for resolving the problem of the Israelite settlement in Canaan. Recent surveys and excavations have uncovered Iron Age I unfortified villages, which were the settlements of the early Israelites in the premonarchic period. Archaeology is now able to present more data for the social and cultural reconstruction of the early Israelite movement.

In the 1950s Aharoni made a regional survey of the heavily wooded area of Upper Galilee; his comprehensive archaeological survey in the rugged mountains revealed a chain of small Iron Age I settlements. Most of the sites encountered had not been occupied before Iron Age I, and according to the evidence, they had been settled peacefully. On a later survey of Judea and Samaria, the occupied West Bank, the Israeli survey team headed by Moshe Kochavi discovered hundreds of small settlements similar to those in Upper Galilee; they, too, had been unoccupied in the Bronze Age.

Aharoni's survey of the northern Negev yielded the same evidence. Concentrating on the Beer-sheba and Arad plain, Aharoni surveyed the northeastern Negev before conducting large-scale digs at Arad, Beer-sheba, Tel Masos, and Tel Ira, and a minor dig at Tel Malhata. There were no Canaanite cities in the northern Negev in the Late Bronze Age. Beer-sheba was settled for the first time in Iron Age I; Arad, Malhata, and Masos were resettled at the same time as Beer-sheba, after a long period of abandonment.

According to the biblical account of the settlement, there were two fortified Canaanite cities in the northern Negev, Arad and Hormah, but there is no archaeological evidence to support this statement. At Tel Arad the occupational sequence extends from the Early Bronze to the Iron Age I, but there are no remains of the Middle and Late Bronze ages. To reconcile the biblical tradition about the existence of Canaanite Arad, Aharoni assumed that it was located at Malhata which had been occupied in the Middle Bronze Age. Tel Masos had also been occupied in the Middle Bronze Age and then abandoned until Iron Age I; Aharoni located the Canaanite city of Hormah at Masos.

Several Early Iron Age villages, recently excavated in modern Israel, have valuable evidence to offer concerning the manner of Israelite settlement in Canaan. Masos, Esdar, Izbet Sartah, Giloh, Ai, and Raddana were typical Israelite villages in the premonarchic period. Their town plans, pillared houses, slope terracing, and other features reflect a sophisticated technology not ordinarily associated with pastoral nomads. Agriculture was the basis of subsistence in Iron Age I villages.

Tel Masos (Khirbet el-Meshash),[13] consisting of three separate settlements, is situated approximately midway between Beer-sheba and Arad. The largest Iron Age I settlement in the northern Negev, it was abandoned after 1000

B.C. Kempinski and Volkmar Fritz conducted excavations at Masos between 1972 and 1975; this was the first joint Israeli-German expedition. Kempinski is convinced that the results of this dig support the immigration model of the German school; Fritz has reservations because of evidence of a high percentage of cattle, which would seem not to support the nomadic hypothesis. In Stratum III, dated to the end of the 13th and the middle of the 12th century B.C., cattle account for one third of the animal stock.

The Israelite settlers at Masos were not simply pastoral nomads from the desert; architectural remains at the site indicate they knew how to build houses. The earliest known examples of the four-room house were found in Stratum II which dates from the mid-12th to the mid-11th century B.C. The typical four-room house consisted of three rooms and a pillared courtyard; a long back room and two side rooms surrounded the central courtyard, which was sometimes unroofed.

The fact that the early Israelites settled in unpopulated regions is proof that their extensive occupation of the land of Canaan was not accomplished through military conquest. In the northern Negev the settlement process began at the end of the 13th century B.C. and continued for more than 200 years. The era must have been peaceful because Masos remained unfortified despite its location on a low hillock. Absence of defensive walls indicates that the security of the settlers was not threatened.

Tel Esdar,[14] a small Iron Age I site about three miles south of Masos, was first discovered by Glueck in 1956. Kochavi's salvage excavation of the tell revealed that Esdar was inhabited in Early Bronze Age II; afterward there was a gap of 1500 years until the site was reoccupied in the Iron Age; the settlement was totally destroyed at the end of the 11th century B.C. A number of houses were built close together in a circle on a flat hilltop at this village; they date from the period of the Israelite settlement in the Negev.

Another Israelite agricultural settlement of the Early Iron Age which is shedding light on the occupation of Canaan is Izbet Sartah,[15] situated on the western slopes of the Samaria hill country. This site and a number of others dating to Iron Age I were discovered during Kochavi's survey of the Sharon Valley; he undertook this survey as part of the excavation project at Aphek. In 1972 Kochavi began a long-term dig at Ras el-Ain at the headwaters of the Yarkon River. The site is identified as Aphek, where the Philistines rallied their troops before fighting two battles against the Israelites. Herod rebuilt Aphek and renamed it Antipatris in honor of his father.

About two east miles of Aphek is a small, unfortified settlement known in Arabic as Izbet Sartah. Izbet is the Arabic designation for seasonal camps; during the summer villagers come from the Samarian hills to cultivate their crops in the Sharon Valley. Sartah is the name of the village. This Iron Age settlement is assumed to be Eben-ezer where the Israelites mustered their army against the Philistine forces deployed at Aphek. The land between Aphek and Izbet Sartah marked the border between the Philistines and the Israelites in the days of the judges.

The identification of Izbet Sartah with Eben-ezer is based in part on the excavation of the site in 1976 when three occupational strata extending from 1200 to 1000 B.C. were unearthed. Stratum II, the most important, revealed the remains of a four-room house, the largest pillared building of this type found in Israel. In the mid-11th century B.C. the site was abandoned for a generation, perhaps the aftermath of the battle of Eben-ezer. Then the settlement was rebuilt and occupied briefly at the beginning of the monarchy before being deserted permanently. A large number of storage pits or silos were discovered at the site; they were typical of many early Israelite settlements. The excavators found two sherds in silo 605, east of the four-room house; the two sherds fitted together making an ostracon with five lines of incised letters. Archaeologists estimate that the silo was originally dug between 1200 and 1050 B.C. On the basis of paleographic analysis the ostracon dates to about 1200 B.C. and contains the oldest and most complete Proto-Canaanite linear alphabet of 22 letters. In all, there are 83 letters in five lines, the final line being the abecedary. Most of the letters are legible, but the first four lines make no word sense. Epigraphists speculate that the ostracon was a student's writing exercise for learning the alphabet.

Commenting on the invention of the alphabet in the second millennium B.C., Frank Cross stated:

> With the creation of the alphabet came the first opportunity for the democratization of culture . . . With the invention of alphabetic writing, literacy spread like wildfire and a new epoch of cultural history may be said to begin with the emergence of the Linear alphabet.[16]

The discovery of the Izbet Sartah ostracon is evidence of a degree of literacy in the period of the judges. The level of literacy is uncertain, but there was a written tradition; writing was practiced among the people at the beginning of the 12th century B.C.

Giloh, an early Israelite settlement southwest of Jerusalem, can contribute to an understanding of the settlement by the tribes of Judah in the area of Jerusalem and Bethlehem. Masos' role in providing evidence about the southern part of Judah is played for the northern region by Giloh. Kochavi discovered this site in 1968 while surveying the Judean mountains; Amihai Mazar[17] excavated Giloh in

1978 and 1979. This Giloh is not biblical Giloh mentioned in Joshua 15; the biblical city would have been located near the northern Negev. Mazar's Giloh is situated in the center of a new suburb of Jerusalem, north of the modern town of Beit Jallah. Giloh was chosen as the name of this new settlement because of similarity in sound between Jallah and Giloh. Baal-Perazim has been suggested as the identification of modern Giloh, but it is not at all certain.

Mazar describes this site as a fortified herdsmen's village; it was occupied only briefly in Iron Age I. The remote location of Giloh may be the reason why it was abandoned after a short time. The site consists of two small mounds with an elevation of about 1500 feet above sea level. This prominence was good for security but not for agriculture. Nonetheless, a double outer wall enclosed the settlement on its southern, eastern, and northeastern sides. Mazar attributes the existence of fortified towns in the central Judean mountains and north of Jerusalem in the 12th-11th century B.C. to the complex ethno-political situation in the Jerusalem region. While Izbet Sartah had a defensive system, Ai and Raddana, two typical highland villages in the early Israelite period, were probably unfortified.

Mazar evaluates the contribution of the Giloh dig to the process of Israelite settlement in Canaan. Following the German school, Aharoni maintained that settlement in the hill country and the northern Negev had been established in the 14th-13th century B.C., before the destruction of the Canaanite cities. The Albright school held that the Iron Age I sites were settled only after the military conquest of the major Canaanite centers. The archaeological evidence does not support Aharoni; Izbet Sartah was an Iron Age I site, Giloh dates between 1200 and 1150 B.C., and the settlements in Upper Galilee are Iron Age I. Mazar sees a relationship between the founding of these Iron Age I sites and the destruction of at least some of the Canaanite cities. The pottery evidence at Hazor, for example, indicates that the sites in Galilee were settled after the destruction of Hazor. Mazar concludes tentatively that the late 13th to mid-12th century B.C. was the period of conquest and settlement; at this time the Israelite settlements came into existence and some Canaanite cities were destroyed.

Between 1964 and 1972 Joseph Callaway[18] excavated et-Tel, the most plausible location of biblical Ai; it was the most meticulous dig in the Kenyon tradition. After the city had been destroyed about 2400 B.C., it lay abandoned until 1220 B.C., when newcomers founded a small village. Other settlements were also established at unoccupied sites in the region at this time; the new settlers apparently met little resistance. The excavations revealed that Ai was an unfortified agricultural village. There are several indications that the residents came from an agricultural background, especially their use of terracing to control soil erosion. Other features of the Iron Age I village at Ai included rock-cut cisterns associated with individual pillared houses, also cobbled streets. The Early Iron Age settlers at Ai were farmers and shepherds; the farmers grew cereal and raised flocks of sheep and goats. Such occupations are not associated with recent immigrants from the desert. This Iron Age IA phase at Ai was abandoned about 1125 B.C.; the Iron Age IB settlers (1125-1050 B.C.) lacked, according to Callaway, their predecessors' experience in village life.

The similarities between Ai and neighboring Khirbet Raddana are striking. Between 1969 and 1974 Callaway and Robert Cooley[19] conducted a salvage excavation at Raddana on the edge of Ramallah. The site was strategically located for security; situated on a hilltop, it was surrounded on three sides by deep valleys. The steep hillsides probably were cultivated. There is ample evidence of intensive agricultural activity at Raddana; the well-planned terraces and the rock-cut cisterns indicate the settlers at Raddana were experienced agriculturalists, especially skilled in hill-country farming. The large number of cereal-processing tools are signs of the agrarian economy of Raddana. The bones of sheep and goats at the site are evidence of the pastoral activity in this village.

The Iron Age I occupation at Raddana had two phases: the first can be dated about 1220 to 1125 B.C. and the second, which came to an end with a violent destruction, from 1125 to 1050 B.C. As an aid in dating, an inscribed jar handle from 1200 B.C. was found in a stratified context on the dig.

The architectural structure at Raddana consisted of compounds of four units, each with three rooms; the units were fortified along the outer side with a sturdy wall. This cluster arrangement of houses suggests an extended family structure within the village. The excavators were attracted to Raddana by hewn pillars fortuitously exposed during road construction. The pillared houses at Raddana were well built; the inhabitants obviously had not come directly from the desert.

Conjectures abound about the identification of Khirbet Raddana. Callaway suggested biblical Beeroth, one of the four cities of the Hivites; Aharoni rejected this suggestion because the Raddana settlement was too small and too short-lived. Aharoni proposed Ataroth-addar, a town on the boundary between Ephraim and Benjamin. mentioned in Joshua.

The east side of the Jordan River is also the scene of new work in Iron Age I. Excavations and surveys have unearthed Iron Age remains, and new sites have been found in the hill country. In a recent article on the archaeology of Jordan and Syria, James Sauer stated:

In agreement with the old reconstruction of Albright and Wright, it can be argued that the distribution and character of the Iron Age IA sites would suggest that they reflect Israelite, Ammonite, and Moabite settlements during the period of the Judges, while the distribution and character of the Iron Age IB sites would suggest that they reflect Philistine or Sea People settlements . . . In the hill country of Jordan, the LB occupation was succeeded by Iron IA occupation, which could well be associated with the Israelite conquest.[20]

In a forthcoming monograph entitled *Highland Villages and Early Israel*[21] Lawrence Stager assesses the various hypotheses on the settlement of Canaan and evaluates the new archaeological evidence. He takes issue with the desert origins of the Israelites, demonstrating that it is invalid to assume a cultural evolution of the early Israelites from seminomadic shepherds to agricultural settlers. Stager favors Gottwald's reconstruction, especially its assumption that the people were well settled in the land and had been living as agriculturalists for a considerable time. Stager draws support for his position from archaeological evidence such as slope terracing, pillared houses, pottery, and language, as well as costume and coiffure depicted on the Merneptah relief of "Israelites." However, in Stager's view, there is not enough evidence to support Gottwald's revolt model. Stager prefers the withdrawal of the primarily agrarian population from the disintegrating city-state system, following Merneptah's campaign and continuing during the influx of the Sea Peoples, and resettlement in the highland frontier in kin-based village and tribal territories.

In addition to the issue of the settlement, recent archaeological evidence can shed light on other puzzling subjects like the Israelite cult; at least archaeology can raise new questions. Concerning the cult of Asherah in ancient Israel, some new extrabiblical data must be taken into consideration. Zeev Meshel[22] made the important discovery at Kuntillet Ajrud, an Arabic name meaning "the solitary hill of the water wells." This remote desert way-station was on the southern border of the kingdom of Judah, 40 miles south of Kadesh-barnea; the site is situated near a crossroad of desert tracks in the vicinity of wells, whence the name of the place. The English explorer Edward Palmer discovered the site in 1869 and made a small sounding.

Meshel conducted an excavation at Kuntillet Ajrud in 1975 and 1976; he uncovered the remains of a main rectangular building and a smaller building. The extraordinary find was not the architecture but the inscriptions therein; they consist of dedications, requests, prayers, and blessings. All are fragmentary, and at present their interpretation is incomplete. These Hebrew and Phoenician inscriptions had been painted on the plaster walls of the building and on two large pithoi or storage jars; others were incised on stone vessels.

The names El and Yahweh, as well as Baal and Asherah, appear in the inscriptions; this evidence points to the religious nature of the Kuntillet Ajrud complex. This Sinai center has been variously described as an Israelite fortress or a caravanserai, but not a temple. Meshel interprets the site as a religious center associated with journeys made by kings of Judah to Elath, Ezion-geber, or southern Sinai. On the basis of epigraphy and pottery scholars date Kuntillet Ajrud from the late 9th to the early 8th century B.C. The inscriptions, designs, and decorations at Kuntillet Ajrud suggest an influence from northern Israel and Phoenicia. Some scholars speculate that the shrine had associations with Athaliah because of her Phoenician connections.

The epithet "Yahweh *smrn*" on one of the pithoi is being

read *somrenu,* "our guardian," by some; others read *somron,* "Samaria," in parallelism with the phrase "Yahweh Teman and his Asherah," which appears on the second pithos. Teman is to be understood as referring to the region of Edom, not to a specific site in the south such as the modern village of Tawilan on the eastern outskirts of Petra. Crystal Bennett, the excavator of Tawilan, has uncovered no evidence of Tawilan as the southern capital of Edom.

Crude drawings accompany some of the religious inscriptions. The "Yaweh-Asherah" inscription and the associated drawing on one pithos have attracted most attention. The inscription may be read, "May you be blessed by Yaweh and by his Asherah." The three figures immediately below the inscription are curious; scholars are interpreting them in various ways, partly because the iconography is not completely clear. Meshel identified the figure in the center as the god Bes, and the figure on the left as another representation of Bes. The ithyphallic dwarf-god Bes was originally an Egyptian demigod, patron of music and dancing. The third figure on the right is a woman playing a lyre while seated on a throne.

In a forthcoming article Dever[23] identifies the woman as the female deity Asherah; he calls attention to her polka dot garment, her coiffure, and the sphinx-throne. He bases his identification of the woman as Asherah enthroned on parallels in Late Bronze Canaanite and Phoenician iconography. The persistence of the Canaanite religion over many centuries in the ancient Near East lends support to Dever's argument.

Other scholars interpret the drawing with the three figures differently. Unlike Dever, Mordecai Gilula[24] ignores the enthroned woman; she may be only a court attendant. He interprets the figure on the left as Yahweh in the form of a bull. Calling attention to the female breasts of the figure in the center, he identifies her as Asherah. The exposed phallus or tail of the center figure may have been a later addition.

Arguing that nowhere in the Hebrew Bible is a pronominal suffix attached to a personal name, many scholars dismiss the interpretation of Asherah as the consort of Yahweh and instead understand "his Asherah" as a reference to a cult object, shrine, or *cella* dedicated to the female deity. In a recent study of the Kuntillet Ajrud inscriptions and their implications, John Emerton[25] concluded that the Asherah was probably the wooden symbol of the goddess, adding that the inscription does not prove that Asherah was considered as Yahweh's consort.

Dever argues that the wilderness shrine of Kuntillet Ajrud is achaeological confirmation for the cult of Asherah as the consort of Yahweh in ancient Israel. Such syncretistic cult was part of the popular religion in contrast to the official religion; Elijah, Elisha, Amos, and Isaiah inveighed vigorously against the former. In support of his interpretation Dever calls attention to the representation of a lion on the pithos with the drawing of the three figures; the lion, a symbol of Asherah, is reminiscent of Asherah's epithet in the Iron Age, "Lady Lion."

A comparable representation appears on a 10th-century B.C. cultic stand which Lapp found in a cistern at Taanach. In 1902 Ernest Sellin discovered at Taanach a large clay incense stand; sixty-six years later Lapp uncovered a clay cult stand, not quite two feet high, lying near where Sellin had found the incense altar. There was in the 10th century B.C. at Taanach a structure related to the local cult; these stands were associated with this structure. Because the stand showed no evidence of burning or incense, Lapp assumed it had been used for libations. More important, this stand, which is in the shape of a hollowed square, has four registers in front; the lowest register depicts a nude female of the Astarte type flanked by two striding lions, whose teeth are bared and tails flying.[26]

Dever[27] draws further confirmation for his interpretation of the deity Asherah from his salvage excavation in 1967 of robbed tombs at Khirbet el-Kom in the southern Judean hills. This Iron Age site has been identified with Saphir of Micah. One of the funerary inscriptions incised in a burial cave at el-Kom reads, "May Uriyahu be blessed by Yahweh, my guardian, and by his Asherah," the same formula found at Kuntillet Ajrud. To date few scholars have published studies on Kuntillet Ajrud; perhaps Dever's convincing article will galvanize more.

The excavations at Lachish, the most important Judahite city after Jerusalem, have occasioned a serious problem in chronology; there has been a hundred-year difference in the dating of Israelite pottery. In 1929 Albright proposed Tel ed-Duweir, and not Tel el-Hesi, as the proper location of Lachish, an identification accepted today by most historical geographers. James Starkey began excavating at the site in 1932 and continued until his death at the hands of bandits in 1938. In 1973 David Ussishkin[28] continued the work of Starkey at Lachish; one of Ussishkin's principal objectives was to settle the destruction date of the controversial Stratum III by concentrating on the city-gate complex near the southwest corner of the mound, where there were a number of superimposed city gates. The first city-gate uncovered by Starkey was dated to the Persian period, designated Stratum I. The Stratum II gate had been destroyed by fire; presumably this was the Babylonian attack on the city. The Lachish letters were found in the debris of the gate-complex at Stratum II. The Stratum III gate-complex had also been destroyed by fire, but the source of this destruction is disputed. Starkey dated it to the Babylonian campaign of 597 B.C.; Albright, Wright, Lapp, Kenyon, Yadin, Holladay and others follow Starkey.

Olga Tufnell[29], who dug with Starkey at Lachish and produced the final report on the project, disagreed with Starkey about the date of the Stratum III destruction. Observing a noticeable difference between the pottery repertoires of Stratum II and III, she concluded they had to be separated by a considerable period of time for typological changes to take place. She also noticed two phases of destruction in the Stratum II gate, assigned to the destruction of 597 and 587 B.C. respectively. In Tufnell's estimation the Assyrians under Sennacherib wrought the destruction of Stratum III in 701 B.C. Ussishkin, many Israeli archaeologists, and others, concur with Tufnell's dating of Stratum III.

More recently Ussishkin has demonstrated by stratigraphic evidence to the satisfaction of many scholars that a destruction date of 701 B.C. for Stratum III accords better with the archaeological data at the city-gate than a date of 597 B.C. It appears that a serious historical discrepancy has now been resolved; the pottery chronology of the Iron Age will also be clarified as a result of Ussishkin's interpretation of the stratigraphy of the gate area at Lachish. The disputed dating of the storage jars with royal Judean seal impressions has also been cleared up. Starkey found over 300 royal storage jars in Stratum III; these jars must have been in use during the reign of Hezekiah.

When Albright[30] led an expedition to Moab and the Dead Sea in 1924, his primary purpose was to clarify the problem of the "cities of the plain." Interest in the question was heightened when Alexis Mallon, a member of the Albright expedition, accidentally discovered the fascinating Bronze Age site of Bab edh-Dhra. In the 1960s Lapp, prompted by the appearance of contraband pottery from

Bab edh-Dhra on sale in the antiquities shops of Jerusalem, began excavations there. Since 1973 Walter Rast and Thomas Schaub have been digging at Bab edh-Dhra and surveying the southeastern plain of the Dead Sea. While surveying, they rediscovered several additional Bronze Age sites; Numeira, where Michael Coogan is digging, es-Safi, Feifeh, and Khanazir, which form a line south of Bab edh-Dhra. As a result, speculation began anew about the location of the "cities of the plain."

In a forthcoming article on the problems of correlating archaeological evidence and biblical sources, Sauer[31] addresses the question of the "cities of the plain." He cautions that identification of these Bronze Age sites with the "cities of the plain" is premature. The evidence to date is too limited; several of the sites have not yet been excavated, and the region southeast of the Dead Sea is still *terra incognita.* Sauer points out that the five sites were not all occupied at the same time; they were not necessarily city sites; they may not be the only Early Bronze sites in the area. He concluded, "In fact, numerous Early Bronze sites exist along the foothills of the Jordan Valley to the north, and there are some which are known along the foothills of the Wadi Arabah to the south, so the five sites are anything but unique."

This rapid and selective review of recent archaeological projects illustrates that biblical archaeology, or the archaeology of Palestine and the Bible, is bursting with energy, ensuring a long life ahead. Archaeology has just begun to make its real contribution to biblical studies.

FOOTNOTES

1. Presidential address delivered at the forty-fifth general meeting of the Catholic Biblical Association held at Siena College, Loudonville, NY, 23 August 1982.
2. *BA* 26 (1963) 122.
3. "On Right and Wrong Uses of Archaeology," *Near Eastern Archaeology in the Twentieth Century: Essays in Honor of Nelson Glueck* (ed. J.A. Sanders; Garden City, NY: Doubleday, 1970) 64-80.
4. "What Archaeology Can and Cannot Do," *BA* 34 (1971) 70-76.
5. R. de Vaux, "On Right and Wrong Uses of Archaeology," 78.
6. *JBL* 32 (1913) 1-53.
7. "Archaeology and the Date of the Hebrew Conquest of Palestine," *BASOR* 58 (1935) 10-18; "The Israelite Conquest of Canaan in the Light of Archaeology," *BASOR* 74 (1939) 11-23.
8. "The Settlement of the Israelites in Palestine," *Essays on Old Testament History and Religion* (Garden City, NY: Doubleday, 1968) 173-221.
9. *The History of Israel* (New York: Harper, 1960).
10. *The Settlement of the Israelite Tribes in Palestine* (*SBT* 2/21; Naperville: Allenson, 1971); "The Israelite 'Conquest' and the Evidence from Transjordan," *Symposia Celebrating the Seventy-Fifth Anniversary of the Founding of the American Schools of Oriental Research* (ed. F.M. Cross; Cambridge: American School of Oriental Research, 1979) 15-34.
11. *The Tribes of Yahweh: A Sociology of the Religion of Liberated Israel 1250-1050 B.C.E.* (Maryknoll, NY: Orbis, 1979).
12. "The Hebrew Conquest of Palestine," *BA* 25 (1962) 66-87.
13. Y. Aharoni, V. Fritz, and A. Kempinski, "Excavations at Tel Masos (Khirbet el-Meshash): Preliminary Report on the First Season, 1972," *Tel Aviv* 1 (1974) 64-74; "Excavations at Tel Masos (Khirbet el-Meshash): Preliminary Report on the Second Season, 1974," *Tel Aviv* 2 (1975) 97-124; A. Kempinski and V. Fritz, "Excavations at Tel Masos (Khirbet el-Meshash): Preliminary Report on the Third Season, 1975," *Tel Aviv* 4 (1977) 136-58; A. Kempinski, "Tel Masos: Its Importance in Relation to the Settlement of the Tribes of Israel in the Northern Negev," *Expedition* 20 (1978) 29-37.
14. M. Kochavi, "Tel Esdar," *Encyclopedia of Archaeological Excavations in the Holy Land* (eds. M. Avi-Yonah and E. Stern; Jerusalem: Masada Press, 1978). 4. 1169-71.
15. M. Kochavi, "An Ostracon of the Period of the Judges from Izbet Sartah," *Tel Aviv* 4 (1977) 1-13.
16. "Early Alphabetic Scripts," *Symposia Celebrating the Seventy-Fifth Anniversary of the Founding of the American Schools of Oriental Research* (ed. F.M. Cross; Cambridge: American Schools of Oriental Research, 1979) 111.

17. "Giloh: An Early Israel Settlement Site near Jerusalem," *IEJ* 31 (1981) 1-36; "Three Israelite Sites in the Hills of Judah and Ephraim," *BA* 45 (1982) 167-78.
18. "New Evidence on the Conquest of Ai," *JBL* 87 (1968) 312-20.
19. J.A. Callaway and R.E. Cooley, "A Salvage Excavation at Raddanah, in Bireh," *BASOR* 201 (1971) 9-19.
20. "Prospects for Archaeology in Jordan and Syria," *BA* 45 (1982) 82.
21. (Chicago: University of Chicago, 1983).
22. *Kuntillet Ajrud: A Religious Centre from the Time of the Judean Monarchy on the Border of Sinai* (Jerusalem: The Israel Museum, 1978).
23. "Recent Archaeological Confirmation of the Cult of Asherah in Ancient Israel," *Hebrew Studies* 23 (1982).
24. "To Yahweh Shomron and His Asherah," *Shnaton* 3 (1978-79) 128-37.
25. "New Light on Israelite Religion: The Implications of the Inscriptions from Kuntillet Ajrud," *ZAW* 94 (1982) 2-20.
26. P. Lapp, "The 1968 Excavations at Tel Taannek," *BASOR* 195 (1969) 2-49.
27. "Iron Age Epigraphic Material from the Area of Kh. el-Kom," *HUCA* 40-41 (1969/1970) 139-204.
28. "The Destruction of Lachish by Sennacherib and the Dating of the Royal Judean Storage Jars," *Tel Aviv* 4 (1977) 28-60; "Excavations at Tel Lachish — 1973-1977: Preliminary Report," *Tel Aviv* 5 (1978) 1-97.
29. *Lachish III (Tell ed-Duweir): The Iron Age* (London: Oxford University, 1953).
30. "The Archaeological Results of an Expedition to Moab and the Dead Sea," *BASOR* 14 (1924) 2-12.
31. "Syro-Palestinian Archaeology, History, and Biblical Studies," *BA* 45 (1982) 207.

Corinthian Bronze

JEROME MURPHY-O'CONNOR, O.P.
Ecole Biblique
Jerusalem, Israel

Were wealthy Romans of the mid-1st century A.D. in the habit of playing word-association games, and had anyone said, "Bronze," the response would certainly have been "Corinth." For over a hundred years Corinthian bronze had been a collector's item, and the passion it could inspire is amply documented.

Verres and Cicero were "proscribed by Antony for no other reason than refusing to surrender to him some pieces of Corinthian ware" (Pliny, *NH*, 34:6). This was in 43 B.C. In that or the following year a graffito appeared on the statue of Octavian, *Pater argentarius, ego Corintharius*, "My father concerned himself with silver, I with Corinthians," because, as Suetonius explains, "it was believed that he caused some men to be entered in the list of the proscribed because of their Corinthian vessels (*vasa Corinthia*)" (*Augustus*, 70:2). In the time of Tiberius Corinthian vessels commanded exorbitant prices (*Corinthiorum vasorum pretia in immensum exarsisse*; Suet., *Tib.*, 34:1), but nonetheless the imperial household had such a collection that a special bureau had to be created to take charge of them; its members were known as a *Corinthiis* or *Corinthiarii*.[1] This, of course, makes the point of the graffito; Octavian had made himself a slave to his collector's greed. Such submersion of more humane instincts by possessiveness enables us to understand why Seneca wrote in A.D. 49, "Would you say that the man is truly human who arranges with finical care his Corinthian bronzes, that the mania (*furore*) of a few makes costly, and spends the greater part of each day on rusty bits of copper?" (*De brev. vitae*, 12:2),[2] an attitude that is perfectly reflected in the irony of his contemporary, Pliny the Elder, *mireque circa id muttorum adfectatio furuit*, "there has been a wonderful mania among many people for possessing this metal" (*NH*, 34:6).

This phenomenon cannot be without interest to those concerned with the sociological background of the New Testament, particularly since Corinth was such an important center. The standard dictionary articles[3] provided many, but not all, of the references and the discussion is highly condensed. Thus, I have thought it worthwhile to undertake a new examination of the dossier, and to provide a modest service by quoting as much as possible of the relevant texts.

The passion that Corinthian bronzes inspired becomes more comprehensible once it is realized that they were not prized for their beauty alone; the metal had an intrinsic value. Writing in the latter part of the 2nd century B.C., Sextus Propertius could bracket it with gold, precious stones, and land:

Nec tamen inviso pectus mihi carpitur auro
    nec bibit e gemma divite nostra sitis
  nec mihi mille iugis Campania pinguis aratur
      nec miser aera paro clade, Corinthe, tua. (*Eleg.* 3:5.3)

[I can look on gold without being consumed by greed
    for it;
I do not quench my thirst from costly jewelled cups;
I have no Campanian lands plowed by a thousand yoke
    of oxen;
It is not my folly to collect bronzes from Corinth's ruin.
Ed. Tr.]

A century later the judgment had not changed, *immo vero
ante argentum ac paene etiam ante aurum Corinthio,* "Corinthian
bronze is valued before silver and almost even before gold"
(Pliny, *NH,* 34:1).

It is difficult to document the origins of interest in
Corinthian bronze. The earliest reference that I have been
able to trace is in Diphilus of Sinope (b. before 340 B.C.) who
makes a parasite say, "When a rich man gets up a dinner and
invites me, I don't stop to notice the triglyphs on the ceiling,
nor do I examine the Corinthian jars (*oude dokimazo tous
Korinthious kadous*), but I watch intently the chef's smoke."
(Athenaeus, *Deipnosophistae,* 236b). The assumption is that
the jars were a prized possession, which it was customary to
admire, but nothing proves that they were made of bronze.

The same sort of ambiguity plagues a reference from
the 3rd century B.C. It is attributed to Callixeinus of Rhodes
(fl. c. 155 B.C.) in a description of a procession which took
place in Alexandria between 278 and 270 B.C.[4] He begins
*echomenoi de touton epompeuon hoi ta chrysomata pherontes,
krateras Lakonikous tettaras,* "next to these in the procession
came those who carried the gold utensils, four Laconian
mixing-bowls," then, after a lacuna, the text continues
Korinthiouryeis duo, "and two of Corinthian workmanship"
(Athenaeus, *Deipnosophistae,* 199e). The first impression that
the Corinthian bowls were also of gold is not necessarily
correct, not only because of the lacuna, but more because of

the peculiar color of Corinthian bronze (cf. below) which meant that it could easily be mistaken for gold.

Fortunately we have a perfectly clear text from the latter part of the 3rd century B.C. A contemporary of the disciples of Theophrastus of Eresus (c. 370-c. 285 B.C.) reports on a banquet in Macedonia at which the guests were given a silver cup to keep, and a gold crown; they were served the first course *en chalko pinaki ton Korinthion*, "on a bronze platter of Corinthian workmanship," *kai meta tauta argyrous pinax heteros*, "and after these a second platter of silver" (Athenaeus, *Deipnosophistae*, 128d). Given the sumptuous character of this feast the Corinthian vessels were certainly not considered common ware.

If Corinthian vessels were known and treasured in Macedonia and Egypt in the 3rd century B.C., it seems reasonable to postulate a much wider distribution. Although a committed philhellene, Scipio Africanus Major (236-184 B.C.) served only in Spain and Africa, yet we are told by Cicero that he dedicated to the sanctuary of the Great Mother at Engyum *loricas galeasque aeneas caelatas opere Corinthio hydriasquee grandis simili in genere atque eadem arte perfectas*, "chased bronze breastplates and helmets of Corinthian workmanship, as well as tall ewers of the same material and artistry" (*In Verrem II*, 4:97). He goes on to underline their value by claiming that Scipio *existimabat ea non ad hominum luxuriem, sed ad ornatum fanorum atque oppidorum esse facta* "he judged them to have been made, not for the luxury of men, but for adornment of temples and towns." (4:98).

The Romans would have come into contact with Corinthian vessels when they moved into Greece during the Illyrian and Macedonian Wars, but real interest in the capital must be related to the sack of Corinth in 146 B.C. (cf. Pliny, *NH*, 34:12 cited below). The various reports say that Lucius Mummius sent back to Rome most of "the votive offerings and works of art" (Strabo, *Geog.* 8:6.23; Pausanias, *Des. Greece,* 7:16.8; Dio Cassius, *History,* 21). None of these, however, explicitly mentions bronze, but the natural assumption that some must have been included receives explicit confirmation from Vitruvius (c. 27 B.C.), *habemus Lucium Mummium qui diruto theatro Corinthiorum ea aenea Roman deportavit et de manubiis ad aedem Lunae dedicavit,* "we find a precedent in Lucius Mummius who destroyed the theater at Corinth and transported these bronze vessels to Rome, and dedicated them, from the spoils, at the temple of Luna" (*De Arch,* 5:5.8)

Vitruvius intends to suggest that such vessels were used in the theater at Corinth as resonance-enhancers, and this has given rise to the hypothesis that these were the "sounding brass" mentioned by Paul (1 Cor 13:1).[5] How Vitruvius knew the purpose of these vessels is far from clear, and the accuracy of his assessment is open to question. The theater at Corinth could hold 14,000 people, and the attitude of the spectators in no way resembled the well-disciplined theatergoers to whom we are accustomed. Just the background noise of such a crowd would have set up vibrations that could not but interfere with the fine-tuning that the resonance-enhancers demanded. Hence, it is preferable to suppose that the vessels mentioned by Vitruvius served a purely decorative function, either on the sides of the stage or at the entrances.

Be that as it may, we must assume that enough Corinthian bronze reached Rome in the immediate post-146 B.C. period to stimulate interest, yet not enough to satisfy the demand. Otherwise, it becomes impossible to explain why the colonists of 44 B.C. (cf. Appian, *History,* 8:136) were aware that there would be a market in Rome for the bronze objects (*chalkomata*) and terracotta reliefs that came to light when tombs were opened during the clearing of the ruins.

Only popular demand could justify the high price they commanded, an aspect that Strabo explicitly emphasizes (*Geography*, 8:6.23). He then goes on to say that interest in the terracotta reliefs quickly waned. Nothing is said about the bronzes, and the only inference possible is that they retained their popularity. The texts from Pliny the Elder and Seneca cited above would even indicate that interest increased.

Inevitably the passion for Corinthian bronze stimulated curiosity regarding the metal itself. What made it different from all other bronze, and how was it developed? Somewhat surprisingly there was a consensus that its development was due to an accident involving fire, but after that point fancy embroidered the details. Petronius certainly had his tongue in his cheek when he made Hannibal responsible; after capturing Troy he burnt all the statues of bronze, gold and silver thus producing a new alloy (*Satiricon*, 50). Pliny the Elder, on the contrary, appears to have been dead serious in postulating that "the compound was produced by accident when Corinth was burned at the time of its capture" (*NH*, 34:6). All of his readers would have understood this to be a reference to 146 B.C., and many must have raised the obvious question: since the city was depopulated, who produced the bronze? However, to develop this refutation is unnecessary, because Pliny contradicts himself; a little later he maintains that by the time of the fall of Corinth all the famous artists in metalwork had been long dead (*NH*, 34:7).

A third accident story is furnished by Plutarch, "a fire consumed a house containing some gold and silver and a great store of copper, and when these were melted and fused together, the great mass of copper furnished a name because of it preponderance" (*Moralia*, 395B). Obviously he did not take this version seriously, because he introduces an alternative with the words *allon logon hemeis akekoamen panourgesteron,* "we have heard a more artful account," and goes on to tell the story of a bronzeworker at Corinth who found some gold and, fearing detection, mixed a little at a time with his bronze thereby making it uniquely beautiful. In the end both tales are dismissed with the words *alla kai tauta kakeina mythos estin,* "both this story and that are fiction" (*Moralia,* 395C).

With the legends out of the way, Plutarch very sensibly continues, *en de tis hos eoike meixis artysis,* "There was apparently some process of combination and preparation" (*Moralia,* 395C), but obviously he has no idea of what it might have been. It is at this point that Pliny the Elder is more forthcoming, for he distinguishes four different types of Corinthian alloy, *eius aeris tria genera: candidum argento nitore quam proxime accedens, in quo illa mixtura praevaluit; alterum, in quo auri fulva natura; tertium, in quo aequalis omnium temperies fuit, praeter haec est cuius ratio non potest reddi, quamquam hominis manu est,* "There are three kinds of this sort of bronze: a white variety, coming very near to silver in brilliance, in which the alloy of silver predominates; a second kind, in which the yellow quality of gold predominates, and a third kind in which all the metals were blended together in equal proportions. Besides these there is another mixture the formula for which cannot be given, although it is man's handiwork" (*NH,* 34:8). The proportion of precious metal may explain Cicero's assertion that Corinthian bronze was "slow to be attacked by rust" (*Tusculan Disputations,* 4:32).

It would be anachronistic to suppose that his description was based on metallurgical analysis,[6] and a little naive to assume that Pliny had access to sources that were unavailable to his contemporary Plutarch. His approach can only have been phenomenological. The objects that he was prepared to accept as of Corinthian origin differed in color. Consciously or unconsciously he was influenced by the monetary value they enjoyed (cf. *NH*, 34:1 cited above), and so articulated the modulations in terms of different proportions of precious metals, notably gold and silver. The validity of this hypothesis would appear to be verified by the fact that he can offer no explanation for the fourth color. By focusing on gold and silver he can only produce three combinations. He could have explained the fourth type by postulating a preponderance of copper, but this would have conflicted with his assumption of intrinsic value.

When an antique becomes a fashion would-be connoisseurs sprout like weeds, and the cupidity of the collector opens the door to the unscrupulous. In other words, the situation is ripe for the appearance of fakes. Petronius makes precisely this point very wittily by making Trimalcion say, *Et forsitan quaeris quare solus Corinthea vera possideam; quia scilicet aerarius, a quo emo Corinthus vocatur. Quid est autem Corintheum, nisi quis Corinthum habeat?*, "Perhaps you will ask how I alone come to possess genuine Corinthian objects. It is very simple. I buy them from a fellow called Corinth! And what is not Corinthian if not stuff that comes from Corinth?" (*Satiricon*, 50) Such exuberant cynicism clearly implies that greed and gullibility went hand in hand. Pliny the Elder would have agreed fully, *mihi maior pars eorum simulare eam scientiam videtur ad segregandos sese a ceteris magis quam intellegere aliquid ibi suptilius*, "It seems to me that the majority of such collectors pretend to expertise in order to separate themselves from the multitude, rather than possess any specialized knowledge in this field" (*NH*, 34:6). Thus, it became imperative to establish standards for the authenticity of Corinthian bronze. Four such criteria appear in the sources.

Many believed that connoisseurs could literally nose out genuine bronze. Martial says of Mamurra, *consuluit nares an olerent aera Corinthon*, "He took counsel of his nose whether the bronzes smelt of Corinth" (*Epigrams*, 9:59.11). It was presumably with the same purpose in mind that Agamemnon bent to closely examine a Corinthian plate at the feast of Trimalcion, because a little later the host says, *ego malo mihi vitrea, certe non olunt*, "I prefer glass, at least it does not smell" (Petronius, *Satiricon*, 50). It is impossible to estimate the value of this criterion, but those tempted to reject it out of hand should remember that many genuine experts in Palestinian pottery will lick it to determine its date.

A second criterion was color. This is clearly articulated by Pliny the Younger in speaking of a statue he has just bought, *aerugo aes ipsum, quantum verus color indicat vetus et antiquum*, "It appears to be a genuine antique, alike from its patina and from what remains of the original color of the bronze" (*Ep.*, 3:6), but the same can be inferred from Plutarch's discussion in *Moralia*, 395B-D. He underlines *tes chroas to kallos*, "the beauty of its color," which he contrasts with the "deep blue" (*cyanos*) tinge of certain statues at Delphi. The subsequent emphasis on fire and gold in the explanations of its origin (cf. above) would appear to suggest that Corinthian bronze was generally thought to be characterized by a ruddy color.

It is perhaps in this perspective that we should interpret the remark of Pausanias, *ton Korinthion chalkon diapyron kai thermon onta hypo oudatos toutou baptesthai legousin*, "They say that Corinthian bronze when red-hot is tempered by this water" (*Des. Greece*, 3:3.3). The water in question is that of Lower Peirene, the principal fountain of the city located just off the agora. Since there was plenty of water available elsewhere in the city (Strabo, *Geog.*, 8:6.21; Pausanias, 3:3.5), the choice of this particular spring must have been prompted by the belief that its water made a specific contribution to the unique character of the bronze. For what it's worth Frazer reports an observation of Gottling that this water leaves an ochre-like deposit, and draws the inevitable conclusion that this may have contributed to the color of the bronze.[7]

What we have seen so far would appear to indicate that the dark-brown of copper was lightened to a reddish hue by the admixture of gold and silver, but it is precisely at this point that we have to be very careful, because Pliny the Elder warns against bronze whose color *iocineris imaginem vergens, quod ideo hepatizon appellant, procul a Corintho,* "approaches the appearance of liver and consequently called by a Greek name *hepatizon* meaning 'liverish'; it is far behind the Corinthian blend" (*NH,* 34:8), though he admits that it is superior to the bronze of Delos and Aegina. In his estimation, therefore, it would appear that the color of genuine Corinthian bronze was lighter than the dark-red of liver, and this is confirmed by his acceptance of a type which is very near silver (cf. above).

According to Pliny, this liver-colored bronze appears particularly *in simulacris signisque,* "in portrait statues and figures" (*NH,* 34:8), and these are excluded by the third criterion, namely, the type of object. He states formally, *sunt ergo vasa tantum Corinthia, quae isti elegantiores modo ad esculenta transferunt, modo in lucernas aut trulleos nullo munditarum depectu,* "The only genuine Corinthian vessels are then those which your connoisseurs sometimes convert into dishes for food, and sometimes into lamps or even washing basins, without any regard for the quality of the workmanship" (*NH,* 34:7). The allusion to plates and bowls in this text is unambiguous, but we must inquire what type of object was capable of being transformed *in lucernas.* A little later Pliny says, *cum esse nulla Corinthia candelabra constet, nomen id praecipue in his celebratur,* "Although it is admitted that there are no lampstands made of Corinthian metal, yet this name specially is commonly attached to them,"[8] and he goes on to give the reason; the destruction of Corinth, *e compluribus Achaiae oppidis simul aera dispersit,* "caused the dispersal of bronzes from a number of the towns of Achaia at the same time" (*NH*, 34:12). This passage fully justifies the use of *transferunt* in the previous one, and incidentally explains why there was some confusion regarding genuine Corinthian objects; they first came to Rome mixed up with artifacts of other provenances. The indiscriminate use of "Corinthian" is underlined by Pliny (*NH*, 34:7).

If, then, we must look for an upright bronze object capable of supporting branched candle-holders, there seems to be no alternative to the assumption that Pliny was alluding to figurines, which he explicitly associates with Corinth. *Signis, quae vocant Corinthia, plerique in tantum capiuntur, ut secumferant,* "Owners of figurines called Corinthian are usually so enamored of them that they carry them about with them" (*NH*, 34:18). *Vocant,* of course, is polyvalent; it could indicate a particular category of figurines determined by their provenance, or it could mean that all figurines were indiscriminately called Corinthian, just as candelabra were. This latter interpretation, however, is made less probable by the contrast between the formulation here and that employed apropos of the candelabra, and would appear to be excluded by a text from Petronius to be dealt with below. Thus, it seems more likely that Pliny believed that certain figurines were genuinely Corinthian. Nothing in the text proves that these figurines were made of bronze but since the adjective "Corinthian" was regularly associated only with this metal and with capitals, only extreme pedantic prudence could accept any doubt on this point.

Pliny gives a number of examples of these figurines. Hortensius, the defense counsel of Verres, had a sphinx, as had the ex-consul Gaius Cestius (mid-1st century A.D.). We know from Quintilian (*Inst. Or.*, 6:3.98) that the sphinx of Hortensius was of bronze,[9] because he also quotes the celebrated retort of Cicero when his opponent claimed that he was no good at riddles, *respondit debere, quoniam sphingem domi haberet.* The Loeb translation — "You ought to be, as you keep a figurine in your pocket" — not only misses the point of the joke, but gives a misleading impression regarding the size of the object. The meaning can only be "You ought to be, because you have a sphinx at home." The connotation of *secumferant,* therefore, must be that the objects were moved when the owners changed residences. Certainly it does not imply that the figurines were very small. No inferences are possible regarding the statues mentioned by Martial, Apollo watching a lizard (*Epig.*, 14:172), and the infant Hercules throttling two snakes (*Epig.*, 14:177).

Somewhat more illuminating is the third example given by Pliny, *circumtulit et Nero princeps Amazonem,* "The emperor Nero also brought about with him an Amazon" (*NH*, 34:48), for he later reformulates this statement, *Strongylion Amazonem, quam ab excellentia crurum eucnemon appellant, ob id in comitatu Neronis principis circumlatam,* "Strongylion made an Amazon, which from the remarkable beauty of the legs is called the Eucnemon, which consequently the emperor Nero caused to be carried in his retinue on his journeys" (*NH*, 34:82). This is the only Corinthian figurine to be attributed to a specific artist. Strongylion is dated to the mid-5th century B.C., and, apart from one group of Muses, his statues were in bronze.[10]

Further inferences regarding these figurines can be drawn from the description given by Pliny the Younger of one he had just bought (*Ep.*, 3:6). *Ex hereditate, quae mihi obvenit, emi proxime Corinthium signum modicum quidem,* "I have lately purchased, with a legacy that was left me, a small

Corinthian statue." That fact that he had to wait for an inheritance hints at the cost of the statue, which represented an old man standing, *ossa musculi, nervi, venae, rugae etiam ut spirantis apparent,* "the bones, the muscles, the veins, and wrinkles are so strongly expressed, that you would imagine the figure to be animated." Since he intended to display it on an inscribed marble base in a temple, the adjective "small" should not be pushed too far. We should probably think in terms of a statue half lifesize.[11]

Pliny the Elder's claim that genuine Corinthian bronze appeared only as bowls, plates and figurines is confirmed by Petronius; from the fused metal of the gold, silver and bronze statues, *fecerunt catilla et paropsides et statuncula,* "they made bowls, dishes, and figurines" (*Satiricon,* 50). At this point it seems appropriate to assemble the terms that have appeared earlier in this article. The most generic is *vas* "vessel" (Pliny, *NH,* 34:7; Suet., *Aug.,* 70; Vitr., 5:5.1) which implies a utilitarian character that is borne out by the other words, *kados* "jars" (Ath., 236b); *krater* "mixing-bowl" (Ath., 199e); *pinax* "plate" (Ath., 128d); *hydraios* "ewer" (Cic., *In Verr.* II, 4:97); *lanx* "tray, plate" (Petr., *Sat.* 50).[12] The *loricae galeaeque aeneae caelatae,* "chased bronze breastplates and helmets" (Cic., *In Verr.* II, 4:97), also have a utilitarian character, but in terms of our sources such objects are exceptional. They may have been attributed to Corinth simply because of the quality of the decoration.

This aspect of Corinthian ware is alluded to in a number of texts. Pliny the Elder's reference to the quality of the workmanship in *NH* 34:7 (cf. above) would seem to imply more than mere perfection of form, and this is confirmed by his claim that all genuine Corinthian vessels were made by famous artists (*ibid.*). In another passage he says, *in Corinthiis aes placet argento auroque mixtum, in caelatis ars et ingenia,* "In the case of Corinthian bronzes we are attracted by (the color which is a) mixture of silver and gold, and in the case of chased metal by artistry and inventiveness" (*NH,* 37:49), but despite the punctuation of the Loeb edition, it is not at all certain that the second phrase refers to Corinthian bronze; the context would rather indicate that it does not. Callixeinus, therefore, is the only one to describe the type of decoration that could be found on Corinthian bronze. Regarding the two mixing-bowls he says, *houtoi d'eichon anothen kathemena periphane tetoreumena zoa kai en toi tracheloi kai en tais gastrais prostypa epimelos pepoiemena,* "these had on the brim seated figures in beaten metal, very striking, and on the neck and around the bowl were figures in relief, carefully fashioned" (Athenaeus, *Deipnosophistae,* 199e).

The quality of such workmanship brings us to the fourth and last criterion of authentic Corinthian bronze, namely, antiquity. Pliny claims that the only artists capable of creating such work had been dead for centuries before the fall of Corinth in 146 B.C. (*NH,* 34:7). The text is far from clear, and he does not immediately give the promised list. We can only assume that he had in mind the list of Greek artists in bronze given in *NH,* 34:49-52, for there he asserts that there were no really great artists after the 121st Olympiad (=296-293 B.C.). The obscurity of his treatment would appear to be a consequence of the rather arbitrary and subjective character of his approach. An unpleasant odor of superiority is easily detected. If we accept his exclusion of portrait statues, one does not have to be a great artist to produce utilitarian articles that are both pleasing to the eye and intrinsically valuable, and Corinth was always famed for its superlative workmanship. One of the reasons why Corinth was wealthy was *malista gar kai entautha kai en Sikyoni eyxethe graphike te kai plastike kai pasa he toiaute demiourgia,* "for both here and in Sicyon the arts of painting and modelling and all such arts of the craftsman flourished most" (Strabo, *Geog.*, 8:6.23; cf. Herodotus, 2:167). Because of this association it is not impossible that some of the craftsmen who fled Corinth in 146 B.C. (Pausanias, *Des. Greece*, 7:16.7) found refuge in Sicyon; the effort of Mummius to winkle them out is unlikely to have been completely successful (Dio Cassius, *History*, 21).

Finally, we come to the question of whether bronze vessels were produced in Corinth after the establishment of the Roman colony in 44 B.C. The textual evidence is meager, but illuminating.

In response to the claim of Trimalcion that he alone possessed Corinthian ware, the narrator says, *expectabam ut pro reliqua insolentia diceret sibi vasa Corintho afferri,* "I expected him to proclaim with his customary arrogance that he had vessels brought from Corinth" (Petronius, *Satiricon,* 50). In itself this statement is ambiguous. It could mean that no such vessels were still available, but equally the sense could be that Trimalcion was not the sort of person to go to such trouble and expense, since his joke (cf. above) makes it clear that he did not value Corinthian ware highly. The balance is weighed in favor of this latter interpretation by the next two texts.

Plutarch, after dismissing as fiction the two stories of the discovery of Corinthian bronze (cf. above), continues, *en de tis hos eoike meixis kai artysis, hos pou kai nun anakerannyntes argyro chryson idian tina kai peritten emoi de phainomenen nosode chloroteta kai phthoran akalle parechousi,* "but there was apparently some process of combination and preparation; for even now they alloy gold with silver and produce a peculiar and extraordinary and, to my eyes, a sickly paleness and an unlovely perversion" (*Moralia,* 395D). At first sight he would appear to be speaking of an alloy made exclusively of gold and silver, but this interpretation is excluded by the context, for he is evidently contrasting the contemporary product with the glorious bronze of yesteryear. Thus bronze was being produced at Corinth at the end of the 1st century A.D. The quality of Plutarch's aesthetic judgment, of course, is open to question — he indicates that others do not agree with him — but there is the hint that, even though the awareness of the use of silver and gold remained, the secret of the precise proportions had been lost.

The last witness is Pausanias. Speaking of the spring of Peirene, he says, *hypo hydatos toutou baptisthai legousin,* "they say that (Corinthian bronze) is tempered by this water" (*Des. Greece,* 2:3.3). The infinitive is in the present tense, so we must conclude that the practice was in operation at the time of his visit (c. 165 A.D.). It is extremely unusual for Pausanias to mention such a mundane detail; in his description of the agora he omits any reference to the many commercial establishments. Thus, he must have been aware of the association of Corinth bronze with the glorious past of Greece, which was his focus of interest. In this respect, it is significant that he does not confirm Plutarch's judgment concerning the quality of the contemporary product. It is unfortunate that there is a lacuna in Pausanias' text in the following sentence, *epei chalkos . . . ge ouk esti Korinthiois,* "since bronze . . . the Corinthians have not" (2:3.3). The suggestion has been made that the reference was to copper and tin, the raw material of bronze, because "there is no slag found in the neighborhood of Corinth and no ancient mines are known to exist,"[13] (for the ancient sources of copper, cf. Pliny, *NH,* 34:2.)

Thus, whatever about the quality of the product, the texts confirm what a little cynicism could have deduced from Strabo's assertion that the bronze objects found in the tombs by the new settlers commanded a high price in Rome (*Geog.,* 8:6.23). It would be asking a little too much of human nature to imagine that some of the wilier colonists did not think of supplementing the supply by local production. Merchants find spiritual satisfaction in meeting a demand. Making a customer happy, of course, is quite a different matter, and one may well wonder if the clients in Rome noticed any difference. Given the demand, assured provenance would have gone a long way toward stilling any doubts.

Be that as it may, early in the history of the colony a bronze smithy was in operation in the area of the Peribolos of Apollo and was connected by channels to the spring of Peirene, i.e. precisely the area mentioned by Pausanias. Sometime later, but within the 1st century A.D., large-scale foundries were opened in the Gymnasium area and west of the agora. The size of the casting-pits in these latter installations indicate that statues were produced, but Roman moulds found in the Central Shops, which divided the agora into two levels, demonstrate that more utilitarian objects continued to be made. Since so much bronze working was carried in the very center of the city, it seems highly probable that there must have been many other installations in the outlying areas. Hence, trade in bronze must be considered to have made a significant contribution to Corinthian commerce in the 1st century A.D.

Despite its legendary character, *Yoma* 38a attests the availability of Corinthian bronze in Alexandria at this period. It was used to fashion the doors sent to Jerusalem to adorn the most striking portal of the Temple, known as the Corinthian Gate from its material (Josephus, *BJ*, 5:201) or as the Nicanor Gate after its donor (*Middoth*, 2:3). Since no text even hints that raw, unformed bronze was exported from Corinth, it seems that the bronze for the doors was obtained by melting down vessels of the pre-146 B.C. period or others recently imported from Corinth.

FOOTNOTES

1. This nomenclature is known only from inscriptions; cf. *Corp. Inscr. Latin.*, VI, nos. 8756, 8757; X, no. 692; and also *PW*, 4:1232.

2. I have paraphrased the first part of this quotation — *Illum tu otiosum vocas* — in order to bring out the technical meaning that Seneca attaches to *otiosum*; it is defined in 14:1, *Soli omnium otiosi sunt qui sapientiae vacant, soli vivunt*, "Of all men they alone are at leisure who take time for philosophy; they alone really live." Where possible the translations are taken from the Loeb edition.

3. Daremberg-Saglio (1887), 1/2: 1507-1508; *PW* (1899), 3:895-896; 4:1233-1234. Unfortunately, H. Payne's *Necrocorinthia* (1931) was not available to me.

4. *PW*, 10:1751.

5. W. Harris, " 'Sounding Brass' and Hellenistic Technology," in *Biblical Archaeology Review*, VIII, 1982, pp. 38-41.

6. In fact there appears to have been no metallurgical examination of Corinthian bronze, apart from the irrelevant analysis of a number of bronze coins, cf. T.L. Shear, "A Hoard of Coins found in the Theater District of Corinth" in 1930, in *American Journal of Archaeology*, XXXV, 1931, pp. 139-151.

7. *Pausanias's Description of Greece*, translated with a commentary by J.G. Frazer, III, London: Macmillan, 1913, p. 24. A belief in the uniqueness of Peirene is attested by the personal observations of Athenaeus, "When I had weighed the water from the Corinthian spring Peirene, as it is called, I found it to be lighter than any other in Greece." (*Deipnosophistae*, 43b). What this would have involved boggles the imagination!

8. Among the booty from the palace in Tiberias which Josephus recovered were "candelabra of Corinthian bronze" (*Vita*, 68). One is also mentioned by Martial (*Epig.*, 14:43).

9. The testimony of Plutarch can be disregarded, because in one text he says it was of silver (*Cicero*, 7) and in another of ivory (*Apothth. Cic.*, 11). Both of these materials are white and according to Pliny, there was a Corinthian bronze in which silver predominated. (*NH*, 34:8, cited above).

10. *PW*, 4/A1:372-373.

11. Certain statues in the Forum at Rome in the 3rd century B.C. were only a meter high. (Pliny, *NH*, 34:24).

12. According to E.G. Pemberton no extant piece of bronze can be attributed to Corinth with certitude. She then continues, "In the later 6th century, Corinth's neighbors, Argos, Sikyon, and Aigina, had developed the technology for casting large-scale bronze sculpture. The practical Corinthians had already created a market in portable goods and made, I suspect, a conscious decision to continue producing those sorts of objects that would contribute to a healthy economy. Corinth thus never developed an important school of bronze sculptors. What work was needed was commissioned from non-Corinthian artists. The city was certainly financially able to hire the best . . .

Large-scale sculpture may bring fame to the individual, but it does not enrich the merchant. Rather, the manufacture and export of the more easily shipped utilitarian wares of high quality, including bronze table vessels, may have been a major source of revenue." ("The Attribution of Corinthian Bronzes," in *Hesperia*, L, 1981, pp. 109-110).

13. Frazer, op. cit., p. 25.

The International God Elohim/Nṯr

CYRUS H. GORDON
New York University
New York, NY 10003

The definitions of monotheism are many;[1] and tomes have been written on Akhenaton as "history's first monotheist."[2] Egyptian "solar monotheism" doubtless had some effect on Israel. The tradition in Genesis 41:45, 50-52 that Joseph married the daughter of Potiphera,[3] a Heliopolitan priest is one of the striking indications pointing in that direction.[4]

Psalm 19:5-6 describes God as the sun coursing across the heavens from east to west. The central figure in the mosaic floor of the Beth Alpha synagogue is a "Helios" drawn in his chariot by horses.[5] There is little doubt that the artists have depicted the God of Israel as the Sun. Whether they reckoned with Psalm 19 as their Scriptural authority is not provable, but they could have made a good case for themselves by doing so.

In the ancient Near East, interethnic and interregional contacts were common from the earliest periods. Since we are dealing primarily with the evidence of written documents, we shall begin with the Early Bronze Age. The Ebla tablets, from the mid-third millennium, include bilingual lists of divine names. Thus the Sumerian god of death and misfortune, Nergal, is equated with the Eblaite Rasap.[6]

The point of this article is that the Egyptian equivalent of Elohim (*qua* the universal and international Deity) is not the Egyptian solar God Rá but Ntr.

Close contact among ethnic groups using different languages, fostering various traditions and devoted to different cults, obliged people to recognize that there is One God who rules the world and all mankind, regardless of each group's parochial affiliations. Homeric Epic is polytheistic; yet when the occasion calls for it, the Iliad (21:103; cf. Odyssey 14:444) speaks of *theos* as "God" (properly spelled with capital "G"), and not as some particular pagan deity. Herodotus (3:40) relates that the Pharaoh Amasis told Polycrates of Samos that *to theion* ("The Deity" = monotheistic "God") is jealous.[7]

Egyptian literature often mentioned Ntr[8] as the universal God who governs the world and controls our destiny. The Middle Egyptian Tale of the Shipwrecked Sailor relates that God is to be thanked (dw', ntr)[9] when one ends a hazardous mission safely. Moreover it is Ntr ("God") who had brought the sailor to the wondrous isle where he was confronted by the Serpent King.[10]

It is particularly in the Egyptian Wisdom Literature that the sages refer to Ntr "God" starting from Old Kingdom times[11] and continuing into Late Egyptian compositions.[12]

The most instructive text to bridge the gap between the Egyptians and Hebrews in this regard is 2 Chronicles 35:21-22. The passage deals with the encounter between Pharaoh Necho II and the Judean King Josiah. Necho tells Josiah that "Elohim" had ordered him to invade and that Josiah should desist from trying to block Necho's advance because of "Elohim" who is with Necho. The biblical text concludes by attributing Josiah's death to the fact that "he would not listen to the words of Necho from the mouth of Elohim."

The "international God Elohim" also appears in the encounter between Abraham and the Philistines of Gerar. The Philistine leaders say to Abraham: "Elohim is with you in all you do, so now swear to me by Elohim" (Gn 21:22).

The international God has definite attributes. For one thing, He maintains nemesis, whereby there is no escaping retribution. Accordingly, if "fear of God" exists in a community, strangers are safe there. But if the people of a community lack the "fear of God," no helpless person is safe there. This is illustrated in Genesis 20 where Abraham gives out misleading information about his wife and half-sister Sarah. Telling the Philistines of Gerar that she was his sister was a deceptive half-truth. When taken to task for not stating that she was indeed his wife, he defended his action by declaring he did not know whether "fear of God" existed in Gerar, for without fear of God (*yir'at-elohim*) "they would kill me for the sake of my wife" (Gn 20:11). Compare Odyssey 9:172-6 which states that the test of God-fearing men is whether they love strangers, whereas men who are not God-fearing are cruel, wild and unjust.

The educated intellectuals of the ancient Near East knew that gods in different areas could represent identical concepts and that therefore the problem might be merely translational. Accordingly, at an Early Bronze site like Ebla, or a Late Bronze city like Ugarit, the scribes knew how to translate the names of deities from language to language. It is not my intention to play down the importance of the Sun god. To the contrary, the pagan cults of the Sun and Moon posed such a threat to the author of Genesis 1, that as pointed out by Professor David Neiman of Boston College, he avoided attributing them to the Creator, Elohim. Instead of making Elohim responsible for the Shemesh ("Sun") cult and for the Yareaḥ ("Moon") cult, the author of Genesis 1:16 has Elohim creating "The Great(er) Luminary" and "The Less(er) Luminary." It is my intention to imply that if Egypto-Hebrew bilingual god-lists come to light, we can expect the equations "Nṯr=Elohim" and "Rʿ =Shemesh" (but not "Rʿ =Elohim").

FOOTNOTES

1. The "monotheism" in the Ten Commandments is in fact monolatry, whereby the jealous God will not allow his devotees to have other gods before Him (Ex 20:3). This is different from the monotheism of Psalm 82 predicting that God will rule the world alone, after the rest of the pantheon dies because of their misdeeds; cf. Cyrus H. Gordon, "History of Religion in Psalm 82" in *Biblical and Near Eastern Studies* (Essays in Honor of William Sanford LaSor), Grand Rapids: Eerdmans, 1978, pp. 129-131. This in turn is not quite the same as Psalm 135:15-17, which insists that all the pagan gods are lifeless statues with mouths that cannot speak, eyes that cannot see, ears that cannot hear, and so forth, because only the God of Israel exists.

2. A relatively recent expression of this to come to my attention is by Donald Redford, on p. 58 of "The Akhenaton Temple Project and Karnak Excavations," *Expedition* 21, 2 Winter, 1979.

3. His name means "He-who-is-given-by-the-Sun."

4. Note that two of the twelve tribal fathers are Ephraim and Manasseh, Joseph's sons born by Asenath, the daughter of an Egyptian Ra' priest (Gn 41:50-52; 46:20; 48:13-20).

5. See the color plate on p. 189 of N. Avigad's article "Beth Alpha" in *Encyclopedia of Archaeological Excavations*, Jerusalem: Israel Exploration Society, Vol. 1 (1975), pp. 187-190.

6. =Ugaritic *Rsp* ="Reshef."

7. Similarly, God is "jealous" in the Bible (Ex 20:5; Dt 5:9).

8. In Late Egyptian, the article *p* ("the") is frequently prefixed, so that "God" is p', ntr, which comes into Coptic as *pnoute* "God." Thus the concept as well as the word for the universal God comes into Coptic from Pharaonic Egyptian in a straight line.

9. Line 5 (Aylward M. Blackman, *Middle-Egyptian Stories*, Brussels: Edition de la Fondation Egyptologique Reine Elizabeth, 1932, p. 41).

10. Lines 113-4: "Lo, God has kept you alive; He has brought you to this wondrous isle" (p. 44).

11. Cf. Etienne Drioton and Jacques Vandier, *L'Egypte,* 4th ed., Paris: Clio (Presses Universitaires de France), 1962, pp. 63-64. Examples are on hand in The Maxims of Ptahhotpe, The Teaching for the Vizier Kagemni, and The Teaching for Merikare (translated in William Kelley Simpson, R.O. Faulkner and E.F. Wente, *The Literature of Ancient Egypt,* new ed., New Haven: Yale University Press, 1973, pp. 159-192).

12. Illustrations are common in the Wisdom of Amenemope. Note H.O. Lange, *Das Weisheitsbuch des Amenemope,* Copenhagen: Andr. Fre. Host & Son, 1925; p. 51 (VIII:19-20), p. 52 (IX:7-8), p. 60 (XI:5), p. 70 (XIV:2), & c.

THE BIBLE AND THE COMMUNITY OF FAITH

Introduction

MIRIAM WARD, R.S.M.
Trinity College
Burlington, VT 05401

One of the most basic and important documents produced by Vatican Council II was the *Constitution on Divine Revelation,* in effect the Council's statement on the Bible. Equally important is what went into the formulation of this document, particularly in the re-writing of Chapter I of the first draft entitled "The Two Sources of Revelation," i.e. Scripture and tradition. (For a perceptive analysis of the process behind this document see Peter Gerard Duncker's article "The Transmission of Divine Revelation According to Vatican II," in *Biblical Studies in Contemporary Thought,* the Tenth Anniversary Commemorative Volume of the Trinity College Biblical Institute.) One might characterize the first draft as simply a continuation of the Scripture-tradition debate of the 1950's which in itself reflected a rather superficial understanding of the nature of revelation. The final text clearly removed the dichotomy of two "fonts" of revelation,

and stressed rather the interrelationship of Scripture, tradition, the Church and the working of the Holy Spirit. The
proclamation of this document had far-reaching positive
effects, especially as regards the Bible and the Community
of Faith, and for ecumenism. From an over-emphasis on
tradition, almost a *Sola traditio,* Vatican II called for a
balance. This, it seems to me, is what Bernhard W. Anderson calls for from the Protestant perspective (where the
Scriptura Sola produced its imbalance) when he asks scholars
for a more balanced approach to biblical theology. It is not
Scripture *or* tradition: but "it is tradition *and* Scripture;
tradition which still makes its theological witness in
Scripture, and Scripture which theologically incorporates
and crystallizes biblical tradition." Readers might recognize
here the underlying debate over the very nature of biblical
theology, understood by some exclusively in its historical-
descriptive dimension, and by others as doctrinal theology.
As in the earlier article by Reginald H. Fuller, Professor
Anderson calls for a more holistic approach.

For thousands of students throughout the United
States the name Bernhard W. Anderson immediately produces the association of *Understanding the Old Testament.* Now
in its third edition, this monumental treatment of the
Hebrew Scriptures, incorporating as it does historical and
archaeological research, literary criticism, and biblical theology reflects Professor Anderson's scholarly competence as
well as his ability to convey the "historical drama reflected in
the pages of the Old Testament" in terms the modern student can both grasp and enjoy. He has written a number of
other books and contributed many scholarly articles to pro-
fessional journals. His teaching has taken him far from
Princeton: to Ghana and New Zealand. Professor Anderson
is an ordained minister of the United Methodist Church.

The article by Professor Anderson that follows is excerpted from his presidential address delivered to the Society of Biblical Literature in 1980. He calls upon his colleagues to reflect on the history of the SBL "not only in the context of forces at work on the North American scene but also in the perspective of the inheritance from Europe, particularly Germany." He lays no claim to having the answer to the two "naivetes" that have characterized biblical methodologies, but he clearly asserts, as was the case of Vatican II, that it is not a question of "either Scripture *or* tradition." The ecumenical implication of this shift by Roman Catholics and Protestants is significant. Some of the barriers erected in the post-Reformation period are removed, resulting in a common ground for a meeting of minds.

Behind every sermon lies an understanding of the nature of the Bible; by its contribution to that understanding, biblical studies can make a crucial difference for preaching. One might guess that these words are a summation of "Sacred Scripture in the Life of the Church," Chapter VI of the same document of Vatican II mentioned above, and indeed they do echo the directives concerning ministering the word, especially through the homily. But these words come from Elizabeth Achtemeier, ordained minister of the Presbyterian Church. They reflect the common concern that all Christian denominations have for faithfully transmitting the word.

Professor of Homiletics, and a specialist in Old Testament theology and biblical hermeneutics, Elizabeth Achtemeier combines preaching, teaching and writing with motherhood. The list of books and articles written both for scholarly journals and popular periodicals inspires one with the same awe as experienced in reading her works or listening to her sermons. They are marked by a creative style of expression.

Although Professor Achtemeier addresses her suggestions to Protestant clergy, she has much to offer those of any denomination whose principal task it is to proclaim the Word of God. Her concerns reflect one of the most urgent calls of Vatican II to priests, deacons, and catechists, but most especially those in the ministerial priesthood acting in the context of the liturgical homily, "to provide nourishment of the Scriptures for the people of God ... and setting their hearts on fire with the love of God." (*Constitution on Divine Revelation*, Ch. VI). Biblical studies and homiletics "go hand in hand, and as the course of one goes, so goes the other," says Achtemeier. And I would add, one of the saddest commentaries on the results of Vatican Council II, is the apathy and neglect accorded the importance of biblical studies for homiletics. Real renewal must bring the Scriptures into the heart of Christian life, and the homily must assume its rightful place of importance.

Tradition And Scripture
In The Community of Faith*

BERNHARD W. ANDERSON
Princeton Theological Seminary
Princeton, NJ 08540

During the past century . . . it has been assumed by critical scholars that in order to take seriously the historical character of the texts one must explore their prehistory as reflected in the various layers of tradition that emerge under historical analysis. In the past many scholars, under the influence of Julius Wellhausen, have perceived the prior stages from a strictly literary point of view, concentrating on the analysis of literary sources, the separation of accretions, and the redaction of the materials into composite wholes. More recently scholars, under the influence of the pioneer of form criticism, Hermann Gunkel, have sought to trace the history of biblical texts behind the compositional stages into the period of oral transmission and to understand how the evolving traditions sprang up within, and were related to, concrete situations in the life of the people. The end result of these studies, if successfully carried out, would be a history of literature from the earliest stages of oral tradition through various compositional stages to the final form of scripture as we have received it.

In all of this, there has been fairly general agreement (complete agreement among scholars is not an historical possibility!) that the biblical scholar must take into account the whole historical, or perhaps I should say traditio-historical, development that led from tradition to scripture. The problem arises when one attempts to become a biblical theologian. Granted that we have to start with the biblical texts that we have received — with scripture — the question is whether it is theologically significant to venture into the prehistory that lies behind the final text. Do such explorations have only the limited value of helping us to understand the genesis and development of the traditions which led toward the final scriptural composition? Or do the pre-compositional levels have theological meanings of their own which not only need to be heard in their own right in the final text but which, in some cases, may be crucial for interpretation?

If I am not mistaken, this is where a major debate is today. Disagreement is over the question as to whether primary theological emphasis should be placed on the tradition *process* or on the final *result* of the process, scripture.

I. The Traditio-historical Process

Consider first the understanding of the relation between tradition and scripture that is advocated by historians of tradition. It was Gerhard von Rad who took with theological seriousness the new kind of *Einleitung* that emerged in the wake of Gunkel's pathbreaking work in form criticism and the history of traditions. It is significant that the first volume of his *Old Testament Theology* appeared with the sub-title, *Die Theologie der geschichtlichen Ueberilieferungen Is-*

raels (1957): *Theology of Israel's Historical Traditions.* What von Rad meant by "history" was not altogether clear, but he did sponsor a subtle theological shift from "history" (in the usual sense, e.g., History of Israel) to traditions about history. Indeed, he advanced a new meaning for the word *Heilsgeschichte* (the history or story of God's saving action), a redefinition that must have disturbed the shades of J.C. K. von Hofmann and his successors. For von Rad the key to *Heilsgeschichte* is *Ueberlieferungsgeschichte,* that is, the history of the transmission of traditions antedating the biblical texts in their final form.

In his bold reliance on a traditio-historical approach von Rad sought to do justice to the narrative mode of expression which, he maintained, characterized Israel's faith from the very first. Since he was basically concerned with theological method, he probably would not have been upset by subsequent objections that his parade examples of the nuclear story ("The Little Historical Credo") come from relatively late stages of tradition. He could have given more attention to early poetic formulations, e.g., the Song of the Sea (Ex15:1-11). His point was that Israel's faith, at whatever level of tradition, is characteristically narrative in style and therefore, as he said in a memorable line, "event has priority over logos."[1] The way to do Old Testament theology is to follow Israel's manner of *Nacherzahlen,* that is, "retelling" the story in ever-new historical situations in which the people found themselves in their movement toward the horizon of God's purpose. When the crust of scripture (say, the Hexateuch) is beaten back into the batter, so to speak, we find this dynamic movement of a people that reappropriated her traditions creatively. The evidence for this is found in the multilayered levels of the biblical texts, their so-called "depth dimension," which the scholar may expose by historical investigation.

Traditio-historical theologians go even further than von Rad by emphasizing the *process* (a good Hegelian term!) of transmission of traditions — the "traditioning process," as it is sometimes called — and thereby open the door for philosophical conversation. This is evident in the essays of a number of the contributors to the international symposium conducted by Douglas A. Knight, *Tradition and Theology in the Old Testament,* for instance the essay by Hartmut Gese on "Tradition and Biblical Theology."[2] Moreover, James Sanders forcefully champions an approach, one that is also influenced by midrashic exegesis, which he denominates "canonical criticism." In various writings, beginning with his *Torah and Canon* (1972), he maintains that the Bible reflects "an existential process" in which people, at various times and in diverse circles, found life-giving value in inherited traditions as they coped with the needs of their historical situation. The growth and development of the literature, according to his view which allows for sociological method, disclose a community on the move, searching for an understanding of its identity and the identity of God and finding in the received traditions both stability and adaptability.[3]

A similar view is advocated by Paul Hanson in his programmatic essay, *Dynamic Transcendence.* He also endeavors to "penetrate behind a surface reading" of biblical texts in order to perceive "the lively process which gave rise to the biblical community's confessions." If we shift our emphasis from "history" to tradition history, and notice the complex character of the appropriation of tradition in any given historical situation, it is possible, he maintains, to understand "the acts of God" in a more satisfactory way. The "lively process" reflected in scripture is one that developed through the years as the community perceived that the new things God did were in keeping with "the creative and redemptive patterns of the past." The fact that "the entire heritage must be related to contemporary experience in a dialectical process of criticism and renewal" not only helps us to understand biblical texts theologically but to find our place in the same unfolding process today.[4]

The traditio-historical approach provides a very attractive view of the biblical community of faith as a people on the way, a "pilgrim people" that was not allowed to settle down in any fixed formulations of the heritage but was constantly summoned into a new understanding of its place in the unfolding drama of the Bible. However, the question arises — and this question has inescapable theological force — as to what happens in the transition from tradition to scripture. That transition, it should be noted, did not occur only at the end of the whole process, at the stage of canonical scripture, but was evident at various stages along the way when words that may have been spoken orally in concrete situations became fixed in writing and thus entered the public domain, where they transcended the living situation in which they once functioned. Isaiah's deposit of his spoken words in writing to be treasured among his disciples (Is 8:16) or Jeremiah's dictation of his oracles to Baruch (Jr 36) provide two glimpses of the transition which took place at various points and in various ways in the history of traditions.

It is to the credit of traditio-historical theologians that they face squarely the problem of the relation between the spoken and the written word, between oral tradition and literature. As an example, take the illuminating essay by Roger Lapointe on "Tradition and Language: The Import of Oral Expression."[5] Like others who belong to this school of interpretation, he too admits the difficulty of penetrating the traditioning process, for our only access to this pre-history is through the final scriptural formulations, and therefore we are led into a realm of uncertainty and hypothetical reconstruction. Can biblical theology, if it intends to be historical in nature, flourish in this shadowy realm? The thing that intrigues me about this essay is that the author, conscious of the Achilles' Heel of traditio-historical investigation, explores the question at the level of linguistics: the relation between the spoken and written word. Primacy, Lapointe argues, belongs to "orality." A living language is one in which the mode of communication is from subject to subject and in which linguistic meaning is given and perceived in a human situation. It follows, then, that written language is relatively inferior: "Written language seems to be a simple transcription of oral language and is as such secondary and relatively accidental."[6] A fateful step was taken when the spoken word, inseparably related to a human situation (*Sitz im Leben*), became the written word and was thereby severed from the concrete situation in which it functioned meaningfully. This transition, says Lapointe in a vivid figure of speech which an OT theologian can hardly ignore, was "a passage probably as important as the passage through the Sea of Reeds."[7] Albert B. Lord, in his reassessment of Homeric literature, also drew attention to the sharp discontinuity introduced when a tradition that was formulated orally was reduced to writing.[8]

Once the matter is stated this way, it is understandable that scholars have sought to go beyond the sacred page and to penetrate the orality of language. The form critical method offered a way to reach into the prehistory of the text, when words were spoken orally and in relation to a concrete human situation, a *Sitz im Leben*. In the spirit of romanticism, Gunkel and his followers (including von Rad) even insisted that the truly creative period of tradition was the oral period, when the word functioned in situations typical of folk life, such as birth, victory in war, cultic celebration, mourning at death, and so on, Yet what happens to human speech when it undergoes the transition from the oral to the written word? (I tremble before this question when I consider the relation between what I say in lectures and what my students take down in notes!) Lapointe described the shift from the oral to the written word as a "passage" as crucial as the passage through the Sea of Reeds — a passage that marked the transition from the old to the new, from a band of slaves to a people with identity. Fixation in writing is a momentous event, for the written product is not necessarily identical with the oral word that it replaces. Indeed, there *is* a profound difference; but one should guard against the romantic notion that the oral word is superior. There are poets who would maintain that the written word, carefully chiseled and nuanced, is the best vehicle for communicating the transcendent meaning of human life. This is true, for instance, of the poem of the Nobel Prize winning poet, Vicente Aleixandre, on "The Old Man Moses" who, from a distance, catches a glimpse of the future that others will inherit.[9] Poetry of this kind is so freighted with verbal power, especially in the original Spanish, that it requires faithful transmission and transcription.

It is striking that so much of the literature of the OT is in poetic form: early traditions like the Song of the Sea, much of the prophetic corpus, the wisdom poetry of Job, etc. The story teller is much freer to expand and improvise than is the poet. To be sure, the "Singer of Tales" (to refer to the title of Albert Lord's book) is bound by the story line, uses fixed formulaic expressions, and speaks in rhetorical cadences; yet each telling of the story is the singing of "a new song" with its audience response. But a poem is not so susceptible to change, owing to its form, its rhythm (if not meter), its unique collocation of words, and its metaphor. It may be marred in transmission, but it requires transmission in its fixed literary form. From a very early period of Israel these two types of tradition undoubtedly coexisted: story material subject to parenetic elaboration and fixed poetic texts (either memorized or written). By the time we reach the poems of so-called Second Isaiah (Isaiah 40-55), we are dealing with the finest poetic art of Israel.

It is significant that James Muilenburg (who from the very beginning of his scholarly career devoted his attention to the poetry of Second Isaiah and whose last work was an unpublished commentary on the first part of the book of Jeremiah [chaps. 1-20] which contains poetry of great power) delivered his presidential address to this society [S.B.L., ed.] on the subject "Form Criticism and Beyond." Contrary to recent interpretation of the address, my esteemed teacher did not advocate moving "beyond form criticism" into a purely literary or rhetorical study of biblical texts. He concluded his address by saying: "We affirm the necessity of form criticism (and that demands appropriate exploration of the prehistory of the text); but we also lay claim to the legitimacy of what we have called rhetorical criticism (and that requires attention to the text itself: its own integrity, its dramatic structure, and its stylistic features)."[10] In his judgment, it was not a sharp either/or. There are many parts of scripture, both narrative and poetic, which may be illumined by form criticism. For traditions when written down still bear the *stigmata* of the spoken word in its concrete situations. As Lapointe observes, Scripture is stamped with the impression of "referents and situations without which it would make no real sense."[11] And these *stigmata* may be theologically significant in the interpretation of what comes to us in final form as scripture.

II. The Final Scriptural Formulation

We turn now to a second approach which has been claiming attention more and more in recent years. According to this view, it is the final scriptural formulation, not the traditio-historical process leading to it, which provides the basis for biblical theology.

Karl Barth was a leading advocate of this view. He recognized that excursions into the prehistory of the text have a limited value and interest. But these ventures should be bracketed when one interprets biblical literature theologically for the community of faith. Barth's scriptural approach is set forth in an excursus on "the history of the spies whom Moses sent to investigate the promised land" related in Numbers 13-14.[12] He recognizes that it is possible to make certain distinctions hypothetically, that is, "'distinctions between that which can be historically proved, that which has the character of saga, and that which has been consciously fashioned, or invented, in a later synthetic view." But these distinctions take us away from the received text. To be sure, we have here a "history," but "the term 'history' is to be understood in its older and naive significance in which (irrespective of the distinctions just mentioned) it denoted a story which is received and handed down in a definite kerygmatic sense." He goes on to say: "To do justice to this sense, we must either not have asked at all concerning these distinctions, or have ceased to do so. In other words, we must still, or again, read these histories in their unity and totality. It is only then that they can say what they are trying to say."

It would probably be a misreading of Barth to suppose that his emphasis on the final text of the biblical narrative demands ignoring the prehistory of the text. He admits that the story contains "a 'historical' element in the stricter sense," that is, the persons, cities, localities, ventures reported. He admits too that the story contains elements of saga, e.g., the depiction of the two men carrying the branch of grapes or the giants who inhabited the land. And further, he says something that sounds like traditio-historical "actualization" (*Vergegenwartigung*): the story of Israel's transition from the wilderness to the promised land was a story that came alive "at a later period — perhaps at a time of the Exile when it was confronted by a dangerous return to its own land." Hence the story displays "the element which has its origin in the synthetic or composite view (fusing past and present almost into one) which is so distinctive a feature of historical writings in Old and New Testament alike." Nevertheless, when all these critical distinctions have been made, he observes, "they can be pushed again into the background and the whole can be read (with this tested and critical naivete) as the totality it professes to be." This is what Rudolf Smend, in an essay in tribute to Barth on "post-critical exegesis," calls "the second naivete."[13]

Barth's interpreters know that he was not a literalist. He took seriously the humanity of scripture and emphasized its rich diversity. His view, however, clearly stands in opposition to the traditio-historical approach as a theological enterprise. Although we may gain some profit from understanding the ongoing history that is reflected in the multilayered biblical texts, this is not the basis for biblical theology. The question of the origin, or dynamic, of the tradition process is not theologically significant, nor is it theologically necessary to know historical and sociological realities present at various stages. Furthermore, the historicist attempt to deal with historical events or historical referents is theologically irrelevant. In fact, this "historicist sense," as Barth puts it in another context, is "a ridiculous and middle-class habit of the modern Western mind which is extremely fantastic in its chronic lack of imaginative fantasy."[14] The theological interpreter is concerned with the final form of the tradition: scripture as read within the community of faith. It takes religious imagination and the power of the Holy Spirit to enter into and appreciate the "genuine history" to which the Bible bears witness — a history in which "the 'historical' and 'non-historical' accompany each other and belong together" and which, in the last analysis, is "non-historical" in the sense that it transcends our creaturely historical distinctions and is seen in its immediacy to God.

This is not the place to go further into the enigma of what Barth means by "history," especially history that is non-historical. There are, however, other movements in both philosophy and literature which, in their own way, emphasize the final text of a writing. Roland M. Frye, an advocate of the New Literary Criticism, has been insisting for some time that biblical scholars should take a leaf from the notebook of secular literary critics who have learned the folly of excursions into the prehistory of a text. In the study of Shakespeare, he points out, the "disintegrators" who tried to explore the precompositional stages ("strata belonging to different dates") have not led us closer to "the authorial originals" but have actually "substituted intricate new understandings which, however subjectively satisfying for a time, have eventually been recognized as learned illusions."[15] And Hans Frei, in his important book on *The Eclipse of Biblical Narrative* — a work which James Barr cites favorably as evidence that biblical theology should shift from "history" to "story"— maintains that the biblical narrative which moves from creation to consummation is not "historical" but "history-like."[16] He compares the Bible to a realistic novel in which the identity of the characters and the intention of the novel are given in the story itself. It makes no sense theologically to look behind the scenes, so to speak, and inquire into a historicity or intentionality outside of the linguistic world of the narrative — in the mind of the author or in the social setting of the time of composition. "The story is the meaning." Attempts to go beyond the story in search of "historical referents" or precompositional stages violate the meaning that is given narratively.

At first glance it seems that Brevard Childs, in his monumental *Introduction to the Old Testament as Scripture,* says something similar in his insistence that the final shape of the text is the basis for theological understanding. In his chapter on the book of Exodus he observes that historical-critical study has shown us the tremendous difficulties that beset a "quest for the historical Moses." "Yet it remains an unexplored challenge," he goes on to say, "whether or not one can speak meaningfully of a 'canonical Moses,' by which one would mean a theological profile of Moses which would do justice to his place within the divine economy."[17] I believe, however, that Childs does not intend "to sever the cord of any historical referential reading of the Bible"; he only insists that the attempt to found theology on "a critical, reconstructed historical sequence" is difficult, if not impossible.[18]

More intriguing is the question of how much Childs is influenced by Karl Barth, under whom he studied systematic theology and, like Rudolf Smend, experienced the lure of "post-critical interpretation."[19] I suspect that in Child's case "the second naivete" (to my knowledge he does not use this language) is different. When it comes to the study of the genesis of the tradition, he stands firmly in the critical school of scholarship. Indeed, he maintains that the various modes of criticism (source, form, tradition, rhetorical, redaction) can help to bring the features of the final text into sharper focus than before. Nevertheless, he maintains that historical criticism in its various modes fails to deal adequately with the theological meaning of *scripture*, that is, the final canonical shape of the various books of the canon. At the final stage of canonicity when the traditions were shaped by usage in the community of faith, scripture reached a transhistorical level — beyond the concrete actualities of the historical time of, say, the Exodus, or Hosea, or so-called Second Isaiah. At this scriptural level, the historical critical method, which seeks to lead us into the prehistory of the text, is no longer applicable and the biblical theologian should move into "post-critical" interpretation. For it is through the canonical contours of the scriptures in their rich diversity that the community of faith hears the word of God.[20]

III. Tradition and Scripture

Here, then, are two radically different approaches to the task of biblical theology. In the case of the traditio-historical approach, the emphasis falls on the theological significance of the movement from tradition to canonical scripture; indeed, one view is that the end-result, canonical scripture, should be regarded as "only an incident, and no more than that."[21] In this perspective, the community of faith is regarded as a people on the way, a people who are constantly being shaped by, and giving shape to, the traditions as they respond to the challenge of new historical situations. On the other hand, in the case of the scriptural approach, the emphasis falls on the end-result of the tradition process, that is, the final literary or canonical shape of the traditions. In this perspective, especially if the canon is taken seriously, the community of faith is defined by the authoritative function of traditions fixed in writing and, at the final canonical stage, in particular books. These opposing approaches, both of which attempt to deal with the historical nature of biblical theology in response to Gabler's appeal, seem to present us with an either/or. At the end of the first hundred years of the Society [of Biblical Literature], we find ourselves in a situation of creative ferment, the outcome of which may be seen in another hundred years by those who inherit our future.

Nevertheless, even at this time, when we can only see through a glass darkly, there are common methodological interests and common theological concerns. It is noteworthy that traditio-historical theologians are also interested in what is called "the second naivete." In an essay . . . which deals specifically with the task of teaching the Bible in universities and seminaries, we read these words (the immediate context relates to teaching in a "confessional" setting):

> Students in the "first naivete" must be pressed toward criticism, and that has been one of the large historic tasks of most seminaries. Students in a critical mood must be pressed to a post-historical "second naivete" which is chastened and knowing.[22]

If students are to be pressed from one naivete to another (the language is not the most felicitous!), then this assumes that their teachers too, even when they use a traditio-historical approach, are concerned with the final form of scripture. Indeed, we should all remind ourselves that our primary task is to interpret the text that we have received, not to substitute some imaginary text created by scholarly ingenuity. The question is whether investigations into the prehistory of the text brings us finally back to the text from which we started, with a literary and theological appreciation that is "chastened and knowing."

For my own part, I welcome the various critical methods that are designed to interpret the text synchronically, not just diachronically, and especially the redaction criticism that helps us to move from analysis to synthesis.[23] Surely a clear verdict of one hundred years of history is that much scholarly work in the past has been too atomistic, too analytical, and not concerned enough with the unity and totality of scriptural units or canonical books. Nevertheless, it is precisely because we deal with the text given to us, as a unity and totality, that we use our historical methodology, with its strengths and weaknesses, in order to understand. True, the final text deserves a place of theological privilege. In regard to Israel's scriptures, that is the text that functioned in the early Christian community and which has been read in the community of faith, both synagogue and church, throughout the centuries to the present. Yet why should the final form of the process of tradition be absolutized? After all, as Rudolf Smend suggests, we may be able to perceive something that those who gave us the text in its final form never saw; and surely we should "use our eyes as best we can."[24]

Granting pride of position to the text in its final form, there are several matters that deserve attention. First, the final text is inseparably related to the history of the community ("Israel" in the case of the Hebrew Bible; the church in the case of the New Testament). The analogy between biblical narrative and the realistic novel breaks down at this crucial point. The prehistory of the novel or the circumstances of the composition of Mozart's music may be ignored as having no bearing on the work itself. But in the case of biblical literature, with some notable exceptions (e.g., Job), we are dealing with works, often composed anonymously, in the history of a people over a period of many generations. In short, the text pulses with the life of a people, and therefore invites historical and sociological inquiry.

A theologian may raise the objection that explorations into the prehistory of the text lead us away from the givenness of the text into the realm of uncertainty and hypothesis. This objection loses much of its force if we seek for illumination of the text, rather than the stubborn, last-ditch defense of hypotheses regarding the prehistory of the text. Hypotheses are necessary, of course, but they are tentative and subject to critical testing; yet this should not lead us into complete skepticism about the precompositional history of traditions and even the earliest period of Israel. Surely the text dealing with the testing of Abraham (Gn 22:1-19) has been illumined by explorations into its prehistory, even though these explorations have to be carried out cautiously and in full recognition of the new meaning that the story gained when incorporated into the epic narrative governed by the history of the promise. Von Rad has helped us to understand that the community was engaged in a significant theological activity in the various stages of the movement that led from oral tradition to scripture. The prehistory of the text was not just an evolution toward its final, scriptural form but the history of a community whose faith was finding expression in forms which became vehicles for expressing its theological understanding. It is important, therefore, to engage in ear training, by whatever methods available, so that we may hear the various theological voices that constitute the choir of the final text. These choral voices may not always be in harmony; in fact, there may be dissonance (contradiction), but all of them should be heard if we are to listen to the witness of the text.[25]

Secondly, the biblical theologian must face the question as to whether the dominant "voice" that speaks in the final form of a text deserves, at least in every case, to be heard as loudly as other voices whose witness has been preserved in the history of traditions. There was a time when scholarship was engrossed with the pursuit of the "earliest"; now the pendulum may swing to the "latest." Even traditio-historical theologians may accord a higher or fuller meaning to the later stages of the process of tradition. Hartmut Gese observes: "This continuing history of tradition can show how, for example, additions to a text — beyond simply replenishing it as may be necessary — can result in an actualization of the text which opens it up to a totally new theological perception."[26] He rightly objects to past scholarly obsession with the origins of primary stages of tradition, as though the stripping off of accretions to a text left us with a residue that is genuine. In the biblical period, he continues, the supplementing of a text had the effect of preserving the old but lifting it up to "a new plateau," "a new ontological level." For example, "through apocalyptic additions a complex of prophetic texts can acquire an altogether new character, representing old truth on a new ontological level." In a particular instance this may be so. Yet it is also possible that the later stages in the history of tradition could blur, obscure, or reverse the theological perception of an earlier stage, in which case one wonders whether the movement which opens up "a totally new theological perception" is a gain or a loss.

Take, for instance, the book of Isaiah. The time has come to go beyond past critical analysis of the book into component parts and to recover some understanding of the integrity of the whole. Isaiah is the end result of a process of tradition, extending from the preaching of the eighth century prophet through his disciples such as so-called Second Isaiah and into the proto-apocalyptic and apocalyptic stages. It may well be that this book provides a good illustration of Gese's thesis that "through apocalyptic additions a complex of prophetic texts can acquire an altogether new character." Be that as it may, it is not certain that the final "apocalyptized" form of the Isaianic tradition is hermeneutically normative. The community of faith which accepts "Isaiah" as scripture may need to turn from this "new plateau" to an earlier, pre-apocalyptic stage if it is to hear "the word of God." The "canonical Isaiah" is no substitute for the "historical" Second Isaiah or the "historical" Isaiah of Jerusalem!

Or consider the case of 'adam in Gn 1:26-28 (also 5:1b-2; 9:6). The creation story has been accommodated to the genealogical scheme that structures the book of Genesis in its final form: five times the formula "these are the generations of" occurs as a superscription in the primeval history (2:4a; 5:1; 6:9 [cf. 5:32]; 10:1; 11:10) and five times in the ancestral history (11:27; 25:12; 25:19; 36:1; 37:2).[27] The result is that in the final composition 'adam has a prevailing masculine meaning, as in the genealogy in Genesis 5 where "he" is the first member in a series traced through the first-born son. Yet the final composition also retains the more inclusive meaning of 'adam given in the once separately existing creation story. Surely it is appropriate for the community which reads the primeval history as scripture to tune in on the prior tradition which sets forth a corporate understanding of 'adam, including "male and female" equally,[28] rather than following the masculine interpretation of the compository stage as was done in the NT (cf. 1 Cor 11:7, "man is the image and glory of God but woman the glory of man").

Or take as a final illustration the parable of the unjust steward found in the Gospel of Luke (16:1-13). It is not clear where the original parable ended, for it has gathered various accretions as the community struggled with its meaning. Are we to conclude that these interpretive accretions have the effect of lifting the tradition to "a new plateau," "a new ontological level"? Or is it the case that these supplements have had the effect of blunting the sharp edge of the story? If the latter is a hermeneutical possibility, then the final text has only a relative claim to authority, especially in the community of faith which reads scripture in the expectation of hearing the word of God.

In the end we return to the note struck almost two centuries ago by Gabler, the reverberations of which are still heard today: "Biblical theology is historical in nature." It is precisely the historical character of the biblical texts which is still the issue, and inescapably related to this is the problem of faith and history or, in the terms of Emil Fackenheim, God's presence and activity in the historical realm.[29] Historical methodology has built-in limitations which make it inadequate for dealing with the biblical witness to transcendence or to divine activity in the historical sphere; but it is a necessary tool for those in the community of faith who take the historical character of the biblical texts seriously.

In this connection, Brevard Childs has put before us a hermeneutical challenge that deserves the most serious consideration. The challenge comes to its sharpest expression in his treatment of Second Isaiah. Reacting against the analysis of the Isaianic corpus into various writings (First Isaiah, Second Isaiah, Third Isaiah, and later accretions), he insists that we should read the book theologically, as the totality that it is scripturally. The theological meaning of the whole is not dependent on scholarly reconstruction of the prehistory of the text or even the relating of passages to historical events or situations in the Assyrian, Babylonian, or Persian periods. "The final form of the literature," he writes, "provided a completely new and non-historical framework for the prophetic message which severed the message from its original historical moorings and rendered it accessible to

all future generations."[30] The movement from tradition to
scripture, in this view, "relativizes" historical particularity
and minimizes historical referents, with the result that those
who were not involved in the original, particular historical
situations can now respond to the religious truth. There is
much to be said for this. Clearly words that were once
spoken or written in concrete situations, say the poetic consolation of Isaiah, chap. 40, or an epistle of Paul, have the
power to speak to future generations, who may know nothing or little of the original, particular circumstances. Childs'
critics rightly point out, however, that this transhistorical
quality is not just a characteristic of the end-result of the
process of tradition but inheres in previous stages along the
way, including the earliest epic and poetic materials.[31] Attributed to Hegel is the wry observation that the past loses its
meaning with the passage of time.[32] But this is not so in the
case of biblical materials which, expressed in the forms of
narrative or poetry, had the power to transcend a particular
historical situation and to speak to future generations.

Nevertheless, this transhistorical quality of the biblical
materials did not eclipse the anchorage of the texts in real
life with its concrete particularity and historical referents.
When tradition underwent the "Reed Sea passage" from the
spoken to the written word, the literature — as we have seen
— retained the *stigmata* of oral speech evoked by concrete
situations. And the same thing is true with tradition which
moved in various literary stages toward final scriptural
formulation. It is not just that Second Isaiah's prophecy
contains "scattered vestiges" of the particular historical situation of a people in the Babylonian exile,[33] but that the
message of the prophet, and hence the meaning for future
generations, is essentially related to that historical situation
into which the prophet spoke Yahweh's word of consolation

and hope. To separate the prophecy from its historical moorings not only leaves us with language that would makeno sense, or would make whatever sense the reader cares to bring to the text, but blunts the cutting edge of the word that the prophet spoke in the name of God.

In conclusion, the relation between tradition and scripture in the community of faith deserves further theological clarification, especially in the case of those who strive for that "second naivete" which is "chastened and knowing." As one who is going on toward that goal (and for one who stands in the Methodist tradition that must be the scholarly equivalent of "going to perfection"!), I submit to you that it is not tradition alone, as though the final canonical text were only an incident in an ongoing process of tradition. Nor is it scripture alone, if that means that the prehistory of the final text discloses only a traditio-historical development. Rather, it is tradition *and* scripture: tradition which still makes its theological witness in scripture, and scripture which theologically incorporates and crystallizes biblical tradition.

FOOTNOTES

*This article has been adapted from the presidential address delivered on November 6, 1980 at the centennial meeting of the Society of Biblical Literature. For brevity a number of footnotes have been omitted.

1. *Old Testament Theology* (New York: Harper & Row, 1962) 1.116.
2. D.A. Knight, (ed.), *Tradition and Theology in the Old Testament* (Philadelphia: Fortress, 1977). See my review essay in *RelSRev* 6 (1980) 104-10.
3. See, for instance, his essay in the *Festschrift* for G.E. Wright, *Magnalia Dei* (Garden City: Doubleday, 1976), "Adaptable for Life: The Nature and Function of the Canon," 531-60; also "Biblical Criticism and the Bible as Canon," *USQR* 32 (1977) 157-65.
4. *Dynamic Transcendence: The Correlation of Confessional Heritage and Contemporary Experience in a Biblical Model of Divine Activity* (Philadelphia: Fortress, 1978); see his chart of an "event" on p. 34; also his essay, "The Theological Signifi-

cance of Contradiction within the Book of the Covenant," in *Canon and Authority* (ed. G.W. Coats and B.O. Long; Philadelphia: Fortress, 1977) 110-31.

5. In Knight, *Tradition and Theology*, 125-42.

6. Ibid., 127.

7. Ibid., 132.

8. A.B. Lord, *The Singer of Tales* (Cambridge: Harvard University, 1964) 124-38. See also D.A. Knight *Rediscovering the Traditions of Israel* (Missoula: Scholars, 1975) 390-91.

9. Quoted in the *New York Times* (Oct. 7, 1977) from "Roots and Wings," an anthology of Spanish Poetry, ed. H. St. Martin.

10. J. Muilenburg, "Form Criticism and Beyond," *JBL* 88 (1969) 1-18. See my essay, "The New Frontier of Rhetorical Criticism," in *Rhetorical Criticism: Essays in Honor of James Muilenburg* (Pittsburgh: Pickwick, 1974) ix-xviii.

11. Knight, *Tradition and Theology*, 140.

12. K. Barth, *Church Dogmatics* IV/2, 478-83. See further R. Smend, "Nach-kristische Schriftauslegung," in *PARRHESIA: Karl Barth zum achtizigsten Geburtstag* (Zurich: EVZ, 1966) 215-37.

13. Essay in *PARRHESIA*, 236.

14. *Church Dogmatics* III/1, 81.

15. R.M. Frye, "Literary Criticism and Gospel Criticism," *TToday* 36 (1979) 207-19.

16. H. Frei, *The Eclipse of Biblical Narrative* (New Haven: Yale University, 1974); see J. Barr, "Story and History in Biblical Theology," *JR* 56 (1976) 1-17.

17. *Introduction to the Old Testament as Scripture* (Philadelphia: Fortress, 1979) 178.

18. Letter dated April 27, 1980.

19. See R. Smend, "Quotations about the Importance of the Canon in an Old Testament Introduction," *JSOT* 16 (1980) 45.

20. See my review of Child's *Introduction* in *T Today* 37 (1980) 100-108, for further discussion of this "transhistorical" dimension.

21. The words are those of the late S. Sandmel, "On Canon" *CBQ* 28 (1966) 207, quoted and discussed by R.B. Laurin, "Tradition and Canon," in *Tradition and Theology*, ed. D.A. Knight, 261-74.

22. W. Brueggemann and D.A. Knight, "Why Study the Bible?" *BCSR* 11 (1980) 78-79.

23. See my essay, "From Analysis to Synthesis: The Interpretation of Genesis 1-11," *JBL* 97 (1978) 23-29.

24. R. Smend, "Questions about the Importance of the Canon," 48.

25. See Paul D. Hanson, "The Theological Significance of Contradiction within the Book of the Covenant," *Canon and Authority* (ed. G.W. Coats and B.O. Long; Philadelphia: Fortress, 1977) 110-31.

26. "Tradition and Biblical Theology," in *Tradition and Theology*, ed. D.A. Knight, 312-13.

27. See further F.M. Cross, "The Priestly Work," in *Canaanite Myth and Hebrew Epic* (Cambridge: Harvard University, 1973) 301-5.

28. See the beautiful and incisive exposition by P. Trible, *God and the Rhetoric of Sexuality* (Philadelphia: Fortress, 1978), chap. 1.

29. E. Fackenheim, *God's Presence in History: Jewish Affirmations and Philosophical Reflections* (New York: Harper Torchbooks, 1972).

30. *Introduction*, 337.

31. See e.g., the reviews by J. Barr and R. Smend in *JSOT* 16 1980.

32. Quoted by Fackenheim, *God's Presence*, 11.

33. Childs, *Introduction*, 325.

The Artful Dialogue:
Some Thoughts on the Relation of Biblical Studies And Homiletics

ELIZABETH ACHTEMEIER
Union Theological Seminary in Virginia
Richmond, VA 23227

There are few subjects more fascinating than the relation of biblical studies to the actual messages that are
proclaimed from the pulpits of Christian churches every
week. Biblical studies and homiletics are intimately related,
although the acceptance of the necessity of the relationship
cannot be taken for granted; we once had a seminary student in Pennsylvania who objected to taking exegesis
courses because it "ruined" his preaching. A few clergy go
through the entire course of biblical studies at a seminary
and nevertheless emerge preaching the same pietism that
they learned in their childhood and youth. Some clergy do
well in biblical courses and yet are so unconscious of their
homiletical methodology and theology that they deliver
sermons actually contradictory to the understanding of the
Bible they otherwise profess. In similar fashion, there are
biblical scholars who carry on their work with no reference
to or explication of its significance for preaching. Such

neglect of the implications of biblical studies for the pulpit is partly due, of course, to the scientific nature of much of historical investigation, where questions of faith and the witness to it properly do not enter in. But some scholars do, it must be confessed, simply avoid the questions raised by preaching.

Nevertheless, it remains true that biblical studies and homiletics go hand in hand, and as the course of the one goes, so goes the other. Karl Barth wrote *Die Roemerbrief* (Eng. trans. *The Epistle to the Romans* [1932]) in 1918 primarily out of concern for preaching, and he therewith radically changed the direction and presuppositions of subsequent biblical study. The necessity of countering the theological sterility of the history-of-religions movement and of proclaiming the Christian gospel in the face of Nazi paganism prompted Walther Eichrodt to write his epic-making *Theologie des Alten Testaments*[1] in 1933-39, and that volume, too, altered the course of biblical research. Similarly, today the yearning to proclaim the gospel in all its fullness has led scholars such as Brevard Childs and Walter Wink to various kinds of dissatisfaction with traditional methods of biblical criticism. The pulpit often has had a profound effect on the course of biblical study.

The reverse is also true: biblical study can and does have great effect on preaching, and nowhere is this more clearly illustrated than in the work-a-day pulpit. For example, if a preacher shares the approach to the Bible of liberal ethicism, which was so characteristic of biblical studies in the twenties and thirties, then the preacher treats the Bible in his or her sermons primarily as a collection of ethical teachings. Or if a preacher views the Scriptures through Wellhausenian eyes, as the record of a natural, progressive development out of the primitive beliefs of the Old Testament to the "higher spiritual truths of Christianity," then that preacher usually denigrates the Old Testament in his or her sermons as "out-of-date" and "legalistic" and "materialistic," or he/she chooses to ignore the Old Testament altogether.[2] If, on the other hand, a preacher attempts totally to ignore the findings of historical criticism, this too shows up in the kind of sermon constructed. Certainly one of the major results of scholarly work on the Bible has been the anchoring of the biblical text firmly in the context of history. Biblical books have been dated, authors or sources identified and located in their periods in time; traditions have been traced back to their earliest discernible roots; ancient Near Eastern history has been outlined; sociological and literary forms have been put in their situations in life; community tendencies have been illumined; word usages and theological concepts have been painstakingly traced through the years. All has prompted the conclusion that the Word of God has been spoken into concrete times at particular places to specific groups and individuals living in unique communities. If the preacher ignores all that historical research or fails to appropriate it, however, he or she often constructs a sermon in which the biblical text is turned into an allegory of life in the twentieth century. For example, Zacchaeus' short stature is made a symbol of some failing in our personalities, or Jacob's awestruck exclamation, "Surely the Lord is in this place and I did not know it!" is turned into an allegory applied to some local American church building. On the other hand, the preacher may fall into moralizing. Ignoring the historical context of the biblical text, the preacher turns it into an "eternal truth" or "principle" which then is foisted off on the congregation in the form of legalism. "Should," "ought," and "must" dominate the sermon, exhortation becomes its tone, and the preacher assumes the role of a modern scribe or Pharisee, beating his or her people over their heads with the law — a law which has been abstracted out of its historical context and translated willy-nilly to the congregation's situation. The context of the gracious working of God in history is left behind, his action is turned into a "principle," and the congregation is exhorted to live a life of righteousness, which the whole biblical story maintains it is impossible for them to do apart from God's work in history.

It is probably fair to say that we are still getting a lot of moralism and allegory in American preaching because some preachers have failed to integrate their study of modern biblical historical criticism with their homiletical and hermeneutical applications of the biblical text. Part of this is the fault of the preacher, of course, but part of it is also due to the failure of the biblical scholar to spell out and to illustrate the significance and applications of his or her work to preaching. The result has often been that the average preacher may know something about form criticism, for example, but has never been taught the implications of that science for using a text in a sermon. Or he or she may go to the other extreme and assiduously study the commentaries, but then end up preaching the view of the commentators rather than the message of the Bible.

There is an artful conversation which must take place between the biblical scholar and the preacher. Behind every sermon lies an understanding of the nature of the Bible, of what kind of literature it is, of how it came into being, of how it can be understood and appropriated by a modern congregation. Biblical studies and homiletics go hand in hand, and perhaps it would help us to relate them in a more fruitful fashion if we looked at the ways in which they are presently being related in preaching in this country. We may then have some indications of directions we should take in the future.

Propositional Preaching

In general, preaching in the United States today takes one of four forms. There is first of all the approach that sees preaching as primarily a setting forth of the truth of biblical propositions; we could in fact label such preaching "propositional preaching." The nature of such preaching is well illustrated in Billy Graham's constant use of the phrase "the Bible says." "The Bible says your sins are forgiven" or "The Bible says Jesus Christ is the Son of God" or "The Bible says we must believe in the name of the Lord Jesus Christ and we shall be saved" or "The Bible says if we do not repent, we are damned." The understanding of the Bible is such that it is a set of "truths" which must be believed, and the purpose of such preaching is really to persuade the hearer to accept the authority of the Scriptures. That done, it is assumed the hearer will become a saved believer. The Bible is imposed upon the congregation as an external authority to which they must submit, and of course, often a doctrine of inerrancy of the Scriptures accompanies such imposition. Faith, then, is the acceptance of the dogma of the Scriptures, involving sometimes only the intellect or emotions, less frequently the whole person. The gospel is largely made up of the proclamation of propositions *about* the Scriptures.

That such preaching has subsequently led thousands of persons into genuine faith in Jesus Christ is not to be denied: those with opposite approaches have no cause for self-righteousness. Nevertheless, leaving all other questions aside, the thoughtful preacher must ask why, if the Scriptures are really a set of propositions, they have been given to us largely in the form of stories. Has God's salvation of his world not been acted out precisely in the form of events? Certainly to state belief, the Apostles' Creed tells a story: "I believe in Jesus Christ, the only begotten Son of

God, who was conceived by the Holy Ghost, born of the Virgin Mary, suffered under Pontius Pilate, was crucified, died, and buried; he descended into hell; the third day he rose again from the dead; he ascended into heaven and sitteth on the right hand of God the Father . . ." This story seems to recapitulate exactly what is given to us in the Scriptures.

The question then becomes, of course: How does the believer come to faith? Is it not by experiencing that the story is his or her story? Is it not by entering into the events witnessed to in the Scriptures and finding that those events are deeds done by God also in his or her own contemporary life — exactly as, for example, Israel entered into the events of her past in her worship and found that God's acts were done for her also in the present? (cf. Dt 26:5-9; 29:10-15) And if that be true, as biblical scholarship has shown that it is,[3] is it not important for the preacher to set forth the story in his or her own preaching, in terms with which the congregation can identify, rather than simply summarizing the results of the story in "propositions" to be believed?

It is precisely the genius of black preaching that even at its most propositional, it has preserved something of the narrative character of the sacred history.[4] Thus the story of the exodus has always been made the oppressed black's story, whether in the slave quarters of the South or in the preaching of Martin Luther King, Jr., or in modern black liberation theology. Negro spirituals — "Go Down Moses," "Swing Low, Sweet Chariot," "We Are Climbing Jacob's Ladder" — as well as Negro literature — Johnson's *The Creation* or the poems of Claude McKay or Baldwin's *The Fire Next Time* — attest to the depths to which the biblical story has penetrated black culture through its preachers, and indeed sustained that culture when it had no other helper. Thus, it has been an understanding of this narrative nature of the Scriptures themselves which has made black preaching so relevant to its people. It is similarly an understanding of the nature of the Scriptures which modern biblical scholarship attempts to foster and deepen.

Thematic Preaching

The second general type of preaching in the United States today is that which is found in most mainline denominations and which could be characterized as "thematic preaching." Such preaching may start with a biblical text, it may deal with a Christian doctrine, it may discuss a topic of the day in the light of Christian belief. But generally, there is a "theme" to the sermon which dominates its thought, and the sermon usually is structured with an introduction, several points (often three), and a conclusion. This is the type of preaching which every middle-class churchgoer has heard from childhood on. If one examines an anthology of preaching, such as James Cox's *The Twentieth Century Pulpit*,[5] this is the kind of sermon most often found in its pages.

The presupposition of such "thematic preaching" in relation to the Bible is that there is a major idea or message which can be distilled out of the text, and the function of biblical criticism for such preaching, then, has been to recover that major theme. That is, biblical criticism has been seen as the necessary tool for uncovering what the text really meant when it was written, and for years it has been the aim of many homiletics teachers to instill in their pupils the necessity of uncovering that actual meaning.

Such a program has encountered many pitfalls. To speak of the most elementary first, busy pastors have failed to do their exegetical homework urged upon them in their seminary training. Very frequently they will study a text until a sermon "idea" is prompted by it. The rest of the biblical passage then falls to the side and the "idea" is developed into a sermon which sometimes uses the text as a pretext, or which often has little to do with the text in its context, or which may impose upon the text a theme largely alien to it. To give authority to such use of the text, moreover, the points of the sermon are supported by appeal to outside authorities — famous personages, psychologists, scientists, poets, writers, congregational experience. As Richard White pointed out in a speech before the 1978 Academy of Homiletics, it is not the authority of the text which is being preached, but that of others acceptable to the hearers, and the congregation seldom is enabled to enter into the saving event to which the text bears witness.

How can it be guaranteed that preachers will preach the text's meaning? That is the question with which professors of homiletics wrestle, and the multiplicity of homiletics manuals on the market testifies to the variety of answers. In most of them it is assumed that historical criticism uncovers the meaning of the biblical passage; the task then is to convey that meaning to the congregation. This brings us to the second pitfall in "thematic preaching."

It is assumed in thematic preaching that there is a "hermeneutical jump" which must be made between the meaning of the text and its meaning for the modern congregation — that is, there is such a jump to be made unless one simply allegorizes or moralizes from the text. Not a little of modern homiletical study has been devoted to the nature of the "jump." How does the meaning of the text in its historical context become relevant in the modern congregation's life? How does the preacher prevent the message of the text from applying only to the past?

Some have thought to answer this question by using the methods of modern communication theory. Thus, Merrill Abbey pointed with approval to Fosdick's method of enlisting the interest of hearers by giving voice to their questions about the teaching of the text (*Communication in Pulpit and Parish* [1973]).[6] Milton Crum, with somewhat different concerns in his *Manual on Preaching*[7] wants every sermon structured in terms of situation of the text/problem for us/resolution in Christian faith and practice. Both are attempts to involve the congregation in the message of the Scriptures.

There are other ways of making the hermeneutical jump. Most preachers try to make it with the use of illustrative material, drawing analogies between the situation of the text and that of the congregation. Recently Richard L. Rohrbaugh made a strong case for the necessity of knowing biblical sociology, in order that such analogies be accurately drawn and the text not be read in terms of an individualistic Protestant ethos (*The Biblical Interpreter*).[8] It seems that the preacher must master yet one more field of biblical science!

Perhaps the most seminal (and risky) for thematic preaching is the suggestion of Leander E. Keck that the meaning of the text is not found solely in the past through historical criticism, but that rather the meaning of any biblical passage grows out of the point where the ancient text and modern congregation meet (*The Bible in the Pulpit*).[9] Such meeting point is found in the person of the preacher. He or she engages in what Keck calls "priestly listening," listening to the words of the text, uncovered by critical study, *on behalf of* the congregation with whom the preacher is one. At that point, in the preacher, past and present come together, and it is the meaning of the text, growing out of such convergence, that forms the content of the message proclaimed. The message today of any biblical text is not simply its ancient meaning. Rather its message is the meaning which it has in relation to a congregation. If this be true, biblical exegesis cannot properly be carried on apart from conversation with the pulpit!

The risk of such a method is that it will force an alien meaning upon the text, and it is finally the canonical meaning of the text which must be the judge of any interpretation of it. But Keck's suggestion certainly gets at the basic fault of all thematic preaching — that of thinking that the message of the Scriptures, illumined by historical study, is a message which speaks only in the past and which must therefore be "made relevant" by some hermeneutical device. The very nature of the biblical record itself belies such a conclusion, for no event or Word of God in the Bible happens only in the past. They continue to speak and to exert their influence on each succeeding generation, so that the present is constantly shaped by past tradition and past tradition is altered by present confrontation with the Word. For example, the exodus in the Old Testament was never considered by the Israelites to be an event which took place only back there in the thirteenth century B.C. It was a concrete historical event which nevertheless continued to happen for each succeeding generation in Israel. It was celebrated as such in the Passover and in the Festival of Covenant Renewal, and it constantly shaped the form and content of the traditions which came after it. The delivery of the exodus into the freedom of the wilderness furnished the content for prophetic pictures of the future (cf. Ho 2:14-15; Ezk 20:33-38; Is 43:19-21; 48:20-21; 52:11-12 etc.). At the same time, other later traditions worked their shaping influence on the exodus story, setting it into the framework of the overarching theme of the promise to the fathers, or interpreting it, as in Deuteronomy, in terms of Yahweh's incomprehensible love.

God's historical deeds continue to exert their influence in the present! The biblical Word continues to speak! That is

what every great preacher has known. And it is when the
exegeted word finds a preacher with language-tools honed
and ready for use, and a heart prepared by faith and prayer
and love, that the necessity for all hermeneutical gimmicks
falls to the side and the thematic sermon becomes proclama-
tional — the channel of God's present active work in judgment and salvation among his people. Historical criticism
serves the function of clearing away misunderstandings of
the text. Above all, it keeps the text from being abstracted
and separated from the concrete actions and words through
which God has revealed himself. But as Gerhard von Rad
has maintained, it is this speaking of the text, often in
surprising ways, that forms the real content of exegesis
itself. The proclamation of the text in the sermon then is for
von Rad simply the same speaking in a different form of
language and confrontation. "I give you about ten to twenty
beginners' sermons," von Rad told his class of fledgling
preachers, "in which you will repeat what you have learned.
Then you will have preached yourselves out. Then if you do
not make the discovery that every text wants to speak for
itself, you are lost. We are dealing with that word that is
sharper than a two-edged sword."[10]

Moreover, it is the full text, with its contextual accretions and later reinterpretations and redactional alterations,
which should speak through proclamation. It used to be
believed in biblical studies that the content of the revelation
given to us was identical with the earliest form of the tradition, and that if we could just get back to the *ipsissima verba* of
the prophet or Paul, back to the original scroll of Jeremiah,
back to the historical words and deeds of Jesus of Nazareth,
we would have the unvarnished Word of God. We now
know, prompted by the study of form and tradition and
redaction criticism, that this simply is not so. For example,
Klaus Koch showed that the original story lying behind

Genesis 12:10-13:1 probably had nothing to do either with
Abraham or with the promise given him by God (*The Growth
of the Biblical Tradition: The Form-Critical Method*).[11] But as the
story now stands in its context of the promise, it serves as a
witness to the working of the Word of God and can so be
received by the preacher, in faith. To give another example,
it is precisely the way in which the gospel writers have
redacted their sources that allows each of them to make his
unique witness to the person and work of Jesus Christ, and
that redaction reveals as much about our Lord as do any of
Jesus' actual historical sayings which may be recovered by
scholars. Thus, the preacher has the responsibility of knowing how to probe the growth of the biblical tradition
through the use of form and tradition and redaction criticism so that all of the text's nuances and emphases may be
heard. He or she then has the responsibility of considering
the particularities of any text in the light of the whole confes-
sion of faith which is the biblical canon, and it is this latter
concern which has been at the center of Brevard Childs'
work.[12]

The Word of God speaks to us, says Childs, out of the
authoritative norm (the canon) of a community of faith (the
people of God), and that whole canon furnishes the
parameters for the covenant people's witness to God's ongoing revelation. Moreover, the text has been given a particular shape within the canon — placed in a particular context
and chronology, interpreted by additions or subtractions to
it and around it, attributed to particular authors or schools
of tradition. These are all definitive of the text's meaning
and the way it is to be interpreted, in Childs' view, and it is
the final shape of the canon, rather than the stages in its
development uncovered by historical criticism, which Childs
wishes to use as the definition of the text's meaning. For
example, Childs would consider a chronological reordering

of a prophetic book to be destructive of the message it now bears in the present shape of the canon, and it is that present shape which is to be the subject of the church's proclamation.

Certainly such a view prompts scholars and preachers to look anew at the message being spoken to the church through the shape of the canon as it now stands, and it raises afresh the question of what it means to have a canon.But I do not believe even a faithful acceptance of the present shape of the canon is adequate without also the careful study of how and when and where texts in the canon got that way and why. It is precisely the careful historical-critical study of the text which has led to the discovery that texts continually reinterpret themselves within the canon itself. That is, it is biblical scholarship which has pointed most forcefully to the continued speaking and reshaping of texts in ever new situations. And it is this dynamic nature of the Word of God itself, bridging every historical gap, that shows the inadequacy of so many of the hermeneutical jumps used in thematic preaching. The Word itself creates the bridge to the people, or it has not been heard as it really is.

Creative Preaching

This brings us to the third form of preaching in the United States today, which is not very widely practiced, and yet which may hold the most promise for the future of preaching, because it can take seriously the effective and dynamic nature of the biblical Word. There is no agreed upon title for this homiletical form, but we might call it "creational" or "creative preaching," because it understands the continuing creative action and speaking of the Word among God's gathered people.

This type of preaching really has two roots. First, it

comes out of that theological movement known as "the new hermeneutic," which was represented by Ebeling and Fuchs and which rested on the philosophy of Heidegger.[13] Much in the new hermeneutic has now passed from general public discussion, but that which remains is a new appreciation of the creative power of language. We learned anew from the exponents of the new hermeneutic that language creates reality — that, for example, when Adam names his world in Genesis 2:20, it becomes "there" for him and he can relate to it. Language has the power to change perception (cf. the slogan "black is beautiful"), or to create a new situation (cf. the liturgical formula, "I announce and declare to you by the authority and in the name of Christ your sins are forgiven, according to his promise in the gospel"). Understood in this manner, the language in which the sermon is framed suddenly becomes very important. The language of the preached gospel can actually be the agent of a new creation, a fact known to Paul long ago of course (cf. 1 Cor 1:21-24), but now newly apprehended and heartening to preachers.

Second, "creational preaching" comes out of the work of C.H. Dodd, Amos Wilder,[14] Robert Funk, Sally TeSelle McFague, Robert Tannehill, to name but a few. The work which these scholars have done is well represented in a brief little book by William A. Beardslee, *Literary Criticism of the New Testament.*[15] In that book, Beardslee points out that literary criticism has moved beyond the historical questions of authorship, date, sources and stages of development, to the question of how the literary forms of the New Testament "worked." That is, how did the forms of gospel, proverb, apocalypse and history (Beardslee deals only with these larger forms) prompt the identification of their readers or hearers with them and how can that original impact be reduplicated through preaching today? In relation to shorter forms, such as parable or apothegm, how was the reader

confronted by them? How did they function? And how can
the same confrontation be achieved in the proclamation of
the biblical message in the modern church?

In short, we have in the contributions of the new
hermeneutic, of form criticism, and of the "new" literary
criticism of the Bible, possibilities offered for preaching
which go far beyond the staid formulas of the usual thematic
sermon. Now we are talking about the creative power of
language and form, through which the congregation can be
enabled to "live" the biblical story so that it becomes their
story, creating the same salvific effects in their lives that that
story first created in Israel and in the primitive church.

There are some homileticians who have now begun to
move out on this frontier. Certainly Fred Craddock's induc-
tive and indirect Kierkegaardian methodologies belong
here.[16] But perhaps Frederick Buechner is the most widely
known among such preachers.[17] Buechner's genius as a
writer is the ability to recast the biblical literature into new
forms of narrative and biography, sometimes successfully
recapturing the original impact of the Scriptures, sometimes missing the full dimensions of their certainty, but
nevertheless introducing us to a compelling homiletical
model.

There are however many others who are also experi-
menting with such creative preaching, and much of their
interest has been centered around the form of the story as
the means of allowing congregational identification with the
gospel. Thus there is a spate of books now appearing on the
market concerned with preaching and narrative, by authors
such as Edmund Steimle, Morris Niedenthal, Charles Rice,
Richard Jensen and James Sanders.[18] Whether there will be
a similar concentration in preaching on other biblical forms
remains to be seen. Certainly many homileticians have writ-

ten on preaching from the parables, but rarely in the context of these new biblical approaches.

Perhaps it should be pointed out that these new developments mark one point at least where biblical scholarship and homiletics have joined forces. The great preachers of the past — Charles Spurgeon, James Stewart, Paul Scherer — also knew and utilized the creative power of language, employing it to bring their congregations vividly and concretely into the story and pericopes of the gospel, that the power of the cross and resurrection might make their people new creatures in Christ.

Certainly the fact that the Word of God, above all human words, creates new situations is that which makes the utilization of the biblical forms in creative preaching so pregnant with possibilities. God has spoken the Word in Jesus Christ that is to be the creator and shaper of all our reality. The challenge to the preacher then is so to employ human language that the full glory and unsearchable riches of that divine creative Word may be made manifest in the lives of God's people.[19]

Experimental Preaching

Finally, the fourth form of preaching in the United States today can be labeled "experimental preaching." John Killenger, William D. Thompson, and Gordon C. Bennett have all written books about it.[20] It encompasses a wide variety of substitutes for the traditional sermon: first-person sermons, dialogue and multilogue sermons, sermons formed from participation by the congregation, press conference sermons, dramatic monologues or multilogues, oral readings, mime, symbolic action, dance, verse sermons, imaginative parables or allegories, dialogues with newspapers or musical instruments, sermons formed from literature or hymns, use of various audiovisual aids in conjunction with the spoken word, folk-masses, religious musical dramas — the list is as endless as the human imagination.

Some of the types listed above have been in use for some time, others are relatively new, but as they have been actually employed by preachers, they can be seriously called into question on the basis of their relation to our understanding of the nature of the biblical Word. Many such forms of experimental preaching abandon the biblical message altogether and become nothing more than artistic or symbolic performances, open to a wide variety of meaning, or interesting human discussions of a current topic of the day. Because such performances occur at stated times of worship on Sunday morning, they are not automatically made into sermons nor do they serve as an adequate substitute for the proclamation of the biblical Word. If the church truly believes that our salvation occurs by our participation in Jesus Christ, then the preaching and liturgical event are going to have to foster that participation, and they can do so only by the presentation of the Word, as that has been handed on to us in the witness of the Holy Scriptures.

There are some forms of experimental preaching which do utilize the biblical Word, of course, but once again these have not been subjected to a rigorous understanding of the nature of the Bible. For example, most first-person sermons engage in a subjective interpretation and psychologizing of the biblical text which can stand up to no scholarly critical scrutiny, and one sometimes suspects that the preacher is using his or her imagination as a substitute for careful exegesis. Also characteristic of many forms of experimental preaching is the fact that they must engage in constant harmonizing of the New Testament traditions, resulting in a homogenized picture of Jesus or of one of his followers to be found in no portion of the Scriptures. New

Testament scholars have gone to a good deal of trouble to clarify the unique witnesses of each of the New Testament writers. When preachers ignore that uniqueness, the cutting edges of the gospel are blunted and rendered ineffective.

There is room for experimental preaching in the church. After all, both Mark and Paul invented new forms to communicate the gospel — Mark the literary form of gospel itself, Paul the form of the distinctively Christian letter — and it may be that our age, so accustomed to the visual and sensual, needs new forms to overcome its dullness of hearing and obduracy of heart. But there is no other word of salvation than that which has been given us in Jesus Christ, and unless he is the Word who is preached, in clarity and simplicity and the creativity of imagination made holy, there will be no divine power at work in our words to save those who believe.

Conclusions

God has promised us preachers that through the folly of the message we preach, he will save his beloved people. We frail and stained earthen vessels have been taken up into the service of God to be his instruments in that incredible task. But the message we preach — the folly of the cross and resurrection — has been given us in particular traditions, in the variety and complexity and humanity and inspiration which make up the biblical witness. If we would truly preach the message, we have to understand its nature. The final purpose of all biblical study is to aid the preaching and work and daily life of the people of God.

How, then, can biblical scholars and preachers join forces more effectively in the proclamation of the Word? How can that artful dialogue between study and pulpit be fostered which will aid us in preaching the gospel? As one who teaches both Bible and homiletics, I want to make only a few suggestions.

First of all, we preachers — and we teachers of homiletics — have great necessity laid upon us to stay abreast of modern biblical study. There is no excuse for approaching some text, in the 1980s, from the standpoint of the biblical research of 1930 or even of 1960. Our major task as Protestant clergy is to be interpreters of the Word of God, and we fail our people if we do not utilize the best tools for interpreting the Word which modern biblical scholarship has to offer. That means keeping our libraries up to date and using library loan-plans, usually available from every seminary — commentaries written in the early nineteen hundreds are rarely sufficient any more! It means taking advantage of continuing education courses on the Bible, and it is incumbent on seminaries and denominations to provide more of those. It means continual, daily, hard research and solid reading in the biblical field. It means fulfilling the ministry of the word given to us, competently and faithfully.

Second, those of us in the biblical field need constantly to approach our task from the standpoint of its implications for preaching and the life of the church. Many biblical scholars are doing this; many are not. And we need to realize that simply learning the methods of textual or literary or form or tradition criticism does not insure the application of those disciplines to a text when it is used in preaching. Preachers need those applications and their implications spelled out for them, in great detail and patience, and perhaps it is the spelling out which we biblical teachers have neglected.

Third, maybe we all need to learn humility in the communion of saints. It is not uncommon for the homiletics teacher in a seminary to be considered a less competent

9

scholar than the biblical professor nor it is uncommon for some biblical professor to be viewed as lacking in commitment to the church. Maybe we need to talk with one another more about our shared task in the faith! Maybe we need to discover that biblical texts take on different meanings in the pulpit than they have in the study, but that the study with its rigorous devotion to truth can powerfully aid the pulpit. It is finally before the judgment of the Holy Spirit, at work in the church, that we all are responsible; and failing him, there really is no lasting worth to what we are doing. So perhaps in sum, our call is to renewed commitment to the triune God, that through the words of the Scriptures handed down to us our people may know and love and serve him.

FOOTNOTES

1. Now translated as *Theology of the Old Testament*, I and II (Philadelphia, The Westminster Press, 1961, 1967).
2. See my further discussion in *The Old Testament and the Proclamation of the Gospel* (Philadelphia, The Westminster Press, 1973).
3. Cf. James Sanders, *God Has a Story Too: Sermons in Context* (Philadelphia, Fortress Press, 1979).
4. See Henry H. Mitchell, *The Recovery of Preaching* (New York, Harper & Row, 1977).
5. Nashville, Abingdon Press, 1978.
6. Philadelphia, The Westminster Press.
7. Valley Forge, Judson Press, 1977.
8. Philadelphia, Fortress Press, 1978.
9. Nashville, Abingdon Press, 1978.
10. *Biblical Interpretations in Preaching*, trans. John E. Steely (Nashville, Abingdon Press, 1977), p. 18.
11. Trans. from the second German ed. by S.M. Cupitt (New York, Charles Scribners' Sons, 1969).
12. See his *Introduction to the Old Testament as Scripture* (Philadelphia, Fortress Press, 1979).
13. See also the works of Walter Ong.
14. See esp. *The Language of the Gospel: Early Christian Rhetoric* (New York, Harper & Row, 1964).
15. Philadelphia, Fortress Press, 1970.

16. *As One Without Authority* (Enid, Phillips University Press, 1971); *Overhearing the Gospel* (Nashville, Abingdon Press, 1978).
17. See his book *Telling the Truth: The Gospel as Tragedy, Comedy, and Fairy Tale* (New York, Harper & Row, 1977).
18. Steimle, Niedenthal, and Rice, *Preaching the Story* (Philadelphia, Fortress Press, 1980); Jensen, *Telling the Story: Variety and Imagination in Preaching* (Minneapolis, Augsburg, 1979); Sanders, op. cit.

OLD TESTAMENT THEMES

Introduction

MIRIAM WARD, R.S.M.
Trinity College
Burlington, VT 05401

Shortly after the Pharisees gathered at Jamnia to map out the future of Judaism without temple or priesthood around the end of the first century, and canonized the collection of their Scriptures as normative for them, the theologian Marcion set in movement a radical interpretation of Paul's teaching on the Law which was to carry its influence even into the twentieth century. For Marcion, the God of the New Testament was new and different from the God of the Old Testament. The Old Testament was to be completely excluded from the Christian Scriptures. Concerned over the unity of the Scriptures, the early Church rejected Marcion's view, and emphatically accepted the canon of the Hebrew Scriptures in the process of placing the stamp of approval on the books received into the New Testament canon.

Although all the articles that follow do not pursue the interrelation between Old and New Testaments as such, they make a statement as to the importance of the Old

Testament in its own right for Christians as well as Jews. Three of the giants in the field of American Catholic biblical scholarship have devoted their scholarly lives to the study of the Hebrew Scriptures.

The publication of *A Path Through Genesis* in 1957, and *The Conscience of Israel* in 1961 were clearly milestones in closing the gap between biblical scholarship and the grassroots mentioned in the preface to this volume. Through his many publications in Spanish as well as English, Bruce Vawter has been an exemplary member of his Congregation of the Mission. Based upon sound biblical scholarship, his popular writings have rendered invaluable service for the non-specialist. Currently chairman of the Department of Theology at De Paul University, Father Vawter has been a visiting professor at Vanderbilt and McCormick Seminary and the Pontifical Biblical Institute in Rome.

In his article "The God of the Hebrew Scriptures," Bruce Vawter challenges Marcionism head-on. While admitting and indeed raising problems which the Old Testament presents for Christian faith, specifically its multiple and diverse characterizations of God, he views them as positive phenomena, having a certain authentic ring, and affording a protection against human arrogance as regards divine revelation.

Readers might want to compare the issue raised by Cyrus Gordon on the international God Elohim with those presented by Father Vawter in conjunction with the challenging words of Herbert Haag whose quotation concludes his article.

For Americans the period of the 1960s was not only one of great literary activity in biblical studies, but one of turmoil and strife over the movement for civil rights for Blacks, and against a war fought thousands of miles away in Vietnam, but seen each evening on the television screens in millions of American homes. With these movements came a conscious- ness-raising of the inherent worth of every human being regardless of race or color, and a questioning of war as a viable method for settling human problems. The extent and depth of this new awareness is unprecedented in world history. That having been said, however, we turn to the prophets of the 8th and 7th century B.C. whose primary goal was to goad the conscience of Israel on some very basic issues regarding human rights.

One of America's leading scholars on the prophetical literature of the Old Testament is Carroll Stuhlmueller, C.P. His doctoral thesis concentrated on "Second Isaiah and his Theology of Creation." He is a member of the Congregation of the Passion, and is Professor of Old Testament at the Catholic Theological Union in Chicago. In great demand as a visiting professor, Father Stuhlmueller is held in high esteem and affection by students in Europe as well as in the United States. As Editor of *The Bible Today*, he performs an invaluable service to the Church through promoting good biblical scholarship on a popular level.

In "The Prophetic Combat for Peace," Carroll Stuhl- mueller examines the different ways that the prophets of Israel fought for peace and justice: those who went to war, and those who condemned war and military alliances. The prophets portrayed God as one concerned with the poor and the oppressed. Using this as a derivative of the moral imperative moving the prophets, Father Stuhlmueller dis- cusses the two ways of prophetic combat for peace and justice: the actions of the prophetic bands or guild prophets who advocated war for justice if all else failed, and those of the prophets represented by Isaiah who condemned war and military alliances. The reader will find echoes of a very modern dilemma posed by liberation theology and by those

who justify guerilla warfare as a viable alternative in over-
coming the institutionalized forms of violence condoned
and perpetrated by governments throughout the world
today.

Because of the scholarly world's preoccupation with the
historicity of the Old Testament, the collection of wisdom
writings has been somewhat neglected until fairly recent
times. In one sense this is surprising, given the direction of
philosophy and theology toward an existentialist approach
to modern concerns. Of all the sections of the Hebrew
Scriptures, it is the body of wisdom writings that speak to the
modern concerns not in the area of international politics,
but in the ordinary life of the ordinary person.

Through the efforts of Roland E. Murphy, member of
the Order of Carmelites, the valuable insights needed today
as much as in the world of Qoheleth, have been kept at the
forefront of scholarship. His many publications on the wisdom literature of the Bible and on the Dead Dea Scrolls, and
his work as editor of and contributor to a number of journals
give Father Murphy a place of preeminence among the
commentators on the sapiential books of the Old Testament. His literary activity has been interspersed with speaking engagements, many of which have been conducted in
ecumenical settings.

In "The Theological Contributions of Israel's Wisdom
Literature," Father Murphy stresses the value of the insights
it provides into daily life and experience. He points out that
the quest for wisdom as in the case of personal moral formation is a daily, ongoing pursuit. At the height of wisdom
thought is the recognition of the mystery of God's activity in
human life. Father Murphy concludes with a wise statement
of his own: "The drive for certainty and security which
characterizes some theological movements has much to
learn from the agony of the sages."

The God Of The
Hebrew Scriptures*

BRUCE VAWTER, C.M.
DePaul University
Chicago, IL 60604

Uncertainty is the law of this life. It is a law that is learnt only reluctantly, even by those who should best know how inexorable a law it is. One may recall how the great H.H. Rowley deplored the passing of critical consensus on the book of the prophet Ezekiel, some twenty-five years ago. It was, he said, a passing "certainly calculated to fill the student with wonder as to whether present-day scholarship has any objective standards" (Rowley). The present writer applauded this sentiment at the time, and complacently contrasted the stability of the rest of OT studies with those of the NT. (As a matter of fact, that "seamless robe of Christ" which was supposed to be the Gospel of John just about at this same time, in great similarity with Ezekiel, was being tentatively regarded as a work of complex redaction, as it has proved to be with many subsequent refinements of the scholars.) Now, however, we have seen how many other OT consensuses have appeared only to disappear as though they had never been, to have had once an ephemeral success that brooked no respectable opposition only to vanish utterly in our days as objects of undeserved derision on the part of later scholars, many of whom never even paid their proper dues to entitle them to assist at the obsequies. One will think immediately, of course, about the source-criticism of the Pentateuch/Hexateuch/Tetrateuch, an enterprise which might even be said to have created modern critical method, which engaged in the past scholars probably of a calibre superior to any of those whom we possess today.

One may also think of other consensuses which other OT studies have dislodged from a previous position that a dozen years or so ago seemed to be unassailable. Martin Noth's reconstruction of the Israelite *amphictyony,* for example, which made so much sense a short generation ago, today can be dismissed even in a deeply conservative journal not on peremptory grounds of infidelity to a revealed word but on eminently historico-literary principles according to which the hypothesis simply does not correspond to fact (Hauser). And what are we to say with regard to even more recent hypotheses which may or may not survive the next decade of scholarly enterprise? With regard to George Mendenhall's notion of the real circumstances of Israel's "conquest" of Canaan, for example, according to which the *Landnahme,* the taking over of the land, essentially is transmuted from foreign invasion into a proletarian revolt of an indigenous population? Or with regard to Margaret Barker's notion of the circumstances of the postexilic Judahite "restoration" in Palestine? If I read her rightly (Barker), she tends to suggest that the canonical text of the OT represents rather a botch of a *pis aller* of historical challenges that should and could have been greeted by far preferable solutions.

These scholarly reversals and revisions present no problem for historical positivists, to whom history is simply a series of unrelated events, a story that has no patterns, no plan, no direction, and is only the record of what supposedly actually happened. They do present problems for those who, without ceasing to be critically historical in their thinking, also wish to believe — on grounds which admittedly are not historical in the positive sense — that there is a theology of history, or, to put it more aptly, that in history the grounds for a biblical theology have been revealed.

Let us consider two propositions, the first of which is somewhat paradoxical. It is paradoxical because it seems that only now is the scholarly community beginning to recognize that OT criticism affects Christian faith quite as much as, if not more than, the criticism of the NT. Along with many others, I once thought somewhat naive the decision of the ecclesiastical authorities made after the publication of Marie-Joseph Lagrange's *La Methode historique* in 1903 that he should confine himself to the "safer" and less "controversial" area of NT rather than of OT research. I am not so sure, now, that the Roman wallahs were not on the right track: the OT did and does present for Christian faith a problematic that is antecedent to and far more complicated than anything that is contained in the NT. To dismiss the enormous problems with which the OT confronts Christian belief requires a complete disdain of history, whether this is expressed by a fundamentalism which has constructed a "salvation history" acceptable to itself but to no disinterested historian, or by a neo-gnostic reinterpretation of Christianity which regards its historical presuppositions to be nothing other than flotsam on the sea of circumstance out of which Christian faith emerged.

The second point is, of course, that the OT does not present one single problem for NT belief in God, but many. Put in another way: the challenge which the OT seems to present to us rises less from the inacceptability of its God-construct than it does from the incompatibility of multiple constructs which may be at war with one another. Before the Christian accepts OT theology as a *propedeuticon* of his own belief, in other words, it appears that he first must put together from the OT documents a theology which the OT itself never produced. This is to ask a good deal.

The problem does not disappear for us simply because it was no problem either for the Tannaim or for the Fathers of the Church. The Tannaim and the Fathers were conditioned by the syncretism of their age to acquiesce in judgments which the pluralism of our age can never permit. Though the judgments which we do make should certainly never be made with any disdain of those made by our fathers in the faith, whether of the NT or the patristic era, of Chalcedon or the Middle Ages, of the Reformation or the Enlightenment, still, in every case we have to do with time-conditioned statements of varying degrees of authority. However authoritative they may be, they remain nevertheless time-conditioned according to the recognizance of a time that is not our own, and which leave us, therefore, always with the duty to solve our own problems for ourselves without any easy bypass of once-for-all solutions frozen in ancient consecrated words of human devising. The Second Vatican Council said no less than this in its decree *Dei Verbum* when it noted of OT revelation the element contained there which is "incomplete and temporary" (Abbott: 122), and also acknowledged that in relation to the Scriptures the Church is "the pupil of the Holy Spirit, concerned to move ahead daily toward a deeper understanding" of the Bible — a paragraph in which the Council insisted upon the vital necessity of up-to-date scholarship *in re biblica* (Abbott: 126). I assume, of course, that what is "incomplete and temporary" has not been so demonstrated once and for all but may be patient of the continued demonstration of ourselves or of subsequent generations assisting the Church in its docility to the better comprehension of the meaning of the word of God, which mainly is a word about God.

The foregoing is prefatory to the proposition that the diverse characterizations of the God of the OT as presented in the OT documents do not add up to a minus but to a plus. For one thing, they carry with them the ring of authenticity as regards divine revelation. If we take as a classic definition of divine revelation that it is the word of God communicated to man in human terms, then we must certainly expect that the communication has come to us in all the vagaries of which the human mind and heart are capable. Capable of encompassing God as of all else, naturally, since God is unknowable to man except in his metaphysical essence, which is a construct of the human mind. And secondly, the variety of OT testimony to God should be cherished as a protection against the human temptation to *hybris,* to the gnostic pretension of total awareness of the divine, an illusion which can provoke disaster not only religious but also, perhaps, civil and political, as our own times may demonstrate. Ignoring this variety may also result in heresy in the most etymological sense of the word, a *hairesis,* a choosing, whether perverse or well-intentioned, which results in what can only be considered a perversion of the message of the OT.

In an article of over a dozen years ago, Morton Smith offered as a definition of the Yahweh of the OT — a god in whose existence "nobody, as far as I know, believes," "a North-Arabian mountain god who traveled in thunderstorms and liked the smell of burning fat" (Smith: 1969, 21). At that time I suggested that if Morton Smith was serious in this summation of the meaning of the God of the OT, either his collection of a "body of documents from the ancient Mediterranean world" (his term for the OT) happened to miss some folios that were in my collection, "or he has gravely misconstrued the character of the literature to whose study he has dedicated his scholarly life" (Smith: 1974, 477). Smith's reading of the OT testimony I cannot with all charity consider to be anything other than in its own way perverse *hairesis* and a travesty of history. Had the Yahweh of Israel been nothing more than what he called him, this Yahweh would surely have taken his place simply as a problematical cipher among the 500 or so other divine names which Mitchell Dahood has discerned in the Eblaite pantheon (Dahood). It is hard for me to believe that by a totally random process Christians' worship of God under the title of "Lord"="Kyrios," which is in turn an "Adonai" or "Yahweh" of the OT, took place in a vacuum of other contenders for supreme lordship in the Ancient Near East. Such a conclusion, however, I admit depends as much, or at least almost as much, upon a presumption of faith as it does upon the empirical evidence.

To pursue the consequences of my proposition: we do not have from the OT a consistent portrait of God as we would expect to have from, let us say, a *Summa* of the Middle Ages or a *Dogmatik* of the twentieth century. Anyone who thinks that we have such a consistent portrait is either ignorant of the OT evidence or has, on grounds of his own, decided to bend the OT evidence to conform to a model of his own construction, which is generally a model that he has extracted less from the NT, from which he thinks it comes, than from a syncretistic "God" concept which is as alien to real history as was the "Theos" of Hellenistic myth or as is the "God" of American civil religion. The second proposition I would like to make is that we have no reason to expect any such consistent portrait, that in fact such a consistent portrait would be a certain sign that the OT sin of idolatry has been committed, namely that we have sought to create

God according to our own image and likeness. As I have said, when we speak the word "God" we enunciate a human construct, a philosophical metaphysics. No one who is unprepared to think in metaphysical terms has any right to expect his idea of God to be given respectability as a term capable of being grappled with by anyone else. This principle applies equally I am sure, to a pre-Kantian medievalist to whom "cause" is the same whether it occurred before time in the beginning of all or refers to a present rearrangement of furniture in his own apartment. Equally it applies to the biblical fundamentalist whose God is grandfather writ large, the God who frowns on extra-tribal vices but certifies the ways of the tribe as most righteous. It applies as well to thinkers for whom "history" is a univocal concept, despite all the qualifications that the past couple of centuries have taught us to apply to it.

As far as the first point is concerned, it is hard to see why there should be problems. Why should the Yahweh of Israel, a Deity worshiped in the north as in the south in the days of the prophets Amos and Hosea at approximately the same time in the eighth century B.C., have been precisely the same in the popular religion of the two nations any more than he was separately for these two charismatic men? Amos looked out on a world, which included Israel, that he could regard only as a *massa corruptionis*, a world for which there could be no redemption. His proclamation of God, therefore, certainly justified by Israel's experience of Yahweh, was one of inexorable retribution, for the nations as well as for Israel. He made a great contribution to theodicy thereby: justice has its demands which are not to be countered by sentimentalist parodies of theology, and if we figure God as the epitome of justice, He cannot be a God who is less than rigorously just. It is hard to agree with various recent commentators who have tried to temper

Amos' message by holding as "authentic" such passages as
9:11-15 which earlier commentators instinctively recognized to be accommodating gestures towards a comfortable
postexilic theological synthesis. The God of Amos, the God
of total justice, is not, to be sure, the only God, but he is God
for all that and he should not be confused with other Gods.

And what of the God of Hosea, Amos' contemporary?
There is no reason to think that Amos and Hosea consciously served other than the one Yahweh of Northern
Israel. Quite apart from the biblical records, the stela of
Mesha, King of Moab, confirms for us that it was only this
Yahweh who was the Deity of Israel. [For what it is worth, I
find convincing the contention that the original name was
Yahw (two syllables; the source of the latter Yahu/o, etc.),
that the *h* terminal of the Mesha stela is a possessive pronoun, and that the tetragrammaton was tendentiously
formed. So Martin Rose (Rose).] Yet what does Hosea tell us
about this God, what revelation of him that had never been
made known to the mind and heart of an Amos? What was
revealed in Hosea, to adopt the phrase of John L. McKenzie,
was a God of "divine passion" (McKenzie).

One can hardly read Hosea 11:8-9 in its context without
becoming convinced that in these verses we have the heart
of Hosea's experience of the God of Amos' wrath expressing
an anguish over his wrath which I am sure would have
shocked Amos and disconcerted him.

> How can I give you up, O Ephraim,
>   how deliver you up, O Israel?
> How can I treat you like Admah,
>   or make you like Zeboiim?
> My heart recoils within me,
>   my pity is stirred.

These are the words of a God not eager but rather reluctant to punish, uncertain in fact of the consequences of what he can do and what he should do. The following lines reinforce this conclusion as this God argues with himself in the same interrogative way:

> I cannot let loose my fury,
> I cannot turn about and destroy Ephraim:
>> for I am God and not man,
>> the Holy One in your midst.

And yet, of course, Hosea's God did destroy just as surely as Amos' did.

Are these separate Gods, the Yahweh of Amos and of Hosea, or are they discrete manifestations of a one God? If this is a hard question for us to decide with all the resources we have of fine distinction and refined hermeneutics, how hard must the question have appeared to an eighth-century B.C. audience — which did not have even a canon of Scripture to fall back upon? What prophet was to be believed? Who had, in Jeremiah's words, stood in the *sod* of the Lord?

It would be tempting to pursue further the varieties of prophetic religious experience, since it is from the prophets of Israel first of all that we expect the confident affirmation: Here is the word of the Lord, here is God revealed. Was the God of the confident, aristocratic Isaiah quite the same as the one who summoned into his service a reluctant Jeremiah and then had to submit to a series of harangues from this unwilling servant that could have been suffered only by a truly divine patience? Were the odd things that Ezekiel did — his so-called "prophetic acts" — and the odd imaginings in which he and later prophets like Zechariah clothed the word of God entirely compatible with the stern and straightforward image of the God projected by a Nathan or an Elijah? Is, in fact, the God of the postexilic Israel proclaimed by Ezra and Nehemiah, the selfsame Deity which Israel had left behind in Palestine and only recovered by the decree of Cyrus the Persian? If so, it was only by a strange metamorphosis in biblical terms, in which not man but God is strangely changed.

Some of the other later literature of the Bible indicates this change. Ezra and Nehemiah, and the Chronicler with them if he is not the same person, have turned Israel into a race rather than a people (which it had been in patriarchal or tribal times) or a nation (which it had become after David and Solomon), or even a religion, which seemed to have been desiderated by the indigenous Palestinian population — certainly larger than the body of "returnees" from Babylonia — who wanted to join with their now distant cousins in restoring Israel on earth. The ecumenical attempt failed, we know. The book of Ruth, among other documents, is monument to the failure, which registers its canonical dissent from not only Ezra and Nehemiah and the postexilic Deuteronomic law but also joins forces with the Pentateuchal traditions to affirm proudly the mixed origins of Israel, united by nothing other than acceptance of a common religious tradition. The tradition, whether fictive (by the Chronicler, certainly, but who can say?) or real (but who, at this remove, can realistically say?), is the all. "In many and various ways God spoke of old to our fathers by the prophets."

Much fairer game, of course, is to be captured in the pursuit of the wisdom literature of the OT. By definition, almost, the wisdom writers do not pretend to utter a "word of the Lord." All that they offer is an opinion. This fact, I suggest, points up the fatal flaw in the theory of "canonical criticism" which has been proposed by, among others, Brevard Childs as a supposed solution to the alleged impasse presented by "biblical theology." For the wisdom literature is certainly part and parcel of the canon, by anybody's definition of the canon. In a review of Childs' *Introduction to the Old Testament,* Robert P. Carroll, after rightly noting that Childs' position amounts to a canon-within-the-canon dogma, observes:

> Given the stress laid on the revelation of *Tora* to Moses on Sinai what difference does it make to that dogma if bound up with it is a copy of Qoheleth with his insistence that the work of God is beyond finding out? . . . If the canonical reading of Job is used as a correction to Proverbs and Ecclesiastes, why should Ecclesiastes not be used as a corrective to Deuteronomy? (Carroll)

Why not indeed? Both Job and Qoheleth were confronted by a *deus absconditus,* but were they appealing or complaining to the same God? One may be permitted to doubt it. For that matter, is the *go'el* of Job 19:25 the God of Israel's redemption as later piety has made him to be? One may be tempted to doubt this very much. But if not so, for whom was Job hoping? Did the Lord create wisdom, build it into his universe, and reveal it to us his creatures, or is the wisdom which governs the world a secret known only to God and forever hidden from man? (Vawter: 1980) When the psalmist says (Ps 37:25)

> Neither in my youth, nor now that I am old,
> have I seen a just man forsaken
> nor his descendants begging bread,

we may well envy this true believer whose life had been happily sheltered from the adverse experiences of other

psalmists, from those of a Jeremiah, a Job, or an Ecclesiastes; but we might also wonder why then his God did
not more resemble than theirs the God of Sirach or the God
of most of the comfortable platitudes of Proverbs.

A fair look at the diversity of the God concept in the OT
can, perhaps, save us from some very wrong decisions.
Years ago, George Ernest Wright pointed out the incom-
pleteness of the OT notion of God (Wright). He did not do
this in the spirit of some modern scholars, who seem to think
that there is a total discontinuity of this concept with the God
of the New Testament. That God was revealed to Israel in
fragmentary and varied ways does not imply that he was not
truly revealed. He was revealed to the extent that he could
be revealed, namely to the extent that the mind of man at
any one time was capable of his conception. At the same
time, the NT has not suddenly rendered pellucid and univocal the opaque and equivocal image of God it inherited —
mainly — from the OT. I am sure there is no profit in
attempting to reconstruct from the NT the mind of Jesus
with regard to his notion of God in terms of the OT which
was his scriptural revelation. The God of the NT who is the
Father of our Lord Jesus Christ we accept from Paul or John
or from some other transmitter of the gospel. He is one or
another or several of the Gods of the OT, and is also doubtless the God — another amalgam — of Hellenistic monotheism. Whoever he is, he does not resolve the problem of
OT theodicy.

I think it unnecessary to drive this point farther into the
ground. Was the God whom the Gospels represent as Jesus'
Father the same as the God whom the same Gospels represent as the object of the worship of the Pharisees? Is the God
of Qumran the God of the OT, let alone the God of the
Gospels? Has any Christian ever read Louis Ginzberg's
monumental *The Legends of the Jews* without being made

vividly aware that he frequently intrudes there upon a totally alien religion with a totally alien God? Is the God of
Islam — whose Islam? — biblical and koranic, similar in any
fashion to the God whom we have extrapolated from whatever parts of the Bible we have chosen?

I offer no solution to these many problems. I merely
repeat that God is what we make him: the old Italian expression is *Dio ha bisogno di uomini.* God has need of men. Without men's thinking and striving, God would remain a mere
noumenon in an unreal world of Platonist idealism. The
Bible, in its record of history and of thought, word and
wisdom, has given expression to the God idea in many
fruitful ways which challenge us to recognize in them not
only the Ground of our Being but also our Savior from
meaninglessness. Were it not for the variegated image of
God as he appears in the OT, however, we should be unprepared for such a challenge. For it is the variety of the OT's
religious   experience   rather   than   any   alleged   basic
homogeneity that accounts for its endurance into our time,
a mirror in which men and women continue to see their
authentic selves seeking to identify God.

I would like to end this excursion with some apposite
words of Herbert Haag, part of his farewell discourse on
retiring from the University of Tubingen:

> Not only is the image of God in the OT more personal
> than that of the NT, it is also incomparably more com-
> plex. The OT knows of a God who is near as well as far
> off, a God who reveals himself and who hides himself, a
> God who is humanly comprehensible and at the same
> time menacing, contradictory, unpredictable, and in-
> comprehensible. It is in such complexity and contrari-
> ety, however, sometimes in one form and sometimes
> another, that man experiences life itself and in such
> complexity he also experiences God (Haag).

* The reader may consult the original article for the list of references. (Ed.).

The Prophetic Combat For Peace: Struggling In The Name Of A Compassionate God

CARROLL STUHLMUELLER, C.P.
Catholic Theological Union
Chicago, IL 60615

Peace and war in Old Testament history cannot be reduced to a simple formula that war is always ungodly because peace is always the divine ideal. Neither can the prophetic statements of Isaiah contain the entire message: "They shall beat their swords into ploughshares and their spears into pruning hooks" (Is 2:4). Several centuries later another prophet, Joel, quoted this same line only to reverse its meaning. Isaiah's idyllic vision of peace now reads: "Beat your ploughshares back into swords, and your pruning hooks back into spears" (Jl 4[3]:10).

A Time of War and a Time of Peace

We are reminded of a statement from Ecclesiastes, the cynical, wise person of the wisdom tradition: "There is an appointed time for everything . . . under the heavens . . . A time to love, and a time to hate; a time of war, and a time of peace" (Ec 3:1, 8).

The seemingly contradictory positions of the prophet Isaiah and the prophet Joel cannot be solved by explaining Joel metaphorically. Isaiah himself was also writing of what "he saw in vision," as the Hebrew introduction (2:1) clearly states, and the poetic language of Isaiah's vision is quite symbolic: "The mountain of the Lord's house shall be established as the highest mountain and raised above the hills" (2:2). God never intended to accumulate more rocks on top of Mount Zion "in the [eschatological] days to come" (2:2). Both prophets then were writing metaphorically, and behind the metaphors there lies a different attitude and a different judgment about war and peace.

A comparison of these two texts from Isaiah and Joel indicates at once that the Old Testament is ensnared in a long, complex history, and within that larger history, prophecy, for its part, had its own tangled evolution. This one example, drawn from Isaiah who prophesied in pre-exilic times between 740 and 690 B.C. and from Joel who ministered to Israel in the post-exilic age somewhere between 500 and 450 B.C., shows that prophecy was not a single, monolithic movement. Yet even in an article as short as this one, the prospects of clear directions, even moral imperatives for peace and justice are not hopeless. If, however, we have pointed out the difficulties of Old Testament history and prophecy, then a signal has been flashed across the bow of our ship of state today, advising us of troubled waters ahead. There is no quick, easy application of biblical texts to the current moral quest for peace and justice. The task, indeed, is difficult and involved, but not impossible.

In order to clarify the prophetic combat for peace, we will first isolate several key religious or moral positions which dominated the origins of the Mosaic covenant, formed its core or heart and were sustained throughout its long course. Whenever they were seriously endangered by compromise or denial, prophets rose to their defense.

Yahweh, Champion of the Poor

Old Testament religion, as is becoming ever clearer from contemporary sociological studies by scholars like George Mendenhall, Norman Gottwald, Frank Frick and Walter Brueggemann, was rooted in a people who would claim no distinctive point of origin, whether national, racial, geographical or cultural. Several phrases in the *Torah* summarize this idea very strikingly: e.g., Israel was "a crowd of mixed ancestry" (Ex 12:38). Ezekiel was even more graphic: "By origin and birth you are of the land of Canaan; your father was an Amorite and your mother a Hittite" (Ezk 16:3). These facts show how the pieces within the jigsaw puzzle of Israelite history turned out weird and awkward.

In their first several hundred years of existence, from the patriarchs around 1850 B.C. all the way to David and Solomon at the turn of the millennium, Israelites possessed only one common trait, their scrambled insignificance. They were a mixed gathering of dispossessed people, former slaves, and indentured servants, mercenary troops, resident aliens, migrant workers, refugees. This sociological condition was due to mammoth international upheavals, the collapse and rise of empires and kingdoms which forced people to migrate or flee for protection, livelihood and basic human dignity. Part of this flotsam on the disturbed ocean waters of the ancient near east gathered to become "Israel." As mentioned already, not till the dynamic age of Kings David and Solomon did this "crowd of mixed ancestry" coalesce into a closely knit, twelve-tribe system. Later during the royal period when low-born Israel began to strut with artificial pomp and to disdain or take advantage of the powerless, the prophetic combat began.

One piece of literature, prophetic in its coloration and influence, was Deuteronomy. Here Israel was reminded:

> It was not because you are the largest of all nations that the Lord set his heart on you and chose you, for you are really the smallest of all nations. It was because the Lord loved you and because of his fidelity to the oath he had sworn to your ancestors, that he brought you out with his strong hand from the place of slavery (Dt 7:7-8).

The deuteronomic rendition of the Decalogue echoed this same attitude. It listed the following reason for excusing slaves from work on the sabbath:

> Remember that you too were once slaves in Egypt, and the Lord, your God, brought you from there with his strong hand and out-stretched arm. (Dt 5:15).

One essential side of biblical religion was its sense of humble, "mixed-up" origins which gradually developed into a theology of election or special choice by God. As Deuteronomy stated very bluntly, this choice could be explained only by Yahweh's love and fidelity for "the smallest of all nations." Yahweh, therefore, became known in the Bible primarily as a compassionate God who — as stated in an early, foundational chapter of Exodus — has "witnessed the affliction of my people in Egypt and heard their cry of complaint against their slave drivers, so I know well what they are suffering" (Ex 3:7). God, therefore, was not intuited first of all as world creator, omnipotent and supremely one, but rather as he himself declared to Moses from a cloud on Mount Sinai:

> The Lord, the Lord, a merciful and gracious God, slow to anger and rich in kindness and fidelity, continuing his kindness for a thousand generations, and forgiving wickedness and crime and sin; yet not declaring the guilty guiltless (Ex 34:6-7).

This theophany was granted as Moses stood on Mount Sinai with the "two stone tablets" of the law in his hands. Here then was the context for interpreting and implementing the *Torah*.

The other key aspects of Mosaic religion can be simply mentioned in passing: (1) earthly life is an "exodus" towards a promised land that always seems to elude Israel, at least in its full promise and hope; and (2) during the exodus, an heroic response can be expected, not daily, of course, but at serious, transitional moments. When Israel, however, found land and prosperity, these turned out to be more than fulfillment; they were as much a risk and a threat, as Walter Brueggemann explains in his book, *The Land*. It is always difficult for a prosperous people to walk humbly before their God and their neighbor and be compassionate towards the poor. At such times prophets summoned Israel heroically upon a new exodus.

This basic thrust of Mosaic religion — a poor, dispossessed people, chosen by God to manifest his compassionate love, continually called onward in its exodus towards the promised future, and summoned occasionally even to heroic response — imparts a unique quality to the biblical quest for peace. It does not seem to be peace at any cost, but peace with human dignity and future hopes for all God's people, particularly the poor. Everyone must remember their origins in poverty and weakness. If this essential quality of biblical peace was compromised, then Yahweh became a warrior, or as the Hebrew expressed it in Ex 15:3, 'ish-milhamah, "a man of war." One of the psalmist's refrains re-expressed the divine epithet thus: "Who is this king of glory? The Lord, strong and mighty, the Lord, mighty in battle" (Ps 24:8). There is, indeed, "a time of war" as there is also "a time of peace" (Ec 3:8).

Another Kind of War — The Combat for Peace

The prophets generally remained with the poor. I say generally, because they too had their own convoluted history, in which one group wandered from their initial call and turned their popularity to self-serving purposes. Then another type of prophet emerged. We can only trace the main lines of this new combat for peace in the name of the poor.

We first meet prophets in biblical literature that developed initially in the northern part of the country; later the group showed up in the southern traditions at Jerusalem. These "guild prophets" generally lived in communities, near important shrines like Gilgal (2 K 1:38), Ramah (1 S 19:22-24; 25:1), Bethel (2 K 2:2-3), Jericho (2 K 2:5,15) and Gibeath-elohim (1 S 10:5). We find them close to the people, sharing their needs and simple joys. The stories in 2 Kings (2-6) for instance, which grew up around these prophetic communities read like the *legenda sanctorum*, the ancient lives of the saints in church history. Miracles abounded, but always the popular kind from everyday life — providing food or cooking-oil, finding a lost axe-head, restoring to life the dead son of a widow, striking enemy soldiers blind. These are poor people's miracles, evoked out of compassion and achieved with little or no ostentation!

The hearts of these prophets were soft towards the poor and often tinged with a touch of humor. The Aramean soldiers who attacked the Israelites at Dothan were not slaughtered but temporarily blinded, and so they lost their way and wandered into the city of Samaria, there to be captured by the Israelites. The prophet Elisha, who directed "operation blindness," then ordered food and drink for them! (2 K6:8-23). Yet humor ceased when the rights of the poor were compromised, their property stolen and their sturdy morals endangered. At this moment prophets stopped at nothing, not even at executions and the collapse of dynasties.

With his own hands, we are told, Elijah slit the throats of the four hundred and fifty prophets of Baal for attempting to corrupt family life with fertility rites and sacred prostitution (1 K 18:40). When King Ahab and Queen Jezebel schemed the death of innocent Naboth, who refused to forfeit his ancestral lands for the embellishment of the royal gardens, Elijah announced the violent end of the entire royal family, even *this* dynasty famous for its exploits like the construction of the magnificent capital city of Samaria (1 K 16:24; ch 21).

The prophet Elisha asssured the fulfillment of this prophecy by charging one of the guild prophets to anoint a new king, the military commander Jehu. Jehu then proceeded to kill the kings of both Samaria and Jerusalem, to order Queen Jezebel to be thrown to her death from a palace window, and to demand the heads of seventy princes "in baskets" (2 K 10:7). The account reeks with so much cruelty that the author could hardly be judged as approving these events. Yet the guild prophets set the action in motion! The prophetic combat for peace had turned into a war for elementary justice.

Throughout other northern traditions, like the "elohist" and the "deuteronomist" accounts in the *Torah*, prophets were intercessors for needy people (Gn 20:7; Nb 11:25), warriors in defence of the weak and oppressed (Jg 4:4-5), but most of all men and women who preserved and defended the spirit of Moses within the religion and lives of the people (Dt 18:15-20; 34:10). This spirit, as we have seen, gathered together a dispossessed people and united them around the Lord's compassionate and gracious love. This concern for justice and peace moved them at times to heroic deeds. To assure the presence of this spirit, prophets lived close to the people, at peace with their everyday lives and solicitous about their basic needs of food, land and self-respect. Like anyone who loves dearly, these prophets summoned all of life's energies to defend these God-given rights and human needs: even to the point of unleashing the forces of violence. These summons were not a call to international war, nor to militarization, not even to a posture of continued readiness for conflict. The guild prophets were reacting to individual cases of serious abuse of human rights where other remedies had failed. In desperate moments, prophets did not consider peace a substitute for justice!

Prophecy, as we mentioned above, had a long and complicated history. Unfortunately, the descendants of Samuel, Elijah and Elisha allowed popularity, prestige and "clout" to go to their head. The guild prophets became fixtures at the royal court (2 S 7:2) and entered fully into palace intrigues (2 K 1:11; Jr 23:9-40). They quarrelled among themselves, so that kings could pit one group of prophets against another group and so be in the comfortable position of choosing the most convenient prophecy (1 K 22). The collapse of prophecy was so complete, that the prophetic word depended on the quality and quantity of food placed in their mouth. According to the Book of Micah:

. . . regarding the prophets who lead my people astray; who, when their teeth have something to bite, announce peace, but when one fails to put something in their mouth, sanctify a war against that one (Mi 3:5).

The "classical"prophets — individuals like Micah who eventually had books to their name — considered it an insult to be associated with the guild prophets. With fire flashing from his eyes and sarcasm spitting from his mouth, Amos retorted: "I am no prophet, nor do I belong to any company of prophets. I am a shepherd and a dresser of sycamore trees" (Am 7:14). The bitter barb in Amos' voice was not lost on Amaziah the high priest. Amos was saying: I am no prophet. I work for a living! A new type of prophet was needed to challenge prophecy. The older type had itself become oppressive of the poor.

Another Kind of Prophecy —
The Moral Imperative of Peace

We center attention upon the prince of classical prophets, Isaiah ben Amoz, and specifically upon the famous Immanuel prophecy in chapters 7-11.

In several important ways Isaiah advanced beyond the Mosaic covenant. The themes of the exodus and Sinaitic covenant drifted out of consciousness; Isaiah, instead, gravitated towards the Davidic covenant, the holy city Jerusalem and its temple. Yet Isaiah remained completely committed to the heart of the Mosaic covenant, the cause of the poor and the needy. In order to correct liturgical abuses, the prophet challenged the people to: "Make justice your aim: redress the wronged, hear the orphan's plea, defend the widow" (Is 1:16). If the city "has turned adulteress," housing a pack of "murderers," where "each one of them loves a bribe" (Is 1:21), these and other crimes are summarized in the statement where widow and orphan have become symbolic of all the poor: "The fatherless they defend not, the widow's plea does not reach them" (Is 1:23). Isaiah, therefore, maintained the most essential quality of Mosaic religion, the Lord's compassionate concern for the oppressed.

Isaiah realized that whether the people were wealthy or poor, they were all in danger of being betrayed by King Ahaz in 736 B.C. The armies of Israel and Syria were invading the kingdom of Judah, intent on replacing the Davidic dynasty with "the son of Tabeel" (Is 7:6). King Ahaz realized that he could not defeat the invaders on the field of battle, so in panic he decided to declare Judah a vassal of Assyria in return for Assyrian military protection.

Without discussing the details, we can agree with scholarly consensus that Ahaz's action was not only cowardly and selfish (he was acting solely for the preservation of the royal family), but it was also useless (for Assyria would intervene only at its pleasure and advantage) and totally immoral (Judah would lose independence, dignity and eventually moral will-power to resist corruption). Isaiah's answer was clear and blunt, "Do nothing!" — every option was immoral — only trust in God! He declared: "Take care and be tranquil, do not fear, nor lose courage" (Is 7:4). "Unless your faith is firm, you will never be confirmed" (Is 7:9). Samuel Terrien translated the latter two lines succinctly: "No faith, no staith!"

Isaiah (30:15-18) wrote his own commentary on this heroic stance of faith. We quote the opening lines:

> For thus said the Lord God,
> the Holy One of Israel:

> By waiting and by calm you shall be saved,
>   in quiet and in trust your strength lies.
> But this you did not wish.

King Ahaz would not be swayed from his decision of making Judah a vassal of Assyria. Judah was now dragged into the international cauldron of intrigue, distrust, greed, cruelty and escalating military adventures. Eventually, Assyria invaded Judah; the erstwhile protector was now wreaking revenge for Judah's failure to pay proper tribute. Isaiah saw in this military expedition of Assyria the chastising, purifying hand of God. The prophet used the image of water. Because Israel had rejected faith in God, symbolized by "the waters of Shiloah that flow gently," God in turn "raises against them the waters of the river, great and mighty, the king of Assyria." Yet, in these destructive floodwaters, Isaiah perceived the presence of "Immanuel — God with us."

When these distant lands armed themselves insolently, formed plans against God and resolved to alter God's designs for Israel, they would be crushed and thwarted, and their plan "shall not be carried out, for Immanuel — is God with us" (Is 8:5-10). When Assyria boasted "by my own power I have done it," God replied through the prophet, "will the axe boast against the one who hews with it?" (Is 10; 13, 15). God would save the poor and humble "remnant of Israel, the survivors of the house of Jacob" (Is 10:20). The Book of Immanuel (Is 7-11) ends with the glorious vision of peace for the once poor and lowly servants of God:

> For the Lord shall judge the poor with justice,
>   and decide aright for the land's afflicted.

> He shall strike the ruthless with the rod of his mouth,
>   and with the breath of his lips he shall slay the
>   wicked . . .
> Then the wolf shall be the guest of the lamb,
>   and the leopard shall lie down with the kid.
> The calf and the young lion shall browse together,
>   with a little child to guide them (Is 11:4-6).

Prophetically, there are crucial moments when no political or military option is morally acceptable. One must take shelter in one's interior conviction of God's concern for the poor and oppressed. The prophetic combat for peace has turned profoundly interior. There are other prophetical movements when God's purifying hand is seen in the reality of military invasion, yet even this insight concludes with God's reducing the insolent invader to an "axe that dared to boast against the one who hews with it." No one may tamper with God's ultimate and central concern for the poor and oppressed.

History Continues

Prophetically, then, there is "a time of war, and a time of peace." Such is the way that the sage Ecclesiastes summed it up after long reflection. In the Old Testament the major question is not so much one of peace at all costs, and it is certainly not one of war if other measures fail. Prophets went to war, and prophets on other occasions condemned war and military alliances. Mosaic religion centered in Yahweh's compassion for the poor and the defenceless and in the Lord's determination to lead the people to a promised land of human dignity and social justice. Only under these conditions could Israel offer acceptable sacrifice in the tem-

--

ple and hurry the day of the Messiah. Yet this day would be carried away in violence (cf. Mt 11:12).

The anointed Savior's name will be "The Lord our Justice" (Jr 23:6). If we obey "what you have been told . . . and what the Lord requires of you," namely: "Only to do the right and to love goodness, and to walk humbly with your God" (Mi 6:8), then the Messiah from lowly Bethlehem "shall be [our] peace" (Mi 5:4).

The Theological Contributions of Israel's Wisdom Literature

ROLAND E. MURPHY, O. Carm.
Duke Divinity School
Durham, NC 27706

Biblical wisdom literature often remains a hazy notion, even for regular Bible readers. For some it suggests a lot of proverbs, somewhat repetitious and sometimes boring, no more perceptive than the common sense insights of many peoples. Or it is summarized as a movement that ended in defeat with the book of Ecclesiastes (all is vanity). Or perhaps it is associated primarily with Job who struggled, like Jacob, with God. These views, impressionistic and superficial, do not arise out of a total confrontation with the wisdom books.

The wisdom books, classified among the *Ketubim* or Writings, have been overshadowed by the Law and the Prophets which develop the great themes of Israel's salvation history. This is partly due to a theological bias about what is important. When the "God who acts" is taken as the dominant motif, the God who established the world in wisdom (Pr 3:19) is less apparent. Nonetheless, it is theologically vital aspects of biblical wisdom which we propose to explore.

At the outset the parameters of Israel's wisdom need to be defined. We restrict ourselves to five books: Proverbs, Job, Ecclesiastes, Sirach, and the Wisdom of Solomon. In recent times considerable research has been devoted to the influence of wisdom on other parts of the Hebrew Bible, but this cannot be considered here.[1] Three of these books can be dated with certainty to the postexilic period: Ecclesiastes (ca. 250), Sirach (ca.180) and Wisdom of Solomon (ca. 50). The date of Job is disputed; in its final form it may be exilic or postexilic. There is good reason to consider as preexilic the collections of sayings in Proverbs 10-29, to which chaps. 1-9 perhaps form a later, postexilic preface. It is important to observe that the bulk of this literature is postexilic, whatever may have been its roots in oral tradition before that time. Hence although one may infer the existence of a court school in Jerusalem, this is largely irrelevant to these books. Qoheleth "taught the people knowledge, and weighed, scrutinized, and arranged many proverbs" (Ec 12:9), and Ben Sira invited his readers to the "house of instruction" (Si 51:23). That is all the information we have concerning the *Sitz im Leben* of these writers. Ultimately the origins of wisdom go back to the insights of tribal elders and the family (cf. Tb 4:5-19), with a probable assist from Jerusalem scribes.[2]

The Listening Heart

In 1 K 3:9, we read that Solomon asks the Lord for a *leb somea*, or a listening heart. In context he is asking for the wisdom to be able to lead the people of God, but the listening heart for which he asks is what wisdom is about: an openness to God, to creation, to experience, to the traditions of the sages. The ideal goes back as far as Ptahhotep, an Egyptian sage of about the 22nd century B.C., who wrote:

He who hears is beloved of god,
He whom god hates does not hear.

The heart of its owner a hearer or non-hearer,
Man's heart is his life-prosperity-health!
The hearer is one who hears what is said,
He who loves to hear is one who does what is said . . .
Teach your son to be a hearer . . .
The fool who does not hear,
He can do nothing at all . . .[3]

Hence it is not surprising to read in Pr 1:8, "Hear, my son, your father's instruction," or in Si 6:33, "If you are willing to listen, you will learn . . ."

What was one expected to hear? A wide range of observations about life and how to cope with it. If the Decalogue covered many concrete ideals of Israelite society, the sayings of the wise were geared to a broader area — the formation of character. Hence, the frequent emphasis on the control of the tongue and indeed all the appetites, on diligence as opposed to laziness, on a sense of responsibility in the discharge of duties. Hearing these admonitions should lead to carrying them out, but the sages also provided motives: "Boast not of tomorrow, for you know not what any day may bring forth"(Pr 27:1).

Biblical "hearing" is the equivalent of obedience, as we learn particularly from Proverbs and Deuteronomy. The urgent preaching tone of Deuteronomy (cf. 5:1; 6:4-5) is matched by the insistence of the sage (Pr 3:1-4; 4:1-10). The issue is praxis, not theory — how is one to live? The fool is not intellectually, but morally, inferior. The essence of folly is to neglect the "fear of the Lord" which is the beginning of wisdom, i.e., it leads to wisdom.

Wisdom As Dialogue

Gerhard von Rad has written that "the most characteristic feature of her [Israel's] understanding of reality lay, in the first instance, that she believed man to stand in a quite specific highly dynamic, existential relationship with his environment."[4] These words describe what is going on in the wisdom movement. The sages analyzed the environment, the created world and its inhabitants, for signs and conclusions about human beings and their activities. They drew analogies and made comparisons between things, living and non-living. Ants are an example of diligence and foresight (Pr 6:6-8). Small things are, if not beautiful, at least wise: ants, rock-badgers, locusts, and lizards (Pr 30:24-28). Even the bee, least "among winged things," reaps the choicest of all harvests (Si 11:3). A dead fly can spoil precious perfume, just as a single slip can ruin much that is good (Ec 9:18). The mysteries of nature were particularly appropriate topics: the way of an eagle in the air, the way of a serpent upon a rock, the way of a ship on the high seas — what do these have in common with "the way of a man with a maiden"? (Pr 30:18-19).

This readiness to learn from nature increased rather than lessened the sages' awe before the mysteries that confronted them, and sometimes veritable hymns concerning the creator of this mystery resulted. Elihu could challenge Job: "Do you know how the clouds are banked, the wondrous work of him who is perfect in knowledge?" (Jb 37:16). And the lengthy reply of the Lord to Job surveys a host of mysterious actions of the Almighty: "Has the rain a father, or who has begotten the drops of dew?" (Jb 38:28). There turns out to be a close relationship between the wisdom meditation and the hymn of praise (e.g., Psalm 104).

Equally striking are the mysteries of human activity

with its ambiguities and antinomies. Silence can be the sign of one who is wise and careful in speech, but even a fool, if he keeps silent, can be considered wise (Pr 17:27-28). A soft word can break a bone! (Pr 25:15). A bitter thing can turn out to be sweet (to the hungry, Pr 27:7). Riches are a constituent part of the "life" that wisdom offered; yet riches can be ambivalent; they cannot compare with virtue (Pr 11:4), and they can lead to sin (Pr 10:16).

Of course there is no one more mysterious in human affairs than the Lord himself. There is the frank admission that no wisdom, no understanding, no counsel, counts against the Lord (Pr 21:30). One may rely upon military might and wise counsellors for victory, but it is the Lord who is ultimately responsible (Pr 21:31; 24:6). Human beings may be certain in their discernment, but it is the Lord who proves the spirit (Pr 16:2; 17:3). And wisdom itself, even if possessed by the wise person, is so vulnerable; more weighty than wisdom or wealth is a little folly (Ec 10:1). And one's grasp on wisdom is so tenuous. One may never really think that one is "wise" — there is more hope for a fool than for such a person! (Pr 26:12).

Another way of understanding this dialogue between human beings and their environment is to say that wisdom theology is creation theology. This is the conclusion of Walter Zimmerli who interprets the wisdom movement as the carrying out of the creator's words, "Be fertile and multiply: fill the earth and subdue it. Have dominion . . ." (Gn 1:28).[5] The divine plan is that humans are to take seriously the world in which they live. Another way of expressing this has been put forth by Claus Westermann.[6] Wisdom is subsumed under God's blessing (Gn 1:22, 28); it is the fruit of the divine blessing and authorized by it.

The recognition that wisdom and creation belong together seems reasonable enough from the point of view of content. But the preoccupation of both Zimmerli and Westermann seems to derive from an embarrassment: what to do with wisdom. Wisdom and creation simply do not fit into the idea of *Heilsgeschichte,* or salvation history, which is taken as the heart of the Bible. Hence, both scholars rooted wisdom in the Torah. G. von Rad travelled another path, finding the theological justification for creation in the prohibition of images (Ex 20:4): "The prohibition, surely, enshrines a decisive and fundamental recognition of the fact that God is theologically transcendent relative to the world, so that the creation narrative must be understood in a certain sense as the immensely diversified exposition of a theological datum which was already embedded in the most ancient form of Yahweh."[7] Yahweh was totally other than the world; he could not be imaged, for he is utterly transcendent. In the structure of the book of Genesis creation is taken over by salvation history, which is pushed back to primeval time (Gn 1-12). This is another way of solving a perennial problem: where does wisdom theology belong?

Perhaps it would be easier to answer the question by granting equal weight to creation/wisdom and salvation history. One may not take the position that the Lord has intervened or revealed himself solely in the sphere of history. Creation also forms a vehicle of revelation. G. von Rad appreciated this and expressed it crisply: "The experiences of the world were for her [Israel] always divine experiences as well, and the experiences of God were for her experiences of the world."[8] Israel did not keep faith and knowledge apart after the fashion of the Scholastic distinction between faith and reason. Wisdom theology is not to be compared with natural philosophy. It never understood itself in this way; rather it was rooted in fear of the Lord. The distinction between faith and reason, or between a (supernatural) revelation in "history" and a (natural) revelation through creation and experience is not recommended by the biblical tradition.[9]

The Kerygma of Wisdom: Life

Nothing less than life, the good life in the here and now, is the promise of biblical wisdom.[10] Observance of the sages' teaching brings "many days and years of life, and peace" (Pr 3:2). Wisdom is called "a tree of life" (Pr 3:18; cf. 15:4), and heeding instruction is the "path to life" (Pr 10:17). This life, of course, was the only life that Israel knew; it was here, on this side of Sheol or the nether world, where one truly lived. The prospect was to have a life full of years, surrounded by family, prosperity and prestige. This meant that one lived in harmony with the Lord, the giver of wisdom (Pr 2:6; Ws 9:1-4). Since the Lord is the creator and sustainer of life (Psalm 104), material possessions are signs of his blessing. For Sirach, good and evil, life and death, poverty and riches, are from the Lord (Si 11:14).

The gift of life is inseparable from the figure of personified Wisdom. It is she who threatens and cajoles human beings to obedience (literally "listening") in order to dwell in security and peace (Pr 1:33). Her threats are marked by divine authority, as she "laughs" at the doom of those who fail to heed her (compare Pr 1:26 with Pss 2:4; 59:9). But in chapter 8 of Proverbs, threat yields to persuasive promise. There she describes her exalted position as firstborn of God's ways, brought forth by God before anything else was created. When the Lord was engaged in creation she was there, an *'amon,* either as "craftsman" involved with God in the creative activity, or as "nursling" playing before him. Whatever be her precise role, she manifests positive joy towards human beings: "and I found delight in the sons of men" (v 31). It is this Wisdom who then proclaims: the one who finds me finds life (v 35).

A similar pattern emerges, but with significant differences, in Si 24. Wisdom is introduced as singing her own praises "in the assembly of the Most High," i.e., in the heavenly court (vv. 1-2). She describes herself: "from the mouth of the Most High I came forth, and mistlike covered the earth" (v. 3), an allusion to her association with the creative word of God (Gn 2:6; Ps 147:15-18). Although she has her throne with God, she travels through creation, even to areas beyond human reach (heaven, the abyss, v. 5). She is looking for a place to take up residence. Finally the Creator tells her: "in Jacob make your dwelling, in Israel your inheritance" (v. 8). She does so: "In the holy tent I ministered [*eleitourgesa*, liturgical worship] before him, and in Zion I fixed my abode." Finally she issues an invitation in a style reminiscent of Lady Wisdom in Proverbs 8.

> Come to me, all you that yearn for me,
>   and be filled with my fruits . . . (Si 24:18-21; cf.
> Pr 32-36)

Who is Lady Wisdom?[11] Israel had differing identifications for her at various times. It has been customary to speak of her as a personification of a divine attribute: "the Lord by Wisdom founded the earth" (Pr 3:19). This notion is too pale to do justice to the process of personification which wisdom enjoys. She is a divine attribute, for she has divine origins and is somehow associated with the Lord in his creative activity. But her orientation is towards human beings. G. von Rad has captured the right nuance: "It is correct to say that wisdom is the form in which Yahweh's will and his accompanying of man (i.e., his salvation) approaches man. Wisdom is the essence of what man needs for a proper life, and of what God grants him. Still, the most important thing is that wisdom does not turn toward man in the shape of an 'It,' teaching, guidance, salvation or the like, but of a person, a summoning 'I.' So wisdom is truly the form in which Yahweh makes himself present and in which he wishes to be sought by man. 'Whoso finds me, finds life' (Pr 8:35). 'Only Yahweh can speak in this way.' "[12] In this view wisdom is not merely the self-revelation of creation, but the revelation of the Lord, that side of God that is turned towards human beings, dwells with them, and enlivens them: "she transcends the created universe and yet eagerly accepts to enter the human realm of existence."[13]

The description of Ben Sira is not less universal, but he is careful to identify wisdom for the Israelite. Concretely, wisdom is Torah: "All this is true of the book of the Most High's covenant, the law which Moses commanded us as an inheritance for the community of Jacob" (Si 24:22). A similar identification of wisdom appears in Dt 4:6-8. But the identification of wisdom and Torah is not meant to limit the possibilities. In the Wisdom of Solomon she returns to a more universal function, while retaining her association with Israel. She is cosmological, in that "she reaches from end to end mightily" (8:1; cf. 6:16, "she makes her own rounds, seeking those worthy of her"). She is explicitly described as a spirit (Ws 1:6; 7:7, 22). She is "an aura of the might of God and a pure effusion of the glory of the Almighty . . . the refulgence of eternal light, the spotless mirror of the power of God" (Ws 7:25-26). More explicitly than Lady Wisdom in Proverbs 8, she is involved in creation as a *technitis* (7:21, "craftsman") who "produces all things" (8:5-6), and is "the mother of all things" (7:12). In short,

There is nought God loves,
    be it not one who dwells with Wisdom (7:28).[14]

When one comes to the New Testament, wisdom motifs continue to appear, especially in the Gospel of John and in Paul. While John uses the term *logos*, or word, the association of word and life (Jn 1:4) remains.[15] Paul can describe Christ as "the wisdom of God" (1 Cor 1:24). From Proverbs to 1 Corinthians the Bible presents a majestic development of wisdom which, while it is capable of a more narrow identification in given periods (Sirach, the Torah) is nonetheless inexhaustible in its understanding. Wisdom is another form of God-with-us and God-for-us.

Wisdom and the Conquest of Death

In contrast to the serene optimism which characterizes the personification of Wisdom and her promises is the actual human condition. The promise of life for Israel was first of all limited by the reality of death, or "existence," if one can call it so, in Sheol (Ec 9:10). But death is not a mere terminus in biblical thought. It accompanies human beings throughout life; it is a dynamic power which pursues them. Death is not merely the inexorable end of human life; it is a daily accompaniment. To the extent that life is marked by suffering and adversity, to that extent it is under the power of death; it is a kind of non-life. Hence when the psalmist cries out that the Lord has brought him up from Sheol, he does not mean a kind of resuscitation or resurrection. He is proclaiming that death has released its grip, in the measure that the psalmist has been restored and given back to meaningful life.

Biblical existence was lived between the two poles of life and death. Despite the promise of wisdom, dying daily in the distress of sickness, adversity, and hostility seems to be too much a part of the human condition to get around, much less to deny. The sages were aware of the limitations of their teaching. They realized that the optimistic system of retribution (wisdom/life; folly/death) which they proposed was not always effective. One way of dealing with this was to admit that the Lord loves the one he reproves, chastises the son he favors (Pr 3:12). But for the most part the standard solution of the sage was the stout affirmation that Wisdom would absolutely ensure life. This thought is echoed throughout Proverbs; it is found in Psalm 37 and also in the speeches of the three friends of Job.

At this point one must admire the dynamic tension that the wisdom literature manifests. The author of the book of Job writes his work precisely to contest the easy solution which he recognized in the predominant strain of wisdom thinking. His hero struggles with non-life and argues with the Lord about the injustice of his situation. He is portrayed as besting the three friends in the dispute which takes place (so the divine verdict in 42:8). But still no "answer" is given to Job. He is vouchsafed a vision of God (42:5) which enables him to live with his adversity, without explanation. What emerges is the possibility of divine presence in the midst of living death.

Qoheleth's judgment is more extreme than that of Job. The extent of the "vanity" which he recognizes human existence to be is stated very clearly in 9:1, "love from hatred man cannot tell." The human condition has never been more movingly described; one cannot tell whether one is loved or hated by God — there is the "same lot for all, for the just and wicked . . ." (9:2). If human existence held out so little, the reality of Sheol after death is the crushing blow. In the face of the remarkable resignation which the Israelite had about the inevitability of death, Qoheleth cried out, "How is it that the wise man dies as well as the fool!" (2:16). The only alternative to a Sheol that is described as a place devoid of work, reason, knowledge, and wisdom (9:10) is the acceptance of whatever lot the Lord gives (5:17-19). There is no way of understanding God's "work" (3:11; 7:13; 8:17; 11:5). It is not surprising that Qoheleth must admit the failure of his effort to achieve wisdom (7:23).

The intense promise of life which wisdom guaranteed seems to have become bankrupt. But not quite. If the problem of suffering never disappears from the human scene, neither does the effort to deal with it. The author of the book of Wisdom comes to it in its sharpest form, the persecution of the righteous — how is one to deal with that? His answer is that the righteous are immortal. But the manner in which he presents this is unique.

The key statement is in 1:15: "justice is undying." Here there appears the old equivalence of wisdom and justice, registered so frequently in the book of Proverbs (10:2-3, 7, 16, 30 etc.). It is in justice or righteousness that the root of immortality is to be found. A description of righteousness is given most concretely in the example of Abraham, who "put faith in the Lord, who credited it to him as an act of righteousness" (Gn 15:6). This is best described by the relationship which the psalmist has with the Lord:

> Yet with you I shall always be,
>   you have hold of my right hand;
> With your counsel you guide me,
>   and in the end you will receive me in glory . . .
> For me, to be near God is my good;
>   to make the Lord my refuge (Ps 73:23-28).

Immortality is the right relationship one has with God. It is not simply extension in time; it does not derive from the human composite, soul or body. The author does not argue from the Greek premise, that the soul is simple, substantial, and undying. He may have shared such a Platonic idea, but it is not the basis on which he affirms immortality. He may even have believed in the resurrection of the body, an idea which emerged in Hebrew thought at least in the second century at the time the book of Daniel was written (Dn 12:2). But such beliefs have only to do with the *manner* of immortality, how life beyond death is made possible. More to the point, he states what true immortality is: a right relationship with God, which simply endures. This relationship, which one might even term a covenant, had not been previously understood as permanent. In Sheol there was no loving contract with God (Pss 6:6; 30:10), but is was he who always had power over life and death, and now it was seen that it was his will to sustain the relationship he had with his creature. On his part, then, life came to be understood as an outright offer. But offer it was, and it needed to be accepted. The acceptance or the rejection was the work of human beings. Acceptance, or righteousness, means that one is undying. Rejection, or wickedness, means that the relationship is severed and one is not truly immortal. This is a remarkably positive conception of immortality. The author is hardly interested in the fate of the wicked. He does speak of their being "in grief" (Ws 4:19), but he does not pursue the point. It is the righteous who are truly immortal. The wicked will realize how wrong they have been, because with great recrimination they will see among the holy ones the just man whom they considered a laughing stock.

> See how he is accounted among the sons of God;
> how his lot is with the saints! (Ws 5:5).

This association with God's family is another expression of what immortality really is. Up to this time one lamented that there would be no praising of God in Sheol (Ps 6:6; Si 17:22 [17]). Now that has been changed; the heart of the next life will be the association with God's holy ones, whose function is praise (Psalm 29; 148:1-2).

Conclusion

A primal theological value of Israelite wisdom is the insights it provides into daily experience, in which a continuous relationship to the Lord is worked out. The casual reader must beware of considering the modest sayings as mere platitudes; they reflect the moral formation that accompanied "fear of the Lord." Moreover, the quest for wisdom is an ongoing one. Neither the earlier nor the later sages say it all. The best of wisdom thought recognizes the mystery of God's activity in human life. The drive for certainty and security which characterizes some theological movements has much to learn from the agony of the sages.[16]

FOOTNOTES

1. For example, it has been argued that the Joseph story (Gn 37-50), Esther, Amos, and the Song of Songs all betray such influence. For a survey of the literature and a critique see J.L. Crenshaw, "Method in Determining Wisdom Influence upon 'Historical' Literature," *The Journal of Biblical Literature* 88 (1969) 129-142, reproduced conveniently in J.L. Crenshaw (ed.), *Studies in Ancient Israelite Wisdom* (New York: Ktav. 1976) 481-494.
2. For differing points of view, see E. Gerstenberger, *Wesen und Herkunft des 'apodoktischen Rechts'* WMANT 20 (Neukirchener Verlag, 1965), and H.J. Hermisson, *Studien zur israelitischen Spruchweischeit* WMANT 28 (Neukirchener Verlag, 1968).
3. Cf. Miriam Lichtheim, *Ancient Egyptian Literature*, 3 Vols. (Berkeley: University of California Press, 1975-1980), I, 74; these are approximately lines 548-575.
4. Cf. G. von Rad, *Wisdom in Israel* (Nashville: Abingdon, 1972) 301.
5. Cf. W. Zimmerli, "The Place and the Limit of the Wisdom in the Framework of Old Testament Theology," *The Scottish Journal of Theology* 17 (1964) 146-158, conveniently reproduced in J.L. Crenshaw (ed.), *Studies in Ancient Israelite Wisdom*, 314-326.
6. Cf. C. Westermann, *Blessing* (Philadelphia: Fortress, 1978) 37-39.

7. G. von Rad, "Some Aspects of the Old Testament World-View," in *The Problem of the Hexateuch and Other Essays* (New York: McGraw-Hill, 1966) 144-165, p. 150.
8. Ibid.
9. The writer has developed this point at length in "Israel's Wisdom: A Biblical Model of Salvation," *Studia Missionalia* 30 (1981) 1-43. Wisdom theology is the necessary (and thus far, missing) biblical basis for the splendid statements of Vatican II concerning the salvation of non-Christians (see *Lumen Gentium,* #16; *Gaudium et Spes,* #22). These statements find theological support in the arguments of Karl Rahner about the *de facto* supernatural order in which human beings find themselves. It is in the area of creation and wisdom theology that a saving faith response is seen to be possible. Biblical wisdom provides such a model, and thus a biblical argument for the theological vision of Vatican II in this matter.
10. Cf. R.E. Murphy, "The Kerygma of the Book of Proverbs," *Interpretation* 20 (1966) 3-14.
11. For more details, see Bernhard Lang, *Frau Weisheit* (Dusseldorf: Patmos, 1976).
12. G. von Rad, *Old Testament Theology,* 2 Vols (New York: Harper & Row, 1962-65) I, 444.
13. The quotation is from S. Terrien, "The Play of Wisdom: Turning Point in Biblical Theology," in *Horizons in Biblical Theology* 3 (1981) 125-153, p. 137.
14. On the emergence of wisdom as a savior figure, see R.E. Murphy, "Wisdom and Salvation" in *Sin, Salvation, and the Spirit,* ed. Daniel Durken (Collegeville: Liturgical Press, 1979) 177-183.
15. For more detail, see Raymond E. Brown, *The Gospel According to John,* AB 29 (New York: Doubleday, 1966) I, 519-524.
16. For a survey of the literature and the main themes that have emerged in the studies of wisdom in the period since World War II, see R.E. Murphy, "Hebrew Wisdom," *The Journal of the American Oriental Society* 101.1 (1981) 21-34.

NEW TESTAMENT THEMES

Introduction

MIRIAM WARD, R.S.M.
Trinity College
Burlington, VT 05401

The New Testament consists of a series of literary texts written within a given historical framework for the early Christian community. They are above all else documents of faith, written for and by people of faith in Jesus Christ. Each one of the New Testament writings therefore, will refer back in faith to the Christ-event. Biblical exegesis concentrates on discovering the religious meaning intended by the author. But they are historical documents, reflecting the changing situations and political climate in which the early Church was born. And because they are documents they contain the diverse literary genres peculiar to the first century.

Modern biblical scholarship concerns itself with all of these aspects of the canonical writings: the historical, the religious or theological, and the literary considerations. The articles included in this section will present some of the current methodologies used by modern New Testament scholars. In no way do we claim an inclusive representation, either of the kind of approach or in the subject matter treated.

We begin this section with a survey-type essay on one of the most misunderstood and misinterpreted elements of the New Testament: apocalyptic.

The classification of the books of Daniel in the Old Testament, and Revelation in the New Testament as "prophetical books" has not helped the understanding of the nature of apocalyptic either as a literary genre or as a distinctive world-view which gave rise to a movement. Although apocalyptic elements are present in some of the prophetical writings of the OT, and although apocalyptic "flows out of" prophecy, the two are not synonymous. Further, because there are apocalyptic elements in many books of the New Testament, there is even discussion among scholars as to whether it is properly a literary genre. Whatever the case, the articles that begin and end this section will help sharpen the reader's awareness of the two aspects of apocalyptic.

Paul J. Achtemeier, like his wife Elizabeth, is an ordained minister of the Presbyterian Church, has been very active on a national and world level of ecumenical discussion, has a most impressive list of publications, translations, and sermons, but unlike Elizabeth, has devoted his scholarly pursuits to *New* Testament study. He is the first non-Roman Catholic to be elected President of the prestigious Catholic Biblical Association. Professor Achtemeier has taught in Switzerland, at Columbia University and Pittsburgh Theological Seminary, and is Professor of Biblical Interpretation at Union Theological Seminary in Virginia.

It is only in recent times that apocalyptic has been given attention as a distinctive movement in late Judaism and early Christianity. It is this facet of apocalyptic, namely, as a way of thinking, a distinctive way of looking upon history and the world that is the topic of the first article.

In his essay "An Apocalyptic Shift in Early Christian

Tradition," Professor Achtemeier focuses on the aspect of apocalyptic as a distinctive world-view. He traces the shift in emphasis from the earlier canonical writings through the synoptic gospels to the fourth gospel by examining the treatment of "the resurrection, the kingdom of God, knowledge and mystery, and other indications of present or future realities." Although one will see that the emphasis is on the "shift" in thinking, nevertheless the underlying reality of a peculiar way of viewing history characterized the writings of many of the New Testament books.

From this survey of New Testament thought along the lines of apocalyptic, we turn our attention next to an example of gospel commentary. But, first, a word about the author.

Donald Senior, C.P. continues the tradition of excellence in biblical scholarship established within the Congregation of the Passion by Barnabas Ahern, Carroll Stuhlmueller, and the late Richard Kugelman. Prolific author and associate editor of *The Bible Today,* and specifically editor of "The New Testament in Review," Father Senior performs an outstanding service in bringing to the attention of readers the notice and evaluation of new publications in biblical studies. Father Senior is currently professor of New Testament Studies at Catholic Theological Union in Chicago. He has lectured and given retreats throughout the United States, Canada, the Far East, and Africa. Father Senior is a member of the Southern Baptist/Roman Catholic Scholars Dialogue sponsored jointly by the United States Catholic Bishops and the Southern Baptist Convention. Readers who want a fine overall view of the gospels in recent biblical research might read Father Senior's *Jesus: A Gospel Portrait.*

Prescinding from, yet building upon the contributions of form criticism, source criticism, and redaction criticism among other methodologies, scholars have moved to consider the wider sociological context as well as the symbolic function of language. "The Eucharist in Mark: Mission, Reconciliation, and Hope," reflects the sensitivities of most recent New Testament research to the "use of metaphor, the power of narrative, and the deep structure of literary forms." Father Senior examines two sets of texts on the feeding stories and the Last Supper, and points out the characteristics of Mark's overall theology in each and illustrates how each text "gives leads to Markan perspectives on the Eucharist."

Central to the faith of Christians is belief in the Resurrection of Jesus. Christians affirm with Paul that "if Christ has not been raised, then your faith is in vain." (1 Cor 15:14). But although the unity of faith in the Resurrection crosses denominational boundaries, there is a diversity of interpretation. This diversity can be seen in the varied treatments and approaches to the Resurrection within the New Testament itself as well as in present-day theological reflection. We include in this collection an article by one who has devoted much time to this topic.

Rev. Gerald O'Collins, S.J., is an Australian by birth, but one who is at home in most every part of the globe. In addition to his native land, he has lectured in England, Ireland, Italy, India, and the United States. His advanced studies were done under Ernst Kasemann, Hans Kung, and Jurgen Moltmann. He is a Professor at the Pontifical Gregorian University in Rome. He has written extensively in the areas of Christology, and the theology of hope, publishing many books and articles in theological journals. Readers will delight in the command of ancient and modern extrabiblical literature which characterizes his writings.

Having written his own book on the Resurrection in 1973, Father O'Collins went on to give us a little gem of a book, *What Are They Saying About the Resurrection?*, in which he sums up the diversity of approaches to the Resurrection in current publications. In the third article of this section, he offers another insight into the "many-faceted mystery of Christ's rising from the dead."

When we turn to Paul, we find that much of his thought derived from his interpretation of the effect of Jesus' death and Resurrection as redemptive liberation. The fourth article (the first of two on Paul) explores Paul's ideals of leadership, on the one hand, and his realism in bridging the gap between belief and practice through his teaching on the formation of conscience on the other hand.

David M. Stanley, S.J., is Professor of New Testament Studies at Regis College, Toronto, and Visiting Professor at the Gregorian University in Rome. From the time of publication of *The Apostolic Church in the New Testament* (1965) to his most recent book, *Jesus in Gethsemane* (1980), Father Stanley has been a moving force within the modern Catholic biblical movement in North America. He is a past President of the Catholic Biblical Association. One of his principal concerns in his lecturing and writing is to relate biblical exegesis to spirituality, as he does in his article here, "Idealism and Realism in Paul: Liberation Christology and Christian Leadership."

While Paul stressed unity and abhorred divisions within the Christian community, the fact remains that he himself was a controversial figure within his own Jewish community. To treat the ethical problem of dissent within a religious community and the moral dilemma which results for both dissenter and those against whom they dissent, we offer a perceptive article by James A. Fischer, C.M.

Former Provincial of the Western Province of the Vincentian Fathers, and past President of the Catholic Biblical Association, (1977), James A. Fischer, C.M., has specialized in the area of biblical ethics. After earning his doctorate at the Pontifical Biblical Institute in Rome, Father Fischer taught in several seminaries, and is presently Professor of Scripture at De Andreis Seminary (Chicago Theological Union). He is an author, retreat director and television commentator. One of his most significant contributions to biblical studies has been accomplished through his lectures given in many parts of the world, in recognition of which he was awarded an honorary degree by Niagara University.

In "Dissent Within a Religious Community: Romans 9-11," Father Fischer uses the example of Paul as a dissenter within his own Jewish community. Paul did not separate himself from them, yet his prophetic message set him at odds with Jewish groups. Father Fischer finds in the literary expression of Paul's situation "basically a series of antithetical images from the past: poetic sayings from the Old Testament." Just as Paul adopted and formed his own self-image on the basis of the prophetic image of his past, so the modern dissenter must be thoroughly convinced of one's self-image of speaking for God or for a higher morality. Fischer says that one is forced to honesty. He draws attention, it seems to me, to a model for the most critical issue of our time: the possibility of nuclear destruction. As increasing numbers of people take the lonely road of dissent, expressing that dissent in civil disobedience, and aware of the consequences of being ostracized, they will need the inner conviction that only faith in the Lord Jesus and concern for the very existence of our planet can give.

"It devolves on sacred bishops 'who have the apostolic teaching' to give the faithful entrusted to them suitable instruction in the right use of the divine books, especially the New Testament . . ." (*Dei Verbum,* Ch. VI, 25) We close this "New Testament Themes" section with an article which has a double significance: its subject matter, and its author. In light of the quotation from Vatican II, let me comment on the author.

Archbishop John F. Whealon represents clergy serving in the hierarchical level of the Church who combine their service with scholarly pursuits. After earning a licentiate degree in Sacred Theology he pursued a licentiate in Sacred Scripture. He then founded Borromeo Seminary for the diocese of Cleveland where he taught Latin, Hebrew and Sacred Scripture. Since 1961 he has been an auxiliary Bishop of Cleveland, Bishop of Erie, and Archbishop of Hartford where he currently serves.

The above quotation from Vatican Council II reminds us of the principal role of the bishop as teacher of the faithful. This role is most often partially fulfilled through delegating the teaching to others who have the time and expertise. Archbishop Whealon's article represents more directly the fulfillment of this responsibility.

Secondly, it seems fitting to close this section of our book with a look at the last book of the New Testament Canon: Revelation. The reader will recall our remarks on apocalyptic made at the beginning of this section in introducing Paul Achtemeier's article. We have in Archbishop Whealon's article an example of greater emphasis on the second aspect of apocalyptic, i.e., considered as a literary genre. Of course one must keep in mind that Professor Achtemeier's formal purpose was to trace the development of apocalyptic beginning with the earlier writings of the New Testament through the gospels, and therefore the emphasis was on the "shift" in thinking. Archbishop Whealon concentrates on a single work of the New Testament whose very name suggests the literary genre of which we speak. The reader will conclude, I think, that the author of Revelation had no intention of giving time tables for events centuries beyond the time of writing, while at the same time the author is very much concerned with a spirit of courage, of faith, and of hope.

An Apocalyptic Shift In Early Christian Tradition: Reflections On Some Canonical Evidence

PAUL J. ACHTEMEIER
Union Theological Seminary in Virginia
Richmond, VA 23227

There has been something of a resurgence of interest in the recent past in apocalyptic ideas and literature. Not only the SBL group that worked so long and fruitfully in this area, but also the work of E. Kasemann, first in his essays, and more recently in his massive commentary on Romans, shows this interest. More recently still J.C. Beker has attempted to incorporate some insights into the apocalyptic nature of much of Paul's thinking into his fine study of Pauline theology, *Paul The Apostle*. If one accepts the notion — and I do — that much of Paul's thinking is shaped by apocalyptic expectations and understandings, one is struck by the fact that in the Deutero-Pauline literature these tendencies are muted, and a reinterpretation of apocalyptic imagery and categories seems to be underway. Awareness of that fact prompts a further question: if there is a reinterpretation of apocalyptic categories as one moves from the Pauline to the later, Deutero-Pauline literature, is there a similar reinterpretation observable in the gospel literature as one moves from the earlier to the later Gospels? It is that question that we shall pursue in this study.

We shall consider, first, some of the components in the shift from an apocalyptic, or better an apocalyptically-shaped outlook in the genuine Pauline epistles to a less apocalyptically-shaped outlook in the Deutero-Pauline material. Second, we shall undertake a similar examination of the Gospels, moving from the earlier to the later examples of this genre, to see whether or not we can discern a similar kind of reinterpretation. A very brief look at some implications growing out of this investigation will conclude the paper.

I am going to make a series of assumptions in this study which I am confident I can defend, but I shall not take the space to do so at this point. With respect to the Pauline literature, I assume the secondary character of Colossians and Ephesians, along with the Pastoral epistles. The remainder I consider to be authentic, with the possible exception of 2 Thessalonians, which I shall here regard as non-authentic. With respect to the Gospels, I assume that Mark is the earliest, that Matthew and Luke used it as a source but independently of one another, that the latter also used a second source in common known as "Q," and that the Gospel of John was written independently of the Synoptics and probably as the last in chronological sequence. Those assumptions will influence the shape of my conclusions, but not the problem.

I also assume as a definition of "apocalyptic" the three items identified by J.C. Beker in his book on Paul; again this topic can be, and has been, argued at great length by those who know a great deal more about it than I do, but for good or ill, I will presume that one is dealing with apocalyptic when the following three elements are present: "(1)

historical dualism; (2) universal cosmic expectations; and (3) the imminent end of the world."[1] That means, as E. Kasemann has observed, that within such a way of thinking, "the world has a definite beginning and a definite end" and therefore "the course of history . . . takes a definite direction and is irrevocable, articulated into a series of epochs clearly distinguishable from each other."[2] For our purposes, I would also accept Kasemann's insight that the opposite of such a view is represented by Gnosticism, since, as he observes, "all Gnosis testifies to the present nature of salvation, and in so doing, diverges from apocalyptic."[3] It is the shift from future to present understanding of aspects of salvation with which we will concern ourselves in this investigation.

It must also be noted that I am limiting myself to the canonical form of the literature under investigation. One could argue that this is an impermissible oversimplification of the problem. What of the material in canonical Mark that antedates its present form in the Gospel? What of the material from "Q" which may not be as old as, or perhaps even older than, Mark? Would not one need first to establish all the traditions on their origin and age, before an attempt can be made to discern trends, such as the attempt undertaken in this article? Yet more than a century of scholarly work has failed to achieve a consensus on precisely such questions as the wording and age of "Q" or the nature of pre-Marcan traditions. To wait until such results are achieved would mean to abandon a project such as this entirely. This is not, of course, to argue that such attempts at specification of pre- and non-canonical material ought to be abandoned. But might it not be the case that the discernment of such a trend as we are investigating in materials we do in fact possess in something like their original form might enable us to discern trajectories that could be useful in finding answers to questions precisely about the pre- and non-canonical forms of the traditions? It is on the possibility that the latter may be the case that this article has been undertaken in its present form.

Finally, by way of caveat, let me make clear that I do not intend to discuss whether or not Jesus himself held apocalyptic convictions. I am investigating the view expressed in certain early Christian writings which were later declared normative, i.e., canonical, and shall not, in this paper, raise the question of the views of the historical Jesus. Any conclusions one may reach from a study such as this would surely have some implications, at least, for questions about the historical Jesus, and I should not want to deny that fact for a moment. It is simply the case that I am not raising that question, and therefore shall not pursue it in this paper.[4]

Involved in all of this, of course, is the problem posed for the primitive Christian community by the delay in the cosmic shift of aeons, i.e., the delay of the parousia. However such apocalyptic expectations arose, they are present in our earliest Christian literature (Paul's letters), and the delay caused problems. One way to solve the problem is to deny there really is a delay. This is the course taken in 2 Peter, where it is asserted that there is no real delay because God reckons time differently than we do, and his "soon," or even "immediately," may take a millennium or two the way we experience time.[5] Thus there is no delay, only a misunderstanding. A second solution is to diminish the importance of the delay by saying that much of what had been expected to occur as a result of the shift is, in fact, already present reality. Salvation has already occurred; our resurrection is a present reality, and therefore the final judgment has already taken place. It is this second explanation with which we shall be occupied in this paper.[6] First, then, Paul's view of the relationship between present and future, between this aeon and the one to come.

From Paul Through the Pastorals

There is no question that Paul is convinced that the apocalyptic change from the old to the new aeon is immediately before him, and that indeed its coming is sure.The eschatological gift of the Spirit has already been given as a guarantee of things to come to those who accept Christ (2 Cor 1:22; 5:5), the form of the present age is passing away (1 Cor 7:31), and the eschatological promises of God, having found their fulfillment in Christ (2 Cor 1:20), are now confirmed (cf. Rm 15:8-12; 1 Cor 1:19). All of that because "the end of the ages has come upon us" (1 Cor 10:11).

Nevertheless, it is equally clear that for Paul, that final transformation still lies in the future. While the resurrection of Christ may have been the first sign of the general resurrection, the first act of the new aeon, as it were, that resurrection remains, to the present, the only act of that first aeon, and one in which Christians do not yet participate.[7] Paul is quite explicit in his argument that for the Christian, participation in Christ's death may be a present reality (e.g., Gal 6:14), but participation in the form of one's own resurrection remains a purely future event.[8] "He who raised Christ Jesus from the dead *will* give life to your mortal bodies" (Rm 8:11); "God raised the Lord and *will* also raise us up" (1 Cor 6:14); "He who raised the Lord Jesus *will* raise us up also" (2 Cor 4:14; emphasis mine). That conviction carries over to, and illumines, the discussion about Christ, in whom the life appeared which overcomes the death introduced by Adam: "As in Adam all die, so in Christ *shall* all be made alive" (1 Cor 15:22); "we have borne the image of the man of dust, we *shall* also bear the image of the man of heaven" (1 Cor 15:49; emphases mine; cf. Rm 5:19). That same point is also made with imagery other than that of bodily resurrection: "We long to put on our heavenly dwelling" (2 Cor 5:2), something we have obviously not yet done; "we want to be further clothed, to have what is mortal swallowed up by life" (2 Cor 5:4-5). Because the general resurrection is future, Paul also speaks of the victory over death in terms of the future. Death continues in the present because it is the last enemy to be overcome (1 Cor 15:26). It is only at the final transformation that death, swallowed up in victory, will lose its "sting" (1 Cor 15:54). That transformation may be coming soon ("we shall not all sleep," i.e. die), but it remains a future event ("we *shall* all be changed," 1 Cor 15:51; emphasis mine). Indeed it is precisely Paul's conviction that the resurrection includes the transformation of the physical body into a body of another order of being (he calls it "spiritual," e.g., 1 Cor 15:44) that makes any notion of present resurrection palpably absurd.

This same unwillingness to speak in any way of present participation in the resurrection, of which Christ is the "first fruit" (1 Cor 15:23), also becomes apparent when Paul speaks of the meaning of baptism. Such participation for Paul is limited to participation in Christ's death. Hence Paul can say that "one has died for all; therefore all have died," and that the result of participation in that death brings about a new kind of life ("that those who live might no longer live for themselves but for him," 2 Cor 5:14-15), but Christ remains the only one about whom resurrection can be spoken of in the past tense (2 Cor 5:15b; the thought is duplicated in Rm 6:4). Paul's discussion of baptism in Romans 6 is perhaps the most compelling demonstration of his unwillingness to speak of the Christian's resurrection as in any way a present reality. The parallelism between entering the water and entering the tomb with Christ, and emerging from the water and emerging from the tomb with Christ, is so perfect as to be unavoidable, yet Paul avoids it. If we *were* united in death, we *shall* be united in resurrection with Christ (Rm 6:5); if we *have died* with Christ, we *shall live* with him (Rm 6:8). If those who have been baptized into Christ have put on Christ (Gal 3:27), and hence have shared Christ's crucifixion to the world (Gal 6:14), they have not yet risen with him in resurrection. The Christian has shared in the dying; at this point, it is Christ alone who does the living which follows such death (explicitly in Gal 2:20: if "I have been crucified with Christ," I do not now live "in him" — rather, "Christ lives in me," i.e., the life remains his; I have not yet taken possession of it). To the last, the resurrection is not something Paul, or any Christian, has "attained"; sharing in Christ's suffering is a present reality, as is "becoming like him in death." But "attain(ing) to the resurrection from the dead" remains in the future (Ph 3:10-12).

With such a view of the resurrection, it is not surprising that in those places where Paul mentions the kingdom of God, the reference to time, when there is such a reference at all, is to the future.[9] This most often takes the form of references to inheriting the kingdom (1 Cor 6:9-10; 15:50; Gal 5:21) although in one place Paul does mention the kingdom in an explicitly apocalyptic passage (1 Cor 15:24; Christ delivers the kingdom to God after destroying all opposing powers).

If an emphasis on wisdom/knowledge can be construed to indicate a present sharing in what otherwise only an apocalyptic future will bring, one would find some counterweight to what to this point has been Paul's exclusively future orientation. Christians can already have the gift of wisdom through the Spirit (1 Cor 12:8), and Paul himself can impart wisdom to those prepared to receive it (1 Cor 2:6, 7). Such wisdom is specifically contrasted with the "wisdom of the world" (1 Cor 1:21; 3:19; 2 Cor 1:12), and is located, indeed incarnated, in Christ (1 Cor 1:24, 30). In both cases its apocalyptic coloration is indicated: it belongs not to the present but to the coming aeon. It is worth noting that Paul discusses wisdom only in his correspondence with Corinth; it would appear to be a response to a problem unique to them, and not something Paul included generally in his preaching.

Paul can also speak of the presence of salvation and glorification, realities which belong within an apocalyptic frame of reference (e.g., Rm 8:30; 10:10), yet they seem to be as much "in process" as they are achieved results (1 Cor 15:2; 2 Cor 3:18). Paul can also, however, identify them as purely future realities (Rm 5:9-10; 10:9 for salvation; Rm 5:2; 8:18; 2 Cor 4:17 for glorification), and references to them as present ought perhaps to be understood in the same way the presence of the Spirit is understood: as the present guarantee of a future reality.

If there is ambiguity about those elements, there is none about the fact that for Paul the judgment of the world and its inhabitants by God is a future reality. If, because of Christ's presence, the old age is already passing away (1 Cor 7:31; cf. 2 Cor 4:16), it will clearly not come to an end before God's final judgment has occurred, with its punishments and rewards (Rm 14:10; 1 Cor 3:8, 13, 14; 4:5; 2 Cor 5:10). When that "day of Christ" will occur is, of course, not known (1 Th 5:2), but only after it has occurred will the new age dawn, with its freedom from bondage to decay (Rm 8:21), its deliverance from divine wrath (1 Th 1:10), and its universal praise of God (Rm 14:11; Ph 2:10).

In sum, if Paul can assure his readers that "now is the day of salvation" (2 Cor 6:2), and that for anyone in Christ the old has passed away and the new has come (2 Cor 5:17), he reserves his sharpest scorn for those who make this their exclusive emphasis and assume that the riches of the new age are already present in their full reality (1 Cor 4:8-9: "All of you, no doubt, have everything you could desire. You have come into your fortune already. You have come into your kingdom — and left us out. How I wish you had indeed won your kingdom . . ." NEB). That reaction makes clear enough, I think, where Paul's major emphasis lay: on the future, when alone the final judgment and the resurrection would occur, God's rule would be universal and visible, and humanity along with the rest of creation would be transformed into a new order of reality. Such elements as were already present were harbingers, guarantees of that glorious future, but no more than that.

When we turn to the Deutero-Pauline letters, however, we find a significant shift in emphasis. We learn, for example, that the "eschatological reservation" with respect to resurrection is gone. As we have been buried with Christ, so we have been raised with him; both Colossians and Ephesians complete the logical extension of Paul's baptismal metaphor (Col 2:12; Ep 2:5-6). Because we have been raised with Christ (Col 3:1), we already "sit with (God) in heavenly places in Christ Jesus" (Ep 2:6), and can be urged to "awake ... and arise from the dead" (Ep 5:14). Interestingly enough, the word *synegeiro* is used exclusively in Colossians and Ephesians. It is not to be wondered that the Gnostics found this view more congenial than Paul's incomplete baptismal metaphor, and therefore interpreted Romans 6 in light of the view found in Colossians and Ephesians.[10]

While these two epistles have little to say about the kingdom, where there is reference to it, it is treated as a present reality. Thus Colossians says that God "delivered us from the dominion of darkness and transferred us to the kingdom of his beloved son" (1:13), as Ephesians, perhaps in reference to the kingdom, says God has "blessed us in Christ with every spiritual blessing in the heavenly places" (1:3).

If less is said here about the kingdom than in Paul's letters, more is said about mystery and the knowledge of it. The author's purpose in Colossians is to see that people have the "riches of assured understanding and the knowledge of God's mystery, of Christ, in whom are hid all the treasures of wisdom and knowledge" (2:2-3; see also 1:25-26; 4:3). Thus, the gospel can now, as revealing such knowledge, be identified as the "word of truth," the possession of which has allowed us to "put off the old nature . . . and put on the new" (3:9-10). Ephesians is more precise about the content of that mystery: it is the inclusion of gentiles into the plan of salvation (e.g., 1:9; 3:4-6). In that case, the epistle's task is described as helping all people to understand that mystery and its repercussions for cosmic reality (3:8-9).

It is, again, hardly surprising that this link between faith and knowledge appealed strongly to the Gnostics, who found precisely in Ephesians and Colossians the keys by means of which to interpret the remaining letters of Paul.[11]

In line with this attempt to describe as present, realities which for Paul had been largely if not exclusively future, Colossians and Ephesians emphasize the fact that Christ has already triumphed over all spiritual foes (Col 2:10b, 15; Ep 1:19, 21). For that reason we too have already died to those "elemental spirits of the cosmos" (Col 2:20), and any enlightenment those spirits have about the true state of reality will have to come through the church (Ep 3:10). While these epistles know that the Spirit functions in the present as the guarantor of future realities (e.g., Ep 1:13-14; 4:30), a view quite in conformity with that of Paul, they have an additional emphasis on the present power of Christ in the believer that is rather unlike Paul. Thus, Colossians can assure us that we have been filled by Christ, in whom the whole fullness of deity dwelt in bodily form (2:9-10; the *RSV* is misleading here), and Ephesians wants its reader to understand the immeasurable greatness of Christ's power which is present in us (1:19). Hence we are now "light in the Lord" (Ep 5:8) and have our redemption, which Colossians defines as our forgiveness of sins (1:13; cf. Rm 8:23, where redemption refers to the transformation of reality which occurs at the shift of the ages). If, therefore, one can still speak of the two ages (Ep 1:21), and of the presence of Christ as the hope of glory (Col 1:27), it is in a perspective weighted in the direction of the present reality of the resurrection and hence of participation in other heavenly realities.

The Pastoral Epistles present a similar, if somewhat more muted, tendency. While the only mention of resurrection is a reference to the false view that it has already happened (2 Tm 2:18; perhaps some gnostic-like tendencies are referred to), and the references to the kingdom understand it as a future reality (2 Tm 4:1, 18; cf. references to future judgment in 2 Tm 4:8 and the future coming of Jesus, 1 Tm 6:14-15; Tt 2:13), there is proportionately an increase in concern with the faith as doctrinal content, something to be known and held to. Even the reference to the resurrection occurs in that context. In addition to the use of the phrase *pistos o logos* (1 Tm 1:15; 3:1; 4:9; 2 Tm 2:11; Tt 1:9; 3:8 — it never appears in Paul; his equivalent is *pistos o Theos*, 1 Cor 1:9; 10:13; 2 Cor 1:18), which relates faith and doctrine linguistically, one hears of being nourished on "the words of the faith and of the good doctrine" (1 Tm 4:6), and finds godliness equated to the "sound words" and "doctrines" of "our Lord Jesus Christ" (1 Tm 6:3). One can therefore train oneself in godliness, here understood as holding to sound doctrine instead of to "godless and silly myths," i.e., false doctrine (1 Tm 4:6-7). As in Colossians and Ephesians, it is the apostle's task to propound such sound doctrine (e.g., 1 Tm 1:1-3; cf. 1:9, where it is also the task of "elders"). What else such a transformation of faith into doctrine may do, it tends to concentrate attention on the present rather than the future, and to that extent could perhaps be understood as a shift away from apocalyptic expectations toward present fulfillment. Doctrine, after all, is a present possession. References to the future (1 Tm 6:18-19; 2 Tm 2:10; 3:1; Tt 1:2) are balanced by references to the present (2 Tm 1:10 — Christ abolished death and brought life and immortality; Tt 3:4-5 — Christ by his appearance "saved us") in a way that was uncharacteristic of Paul, where "heavenly realities" remained a thing of the future.

Our survey of the Pauline literature has thus disclosed a shift in apocalyptic expectation away from the future and into the present with a corresponding increase in emphasis on realities which are now at work in the world. We saw this in relation to the idea of the general resurrection, and if somewhat less in regard to the kingdom, then certainly more in respect to the knowledge of mysteries and the possession of wisdom. If the difference is, to some extent at least, in degree rather than in kind (e.g., wisdom), in other instances it is in kind (e.g., resurrection). If the shift was less pronounced in the Pastorals, we saw even there a kind of balancing of emphases on present and future; even the emphasis on marriage shifts from Paul's: avoid it if possible (1 Cor 7:26, 29) to the Pastorals': by all means use it to solve the problem with younger widows (1 Tm 5:14).

We must now turn to the second part of our task, viz., to inquire whether a similar shift along similar lines is visible as we move from earlier to later Gospels.

The Gospel View

We shall follow the same pattern in our investigation of the Gospels as we did when we looked at Paul, i.e., resurrection, kingdom of God, knowledge and mystery/mysteries, and other indications of present or future realities.

There are, of course, no accounts of the appearance of the risen Jesus in Mark, although it is clear that Mark knew he had risen (e.g., 16:6). What it may mean that Matthew and Luke add them, as later tradition felt compelled to add them to Mark, we will discuss when we come to Matthew and Luke. Otherwise, with few exceptions — Jesus is falsely identified as a risen John the Baptizer; Jesus assumes, contrary to the Sadducees, that the dead will rise — the word is applied to predictions of Jesus' own resurrection.

The kingdom of God for Mark is resolutely future. If the scribe who knew that love is superior to burnt offerings was not far from the kingdom, he was not in it (12:34); and if the disciples have been given the secret of the kingdom, they have not yet been given the kingdom itself (4:11). The theme of Jesus' preaching is the approach, not the presence, of the kingdom (1:15), as Jesus' whole career is probably to be understood in Mark as the working out of that programmatic announcement, as it was also to be the career of Jesus' disciples (6:12). To be sure, the kingdom was coming soon — within one generation (9:1) — but even casual references to it make clear its futurity (e.g. 9:47; 10:15, 24-25; 14:25; 15:43). Those parables that are identified as speaking of the kingdom point to the relation between present acts and future outcomes (4:3-9, 26-29, 30-32; 12:1-11) — thus underlining again the coming, not the presence, of the kingdom. Even the exorcisms, to the extent they are related to the coming of the kingdom, function as a sign of its coming, rather than as a sign of its presence. Satan's power, if challenged, has not been eliminated. He can still snatch away the word which has been heard (4:15). If the presence of the kingdom means Satan's defeat, it is not yet present, since his defeat has yet to occur.[12]

The categories of mystery and knowledge are also of minor importance for Mark. The two are not connected in Mark 4:11 (the only use of the word "mystery" in Mark), and "knowing" refers more often to perceiving the importance of an event than the comprehension of some content (disciples fail to perceive, 6:17; Jesus does not want to be recognized, 5:43; 7:24; 9:30; things are perceived, 5:29; 12:12; 15:10, or known, 13:28-29, as a matter of course; things are ascertained, 6:38; in no case is "knowing" used in any technical sense).

There are, of course, indications that the kingdom is very near; Elijah has already come (9:12), and Satan is being robbed (3:27). Those who have left family for Jesus and the gospel already receive as reward a larger family (10:28). Demons wonder aloud whether their apocalyptic doom has dawned (1:24; cf. 3:11). Only if Jesus were casting out demons by the power of the prince of demons, however, would it mean that Satan's kingdom has collapsed (so 3:23-26). There is, to be sure, a new situation in Jesus' presence (2:21-22) which people recognized (e.g., 2:12), but the full reality remains future. It is Elijah who has come, not the kingdom, and Elijah/John's message points to the future, not the present (1:7). The reward of good, if startling, acts remains in the future (9:42-48; cutting off offending body parts). If the shift of aeons will happen in Jesus' generation (13:30), it has not occurred yet (14:62; cf. 13:26), and no one knows precisely when in the future it will (13:32-33). If Jesus will give no sign about himself (8:11-12), there will be cosmic signs in the future that will allow no questioning that the time of the kingdom has finally come (13:24-27). His followers knew well enough that the kingdom had yet to come; they had time to ask for special treatment when it did (10:35-40). The parables made it clear enough; only at the end does the resolution come. There is no proleptic realization of the harvest before it occurs. Until it comes, its reality may be anticipated, but not enjoyed. The emphasis is on a future reality, and the shadow it casts before it remains just that, a shadow, and not the substance.

When we come to Matthew and Luke, some subtle changes have occurred. Let us consider them in that order.[13]

It is clear enough that Matthew shares the apocalyptic notion of two ages, since he refers to the present as well as the future age (e.g., 12:31-32; 13:39, 40, 49; 24:3; 28:20).[14] Any changes in eschatological outlook will, therefore, occur within that apocalyptic framework. There are such changes vis-a-vis Mark, however.

There are, in the first instance, accounts of the appearance of the risen Jesus. However one may want to account for their generation, their inclusion in Matthew indicates, I would want to suggest, a tendency toward seeing this harbinger of the new age (i.e., the resurrection of the dead) already being accomplished in this age. Christ's appearances make clear in a vivid way the reality, already in the present age, of that aspect of the future age. But not only Christ's resurrection. Matthew also notes further apocalyptic fulfillment in relation to the resurrection in the events he describes as contemporaneous with it: both the details of the resurrection of Jesus himself (28:1-4 — the earthquake, perhaps caused by the angel) but also a more general resurrection, verified by eye-witnesses (27:51b-53). Thus the reality of the new age is already introduced! The final pronouncement in the Gospel promises in a way unknown from

Mark the continuing presence of Jesus (28:20b), thus introducing the reality of the coming age into the present one.
With respect to the kingdom of God (kingdom of
Heaven in Matthew), the change is not so pronounced. The
kingdom lies in the future. That is so much taken for granted
that in even casual references, where the futurity is not the
point, it is presupposed (e.g., 5:19, 20; cf. also 10:17; 16:28,
where the "Son of Man coming in his kingdom" is equivalent
to the coming of the kingdom of Heaven, as 13:41, 43 make
clear). The coming will occur within Jesus' generation
(16:28). Two sayings, both from "Q," have been interpreted
by some scholars as meaning that the kingdom is already
underway (11:12; 12:28), but the sayings will also sustain an
interpretation that limits this coming to the future.[15] If the
struggle against Satan is portrayed in these passages as
being underway, it is nevertheless not yet completed, and
hence the new age remains future.

With respect to knowledge, there are some further, if
also subtle, shifts. The disciples are no longer pictured as
largely, if not completely, incomprehending. Where Mark
implies the disciples have misunderstood the parable of the
sower (4:13), Matthew has a blessing (13:16-17) on them
because they have understood.[16] The parable session as a
whole is concluded with an undisputed claim by the disciples
that they have understood (13:51). On at least two other
occasions, Matthew adds a comment making clear that the
disciples understood the events in which they participated
(16:12: they understood the "leaven"; 17:13: they understood about John the Baptizer). Underlying this is the subtle
but I think highly significant change in what it is that distinguishes disciples. It is not, as in Mark, that they have been
given the secret of the kingdom, an idea of some inherent
unclarity. In Matthew, they have been given to know the
secrets of the kingdom. Knowledge is now the key category,

and the disciples bear that out in Matthew's account. To that extent, at least, the new age makes its presence felt as reality now.

Again, Matthew is clear that the kingdom is future, if imminent. This notion, taken from Mark (e.g., Mt 16:28; 23:34 — "in this generation") is reinforced (10:23 — it is to come before the mission to Israel is completed). Even sentences of holy law point to the "imminent invasion of the Parousia."[17] The judgment accompanying its coming also plays its part in making clear that the kingdom is not yet (e.g., 10:40-42; 12:36-37; so esp. some parables: 13:24-30; 13:47-50; 25:31-33), as does the reference to cosmic signs which must precede its coming (24:26-31). In one instance, a reference to the present reality of the kingdom is deleted from the Marcan source (a reward for leaving family seems to be solely future: cf. Mt 19:27-29 with Mk 10:29-30).

Such a change is balanced by others, however, that point in the opposite direction. In addition to the massive evidence that Jesus fulfills Scripture and therefore is himself the new reality, the demons wonder whether Jesus' activity against them means an acceleration of the apocalyptic timetable (8:29: "have you come against us *before the time?*"), and the assignment to Peter and the church of the apocalyptic keys (16:18-20; cf. 18:18-20 — the keys do after all control access to the new age) shows Matthew's inclination to see in the church the presence of the new reality. Such an idea is further supported in 10:41, where the Lord is present in the activity of those who proclaim the gospel.[18]

Much has been written about Luke's attempt to come to terms with a delayed parousia, attempts which include the presence of the Spirit as substitute for the new age, and a new periodization of the history leading up to that age.[19] Here, clearly, there is movement toward accounting for the delay with an emphasis on the present reality of the new age.

If, as we suggested, appearances of the risen Jesus also belong to such a view, Luke's accounts give further evidence of the "apocalyptic shift"; the risen Christ, capable of eating (24:41-42), promises "power from on high" (24:49), a promise fulfilled at Pentecost (Ac 2). The general resurrection, of course, remains a wholly future event (e.g., 14:14; 20:34-37).[20]

With respect to the kingdom, Luke, as other Synoptics, awaited a sudden incursion of the kingdom (12:40; 17:26-36) within Jesus' generation (9:27; 21:31-32), and thus anticipated a "speedy vindication of God's elect" (18:7-8b). Its coming will include a necessarily future judgment (e.g., 10:13-15; cf. 3:15-17). But there are also hints that Luke thought of it as being already present. Rewards for leaving family are, as in Mark, already available (18:29-30), and if the "kingdom among you" (17:20-21) is, as the context shows, to be understood in the future sense,[21] it is nevertheless clear that in one case at least, Luke's special material recalls Jesus announcing the kingdom as already given to the disciples (12:32; the verbs are in the aorist: "it *pleased* your Father to *give* you the kingdom")

As in Matthew, there is in Luke increased, if subtle, emphasis on knowledge. Lawyers face the accusation from Jesus that they took away from the people the key of knowledge, and the saying about things hidden and revealed, present both in Mark and in "Q," is given twice in Luke, but both times in the form that nothing hidden will not be made *known* (8:17; 12:2). As in Matthew, the disciples have the gift of *knowing* the mysteries of the kingdom, as a gift confirmed when the risen Christ, as his final act on earth, opens the minds of the disciples to understand Scripture (24:45). To that extent, one suspects, Luke felt that the reality of the new age, present in Christ, was also now present with the disciples.

There are, of course, numerous indications that Luke held to the idea of a future consummation, preceded by cosmic signs (21:8-28), yet coming in a way that confutes all attempts to reckon its time (12:40-48), and bringing with it appropriate rewards and punishments (e.g., 6:35-38; 14:14; 16:9). Yet the evidence is unmistakable that some of those future realities are being moved into the present. There is the fulfillment motif (e.g., 4:18-21, 23-27); and Jesus' response to the question of John ("Are you the coming one?"), turning on miracles worked in response to the query, points to Luke's understanding of miracles as sharing in the power of the kingdom (7:18-23; Luke's addition of v. 21 and the use of the aorist in v. 22 underline his view). Jesus' comment that he saw Satan fall "like lightning" from heaven, unique to Luke, indicates that exorcisms also share in the apocalyptic defeat of the one who rules this age (10:18), an insight confirmed by v. 19 which describes the power now given to Jesus' followers (it is "over all the power of the enemy").[22] The adaptation of "Q" in 12:8-9 (acknowledging or denying the Son of Man has consequences), so that all references to apocalyptic events and the coming of the Son of Man are eliminated, and the placing of it in a context of present activity (esp. vv. 10-21) making it appear the consequences are immediate, not necessarily future, shows a similar bent,[23] as does the added material about the Baptizer's message, which assumes a continuation of society, not its imminent end (3:10-14).

In a similar way, Luke puts his added account of the mission of the Seventy into a context in which their announcement that "the kingdom of God has come near you" (10:9, 10) could mean nothing less than their announcement that Jesus was coming and thus that where he was, there the kingdom also was (cf. 10:1 — Jesus sent them "into every town and place where he himself was about to come").

Talbert's observation that "in Luke-Acts *sozein* applies almost exclusively to the present" also shows this tendency.[24] If one adds to that, Jesus' statement to the penitent thief on the cross that his entry into paradise was indeed imminent ("this day," 23:42-43), one has a picture of immediate access to the kingdom in the presence of Jesus, an emphasis which can only be described as different from that of Mark.

It is when one comes to the Gospel of John that the kind of shift we found from Paul to the Deutero-Pauline literature becomes most evident.[25] This is apparent already in the area of resurrection. Jesus appears, and gives to the disciples what in Luke they receive only later: the Holy Spirit (20:19-23). What for Luke is an event in the life of the church is moved forward in John into an event in Jesus' life. Jesus' prediction that the time is coming when the dead, on hearing God's voice, will come forth from the tombs, an event clearly belonging to the apocalyptic shift of the ages, becomes reality when Jesus summons Lazarus from the tomb; I take the similarity between these two passages to be other than accidental (5:28-29a — in both there is a cry, and the dead emerge). Jesus' announcement that he is the resurrection and the life, in correction of Martha's specific reference to the apocalyptic event, confirms John's relocation of resurrection for the Christian from future to present (11:23-26a).

Although John used the phrase "kingdom of God" sparingly (3:3, 5 only), it seems clear that the function of the kingdom is taken over in John by the reality designated "eternal life." That such eternal life is also a present reality needs only to be mentioned to gain assent from those who know John's Gospel (e.g., 5:24; so also is divine sonship a present reality, 1:12).[26]

There is a significant increase in John over the Synoptics in the emphasis on the role of knowledge. It is knowledge of God that separates good from bad in John (e.g., 17:25). Those who cannot understand Jesus thereby make clear that they are not his followers, but rather his opponents, who belong to, and are characterized by, the "world," almost surely the Johannine equivalent of the apocalyptic "this world" or "this age" (e.g., 8:27, 43, 55; 16:3). The disciples, on the other hand, are precisely the ones who do understand (e.g., 8:31-32; 10:14-15, 27; 17:7-8). If for a time such understanding eludes them (e.g., 10:6), John makes clear that this period will end with Jesus' resurrection. At that point, one is tempted to say, apocalyptic wisdom will be the disciples' possession (e.g., 12:16; 13:7; 14:20). Indeed, it is precisely such knowledge which constitutes, or at least, characterizes, the apocalyptic gift of eternal life (17:3).

One must be careful, however, not to overstate the case. References to the future and what it brings for the believer and unbeliever alike abound in John. The general resurrection (5:28-29) occurring on "the last day" (6:39, 40, 44, 54), salvation (10:9), eternal life (10:28), judgment (12:48) — all are to occur in the future, when Jesus returns for his own (14:3).

Yet if some things remain for the future, they are overwhelmed, even swallowed up, by the present. In some cases both present and future are mentioned (e.g., 6:54: the one who eats *has* eternal life and *will be raised up* on the last day; a similar play on dying and not dying appears in 11:25). Far more often, however, it is solely the present on which emphasis is laid.[27] Jesus' glory was visible to his followers (1:14; 2:11; 13:31), and the judgment awaited at the turn of the ages has already taken place (3:18-19; 12:31; cf. 5:26-27), as has the receiving of eternal life (5:24; 6:47; cf. 8:51). Those who accept Jesus already enjoy the food of the messianic banquet, which stills all further hunger and thirst

(4:14; 6:35). The passing from the darkness of ignorance into the light of knowledge and life, again a figure of the turn of the ages, occurs in John with the coming of the Paraclete. What is confusing to the disciples during Jesus' incarnate life is clarified with the coming of the Paraclete, which turns what was future during Jesus' lifetime into the "present time" of the church. If Jesus must go away before the Paraclete can come (16:7), then after he has gone and is risen, it does come (20:22), bringing with it judgment (cf. 16:6), truth (15:26; 16:13), or whatever the disciples may request (16:23; cf. 15:7, 16). Indeed, it may even be that Jesus himself returns as the Paraclete (14:28, in the context of the coming of the Paraclete). Therefore, for John, the eschatological harvest is now (4:35) and the disciples may participate in an activity (4:38) which in the synoptic parables was a symbol of the apocalyptic future. Here clearly, what was once awaited at the time of the parousia is now declared to be within the grasp of contemporary believers.

Conclusions

Our cursory examination of the shift that apocalyptic thinking underwent in the primitive Christian community as shown in some of the literature it produced — the Pauline letters and the Gospels — shows that to some extent at least both types of literature solved the problem of the delay in the shift of aeons in a similar way, viz., by declaring that much of what had been awaited in the future was, in fact, to be understood as present reality. The shift observed between the genuine letters of Paul and the Deutero-Pauline material was duplicated most clearly in the shift from the Synoptic to the Johannine perspective, although hints of that shift were already present as the Synoptic tradition moved from its initial formulation in Mark to its expansion in Matthew and Luke.

The similarity of that shift in apocalyptic thinking obviously has many implications for our understanding of the growth and development of tradition within the primitive Christian community, and even beyond its confines. While a careful examination of those implications lies beyond the scope of our present investigation, we may briefly sketch out two that come immediately to mind.

First, the existence of such a similar development within two types of tradition that had no evident literary connections with one another (i.e., the Pauline materials with the gospel material) may point to a tendency more widespread and uniform within the primitive church than might have been suspected. Such a move from future to present would lie along a trajectory that would finally make a gnostic solution seem not only plausible but desirable, and would indicate why that way of understanding reality appeared so fascinating to many who were attracted to the Christian faith.

Second, if the movement we have noted has been accurately traced, then the enthusiasm to which Käsemann, among others, has given so much attention was not the original, but a derivative form of primitive Christian faith. It is not the case that Paul represented an interruption in the stream of enthusiasm which led from his opponents in Corinth to the community behind Colossians and Ephesians; instead, the latter community represented an outgrowth from the Pauline and resulted from the delay in the return of Christ. Such a way of understanding the trajectory is borne out by the similar trajectory found in the Gospels, from earliest to latest.[28] Whether or not the movement of apocalyptic thinking, from future to present, however, is an accurate tracing of movement within the primitive Christian traditions, only further, and more detailed study will reveal.[29]

FOOTNOTES

1. J.C. Beker, *Paul the Apostle* (Philadelphia: Fortress, 1980) 136.
2. E. Kasemann, "The Beginning of Christian Theology," *New Testament Questions of Today* (London: SCM, 1969) 82-107, esp. p. 96.
3. E. Kasemann, "An Apologia for Primitive Christian Eschatology," *Essays on New Testament Themes* (*SBT* 41; London: SCM, 1964) 169-95, esp. p. 172.
4. That consequences from this kind of study can be drawn relative to the views of the historical Jesus is shown, e.g., by Kasemann's articles, "On the Subject of Primitive Christian Apocalyptic" and "The Beginnings of Christian Theology," where he has much to say about Jesus' views. See also the work of R.H. Hiers, *The Kingdom of God in the Synoptic Tradition* (Gainesville, FL: University of Florida, 1970), where conclusions different from those drawn by Kasemann are presented.
5. On this whole question, see J.J.M. Roberts, "A Christian Perspective on Prophetic Prediction," *Int* 33 (1979) 240-53 esp. pp. 250-51. See also E. Kasemann, "On the Subject," 131; R.E. Brown, *The Gospel According to John* (AB 29, 29A); Garden City, NY: Doubleday, 1966) cxx.
6. A third solution is to assume that it is indefinitely delayed, and hence no longer important. That is what H. Conzelmann proposed was the case with Luke; on that point, see C.H. Talbert, "Shifting Sands: The Recent Study of the Gospel of Luke," *Interpreting the Gospels* (ed. J.L. Mays; Philadelphia: Fortress, 1981) 197-213; E. Kasemann, "On the Subject," 131.
7. Ibid., 134.
8. This is, of course, the key element in Paul's "eschatological reservation," a term coined by Kasemann (ibid., 132) for an element of Pauline theology known to many independently of Kasemann.
9. Paul does on occasion seem to speak as though the kingdom were present: Rm 14:17; 1 Cor 4:20, but the context makes clear, I think, that he means the way the future kingdom ought to affect the present behavior of those who anticipate its coming.
10. E.H. Pagels (*The Gnostic Paul* [Philadelphia: Fortress 1975] 119) uses the teacher of Rheginos as an example.
11. Ibid., 115, 160, 164.
12. R.H. Hiers, *The Kingdom of God*, 34, 42, 48; see also J.M. Robinson, *The Problem of History in Mark* (2nd ed.; London, SCM, 1962).

13. One could expect, and appropriately, a consideration of the apocalyptic/ eschatological features of "Q." Assuming it is chronologically parallel with Mark, it would help us in plotting changes. Yet the difficulty in isolating the actual wording of "Q" with any degree of accuracy lessens the value of such a consideration for our purposes. That the general lines of "Q" reflect those of Mark in the keen anticipation of the future, with no real idea of experiencing the coming kingdom in the present, can be gathered from a study such as that by R.A. Edwards, *A Theology of Q* (Philadelphia: Fortress, 1976). The differing evaluations of Jesus' death and the emphasis in "Q" on the collected "wisdom" of Jesus do not alter the intense eschatological anticipation which characterizes the material. Absence of overt apocalyptic speculation does not mean "Q" knows nothing of the change of aeons. On the contrary, the silent assumption that such a change is imminent argues that absence in this case means presupposition, rather than lack of awareness. Only on the apocalyptic assumption of a change in aeons does the eschatological eagerness of "Q" become understandable.

14. I owe these references to R.H. Hiers, *The Kingdom of God*, 32, 79.

15. Such an interpretation has been vigorously defended by R.H. Hiers (*The Kingdom of God*) in the relevant chapters.

16. Matthew has used a "Q" saying that reflects the prophecy-fulfillment motif to show that, contrary to Mark, the time is already present when the disciples can understand. On the meaning of this saying in "Q", see R.A. Edwards, *A Theology of Q*, 44-47.

17. The phrase is from E. Kasemann, "The Beginnings," 92. Kasemann suggests that, if Matthew did not actually invent the form, he at least gave it its fullest utilization (p. 93).

18. On this point, see E. Kasemann, ibid., 90-91.

19. In addition to H. Conzelmann, see C.H. Talbert, "Shifting Sands," and more recently J.A. Fitzmyer, *The Gospel according to Luke I—IX* (AB 28; Garden City, NY: Doubleday, 1981), ad loc. Fitzmyer agrees with Conzelmann and Kasemann (pp. 18-19), but with modification (pp. 20-21).

20. I do not find the ambiguity in this verse about whether the "sons of the resurrection" have still to be raised or are already raised which R.H. Hiers (*The Kingdom of God*, 86-87) does. Verses 35 (those who are accounted worthy to attain to that age and to the resurrection from the dead) and 37 (proof of the resurrection from Scripture) convince me that Luke means the resurrection that accompanies the apocalyptic shift in aeons. If there is a question, it is only, as Hiers also notes, whether abstaining from marriage now characterizes those accounted worthy to be raised then.

21. I think R.H. Hiers (*The Kingdom of God*, 22-29) has shown this to be likely.

22. Hier's argument (*The Kingdom of God*, 50-56), that it refers to the future downfall of Satan, is correct in that Satan's rule is not yet ended in the normal apocalyptic sense, but v. 19 suggests some proleptic presence of the kingdom, in my judgment.

23. Although the reference to the Son of Man in 22:69 omits mention of this coming, only including the statement that he will be seated at the right hand of the "power of God," it does not necessarily imply the presence on earth of that Son of Man. Indeed, it implies just the opposite.

24. C.H. Talbert, *Interpreting the Gospels*, 206.

25. Obviously this helps the comparison only if John is the latest of the Gospels, rather than, as is now and again suggested, perhaps even the earliest. If John did, in fact, know one or more of the Synoptic Gospels, the case would be strengthened for this kind of development in apocalyptic thinking from future to present.

26. See R.E. Brown, *The Gospel of John*, cxvii–cxviii.

27. For a similar judgment on what is happening in John, see E. Kasemann, "On the Subject," 131.

28. The fact that "Q" apparently had no account of Jesus' passion and resurrection rules it out as evidence for the kind of pre-Pauline "enthusiasm" Kasemann posits as a theological movement in the very earliest period of the Christian community.

29. Thanks are due to James L. Mays for a careful reading of an earlier draft of this article. As usual, I benefited from his encouragements and suggestions.

The Eucharist In Mark:
Mission, Reconciliation, Hope

DONALD SENIOR, C.P.
Catholic Theological Union
Chicago, IL 60615

Contemporary liturgists emphasize that in order to
grasp the full meaning of the liturgy one must be sensitive to
the power of its medium: gesture, symbol, music, word. It is
not enough to be doctrinally acute and ritually correct; to
experience Eucharist one must be open to the texture of its
presentation.

A similar conviction guides contemporary biblical
studies, especially in the area of gospel research. Scholarship has evolved from a consuming interest in the history
and development *behind* the text to savor the language and
literary power of the text itself. The use of metaphor, the
power of narrative, the deep structure of literary forms:
these are some of the new interests of contemporary gospel
study.

This article . . . will attempt to join the interests of
liturgy and Scripture by examining some passages of Mark's
Gospel related to Eucharist. In Mark's Gospel, of course,
there are no abstract discussions of Eucharist; references, if

they are present, must be detected in the symbols, metaphors and movement of Mark's narrative. By close attention to the fabric of Mark's story we might be able to detect what the experience of Eucharist meant for his community, or at least what the evangelist wanted the Eucharist to mean.

Two sets of texts will be examined: the feeding stories of 6:30-44 and 8:1-10 and the Last Supper of 14:12-31. Basic concerns of Mark's overall theology are exhibited in each text and each of these texts gives leads to Markan perspectives on the Eucharist.

One Bread for Two Peoples: Eucharist and Mission in Mark 6:30-44 and 8:1-10

Almost all recent interpreters of Mark's Gospel recognize that discipleship is a major concern of the evangelist. Each of the Gospels portrays the disciples as those characters in the narrative with whom the Christian reader can identify in a special way. In the disciples' call, their ongoing relationship with Jesus and the mission offered to them, Christian readers are able to discover dimensions of their own Christian existence. The uniqueness of Mark lies in the particular tones he gives to his portrayal of the disciples.

There is little question that Mark, along with the other gospel writers, affirms important positive features of the disciples. They are called to "follow" Jesus and to share in his eschatological mission of "fishing" for people (Mk 1:16-20). They are privileged witnesses of his powerful mission and the recipients of his private instruction (4:11, 34; 7:17; 10:10, etc.). They are promised their rewards in the final days (10:29-30). The "Twelve" are formally commissioned (3:13-19), sent out on mission (6:7-12), and experience the success of that mission (6:13, 30). As Ernest Best has insisted, these positive traits must not be overlooked in any assessment of discipleship in Mark (E. Best).

Yet the peculiar contribution of Mark seems to lie not in the positive affirmations about the disciples — a point he shares with the other Gospels — but in their *negative* traits, an emphasis much more pronounced in Mark than in any other Gospel (cf. J. Tyson, T. Weeden, R. Tannehill, etc.). There are numerous incidents in Mark's account where the disciples cannot comprehend Jesus or his mission and even occasions when their own viewpoint seems to stand in opposition to that of Jesus. To cite some of the more obvious examples: they fail to understand the parables of Jesus' teaching (e.g., Mk 4:13; 7:18); they are baffled by Jesus' walking on the water (Mk 6:51-52); they exhibit exclusive attitudes, for which Jesus corrects them, as in the case of the exorcist of 9:38-41 and the children of 10:13-16; after each of the Passion predictions, the disciples display attitudes diametrically opposed to the self-donation that is a hallmark of Jesus' own teaching and example (cf. Mk 8:32; 9:32-34; 10:35-45). The most glaring examples come in Mark's Passion narrative where the disciples are presented as abject failures: one of the Twelve becomes Jesus' betrayer (14:10-11), the leader of the disciples publicly denies knowing him (14:66-72), and all sleep during Jesus' critical prayer (14:32-42) and flee in panic at the moment of his arrest (14:50), including one who bolts away without his clothes (14:51; cf. H. Fledderman). In Mark's story none of the chosen disciples are present at the crucifixion of Jesus, the event which is obviously the center point of the entire Markan story.

Many interpreters see this mass of evidence falling into a perceptible pattern: the disciples move from a "lack of understanding" during the Galilean ministry of the first eight chapters, to more overt "misunderstanding" during the journey narrative of 8:22 to 10:52, and finally to "failure" in the passion story of chapters 14 and 15 (cf. Tyson, Weeden, Tannehill, Perrin). This movement indicates that the failure of the disciples is a deliberate literary and theological construction of the evangelist.

Although there is widespread agreement that Mark does, in fact, emphasize the failure of the disciples, there is little consensus of *why* he does so. It is generally agreed that by his negative image of the disciples Mark intends to critique attitudes or stances within his own community, but hypotheses about the nature and extent of Mark's target differ widely.

My own viewpoint is that Mark does *not* intend to focus on a single faction or doctrinal aberration by means of his discipleship material. The Gospel is not ultimately a polemic; it remains "Gospel," that is, a broadly based proclamation to his community (cf. R. Pesch, R. Martin). The disciples, both in their positive and negative features, are *representative* of Christian responses and attitudes; some to be affirmed as the heritage of all Christians, others to be exposed and critiqued as deviations from authentic Christian existence.

It is at this point we can turn to the feeding stories of 6:30-44 and 8:1-10; here, too, are important instances of discipleship failure. On at least two occasions, Mark indicts the disciples for their inability to *understand about the loaves.* After the account of Jesus' walking on the water, Mark notes that the disciples fail to understand the meaning of this manifestation of Jesus' identity because "they did not understand about the loaves, but their hearts were hardened" (6:52), a reference to the feeding story (6:30-44) that had immediately preceded the sea story. An even more pointed indictment comes after the second feeding story. The disciples misunderstand Jesus' reference to the "leaven" of the

Pharisees (8:15); they presume he is speaking about the sparse provisions ("only one loaf" 8:14) they had brought with them in the boat. Jesus' reply to the disciples is strongly stated; their lack of perception is explicitly connected with the two previous feeding stories:

> ... Jesus said to them, 'Why do you discuss the fact that you have no bread? Do you not yet perceive or understand? Are your hearts hardened? Having eyes do you not see, and having ears do you not hear? And do you not remember? When I broke the five loaves for five thousand, how many baskets full of broken pieces did you take up?' They answered, 'Twelve.' 'When I broke the seven loaves for the four thousand, how many full hampers of fragments did you collect?' And they said to him, 'Seven.' And he said to them, 'Do you not yet understand?' (8:17-21).

Note that Mark is drawing attention to *both* feeding stories; the disciples' lack of perception (these same images of "seeing" and "hearing" are used as metaphors for a lack of faith in Mark 4:12, drawing on the quotation from Isaiah 6:9-10) is related to Jesus' power to multiply sufficient provisions ("five . . . for the five thousand"; "seven . . . for the four thousand") into an abundance on two different occasions ("how many baskets full of broken pieces did you take up?").

What then is the disciples' problem about the loaves and how does this help us understand an important dimension of Eucharist in Mark's Gospel?

First of all, it has long been obvious to interpreters of Mark (and we may presume to Mark's first readers) that the evangelist relates the feeding stories to the Eucharist. The actions of Jesus in both stories — "taking" the loaves, "looking up to heaven," "giving thanks," "breaking bread" and "giving" it to the disciples (cf. Mk 6:41 and similar words in 8:6) — and the reference to the abundance of "fragments" *klasmata* (6:43; 8:6), a term used in later liturgical texts to refer to the Eucharist, brings the feeding stories into a clear relationship with the institution account of 14:22-26 and with the liturgical experience of the early community (Donfried, Van Canghe, etc.). In other words, Mark sees several layers of meaning in these feeding stories: they are obvious messianic deeds, recalling the feeding of Israel in the desert (Ex 16) and the final eschatological feeding at Zion (Is 25), and they display the power of Jesus on behalf of a needy people reflecting the mighty acts of Elijah the prophet. And now they are seen as reflective of the post-Easter experience of the community, encountering the nourishing power of the Risen Lord in their midst.

These interpretations, we may presume, were already part of the feeding story as it came to Mark. But in Mark there are *two* stories, and it is on this point that the specific interests of Mark emerge. Whether Mark created a second story or whether two came to him in the tradition must remain a moot point, cf. on this Donfried (one story) and Achtemeier (two stories in connected miracle "chains"). In any case it is Mark who has placed these stories in their present narrative framework. The first story (6:30-44) follows a section in which Jesus has encountered the unbelief of his own village (6:1-6) and then sent the Twelve out on mission (6:7-13, 30-31). A flashback to the death of John seems to suggest that the fate of the Christian mission, as with the fate of Jesus himself, will be to encounter opposition and death (6:14-29). The feeding story that follows takes place in *Jewish* territory, but the mission issue has already been raised (Kelber).

The placement of the second feeding story is equally auspicious. It caps a journey begun in 7:24 ("And from there he arose and went away to the region of Tyre and Sidon ...."). The immediately preceding scene (7:1-23) is the long controversy with the Pharisees over cultic purity and dietary laws, culminating in the radical declaration that "all foods are clean" (7:19). The encounter with the Greek woman in 7:24-30 where her faith overcomes the "children first" (7:27) principle of salvation history clearly shows that Mark sees this entire section as a portent of the Gentile mission of the community (Kelber, Hahn).

The second feeding, then, is clearly a feeding of *Gentiles;* Jesus returns to Jewish territory on the other side of the lake only in 8:10. Thus the Markan Jesus feeds both Jews *and* Gentiles.

It is equally significant that Mark has made both feeding stories discipleship stories as well. In both instances the disciples propose sending the crowds away rather than attempting to feed them (6:35-36; 8:4). In view of Mark's comments in 6:51-52 and 8:17-21 there is no doubt that he interprets the disciples' reactions as less than innocent. Even though Jesus involves them in the process of feeding the crowds (in both instances the disciples are instructed to distribute the loaves to the crowds: cf. 6:41; 8:60), they have not understood that the mission of Jesus is to feed *both* Israel and the Gentiles.

In other words, the disciples' lack of understanding probed by Jesus in 8:17-21 concerns the inclusive mission of the community; the church is to encompass both Jew and Gentile. The numbers referred to may also symbolize this: The "twelve" baskets (8:19) being an obvious symbol of the twelve tribes of Israel, and the "seven" (8:20), a possible reference to universalism (Van Canghe, Harrington).

For our purposes, it is important to note that by means of these stories Mark has related the universal mission to the *Eucharist.* It is only natural that the tensions experienced in the early community over the profound pastoral issue of the mission to the Gentiles should have come to a head at the Eucharist. The struggle to open up the community's horizon to outsiders would have created a parallel set of tensions *within* the community, between Jewish Christians and Gentile Christians. Other New Testament texts clearly relate controversy about the mission to the question of shared "table fellowship" between Jew and Gentile, as in the Cornelius story of Acts 10-11 and in Paul's accusations against Peter in Galatians 2:11-12.

In the face of such tension, Mark seems to be reminding his community that its own universal mission was rooted in the messianic mission of Jesus; Eucharistic table fellowship meant one bread for different people, just as Jesus, with insufficient provisions, fed the hungry multitude on both sides of the lake. The disciples in the Gospel story failed to grasp the meaning of the feeding stories, with disastrous consequences for themselves; the disciples of Mark's own community should be careful not to repeat such obtuseness.

The Bond of Discipleship: Broken and Healed: Mark 14:12-31.

Following the lead Mark gives the reader in the feeding stories, we now turn to another "bread" story, that of the Last Supper; by paralleling the actions of Jesus in both sets of stories Mark draws our attention to both.

As in the case of the feeding stories, attention to the narrative framework supplied by Mark helps bring out new dimensions of the Institution story and may also help us sense deeper tones of the eucharistic experience of the Markan community. Traditional exegesis of this passage has focused heavily on historical issues (Did Jesus celebrate a final meal with his disciples? And was it a Passover meal? Is

the Synoptic or Johannine chronology to be preferred? etc.)
or on doctrinal issues (How much of later sacramental theology is reflected in this text? Is a theology of real presence or
sacrifice present? etc.). But attention to the narrative setting
points to other issues that may have been more specific to
Mark.

Many scholars (e.g., Donahue, Perrin, etc.) credit Mark
with placing the supper story in the context of the Passion.
The farewell meal of Jesus with his disciples becomes part of
an ongoing passion story that will move from the introductory scenes of chapter 14 through the account of the
arrest, trials, death, burial and finally, the discovery of the
empty tomb. If we give Mark credit as the storyteller who
shaped large portions of this passion narrative into its present configuration, then it is very illuminating to note the
immediate context he gives the supper story: it is surrounded
by predictions of radical discipleship failure. In 14:17-21,
Jesus predicts his betrayal by Judas, "one of the Twelve"
(14:20); in 14:27-31, he predicts the denial by Peter and the
desertion by all the disciples. This is a clear instance of what
J. Donahue calls Mark's "sandwich" technique (Donahue).

These poignant predictions of discipleship failure serve
as a vivid counterpoint to an emphasis on the bond between
Jesus and his disciples that is a natural part of the whole
supper story. Mark dramatizes preparations for the meal
(14:12-17): it is the Passover and Jesus intends to eat this
special feast with his disciples (14:14). The preparations
underline both the solemnity of the occasion (14:12-17) and
the union between Jesus and his followers (14:12, 14, 15,
17). The meal itself has obvious significance as a bond between Jesus and the disciples, a point made explicit in the
text: all eat the bread broken (14:22) and all drink of the cup
(14:23), all sing a hymn together (14:26). This emphasis on
the bond of table fellowship is poignantly contrasted with an

emphasis on the bond *broken* in the predictions: the betrayer is characterized as "one of you . . . one who is eating with me" (14:18), as "one of the twelve," "one who is dipping bread into the dish with me" (14:20). The resistance of Peter and the disciples to Jesus' prediction of their failure (cf. 14:29, 31) also draws attention to the bond about to be broken.

However, along with an emphasis on discipleship failure in the supper texts, Mark also stresses the *triumph* of Jesus and ultimate *reconciliation* with the disciples. This is a point often underplayed in recent interpretations of Mark, so it deserves careful attention. Even though there are good reasons for concluding that the institution account is a pre-Markan tradition, this does not mean it is unrelated to previous motifs of his story. First of all, the theme of self-donation ("take; this is my body" "this is my blood of the covenant, which is poured out for many" 14:22-24) which is surely one level of meaning in the words of institution echo the tone and content of several of Jesus' sayings earlier in the Gospel. Self-donation on behalf of the many characterizes the mission of the Son of Man (10:45) and it is to be the attitude of the disciples who must "deny themselves and take up their cross and follow me" (8:34), who must "lose their lives for my sake and the gospel's" (8:45), who must be "the last of all and servants of all" (9:35), who must abandon all to follow Jesus (10:28-29), who must "drink the cup" Jesus drinks and be baptized with his baptism (10:38) (both the "cup" and "baptism" are allusions to his self-giving death on behalf of others).

In view of these important texts it is not surprising that at the final fellowship meal, the Markan Jesus describes his impending death in the terminology of self-donation: his person and mission are bread and wine given as life-giving nourishment on behalf of the many (14:22-24).

Note, too, that Mark's supper story emphasizes the

ultimate efficacy of Jesus' mission. A solemn dominical saying promises that Jesus will drink the wine of the covenant "new in the Kingdom of God" (14:25). Again, important links with deep currents of Mark's Gospel are forged. Mark, in concert with the other synoptics, presents the coming of the Kingdom as the keynote of Jesus' entire mission (1:14-15). The mystery of that Kingdom was shared with the disciples (4:11) and its coming in power is assured (4:28, 32; 9:1; 13:26; 14:22).

The saying in 14:25 takes into account Jesus' impending death: "Truly I say to you, I shall *not drink again* of the fruit of the vine *until* . . ." But beyond death comes the sure victory: "when I drink it *new in the Kingdom of God.*" It should be noted that this same affirmation — reality of death but assurance of victory — characterizes most of Mark's references to Jesus' death, particularly those predicted by Jesus himself. The Son of Man will be handed over to death, but on the third day he will be raised up (cf. the passion predictions of 8:31; 9:31; 10:33-34).

This emphasis in the supper story on the ultimate victory of Jesus (an obvious theological assumption of the entire Gospel of Mark) is paralleled by an assurance of the ultimate rehabilitation of the *disciples.* Here, again, is an important aspect of Mark's supper story sometimes overlooked because of the novelty of Mark's emphasis on their failure. In 14:27, the Markan Jesus predicts the breakdown of the disciples: "You will all be scandalized, for it is written, 'I will strike the shepherd, and the sheep will be scattered.'" But that prediction of failure, which fulfills the scripture (cf. also 14:49), is matched by a dominical saying of equal weight and surety: "But after I am raised up, I will go before you to Galilee" (14:28). A promise of failure is followed by a promise of reconciliation and renewal.

This promise is the one repeated by the "young man" at

the empty tomb in 16:7, "But go, tell his disciples and Peter that he is going before you to Galilee; there you will see him, as he told you." Recent scholarship is sharply divided on the interpretation of Mark 16:1-8: is it to be understood as an effective promise of reconciliation for the disciples, or should the women's silence as they leave the tomb (16:8) be taken as a final instance of discipleship failure, with the result in Mark's story that the disciples never get the message of resurrection and, as a result, remain in their disarray? (Perrin, etc., Weeden, etc.)

As R. Meye and others have argued, however, the ambiguities of a single verse should not cancel out sureties provided by the rest of the Gospel. Here is where the supper texts are so crucial: the evangelist has already taken into account the failure of the community (14:27), but places alongside that Jesus' equally efficacious promise of reconciliation (14:28). The Son of Man will come in power (13:26) and will drink the wine of fellowship new in the Kingdom of God (14:25). These texts and the whole brunt of chapter 13 which presumes the ongoing and world-wide mission of the community (13:10) should determine the interpretation of 16:1-8. The women's "fear," "silence" and "ecstasy" (16:8) as they leave the tomb should be seen as an expression of awe resulting from their encounter with the power of God and his heavenly messenger, not as a subtle device by which the evangelist overturns his entire theological and narrative construction with a sudden O. Henry-like ending.

Therefore, the ending of Mark's Gospel is an efficacious promise of reconciliation: the "disciples and Peter" (the order in 16:7 may reflect the order of the failure in the passion story) are to return to Galilee, the place of the mission (Van Canghe). There they will "see" and be reconciled with the Lord they had failed. Thus the promise made by Jesus at the supper before his death is triumphantly ratified by a heavenly messenger at the tomb after Jesus' resurrection. Jesus overcame death, not only the death that destroyed his body but the death that engulfed his fragile community in the passion story.

If this interpretation of the Markan story has merit, then it can be said that the evangelist has linked the institution account with themes of discipleship failure *and* discipleship reconciliation. At the table of the Lord, both the impending failure and the ultimate hope of the disciples are revealed. Here, I would suggest, is an important glimpse into the Eucharistic experience of the Markan community. Why such emphasis on failure and on reconciliation in connection with Eucharist? Many interpreters of Mark have suggested that the Gospel was composed for a community that had suffered persecution. This may be deduced from the strong emphasis on the passion, as well as from explicit references to persecution in 4:17; 10:30; 13:9-13; etc. The reference in 4:17 has particular importance, I believe. In an allegorical interpretation of the sower parable, the evangelist explains the seeds sown on rocky ground as those "who when they hear the word, immediately receive it with joy; and they have no root in themselves, but endure for a while; then, *when tribulation or persecution arises on account of the word, immediately they fall away*" (4:16-17). Mark's community knew persecution and it also knew the bitter experience of apostasy: the persecutions created martyrs but also failures, undoubtedly with bitter consequences for relationships within the community.

If this was the case, then we can surmise why Mark links this issue with Eucharist. Although we have no explicit information about the cultic life of Mark's community, it seems reasonable to suppose that the gatherings of Christians to celebrate agape meals or the Eucharist were in relatively small groups or house churches. For someone to break this kind of bond through apostasy, perhaps even by collaboration with the persecutors, or public renunciation of one's ties with the Christians, would be a stunning blow to the community's morale and a source of bitter alienation between those who remained in the community and those who fled. It does not take much imagination to reflect that the Eucharistic meals might well become the arena in which these tensions exploded: between those who stayed and those who had fled but now wanted reconciliation, or between those who stayed and the relatives and friends of those who had apostatized. Second repentance, as we know from Hebrews and other texts, was a stumbling block for the early Christian community.

Does Mark intend to deal with this source of pain and alienation in his community in the way he tells his story of the passion? Should the community be so easily disillusioned with the failure of the disciples? Could reconciliation be refused to members of the church who had panicked and fled or publicly renounced their faith or even betrayed it, when Jesus himself had offered reconciliation to his own apostatized disciples, who, by the way, went on to become the foundation of the community?

Eucharist:
Mission, Reconciliation, Hope

The issue of mission and persecution which we have detected in the Eucharistic texts of Mark lend credence to the traditional assignation of Mark's Gospel to Rome. From Paul's correspondence we know that the role of Jew and Gentile in salvation history, and the scope of the Christian mission were issues debated in the Roman church. We also know from other sources that the Roman church suffered persecution under Nero. And we can also detect in Mark's passion theology tones not unlike that of Pauline theology (Martin). The Roman origin of Mark cannot be proven, of course, but this locale, shortly after the persecution of Nero, seems as reasonable a hypothesis as any.

More to the point of this article is the intriguing fact that the evangelist has linked Eucharistic texts with some of the most painful pastoral questions of his church: mission and reconciliation. Both involved deep divisions that may have erupted at the Eucharistic celebration; both involved painful alienations which could only be healed and ultimately reconciled in the table fellowship of Eucharist. There, Jew and Gentile could share the one bread; there, too, a sadder-but-wiser church could repent of its failures and once again take up the bond of discipleship. The source of hope in both instances was not to be found in the fragile disciples themselves but in the compasion and strength of the Risen Christ.

FOOTNOTES

Achtemeier, P. 1970. "Toward the Isolation of Pre-Markan Miracle Catenae," *Journal of Biblical Literature* (89), 265-291.

Best, E. 1977. "The Role of the Disciples in Mark," *New Testament Studies* (23), 377-401.

——— 1981. *Following Jesus: Discipleship in the Gospel of Mark* (Journal of New Testament Studies; Supplement 4; Sheffield: University of Sheffield Press).

Donahue, J. 1973. *Are You the Christ?* (Society of Biblical Literature Dissertation Series 31; Missoula: Society of Biblical Literature).

——— 1976. "From Passion Traditions to Passion Narrative," in *The Passion in Mark* (W. Kelber, ed.; Philadelphia: Fortress), 1-20.

Donfried, K. 1980. "The Feeding Narratives and the Marcan Community," in *Kirche* Festschrift fur Gunther Bornkamm zum 75. Geburstag. (D. Luhrmann & G. Strecker eds.; Tubingen: J.C.B. Mohr), 95-103.

Fledderman, H. 1979. "The Flight of a Naked Young Man (Mark 14:51-52)," *Catholic Biblical Quarterly* (41), 412-418.

Hahn, F. 1965. *Mission in the New Testament* (Studies in Biblical Theology 47; Naperville: Allenson).

Harrington, W. 1979. *Mark* (New Testament Message 4; Wilmington: Michael Glazier).

Kelber, W. 1974. *The Kingdom in Mark* (Philadelphia: Fortress).

Martin, R. 1973. *Mark: Evangelist and Theologian* (Grand Rapids: Zondervan).

Meye, R. 1969. "Mark 16:8 — The Ending of Mark's Gospel," *Biblical Research* (14), 38-43.

Perrin, N. 1976. "The Interpretation of the Gospel of Mark," *Interpretation* (30), 115-124.

_____ 1977. *The Resurrection According to Matthew, Mark, and Luke* (Philadelphia: Fortress).

Pesch, R. 1980. *Das Markusevangelium* (Vol. 1; Freiburg: Herder).

Tannehil, R.C. 1977. "The Disciples in Mark: The Function of a Narrative Role," *Journal of Religion* (57), 386-405.

_____ 1979. "The Gospel of Mark as Narrative Christology," *Semeia* (16), 57-59.

Tyson, J. 1961. "The Blindness of the Disciples in Mark," *Journal of Biblical Literature* (80), 261-268.

Van Canghe, J-M. 1972. "La Galilee dans l'evangile de Marc: un lieu theologique?" *Revue Biblique* (79), 59-75.

_____ 1974. "La multiplication des pains dans l'evangile de Marc. Essai d'exegese globale," in *L'Evangile selon Marc: Tradition et Redaction* (M. Sabbe, ed.; Leuven: University of Leuven Press), 309-346.

Weeden, T. 1971. *Mark: Traditions in Conflict* (Philadelphia: Fortress).

Christ's Resurrection
As Mystery Of Love

GERALD O'COLLINS, S.J.
Gregorian University
Rome, Italy

Living in the land of Dante has made me realize that something essential was missing from the scheme of interpretation models which I presented in *What Are They Saying about the Resurrection?*[1] That book outlined and developed six such models for reflecting on the many-faceted mystery of Christ's rising from the dead: his resurrection as (historical) event, as redemptive, as revelatory, as the ground for faith, as the divine promise which grounds hope, and as the trigger and content for the Church's proclamation (pp. 7-10). What that list lacked was the model of love. My main justification for the gap comes from the fact that theological reflection on Christ's resurrection in terms of love has been slight or simply absent. In this article I plan to review first the little I have found written on the topic and then suggest ways for interpreting the resurrection as a mystery of divine and human love.

I

Some authors who use love as a major or even primary focus when discussing other Christological mysteries fail to do so when they come to the resurrection. Hans Urs von Balthasar is a case in point. His classic *Love Alone*[2] pointed the way for a theology largely developed around the divine glory and love in *Herrlichkeit* (1961-1969) and *Theodramatik* (1973-1978). *Love Alone* presents the incarnation (p. 45) and the crucifixion (pp. 94-95) as mysteries of love, but does not really do the same for Christ's resurrection. At best this is only hinted at when von Balthasar describes both the crucifixion and the resurrection as "the dramatic appearance of God's trinitarian love" — that is to say, the revelation of "the Trinity's loving struggle for mankind" (p. 120). Even this partial and passing link between love and the resurrection loses its impact, when the author at once switches to another idea, the power at work on the dead Jesus and then on his disciples:

> It was not a harmless 'teaching' which tore the decomposing corpse of the sinner (!) from the grave that had been sealed for three days and which roused the disciples whose courage had gone, transforming them into witnesses to the Resurrection throughout the world (p. 120; translation corrected).

The *Von Balthasar Reader*[3] provides a 50-page introduction and includes 112 representative texts to offer a comprehensive view of his key themes. In the context of the resurrection as trinitarian event, von Balthasar remarks that "God the Father . . . with the resurrection of Jesus . . . established the primitive Christian core of dogma: God is love" (p. 113). Apart from this, the *Reader* neither reports nor quotes any exposition of the resurrection in the key of love. Von Balthasar's contribution to theology lies elsewhere.

If one examines the various writings on Christ's resurrection by von Balthasar's great contemporary, Karl Rahner, the yield on love is likewise slight. Apropos of the experience of the disciples at the first Easter, he observes in passing that this "experience includes the encounter" with Jesus' "love and fidelity."[4] But generally when he deals with the resurrection, Rahner's interests are different: the inner relationship of Jesus' death to his resurrection, the revelation of the resurrection, the role of transcendental hope in the free act of accepting the resurrection, and so on.[5]

In a section (pp. 230-237) of his *Introduction to Christianity*[6] Joseph Ratzinger briefly expounds belief in the resurrection as "faith in the love that has conquered death" (p. 237). He finds "the basic problem of human existence" in the fact that love demands indestructibility. But "this cry of love's cannot be satisfied . . . it claims eternity but in fact is included in the world of death." If we confront this common human problem, we can see how faith in Jesus' resurrection means believing in "the greater strength of love in the face of death" (p. 230). Ratzinger interprets the link between love and death as follows:

> Only when someone values love more highly than life, that is, only where someone is ready to put life second to love, for the sake of love, can love be stronger and more than death (p.232).

Specifically, "Jesus' total love for men," which led him to the cross, was "perfected in total stepping-over to the Father" and thus became stronger than death, because in this passage he was taken up and totally "held" by the Father (p. 233).

In what precise way does Ratzinger hold that love effected the resurrection?

(a) Apparently the central point is the Father's love towards Jesus. What Ratzinger says later about our hope for resurrection and God as "the lover" who in the face of death "has the necessary power" (p. 271) seems also to be the main thrust of the argument here. In the case of the Father's love for Jesus, "the power of love for another" was so strong "that it could keep alive not just his memory, the shadow of his 'I,' but that person himself" (p. 232). In that way Jesus was enabled to overcome death by "living on in another," whose love took the beloved Jesus "into its own being," and thus made possible "this existence in the other" (p. 233).

(b) What role did Jesus' own (human) love play — and, in particular, his "total love for men"? Seemingly Ratzinger suggests that it also brought about the resurrection. As we have seen above, Jesus was someone who valued love more highly than life. Where (and only where) someone is ready to put life second to love, love can prove stronger than death. At the same time Ratzinger rules out the possibility of other human beings, apart from Jesus, exemplifying this power: "Our own love, left to itself, is not sufficient to overcome death; taken in itself it would have to remain an unanswered cry" (p. 234). This argument clearly raises a question about the human powers of the historical Jesus. Did his generous, "total" love in some way literally effect his own personal, glorious resurrection? Did Jesus rise because his (human) love not only "demanded" that from the other (his Father) but also in and of itself proved stronger than death? It is not altogether clear that Ratzinger is saying this. I return to the point shortly.

(c) In any case Ratzinger's statement about Jesus' love (which sounds like a general principle), "*only* where *someone* is ready to put life second to love . . . *can* love be stronger . . .

than death" (italics mine), obviously needs some qualifications. It is certainly not meant to rule out resurrection for those human beings and Christians who do love others but not in a way which shows that they are truly ready to put life second to love. (Apropos of this, the judgment scene in Matthew 25:31-46 presents the righteous as being rewarded with eternal life not because they have literally surrendered their lives through love, but because they helped the hungry, the sick and others in need). Nor should the statement "only where someone . . ." be taken to exclude in principle the resurrection for judgment of those who, so far from putting life second to love, have sinned grievously against love. Despite "only," "someone" and "can," Ratzinger intends the statement not so much as a general axiom, but as a comment on the way Jesus' destiny once and for all put an end to death's power and opened up a new, definitive life. In that unique case the power of love proved stronger than death and brought for all human beings the new stage of risen life. Hence the resurrection means that "he [Jesus] who has love for all has founded immortality for all . . . *his* resurrection is *our* life." His love and only his love, "coinciding with God's own power of life and love, can found our immortality" (p.234).

In Ratzinger's brief treatment of the credal article, "rose again from the dead," the following links between love and Jesus' resurrection are made: God (the Father) was "the lover" who had the power to raise Jesus to new life — point (a); through the divine power Jesus' love proved life-giving for others — point (c). What is not totally clear is whether Ratzinger wants to maintain point (b) — that Jesus' self-giving (human) love also worked as a this-worldly cause to effect the resurrection.

Bela Weissmahr certainly does intend to hold (b). He argues that Jesus' utter surrender in love worked as an immanent cause in producing the resurrection or at least the great sign of the resurrection, the disappearance of his corpse from the grave. Ultimately the resurrection was a creative act of God, but Jesus' unique (human) love for God and neighbor also came into play to bring about that effect.[7] This interesting thesis is unfortunately not developed very much, even if the other matters which Weissmahr discusses have some relationship to love. The author remains faithful to the title of his article, which does not promise to restrict itself to the power of love.

Thus far I have sampled some contemporary Catholic writers. Apart from eight pages by Ratzinger and a briefly stated thesis by Weissmahr, there is scarcely anything to mention about attempts to elucidate Jesus' resurrection in terms of love. In his 1979 survey article on "The Resurrection of Jesus in Catholic Systematics" (see n. 5), John Galvin covers such authors as Rahner, Walter Kasper, Hans Kung, Edward Schillebeeckx, Jon Sobrino and von Balthasar, but (apart from a footnote reference to Weissmahr's article) has nothing to report on the theme of love. Recent discussions of the resurrection have dealt with other issues like the very nature and meaning of "resurrection," the relationship of Jesus' dying and rising, the question of the empty tomb, and the revelation of the resurrection. An earlier, two-part study of the theological and exegetical writing on Jesus' resurrection (coming from a wide range of Christian authors) also had nothing to say about the topic of love.[8]

It occurred to me that Teilhard de Chardin might have analyzed the resurrection in the light of love. After 1930 he worked out a view of love as the force in a world which is dynamically converging towards Christ, the one Omega point and unifying goal of everything. Then Teilhard often expressed a wish to die on the day of Christ's resurrection; in fact he did die on Easter Sunday 1955.

Drawing on the letters of Saint Paul, he wrote about the "cosmic attributes" of the risen Christ.[9] He saw the resurrection as a cosmic event in which Christ overcame matter's resistance to spiritual ascent, effectively assumed his functions as center and focus of the universe, and guaranteed the upward and forward development of the cosmos.[10] Nevertheless, Teilhard did not normally have a great deal to say about the resurrection precisely as such. Rather, he spoke much more of the incarnation as it dynamically unfolded towards its future completion[11], and was flanked by creation, on the one hand, and by Christ's redeeming death, on the other. Hence even though Teilhard acknowledged the risen Christ as the "Personal Heart of the Cosmos" who inspires and releases the basic energy of love which progressively carries both humanity and the universe towards its future goal,[12] nevertheless, he did not tend to associate love explicitly with the event of the resurrection. A note on the mystery of love from his unpublished personal retreat in 1945 typifies a mind-set which turned more easily towards Christological mysteries other than the resurrection: "Creation — *the generative aspect;* Incarnation — *the unitive aspect;* Redemption — *the laborious aspect.*"[13]

The present Pope draws some lines between the resurrection and God's merciful love in his encyclical letter, *Dives in misericordia* (30 November 1980). John Paul II speaks of "the Son of God, who in his Resurrection experienced in a radical way mercy shown to himself, that is to say the love of the Father which is *more powerful than death*" (n. 8). In this event which he personally experienced Jesus revealed a merciful love, which continues to show itself more powerful than death (and sin) for all who live "in a world that is subject to evil." Christ "has revealed in his Resurrection the fullness of the love that the Father has for him and, in him, for all people" (ibid). Here the papal teaching turns on two notions (experience and revelation) which surface throughout the whole encyclical. At the same time, even though John Paul II expounds the resurrection in the key of love, the treatment is slight and occurs in an article (n. 8) which places considerably more emphasis on Jesus' cross as the sign of God's merciful love.

To conclude this first section I should also mention Rosemary Haughton's *The Passionate God*,[14] an imaginative attempt to interpret the essentials of Christian faith through the idea of romantic love. She calls Chapter 4, "Resurrection" (pp. 129-173), "the center of the book" (p. 129). Yet much of this chapter is spent exploring other, albeit related, themes like the role of Mary, the training of the disciples, and the passage to Calvary of a Jesus who was driven by "the inner logic of Romantic passion" (p. 146). Apropos of the resurrection, the most significant thesis affirms Jesus' liberation to love his Father in a complete fashion: "the resurrection" was "the moment of breakthrough, the explosion of fully reciprocated love" which knew "itself free of all restriction." At last Jesus could "give back to the One he loved the unshackled fullness of love" (pp. 152f). In a later section of the book Haughton examines the life experienced by those baptized into the paschal mystery. There she speaks of the resurrection as "the leap by which the body of Jesus begins to live in those bodies of his lovers" (p. 230). They are moving towards the final consummation which she calls "the unimpeded outpouring of divine love" (p. 231). Haughton thus offers a few suggestive hints towards a presentation of Christ's resurrection in terms of love. But her book delivers its principal message elsewhere — in the reflections on the incarnation, "the supreme and constitutive instance of passionate breakthrough" (p. 130).

II

Having produced some evidence for my theory that little has so far been developed on Jesus' resurrection as a mystery of love, I want to consider what such an approach could entail, Not surprisingly it is a matter of exploring a number of relationships: that of the Father towards the crucified Son, that of the risen Jesus towards his Father, that of the Holy Spirit towards the Father and the Son, that of the risen Jesus towards all men and women, and that of human beings towards the risen Lord.

To expound in any detail the Father's love which the crucified Christ experienced in the resurrection, one needs some account of what love involves. Here I do not wish to indulge an enormous parenthesis and discuss at length what philosophers, theologians and others have written on the various forms of love — from Plato, the Song of Songs, the *Bhagavadgita,* John and Augustine in the ancient world, through Abelard, Bernard, Aquinas and Dante, down to Martin D'Arcy, de Rougemont, C.S. Lewis, Nygren and Spicq in our own century.[15] My own reading and reflection suggest the following working description of what true Christian love (and indeed genuine human love) should involve.

(1)   Love wills the good of others; it acts and works for their welfare. The New Testament clearly privileges this aspect of love. To a lawyer who questions him about inheriting eternal life, Jesus tells the parable of the good Samaritan and twice insists on the activity of love in the service of God and neighbor: "*Do* this, and you will live . . . Go and *do* likewise" (Lk 10:28, 37). Paul's version of love in 1 Corinthians uses fifteen verbs to present the active ways in which love expresses itself (1 Cor 13:4-7). 1 John likewise indicates that "love must not be a matter of words or talk; it must be genuine, and show itself in *action*" (1 Jn 3:18).

(2) Common experience constantly illustrates love's power to deliver others from all kinds of evil and danger. It can heal human wounds, both great and small. Love brings to life those who have suffered spiritually, psychologically and physically. Love acts to transform persons who in different ways have become disfigured; love can make the ugly beautiful.

(3) Love not only saves and changes what is already there, but it also generates and creates what does not yet exist. Human procreation is the usual paradigm for this generative and creative power of love.

(4) Besides "being for" others, love also welcomes others and desires to "be with" them. Where hatred breaks down interpersonal communication and rejects the presence of others, love seeks the presence of those whom it loves and communicates with them (Jn 5:20; 15:15).

(5) Finally, love intends to be eternally faithful. It affirms immortality and wishes that its object would never die. In "A Metaphysic of Hope" Gabriel Marcel illustrates how the communion of love maintains indestructibility. To "love someone is, in effect, to say, 'You will not die.' "[16]

Ever so much more could be said if one wanted to cover the whole ground very thoroughly. But even this brief, working description of love allows one to elucidate that love which Jesus experienced after the crucifixion when the Father raised him from the dead (Gal 1:1, etc.).

1. On Calvary the cry of abandonment (Mk 15:34) brought no powerful word from heaven; the divine help was not forthcoming. But in the resurrection the Father's love showed itself supremely active. In raising the dead Jesus it worked for his ultimate welfare and highest good.

(2) That love "healed" Jesus who had suffered the final wounding of death. It saved him from definite decay and destruction (Ac 2:24-31). It brought him to new and

everlasting life. Love transformed Jesus who had become disfigured and ugly, "a man of sorrows" who "had no beauty, no majesty to draw our eyes, no grace to make us delight in him" (Is 53:2f). In resurrection he was taken up into the radiance of divine glory (Lk 24:26; Jn 17:1; Ph 2:9-11; 1 Tm 3:16; 1 P 1:21).

(3) Within the life of the Trinity the Son is not created but eternally begotten — from all eternity born "from the womb of the Father" (the Eleventh Council of Toledo; DS 526). In the language of Nicaea, "there never was (a time) when he was not" (DS 125). With the earthly Jesus, however, a real death meant that there came "a time when he was not." In the resurrection the Father's love *re*generated and *re*created to new life the dead Jesus whose human existence had been terminated by crucifixion.

(4) To describe the resurrection as the Father's full and final welcome to the incarnate and crucified Son might sound poetical rather than properly theological. Nevertheless, it seems a reasonable gloss on that "going to the Father" (Jn 13:1, etc.) which runs as a leitmotiv through the last discourse in John's Gospel. Likewise the image of "being exalted at the right hand of the Father" (Ac 2:33f; Rm 8:34; Ep 1:20; etc.), besides indicating how the risen Christ is revealed in his divine glory and saving power, also points to his Father's receiving him into a full presence and perfect communion of life (Rm 6:10). Jesus' interpersonal communication with the One whom he called "Abba" was interrupted by death, only to be restored in a new and final way.

(5) Lastly, in raising Jesus from the dead, the Father showed the fidelity of his love (cf. 2 Cor 1:18). To name Jesus as "the Son whom I love" (Mk 1:11; 9:7) was tantamount to saying, "I will not abandon him to death" (see Ac 2:25-31). Human beings speak brave words of love, but know their weakness in the face of death. The Father's word

of love, however, was powerful when spoken over the corpse laid to rest near Calvary: "You will not perish in death but will live forever."

What then of Jesus' love for his Father and his "total love for men"? (Ratzinger; see also Weissmahr) During his ministry that love drove Jesus to be utterly subject to his Father's will and to be completely available for the service of those who needed mercy and healing (Mk 10:45a; Lk 22:27). In a reckless way Jesus gave himself totally to the service of the present (Mt 12:28 par) and future (Mt 8:11 par) rule of God, that final offer of salvation for sinful and suffering men and women. He identified himself with the divine concern to forgive and save human beings.

In *Interpreting Jesus*[17] I drew together the evidence for maintaining that Jesus anticipated and accepted the violent death to which his ministry of obedience and service led (pp. 79-92). His love proved to be not only dangerous for him but also deadly. He surrendered and gave himself away in love. This meant pain when others refused to respond (Lk 13:34; 19:41), loss of freedom (Mk 14:43ff), and finally the radical diminishment of death. All of this raised and left open the question: Could such love for God and neighbor ever bring personal fulfillment and happiness? Or did (and does) truly self-forgetful love ultimately produce only self-loss and self-destruction?

The resurrection showed that the "going-out-to-others" and "being-for-others" which Jesus practiced, even at the cost of his life, finally meant a "coming-to-himself." His self-forgetfulness brought the ultimate self-fulfillment of risen life. His earthly existence, which had been lived and lost in love, was raised to its definitive state as the supreme case of losing and finding one' life (Mk 8:35 par). His loving fidelity to his Father and to those he served made him give up all — only to receive all through the Father's fidelity to him. The utter self-giving of Calvary was more than matched by the greatest gift of all, the transformation of resurrection.

As raised to new life, Jesus could give back to his Father a "fully reciprocated love" (Haughton). Their dialogue, which at the level of Jesus' humanity had been interrupted by death, could now be resumed in a full and final way. In the resurrection Jesus "experienced the love of the Father" (John Paul II), and could thus respond in love — giving as well as receiving.

This fresh and final dialogue of love consummated a life and death in which Jesus' relationship with his Father and with the human beings he served had been empowered by the Spirit (Mk 1:10, 12; Lk 4:14, 18; etc.). As the personal agent of the resurrection (Rm 8:11), the Holy Spirit could "spiritualize" Jesus' humanity to the ultimate degree (1 Cor 15:42ff) and restore in a transformed way that dialogue between Jesus and his Father which death had broken off. In these terms we can call the resurrection a trinitarian event of love — with the Spirit as the personal exchange of love between Father and Son.

Here I want to distance myself from the versions of the paschal mystery developed by Jurgen Moltmann[18] and Eberhard Jungel.[19] Moltmann's understanding of Jesus' passion, death and resurrection sees it all primarily as an event within God: the human history of pain is part of the history of the Trinity. In the passion Christ experiences the pain of being temporarily abandoned and cursed by his Father. Yet the Father is equally affected by the suffering of the crucifixion: "The Son suffers dying, the Father suffers the death of the Son. The grief of the Father is just as important as the death of the Son."[20] The Holy Spirit intervenes to reconcile Father and Son and re-establish the trinitarian community of love.

Jungel interprets the paschal mystery as a story of dynamic love which moves from life to death for the sake of a richer and deeper life to come. To achieve a much deeper union of love with the Son (and through the Son with the whole human race), the Father is willing to sacrifice his relationship with the incarnate Son. At the moment of Jesus' death the union between Father and Son is recovered, when as the bond of love the Spirit reunites Father and Son (and goes on to work as the power of love in human hearts and minds).[21]

There are many problems with the interpretations of Moltmann and Jungel. In both cases God ceases to be immutable and is intrinsically changed through the death and resurrection of Jesus. It is hard to see how Moltmann — at least in *The Trinity and the Kingdom of God* — escapes lapsing into tritheism. Further, his version of the nature of love incorporates suffering (even suffering deliberately and directly inflicted on the beloved) to such a degree that one wonders whether the risen Christ and those who share in his resurrection will ever be rid of suffering even in their risen state. Apropos of Jungel's approach to the paschal mystery, I cannot help asking: What stops the Father from imposing more crucifixions on the incarnate Son, so as to improve their relationship still further?

To complete this sketch of Jesus' resurrection as mystery of love, I want to add something on his relationship to humanity and the cosmos. The resurrection brought a liberation from the normal, earthly limitations of time and space. During his ministry Jesus' loving service of others had been limited by the ordinary conditions of human life. The radical transformation of resurrection liberated him to be actively present everywhere, so as to affect lovingly (and often mysteriously) the lives of all men and women, to fashion a community of love which the New Testament presents through the figure of the groom/bride relationship (Ep 5:25ff; Rv 21:9), and to pour into the hearts of believers the Spirit of love (Jn 20:22; Ac 2:33; Rm 5:5; etc.). With his earthly body Jesus had reached out to heal the sick, forgive sinners and communicate the saving truth of God. Through his risen body he ministers really, if under signs, in the whole sacramental system of the Church. The gift of his risen presence in the Eucharist aims to bring his disciples to everlasting life (Jn 6:4ff), that final consummation which is "the unimpeded outpouring of divine love" (Haughton).

By its very nature love looks for or at least invites reciprocity. Here we can apply to the situation of the resurrection some reflections which von Balthasar offers about the incarnation. He notes how a "glorious" or beautiful object attracts us. At the same time, the object we love always appears wonderful and glorious to us. In brief, what is glorious draws forth our love, and what we love is or becomes glorious. Von Balthasar observes that this convergence of love and glory (or beauty) is exemplified in the incarnation, "where the divine Logos *descends* [italics mine] to manifest and interpret himself as love, as *agape,* and therein as the Glory."[22] This relationship between love and beauty, which Saint Augustine classically formulated in his *Confessions* (X, 27), bears strikingly on the situation of those who reciprocate the risen Christ's love.

After Jesus has risen and ascended (Jn 20:17) to his final glory (Jn 17:1), John's Gospel reports Peter's protestations of love for his risen and glorified Lord (Jn 21:15-17). Radiantly exalted, Christ draws worship and wonder from the universe (Ph 2:9-11; Rv 1:12ff). Some Easter narratives, even though they do not explicitly state this, certainly hint at the risen Christ's glory and beauty which attract our human love (Lk 24:13-35; Jn 20:11-18).

John's Gospel also calls to mind another dimension of the human response in love to the paschal mystery. Love makes it possible for the beloved disciple to "see" the empty tomb and on the basis of such an ambiguous sign to reach Easter faith (Jn 20:8). Love makes that disciple sensitively aware of the risen Lord's presence and capable of identifying the stranger on the beach at dawn: "It is the Lord" (Jn 21:7).

In the case of any Easter faith there is something of what Rahner calls the "circumincession of knowledge and love."[23] What he says about our relationship to mystery as such can be properly applied to the insight and love involved in a faith relationship to the Easter mystery. Because of the mutual conditioning between knowing and willing, love enables us to recognize the truth and know Christ's resurrection. The ultimate "incomprehensibility" of this mystery "forces knowledge to surpass itself and both preserve and transform itself in a more comprehensive act, that of love." This mystery is "the goal where reason arrives when it attains its perfection by becoming love" (p. 43). In short, by remembering the role of love, we both respect the freedom of Easter faith and the mystery with which we freely relate through that faith.

At the beginning of *La Vita Nuova* (II) Dante recalls the decisive moment in his boyhood *"quando a li miei occhi apparve prima la gloriosa donna de la mia mente"* ("when the woman whom my mind beholds in glory first appeared before my eyes"). The lifetime he spent exploring and interpreting his love for Beatrice hints at the challenge of Christ's resurrection. That mystery of divine love simply transcends any rational explanation to be readily comprehended by our minds. Easter first happened through the freedom of God's love and will never cease to invite the free, life-long commitment of our love.

FOOTNOTES

1. New York, 1978.
2. New York, 1969; the original, *Glaubhaft ist nur die liebe*, first appeared in 1963.
3. Ed. M. Kehl and W. Loser (New York, 1982).
4. "Resurrection," *Sacramentum Mundi* 5, p. 329; ‡*Encyclopedia of Theology* (London, 1975), p. 1438.
5. For a summary and a bibliography of Rahner's writings on the resurrection, see J.P. Galvin, "The Resurrection in Catholic Systematics," *HeyJ* 20 (1979), pp. 123-45, at pp. 125-30.
6. New York, 1969.
7. B. Weissmahr, "Kann Gott die Auferstehung Jesu durch innerweltliche Krafte bewirkt haben?", *Zeitschrift fur katholische Theologie* 100 (1978), pp. 441-69, especially pp. 456f.
8. R.C. Ware, "The Resurrection of Jesus," *HeyJ* 16 (1975), pp. 22-34, 174-94.
9. *How I Believe* (New York, 1969), p. 80.
10. See C.F. Mooney, *Teilhard de Chardin and the Mystery of Christ* (London, 1964), pp. 120, 135.
11. *The Divine Milieu* (New York, 1965), p. 30; *The Future of Man* (New York, 1964), p. 33.
12. For details see R. Faricy, *All Things in Christ: Teilhard de Chardin's Spirituality* (London, 1981), pp. 13-31, especially pp. 17ff.
13. Quoted by R. Faricy, ibid., p. 45.
14. London, 1981.
15. For various philosophical and theological approaches to love see: J. Cowburn, *Love and the Person* (London, 1967); R. Carpentier and W. Molinski, "Charity," *Sacramentum Mundi* 1, pp. 284-94; M.C. D'Arcy, *The Mind and Heart of Love* (London, 1945); R.O. Johann, *The Meaning of Love* (Westminster, Md, 1955); C.S. Lewis, *The Four Loves* (London, 1960); E.V. Vacek, "Scheler's Phenomenology of Love," *Journal of Religion* 62 (1982), pp. 156-177; D.D. Williams, *The Spirit and the Forms of Love* (New York, 1968).
16. *Homo Viator* (London, 1951), pp. 29-67, especially pp. 57-63.
17. London and Ramsey, N.J., 1983.
18. *The Crucified God* (London, 1973); see also *The Trinity and the Kingdom of God* (London, 1981).
19. *Gott als Geheimnis der Welt* (Tubingen, 1977).
20. *The Crucified God*, p. 207.
21. On Moltmann, Jungel and the somewhat similar approach of von Balthasar see J.J. O'Donnell, "The Doctrine of the Trinity in Recent German Theology," *HeyJ* 23 (1982), pp. 153-167; see also the document from the International Theological Commission, "Theologia-Christologia-Anthropologia," *Gregorianum* 64 (1983), pp. 5-24.
22. *Love Alone*, p. 45.
23. "The Concept of Mystery in Catholic Theology," *Theological Investigations* 4 (London, 1974), pp. 36-73, at p. 42. See also my *Easter Jesus* (new ed.: London, 1980), p. 137, and *Fundamental Theology* (London, 1981), pp. 147-49.

Idealism And Realism in Paul: Liberation Christology And Christian Leadership

DAVID M. STANLEY, S.J.
Regis College
Toronto, Ontario, Canada M4W1K4

One of the distinct impressions which one receives from even a cursory reading of the Pauline correspondence preserved in the New Testament is that the "historical Paul" was, through his apostolic career, continually caught up in controversy. Indeed, it is not difficult to sense that, whatever love and loyalty he inspired in most of the members of the churches he himself had founded, to the generation or two immediately following his death, Paul undoubtedly appeared as a controversial, if not totally suspicious, figure. This conclusion seems inescapable when one studies the post-Pauline literature, for example, Acts and the Pastorals. For in the interests of defending the Paul of history against censure, or — what is worse — oblivion, the authors of these documents have painted a picture, more than life-size, of the Apostle of the Gentiles. In a word, they have created a figure on the heroic scale, the "legendary Paul," which cannot always be reconciled with the Paul of the genuine letters.

The problem is compounded, of course, by the fact that there is as yet no real consensus amongst contemporary Pauline scholars as to precisely which of the letters ascribed to Paul (apart from the Pastorals and Hebrews) came in reality from his pen.

Granted, on the evidence of the letters that "there is a considerable gap between what Paul has handed on to his churches as having himself received from the Lord and the living out of his preaching by the members, is it possible to discover and describe what Paul would regard as the point of equilibrium between orthodoxy and orthopraxis?"

Before attempting to answer the question, two *caveats* appear to be in order. In the first place, in the absence of any documentation from the "other side" of the various controversies in which Paul became embroiled, one can only make an educated guess as to the concrete historical situations out of which they arose. In fact, as early as the mid-second century of the Christian era, this warning was issued by the author of 2 Peter, when he admitted that the letters of "Paul, our friend and brother . . . contain some obscure passages, which the ignorant and unbalanced misinterpret to their own ruin" (2 P 3:15-16). And secondly, we are left very much in the dark as to the resolution, successful or otherwise, of practically all these controversial issues. What, for instance, was the outcome of Paul's confrontation with Peter at Antioch? (Gal 2:11-14). Indeed, how did those volatile Celts themselves react to this angriest of Paul's letters, whom he addresses as "You fools of Galatians! you must have been bewitched!"? (Gal 3:1). Did Paul succeed in reassuring the Christians of Thessalonica about the fate of their friends who had died before the parousia? How did Paul's beloved Philippians heed his intemperate warnings to "beware of those dogs and their evil machinations" (Ph 3:2), those "enemies of the cross of Christ . . . whose god is their belly, whose glory is in their shame"? (2:18-19). What success was ever achieved at Corinth by Paul's letters, of which two are most certainly lost? One final observation is in order here . . . it appears appropriate to restrict our discussion to the notion of Christian leadership, which Paul evolved — not only despite, but because of — the gap he so valiantly attempted to bridge between the ideals set forth in his gospel and the living-out, by the Christians of the churches he had founded, of what he proudly and consistently referred to as "my gospel" (Rm 2:16). For, to the naive Galatians, he peremptorily dismissed any "other gospel" as perversion of "the gospel of Christ" (Gal 1:6-9), stating unequivocally that "the gospel proclaimed by me is no mere human invention. Nor did I receive it from any human being, nor was I taught it in any other way than by a revelation from Jesus Christ!" (Gal 1:11-12). And he angrily takes issue with his fractious Corinthians, who have accepted "a certain visitor, who proclaims a Jesus other than the Jesus we proclaimed," and thus "have received a spirit opposed to the Spirit already given to you, a gospel at odds with that you have already accepted" (2 Cor 11:4).

Spiritual Leadership

Since these (and other) intemperate statements of an angry Paul may well give any reader the false impression that the Apostle, in his zeal for orthodoxy, was betrayed into confusing leadership with apostolic authority, as has happened not infrequently in the course of the history of the Church down to our own day, we cite here the shrewd observations of the distinguished American moral theologian, Richard A. McCormick, S.J., regarding the crucial necessity of avoiding "a constant tendency in the past to identify authority and leadership in the Church." He notes the paradoxical result that:

The more there is reliance on mere authority, the less one does those things required of true leadership . . . This careless identification of leadership with office yields two remarkable results. First, an independent value is attributed to mere office, with, of course, a dominant concern for the prerogatives of office and a corresponding insensitivity to the goals it serves. Secondly, we begin to experience the controlled group or society . . . dominance of the negative in teaching . . . avoidance of risk in decision-making . . . enslavement to the traditional formula in theologizing, secretiveness in the use of power.

By contrast, "True leadership, in whatever form it is found, calls forth the best in those led. It *liberates* them into the fullness of their potential as individuals and as a group." And he continues with a description of theological leadership:

A man is a theological leader because of the depths of his insight into the faith and the power of his communication of these. Now depth of insight and power of communication constitute leadership precisely because they liberate us from the confinements of our own imaginations and formulations, from our ignorance and doubt . . . We are all victims of the oppression of our own limitations and need liberation to that extent.[1]

It is the contention of the present writer that such a conception of spiritual leadership was verified in Paul of Tarsus; that, in fact, his ideals of leadership derived from what is perhaps his dominant interpretation of the effect of Jesus's death and resurrection, redemptive liberation, and that, finally, the chief means Paul used to aid his Christians in bridging the gap between "orthodoxy and orthopraxis" were his teaching on the formation of the Christian conscience and his insistence, with those churches he himself had founded, upon the imitation of himself, as well as his stress upon the significance of "testing," "discerning," "examining" one's own Christian self-awareness, itself the effect of the indwelling dynamism of the Spirit of God. We shall begin, however, with a concrete verification, in one delicate situation faced by Paul, of the kind of spiritual leadership described by Fr. McCormick: Paul's brief note to the little "house-church" in Colossae, denominated (not quite accurately) as "to Philemon."

Paul As Spiritual Leader

From the start of this short letter, Paul eschews any injunction on the basis of his apostolic authority, although he somewhat playfully alludes to such a possibility at several points (vv. 8, 14, 21). He deliberately avoids his customary style in the letter's address, "Apostle," substituting instead "prisoner of Christ Jesus," while designating Timothy as "the brother." The so-called "Thanksgiving" evinces several novel features, which illustrate the *personal* nature of Pauline leadership. "I keep hearing of the love and the faith you display towards the Lord Jesus and towards all the saints" (v. 5). This unprecedented inversion of love and faith underscores the foundation upon which Paul has chosen to support his plea that Onesimos, the runaway slave, be returned to him by Philemon, and, still more, the all but unexpressed request for Onesimos's manumission. "It is with full confidence in your compliance that I am writing to you, knowing you will do even more than I am asking" (v. 21). Paul summarizes the prayer he had made before writing as a request "that your participation in the faith may spring into action by the recognition of *every good thing* [natural, no less than supernatural], abiding in us both in relation to Christ" (v. 6). Philemon is twice addressed as "brother," and is not allowed to forget that the runaway, now a newly baptized Christian, is "my child, whom I have begotten in prison" (v. 10); and hence Philemon's "beloved brother, immensely dear to me — and so much more to you, both as a man and as a Christian" (v. 16). For, as Paul humorously hints, as he sends, over his own signature, his I.O.U., the owner of the slave is in fact in debt, for his own entry into the Church, to the Apostle: "not to mention the fact that you owe yourself to me!" (v. 19).

Aware that Philemon, a wealthy man in whose grand house this tiny Colossian congregation meets for worship, is well acquainted with the language of commerce, Paul playfully makes abundant use of legal and commercial language. He refers to Onesimos as "your proxy in serving me in prison" (v. 13), and declares that "he has been separated from you for a brief spell" (a euphemism for "he ran away"), "in order that you might get him back as payment in full"; since Onesimos, now a Christian, has become truly Philemon's brother, instead of slave. "I, Paul, am signing my own hand — I will repay!" (v. 19). Then he adds his subtle plea that Onesimos be manumitted: "Yes, brother, for my part, I could wish as a Christian that you, also a Christian, would let me have this favor from you. It is with full confidence in your compliance that I am writing to you, knowing you will do even more than I am asking" (vv. 20:21).

The almost forced gaiety of Paul's tone throughout his note suggests how sensitive he is to Philemon's bitterness and resentment at being cheated by this slave. For this eminently successful business man, it will be next to impossible to accept Onesimos back into his household and his confidence, as his chattel, let alone as his brother "in Christ." Paul exemplifies the genuine qualities of a leader, as he seeks by every means in his power to liberate Philemon from his rancor and malevolence, and bring him to free this treacherous slave. Paul's seriousness in attempting the impossible may be gauged by his abundant use of the language of Christian mysticism, "in Christ," "in the Lord."

It is, moreover, to be noted that Paul's leadership is directed also towards the community, in this issue which chiefly concerns the slave's owner. The letter begins and ends as a communication to the entire congregation. This is not simply a matter of epistolary form, or etiquette. No one is more aware than Paul that in the Church, "Christ's body" (1 Cor 12:27), personal affairs are no longer merely private. He must prepare the church at Colossae to receive Onesimos as "a beloved brother"; and this demands that this little group, which undoubtedly shared Philemon's furious resentment over the flight of this slave, must also be liberated by growing in love, in the first place, and also faith, if this augment of one is to become true growth "in Christ."

The Freedom For Which
Christ Has Set Us Free (Gal 5:1)

The death and resurrection of Jesus is the focal point in Pauline thought, as may be seen by the fact that Paul employs some ten different symbolic expressions to describe its effects upon Christian existence. Of these, the three most significant are undoubtedly "new creation" (Gal 6:15; 2 Cor 5:17), "reconciliation" (2 Cor 5:18-19; Rm 5:10-11; 11: 25; see Col 1:20-22; Ep 2:16), and "freedom in Christ" (Gal 2:4; 5:1, 13; Rm 6:7, 22; 8:2, 21). I venture to suggest that this last was the most congenial to the Apostle, especially when one includes its antithesis, "slavery," which paradoxically Paul uses to express the same reality, his being in union "with Christ." In fact, one receives the impresssion that he not infrequently thought of his confrontation by the risen Christ on the Damascus road as his own liberation. "Am I not a free man? am I not an apostle? have I not seen Jesus our Lord?" (1 Cor 9:1); and further on, "I am a free man, and own no master!" (v. 19). He dwells at some length upon the present effects of this liberation from his former religious life as a Pharisee (Ph 3:7-15), which has freed him to pursue Christ his Savior. Paul makes use of the metaphor of the foot-race from the Greek Games to describe his new Christian freedom:

> Not that I have already won [the prize]. I have not yet attained perfection. On the contrary, I keep running hard to reach the goal, by virtue of my being overtaken by Christ Jesus. No, brothers! I do not judge myself to have reached the goal. One thing only I bear in mind. Forgetting what lies behind, I press on eagerly to what lies ahead: I run hard towards the goal for the prize of the call heavenwards by God in Christ Jesus (Ph 3:12-15).

While this foundational experience, his meeting with the risen Lord, can be depicted by Paul in terms of God's creation of light (2 Cor 4:6), and presented as God's act of "reconciling" ("All this comes from God who reconciled me to himself through Christ and gave me the ministry of reconciliation" — 2 Cor 5:18), it is also true that this momentous meeting contributed significantly to Paul's image of Christ as Liberator, who imparts freedom through his gift of the Spirit: "for where the Spirit of God is present, there freedom exists" (2 Cor 3:17). In fact, as he reminds the Galatians, who stand in peril of a new enslavement by judaizing missionaries, "We are not, my brothers, children of the slave-girl, but of her that is free. It was for freedom that Christ has freed us: stand firm, then, and refuse to be entrapped once more in a yoke of slavery" (Gal 4:31ff). "You have received the call to freedom, brothers: only do not turn that freedom into license of your earthbound self; rather through love become enslaved to one another" (Gal 5:13).

In the letter to the Roman community, Paul sums up the effects of Jesus' death and resurrection as the liberation of mankind from the tyranny of Sin and Death, personified as enemies of all Adam's children (Rm 5:15-19). In this passage, it should be noted, Paul puts special emphasis upon the *moral* aspect of Christ's work by stressing his obedience to the divine will. Accordingly, in the new Christian life, the liberating effects of the Christ-event demand an ethical response: "By being freed from Sin, you have become enslaved to Righteousness" (Rm 6:18). This gracious gift of God in Christ means also that the Christian is now free from the Mosaic Law: "As a result, my brothers, you have been put to death to the Law, through Christ's body, so as to belong to Another, to him who rose from death, that we might bear a rich harvest for God" (Rm 7:4). Somewhat later Paul depicts this divine act of graciousness as liberation: "There is consequently no verdict of condemnation for those in union with Christ Jesus. For the 'law' of the Spirit of life in Christ Jesus has liberated me from the 'law' of Sin and of Death" (Rm 8:1-2). Finally, Christ the Liberator has freed the believer from his earthbound self: "For none of us can live for himself, and no one dies by himself. If we are alive, we are living for the Lord; if we are dying, we are dying for the Lord. Hence, whether we live or whether we die, we are the Lord's" (Rm 14:7-8). "He died," Paul stated to the Corinthians, "in order that those who are alive might no longer live for themselves, but for him who died and was raised on their behalf" (2 Cor 5:15).

The consequences of this seminal insight into the liberating effects of Jesus' death and resurrection may be observed in Paul's dealings with the churches under his care. Whether he is encouraging and exhorting these communities, or correcting and reproving them, he constantly displays the greatest reverence and respect for the presence in them, individually and collectively, of the liberating Spirit of Jesus. He takes care to "recommend" his injunctions or reproof by giving reasons, drawn from revelation and elsewhere, for his use of authority. Above all, even when he is angry (as in Galatians) or hurt (as in 2 Corinthians), he strives manfully to exercise authority as an expression of the single command to love one's neighbor as oneself (Gal 5:14; Rm 13:8-10). We are given a precious glimpse of Paul's genuine leadership in his directives to Corinth regarding the formation of the Christian conscience.

The Formation of a
Christian Conscience

It may be fairly stated that Paul not only introduced the term conscience (*syneidesis*) into Christian vocabulary, but contributed largely to the theological development of the concept. The word was not in common use in hellenistic Judaism, but it figured prominently in Stoicism and Epicureanism. Paul, however, gave the word a meaning very different from the sense it had acquired among the Stoics, whose pantheism excluded the notion of a personal God. For him the obligation to act in accordance with conscience derived from the divine will. To the mind of the Epicurean, conscience passed judgment upon actions once they were posited; it was not, therefore, a source of moral obligation.

Paul was himself blessed with a robust conscience, as is clear from 1 Cor 4:3-5. In that passage he asserts that an examination of his conscience reveals that he is free of sin, "Yet not for that reason am I justified. The one who judges me is the Lord!" The Apostle here reveals his awareness of the danger of turning an examination of conscience into a process of self-justification; and so he asserts categorically that his state of sinlessness is the effect of Christ's justifying action upon him. To read Rm 7:7-25 as an autobiographical sketch is to misinterpret Paul, by viewing him as a sort of Hamlet.

In his first extant letter to Corinth, the Apostle has devoted considerable space to a question which may, on a superficial reading, appear to the present-day reader as a kind of museum-piece: whether the Christian is permitted to eat meat that had been sacrificed in pagan shrines to idols (1 Cor 8:1-11: 1). If, however, these chapters are read with attention, one discovers that they contain an invaluable treatise on the formation of a Christian conscience. Paul was obliged to deal simultaneously with the "enlightened" believer ("the robust") and the person who is scrupulous, yet easily led astray by the example of others ("the insecure"). There is much that needs correction and development in either type of conscience. The man with the so-called enlightened conscience boasts, "we all possess knowledge." Paul grants the claim, but generally attempts to bring such a one to see that mere theoretical knowledge without love and concern for others simply "breeds conceit" (1 Cor 8:1-2); it lacks "the love that builds," which helps the neighbor to grow. More importantly, it is as yet ignorant, because "it does not know God's will" (*kathos dei*). Such love is, of course, a gracious gift of God's own love: "If a person loves God, such a one has been known [in the true sense] by him" (v. 3)."By loving us, God makes us lovable," says St. Augustine.

As he lacks real love, "the robust," reveling in what he wrongly regards as his Christian freedom, needs to be reprimanded. Thus, while Paul grants, "Certainly food will not bring us into God's presence," still he warns "the robust" to "Be careful that this freedom of yours does not become a pitfall for the insecure" (vv. 8-9). Indeed, "this knowledge of yours is utter disaster to the insecure, the brother for whom Christ died! In thus sinning against your brothers and wounding their conscience, you sin against Christ" (vv. 9-11). In the sequel, Paul bring arguments from Israel's experience in the exodus (1 Cor 10:1-11), as well as from his own apostolic example (1 Cor 9:3-23), to instill in "the robust" a greater concern for the weaker consciences in the community, while inculcating the need of Christian prudence.

The "insecure" Christian, on the other hand, is precisely weak *in faith*; specifically, he cannot bring himself to believe in God's almost irrational love for himself, as well as in the goodness of the creation. It is interesting to recall a text (Rm 14:23) where Paul actually uses "faith" as a synonym for "conscience." "A man who has doubts is guilty if he eats, because his action does not arise from his *faith*; and anything that does not come from *faith* is sin." Such a person needs to convince himself that he, personally, is the object of God's love that has been demonstrated by Christ's saving death. Such a one must come to realize that he is in truth "the brother for whom Christ died." Only in this way can he form a genuinely Christian conscience, and so be *liberated* through accepting in faith the fullness of God's self-revelation through love.

It is helpful to recall that Paul is dealing here with what is specifically a *Christian* problem, which could not arise for the devout Jew who had, in the Law of Moses and in the 618 precepts of pharisaic Judaism, norms or rules that governed the entire gamut of his actions. Paul's awareness that the Mosaic Law no longer bound the Christian brought him to see the necessity of following one's conscience, and thus for himself as apostle, the duty of forming the Christian conscience of those in his care. Finally, it is to be remarked that Paul concludes this discussion with the injunction "Become imitators of me, since I am [an imitator] of Christ" (1 Cor 11:1). This notion of "imitation" is found, in the New Testament, exclusively in Paul's authentic letters and in certain post-Pauline writings that evince Pauline influence (Ep 5:1; Heb 6:12; 13:7), where, however, the notion of imitation has undergone certain modifications. Since this continual invitation to imitate himself, issued to those communities he had founded, is another means Paul employed to bridge the gap between orthodoxy and the living-out of the gospel, we must examine its meaning.

Become Imitators of me,
    as I am of Christ (1 Cor 11:1)

This habit of urging the imitation of himself, peculiar to Paul, was a practice adopted by the Apostle only towards those Christian foundations he himself had assembled, the communities of Thessalonica, Philippi, and Corinth. It never appears in the other authentic Pauline letters. Thus it was proposed only in the context of those intensely personal relationships, which caused him so much joy and grief. It should be observed, moreover, that Paul nowhere speaks of the imitation of Christ without urging in the first place the imitation of himself (1 Th 1:6-7; 2 Th 3:7-9; Ph 3:17; 1 Cor 4:15-16; 11:1). The Apostle was deeply sensitive that, as human beings, we stand in need of a concrete example of Christian values. Further, he was well aware that, in a very real sense, it is impossible to imitate Jesus, particularly in his career as redeemer. Thus, it is instructive to note that, when he cites an early Christian hymn which extols that saving career of Christ (Ph 2:6-11), he avoids suggesting that the Philippians are to imitate his achievement. Finally, Paul also knows that this imitation of himself, and *through him* the imitation of Christ, is not some kind of external copying. Rather it is an experience, mediated by these Christians' personal knowledge of Paul. Thus it is akin to that "intimate knowledge of our Lord, who has become man for me," which St. Ignatius bids the retreatant beg for in the second week of the Spiritual Exercises. Such knowledge is perceived consequently as a gracious gift of God. This imitation of himself to which Paul invites his communities is the result of a shared experience of faith, with him who fathered them in that faith: "You have not a plurality of fathers, since, as regards your union with Christ, it was I who fathered you through the gospel. Accordingly, I beg of you, become imitators of me" (1 Cor 4:15-16). Such was the nature of the apostolic charism with which God had gifted Paul that (as he knew) this imitation of himself would lead his communities to an ever deeper knowledge of Christ his Lord. For it was for Christ, not himself, that Paul made disciples. Here again, through these exhortations to imitate himself, we see Paul exercising his spiritual leadership.

Discernment of Spirits
(1 Cor 12:10)

Ignatius Loyola was led to compose *The Spiritual Exercises* out of the conviction that his own experiences of God and of Christ in the castle of Loyola, at Manresa and the river Cardoner, and at La Storta, despite their often deeply mystical character, could be useful to other Christians bent upon "seeking and finding the will of God." Thus his statement of purpose ("the conquest of self and the regulation of one's life in such fashion that no decision is made under the influence of any inordinate attachment"), admittedly bleak in its formulation, indicates the goal to which he desired to assist the exercitant: a truly spiritual experience of Christian freedom. Because the aim is an experience of *liberation,* the retreatant must be released from the strictures of "the death-dealing letters" (2 Cor 3:6) and guided towards the leading of "the life-giving Spirit" by the art of "the discernment of spirits." Because the experience is Christian (the antithesis of egocentrism) this discernment is to be carried out while contemplating the mysteries of Jesus' earthly history. Because the experience is *spiritual,* it can be attained primarily under the infallible guidance of the Holy Spirit and only secondarily with the assistance of a director. I recall here these salient features of Ignatian spirituality in order to introduce a brief discussion of the Pauline phrase, "discernment of spirits" (1 Cor 12:10), since that spirituality bears several striking points of resemblance to Paul's, being the product of mystical experiences analogous to those of the Apostle.

The two chief obstacles to Paul's preaching of the gospel were undoubtedly the judaizing tendencies of certain Jewish-Christian missionaries and the pagan philosophy of Stoicism. To explain the violence of Paul's opposition towards the first group is difficult: the precise identity of these adversaries (were they Jews as well as Jewish Christians?) is impossible to ascertain, and their teaching concerning the necessity of the Mosaic Law for salvation would appear tinged with some sort of incipient gnosticism. The challenge offered by the spread of popular versions of Stoicism in the hellenistic world lay not in its pantheism, but rather in its lofty ethical ideals, especially its advocacy of the flight into inwardness as the means of achieving the preservation of the self.

Paul appears to have correctly diagnosed the chief peril in both these errors as an attack upon "our freedom in Christ Jesus" (Gal 2:4). He seems to have Stoic *apatheia* (the flight into inwardness) in mind in his remarks to the Corinthians: "I am free and acknowledge no master. Yet I have made myself a slave to all men, in order that I may win the majority of them" (1 Cor 9:19). And to the Galatians: "You have received the call to freedom, my brothers . . . yet through love you must become slaves to one another" (Gal 5:13). His reiterated and passionate declarations that the Christian has been liberated from the hobbling shackles of the Law sprang from his conviction of the opposition between it and the Spirit. "If you are led by the Spirit, you are not subject to the Law" (Gal 5:18). He was well aware that the present earth-bound condition of every human being (*sarx*) was only aggravated by the Law that was powerless to save (Rm 7:7-25).

The liberating effects of Christ's saving work were communicated to the believer by the Spirit. "For our part, it is upon the Spirit by means of faith that we base our hope for the uprightness we await. By contrast with our union in Christ Jesus, circumcision can have no more effect than the lack of it. What counts is faith that is operative through love" (Gal 4:4-5). This text picks out the four vital elements in Christian freedom: faith, hope, love — and their source, the Spirit.

Attention then to the operation of the indwelling Spirit of God is essential to the ongoing process of liberation, since the Spirit is the source of the believer's consciousness of his true identity as an adoptive child of God (Gal 4:6; Rm 8:14-16). "We, however, have not received the spirit of the world but the Spirit who comes from God, in order that we may recognize God's gracious gifts to us" (1 Cor 2:12). The Spirit is at the heart of Christian affectivity expressed in prayer (Rm 8:26-27). Hence, Paul knows that the activity of the Spirit through the mind, heart, and sensibility of the Christian is to be held in deep reverence. "Do not stifle the Spirit: do not despise prophecy" (1 Th 5:19, 20).

At the same time, Paul is fully aware that, because the Spirit operates through the affective as well as intellectual faculties, these "spirits" are ambiguous, and must be discerned for what they are by "testing" and "discriminating" (2 Cor 13:5). Thus to the text just cited Paul adds immediately: "Bring them all to the test; then guard what is good and avoid the evil of whatever kind" (vv. 21-22). In his first letter to Corinth Paul discusses various criteria that are needed in successful discernment. Those gifts of grace that are orientated to the "building up" of the community are to be preferred to more personal charisms. Prophecy and all forms of Christian teaching hold a high place, while love remains "a more excellent way" (1 Cor 12:13). Paul puts this community on guard against the ambivalent character of certain manifestations of religious enthusiasm, which might easily be confused with the ecstatic frenzies induced in the hellenistic mysteries (1 Cor 12:1-3). He reminds the church that "No one can say, 'Jesus is Lord', except under the influence of the Holy Spirit" (v. 3). This primitive Christian *credo*, the epitome of true Christian belief, cannot be meaningfully uttered apart from faith, the Spirit's gift. Moreover, for genuine discernment, love is also essential. "And this," Paul writes to his Philippians, "is my prayer for you: may your love yield an ever richer harvest of true knowledge and a perception of every kind, so that you may test what is most worthwhile" (Ph 1:9-10).

Today's reader of Paul's letters may sense disappointment at the relatively little space in them devoted to discernment. It is a salutary reminder that this great theologian of Christian liberation was convinced that a restrictive set of regulations in this delicate matter would be totally inconsistent with his supreme confidence in the Spirit of God for the guidance of his Christians to true "freedom in Christ Jesus."

FOOTNOTES

1. Richard A. McCormick, S.J., "Notes on Moral Theology," in *Theological Studies* 33 (1972), pp. 101-102. This is the author's preface to his paper on "Leadership and Authority," in *Proceedings of the Catholic Theological Society of America* 36 (1971).

Dissent Within A
Religious Community: Romans 9-11

JAMES A. FISCHER, C.M.
Kenrick Seminary
St. Louis, MO 63775

Dissent has always been an ethical problem for both the dissenters and those against whom they dissent. When either party is a Christian, the Bible is apt to be cited as justification for one stand or another. This has been particularly true of dissent within the Christian Church, local or universal, diocesan or religious community. That the Bible has some relevance to the questions discussed may be granted. However, the way in which the Bible is relevant is as difficult to define in this particular problem as in the more general question of the relevance of the Bible to "Christian" ethics.

An attempt will be made here to examine one example of religious dissent within a religious community and to locate this within a larger context of an approach to the total ethical problem. The example concerns Paul as a dissenter within his own Jewish community. Paul never separated himself from the community into which he was born. As the Acts of the Apostles testifies, he continued until the end of

that story to preach first to synagogue Jews. At the time the
Epistle to the Romans was written (circa 55 A.D.) there was
no completely clear separation between the groups of Christians and Jews. Yet Paul's prophetic message set him at odds
with the Jewish groups. It was an uncomfortable relationship for him.

Romans 9-11: Integral

The relevance of Romans 9-11 has usually tested the
mettle of commentators. To some it has seemed a fragment
from a lost letter; to others it has appeared as an abstract
treatise on "the Jewish Question." The approach taken here
is that Romans 9-11 is an integral part of the Epistle as an
application of some of the basic insights of the first eight
chapters to a personal problem of Paul. As usual, Paul is
aware that his own problems are the problems of many of
his audience also, but the approach is through the personal
dimension.

The methodology used here has developed out of a
more general consideration of the relevance of the Bible to
ethical topics. It begins with the observation that most human decisions are reached more on the basis of images than
of reasoning. Whether the problem is a national one, such as
the Iranian crisis, or a personal one, the nub of the problem
is probably one of self-imaging however that may be wrapped up in abstract rationalizing. On this level the Bible
becomes relevant if authentic images bearing on the decision can be located both in the text and in the decision-maker. The Bible as literary work generally conveys its message in images rather than abstract or legal sayings. Indeed,
the legal sayings themselves simple mirror the way in which
the law-maker and society image the people for whom the
laws are made. Behind these literary images are the

psychological self-images which the authors used to express themselves, and behind these psychological self-images are those enduring pictures in which men have tried to express their inner nature. In contemporary ethical studies this final level of images is often referred to as "character," "root of being," "vision," "value," etc.

Antithesis And Paradox

These images challenge one another both in the biblical text and in the decision-maker. Antithesis and paradox are frequent literary ways in which the author seeks for understanding. The same conflict goes on in the decision-maker; without a conflict there would be no problem. The dynamism in the conflict eventually concentrates on a necessity for an act of faith. Far from being cut and dried, Christian ethics is a continual challenge to gain a deeper understanding of what is involved in the stance which the Christian takes. The only place that the Christian can find peace eventually is in surrendering self to a person who is ultimately responsible for the problem. This is the point on which the Bible, Old Testament as well as New, continually operates. It is "revelation," i.e., it discloses the presence of God. Whatever the abstract reasoning may be which leads to preferring one decision over another, the Christian must finally make an individual decision in faith. Otherwise, it is not a Christian decision. In effect, the Bible is better at challenging the decisions one makes than at presenting a solution to problems. It is within this general framework that Paul's problem of dissent is to be considered. He carried out a ministry which provoked his brother Jews because he was convinced that he had been given a mandate from God. He discovered that they were unwilling to listen and rejected him.

Outline of 9-11

A brief and somewhat conventional outline of the passage will serve as a reminder of what is in these chapters and locate the material to be used later. The whole matter might be entitled: The Problem of God's Freedom and Power in Choosing a People.

1. Blessings are a free act of God's limitless power

        a. All nations are blessed through Israel even though Israel is not now blessed since that is God's free choice — Rm 9:1-13.

        b. What God's free choice is now is that his name be announced to all the world — Rm 9:14-19.

        c. He achieves his purpose despite human opposition or weakness; he shows his glory by choosing us whom he prepares for glory — Rm 9:19-29.

        d. We cooperate by faith in Jesus, a rock of scandal; we do not rely on our own works — Rm 9:30-33.

2. Disbelief is an act of man

        a. Sincere belief was rare among the Jews, but not unknown — Rm 10:1-13.
        b. The unbelief of the Jews has led to the believing of the Gentiles — Rm 10:14-20.

3. Can God save the Jews?

      a. Questions and answers — Rm 11:1-12.
      b. An admonition to Gentiles: don't boast! — Rm 11:13-24.
      c. Explanation of the mystery of salvation — Rm 11:25-32.
      d. Final doxology — Rm 11:33-36.

Literary Analysis of the Images

Romans 9-11 abounds in images, most of which come in pairs. Isaac-Jacob, Moses-Pharaoh, the talking pot and the potter, Christ and the Law, the broken branches of the olive tree and the engrafted branches, friends-enemies, the people-the remnant, etc. The central contrasting image seems to be "no-people" — "my people" (Rm 9:25). These are not abstract terms, but names for definite entities taken from the prophetic preaching. In the prophetic vocabulary "my people" was Israel as it perceived itself; the odd expression "no people" was clearly the non-Jew who had no entity before God. The paradox was that the prophets so often converted the identities involved. Paul employs a great number of sub-images in the passage to picture the same reality. Thus Rm 9:22-23 contrasts "vessels of wrath" and "vessels of mercy"; Rm 9:30-32 has the "Israel of works" and "nations of faith"; Rm 9:25 sets side by side "not loved" and "Beloved"; Rm 9:8 has "children of flesh" and "children of promise"; Rm 10:17-18 and 11:8 image the community as "non-hearing" and "hearing"; Rm 10:4 speaks of "the Law" and "Christ" as the end of the Law. In summary, as Paul looks at the community to which he belongs, he sees them as consciously boastful of ethnic background, achievement, and law-abiding although they know that all has not gone well and yet on the other side he knows that they have experienced mercy, that they have a stability in faith in a promise and that they experience the presence of Christ as the "end" of the Law. All of this is expressed in a series of images which were not spun off by Paul as literary approximations but which had a concrete entity before he used them.

Nor is Paul uninvolved in the images. Each of the three chapters begins with a statement of his personal and emotional involvement:

> 9:1 "I speak the truth in Christ: I do not lie. My conscience bears me witness in the Holy Spirit that there is great grief and constant pain in my heart."
>
> 10:1 "Brothers, my heart's desire, my prayer to God for the Israelites, is that they may be saved."
>
> 11:1 "I ask then, has God rejected his people? Of course not! I myself am an Israelite, descended from Abraham, of the tribe of Benjamin."

Romans 9-11 is not an abstract treatise on the "Jewish Question," but a problem for Paul.

Opponents

The same conclusion must be reached by asking: who is the imagined opponent in the diatribe sections of the passage? Diatribe (a technique of popular preachers in asking questions and giving succinct, often ironic answers) appears first in Rm 9:14 and 30 with the standard introduction: "What then shall we say?" and a following set of answers. These questions concern God's governance of the world: Is God unjust? Why does he find fault? Do the Gentiles succeed by failing and the Israelites by working? Rm 10:14, 15, 18, 19 use diatribe in a series of questions which ask "how" or begin "But I ask . . .". They all concern the question of how it was that Israel received the message of God but did not act on it. Rm 11:1, 2, 4, 11 are questions introduced by "I ask"; Rm 11:7 is introduced by "What" and Rm 11:15 by "Who." The center of the questioning concerns whether God has forsaken his people. It is impossible to identify from historical evidence the audience who might have posed these questions and it is somewhat irrelevant to the diatribe technique to do so. The personal references at the beginning of the chapters give an indication that Paul, like other preachers who employ diatribe, was posing problems which first arose within himself and which he felt would be questions that his readers had or should have had.

To exemplify, Rm 11:14-21 raises the question whether the Good News has been preached to the Israelites since they have not responded. It was a perplexing problem to Paul since he had just reflected on his own self-image as a preacher to the nations: "I say this now to you Gentiles: Inasmuch as I am the apostle of the Gentiles, I glory in my ministry" (Rm 11:13). That mission had been successful. On the other hand, he had frequently referred to himself as an Israelite and a preacher to them (cf. Rm 9:1-5; 10:1-2, 13; 11:1-2). They had not listened. It is precisely in this conflict of images within Paul, the successful preacher to the nations and the spurned preacher to Israelites, that the conflict arose.

The Challenge

The literary images point to the conflict within Paul. The mystery of choice and rejection arises from the way in which the situation is pictured. Yet there is a paradox. The Israelites are not rejected (Rm 11:1-3). It is not ethnic descent or performance on the basis of the Law which makes a true Israelite. Within "my people" is a remnant and a Gentile group of hearers. Even the non-hearers have a future (Rm 11:25-29). The paradox is expressed in a literary way by the contrasting words which form the center of the discourse. Thus in Romans 9 the words with multiple uses center around the contrast between mercy (Rm 9:9; 15, 16, 18, 23) and wrath (Rm 9:15, 17, 19, 28). At the end of this chapter a new concentration begins and continues into Romans 11. This is based on faith (Rm 9:30, 33; 10:6, 8, 9, 10, 11, 14, 16, 17) and justness (Rm 9:30; 10:3, 4, 5, 6, 10). the antithesis to this is Law and works (cf. Rm 10:4 for law; the rest comes from the context). Concentrating on Romans 11, this centering of words on faith and justness indicates that the challenge of the opposing images must somehow result in a deeper insight into what faith and justness really mean. This can then be fed back into the images and a hermeneutic loop results which eventually culminates in the doxology which ends the whole passage.

Paul and the Jews

To put this in terms of decision-making, Paul was confronted with the problem of how he could continue to perform a God-given mission to his own people when it seemed to be totally fruitless. He could see himself quite clearly as an apostle to the nations and he could see them responding. He could see himself as a prophet admonishing them (cf. 11:13-24) against overconfidence, and that was just a matter of common sense. But when he pictured himself as preaching to his own people, he cringed. Had God's word failed? They had certainly heard the word of God from Moses on and they were zealous for it (Rm 10:1-7). But somehow they had never made the connection that Jesus was "the end of the law" (Rm 10:4). The Gentiles, who didn't even pretend to understand this, seemed to have arrived at understanding. Isaiah had experienced the same thing: "All day long I stretched out my hands to an unbelieving and contentious people" (Rm 10:21 quoting Is 65:2). Indeed, this message of rejection had been part of Isaiah's inaugural mission (cf. Is 6:9-10). Paul could not avoid the prophetic image. The mission was to preach; it was not to preach successfully. That had its mysterious place within God's design as Chapter 11 goes on to say. But the preacher does not fully understand the mystery. He could only join himself to God as an apostle, but not as a counselor (Rm 11:34).

Continuing Revelation

A good deal of attention has been given to technical details to vindicate that the contemporary application is not an exercise in subjective eisegesis. The text portrays Paul caught in a conflict of images as prophetic preacher. The literary expression is basically a series of antithetical images from the past. These chapters contain more quotations from the Old Testament than any other Pauline passage; poetic sayings from Deuteronomy, Psalms, Isaiah and Jeremiah abound. Paul's identification with those previous Israelites is strong. The final stance which Paul adopted depended on how he pictured Israel and Israel's prophets in previous ages. It was the images which were trans-temporal in his time.

Our application depends on the same transference of images. How the present author and reader react to the material presented here depends far more on self-imaging and self-understanding than on logical argument. Any dissenter worthy of the name must have a self-image of being a spokesman for God or a higher morality, and probably creates that impression. Yet such a position tests the honesty of any human being. Actual experience of protesting reveals unsuspected and cunning self interests. The desire to win an argument, to vindicate a position, to manipulate policy, to demonstrate superior knowledge inevitably intrude. In the final analysis, there is no way of proving infallibly that one is right in the *ad hoc* situation. Yet the protester must adopt an unambiguous stance, knowing all this. The test of the prophetic image is important: the prophet speaks for God and knows that he will not be heard. Such was the tradition of old: Jesus quoted the proverb, "No man is a prophet in his own country." The test of honesty (but not of rightness) is whether one is willing to be ignored.

Yet this is not all that is involved. Since the protesting is within one's own community, the reactions are not neutral but predictably unpleasant. Can one ignore the message because of personal loss? What shall be one's stance towards those who do not hear? It is easy enough to dismiss them as a "no-people." But is this true? One's own community is still one's own community. More to the point, it is God's community. As Paul realized, God had not rejected his own people. Conversely, God had not canonized them. One may say that these are good people. They may not be. They are simply chosen and chosen for mysterious reasons.

In the end, one can only make a decision out of faith. The images from the past illuminate one's own self-images, good and bad. Such images are human psychological drives which can both exalt and debase. Behind them somewhere lies an ultimate reality of who the protester really is before God. In facing that reality one defines both one's potential and one's limitations. One is forced to ask if one is really honest. If the answer is yes, then the only part of the mission which is visible is that I am convinced that my decision somehow connects me with God, whether it is objectively right or not. I know no more than an honest conviction and a willingness to allow God to act. "For who has known the mind of the Lord? Or who has been his counselor?" (Rm 11:34). Even less can one manipulate the outcome and expect a reward. "Who has given him anything so as to deserve return? For from him and through him and for him all things are. To him be glory forever. Amen" (Rm 11:35).

FOOTNOTES

B.C. Birch and L.L. Rasmussen, 1976. *Bible and Ethics in the Christian Life.* Minneapolis: Augsburg.

H. Edward Everding and Dana Wilbanks, 1975. *Decision Making and the Bible.* Valley Forge, PA: Judson.

James A. Fischer. "Pauline Literary Forms and Thought Patterns," *CBQ* 39 (1977) 209-23; "Ethics and Wisdom," *CBQ* 40 (1978), 293-310.

Robert W. Funk, 1966. *Language, Hermeneutics and Word of God.* New York: Harper.

James Gustafson. "The Place of Scripture in Christian Ethics: A Methodological Study," *Interpretation* 24 (1970), 430-55.

Ernest Kasemann, 1971. *Perspectives on Paul.* Philadelphia: Fortress.

John A.T. Robinson, 1979. *Wrestling with Romans.* London: SCM Press.

New Patches On An Old Garment: The Book Of Revelation

JOHN F. WHEALON
Archbishop of Hartford
Hartford, CT 06105

The popularity, fascination and challenge of the last book in the New Testament continue undiminished in this 20th Christian century. As in previous centuries, Bible groups of fundamentalist type continue to discover in this book signs of their times and indications of the imminent end of the world.

With recent greater interest in the Bible by some Catholic laity, prudent guidance from biblical scholarship is needed in interpreting Revelation. Happily, a Task Force on Apocalyptic Tradition was formed within the Catholic Biblical Association and met from 1973-76. Some studies of this Task Force were published in the July 1977 *Catholic Biblical Quarterly*.

Among the conclusions of this study the following are noted: (1) Revelation as a whole has the form of the early Christian apostolic letters, such as the Pauline letters, within which are set prophetic-apocalyptic visions, symbols and patterns (Fiorenza:358; Pilch:35-43); (2) Revelation must be interpreted in terms of the historical context in which it was composed (Collins:241).

These conclusions are to be kept in mind for any critical analysis of Revelation. The entire book with all its parts is an inspired, Christian book of the New Testament, with reference to the Gospel of Jesus Christ. If parts of the book were originally Jewish, they were — like the first Christians — baptized and became Christian.

In this article we will argue that the parts of Revelation enclosed by the epistolary introduction and conclusion were originally a Jewish apocalypse, preserved without major editing. The Jewish apocalypse was presented with a small number of parenthetical glosses that interpreted the Jewish text for Christian readers.

This article, consequently, is an expression of that which Fiorenza describes as the "compilation theory": "The various *compilation theories* maintain that the present text of Revelation lacks an inner cohesiveness and conscious order because it consists of a number of Jewish and/or Christian sources which were more or less skillfully combined by one or more redactors. Revelation consequently manifests the same editorial process as other Jewish apocalypses which were revised or edited by Christian writers . . . Those scholars who consider that the basis of our present text is Jewish or stems from very early Christian sources usually attribute chs. 1-3 and the epistolary framework to the final Christian redactor." (Fiorenza:346).

Problems in Interpreting the Text of Revelation

There are two areas in which Revelation has presented persistent difficulties for Christian interpreters. The first can be described as the non-Christian qualities of most of the book. The epistolary introduction, (Chs. 1-3) and conclusion (22:8-21) are Christian writings. They are Christian in concept and Christian in terminology. Special Christian words such as *Iesous Christos, Ioannes, Ekklesia, Charis, Agape* and *Uios Theou* are found only in these sections, and not in the much longer central section (Ford:43-45). But from the start of Ch. 4 to verse 7 of Ch. 22, Christian concepts and terminology are infrequent, and are found in clauses that are artificially related to the context. In this larger, central section of Revelation the usual Christian virtues are conspicuously absent. The second problem is the identity of the Messiah. The Messiah is described in Revelation as a military leader, a fighting warrior who crushes enemies. The contrast between the non-military and apolitical Jesus of the Gospels and the fighting Messiah of Revelation is dramatic.

The woman of Ch. 12, though mother of the Messiah, is not the mother of Jesus known to Christianity through the Infancy narratives. The gentiles or nations are at times described in a pejorative fashion indicative of a Jewish rather than a Christian viewpoint (see Rv 19:18-19). The lamb, slain and yet living (Rv 5:6), was slain in battle and yet lives to fight again and conquer. This is a concept certainly analogous to the risen Christ. As Ford notes, the proclamation of the Lordship of Jesus is absent from the central text, and the new Jerusalem does not have Christ as its cornerstone (Ford:17; 333-4). The doctrine of the millennium, Rv 22:2-3, is found in Jewish apocalyptic literature but has been a major problem for Christian theology. These several considerations concerning Rv 4:1-22:7 point to a non-Christian origin of this text.

That Christians accepted and adapted Jewish apocalyptic writings has been shown as not uncommon. As is noted by Russell, the Jewish apocalyptic traditions were so generously embraced by the early Christian Church that apocalyptic was eventually looked upon as more Christian than Jewish (Russell:27).

The reasons for the popularity of apocalyptic in early

Christian circles are evident. The early Church developed in the diaspora and used the LXX, with its presentation of Daniel. The early Christian thinkers found a welcome compatibility in some apocalyptic doctrines — the view of the present age as ending and God's final age as imminent, the anticipation of the coming of the Messiah, the messianic Kingdom, the woes of the last days, the divine judgment of the world, the resurrection of the dead, the future rewards of the saints and punishment of sinners (Russell:34). These were welcomed by followers of Jesus as familiar doctrines; texts containing those doctrines were warmly received.

It is known that some Jewish apocryphal writings were edited by Christians. Such, according to Russell, were the Sibylline Oracles, Testaments of the XII Patriarchs, II Esdras (Russell:34-35). Ford lists the Christian interpolations in the Books of Adam and Eve, the Martyrdom of Isaiah, I Enoch, Testaments of the XII Patriarchs, the Jewish Sibyllines, III Baruch and the Psalms of Solomon (Ford:22-26).

Because of these indications that Rv 4:1-22:7 was in original form a Jewish document, our task is to identify and analyze Christian additions and editing to that document.

Noting the obvious transitional phrases in 4:1 — the words "after this" and "which I heard earlier" — the individual who reads this text as a Jewish document will not find many clearly Christian ideas. Those clearly Christian are:

1. Rv 11:8 — the words "where also their Lord was crucified" are used in reference to a city which is undoubtedly Jerusalem. Grammatically this clause is an awkward appendage at the end of a relative clause. The appendage is introduced not with a second relative pronoun, and the position of *kai* makes this an added thought. It is justifiable to see this as a parenthetical explanation for the benefit of Christian readers. These words could be eliminated without upsetting the grammatical structure.

2. Rv 12:17 — the words "and having the testimony of Jesus" are a second appositive clause, appended to the end of the sentence. These words are duplicative and could be eliminated without affecting the grammatical structure of the sentence. Ford notes that these words are considered an addition by Wellhausen and Weiss (Ford:193).

3. Rv 13:8 — the words "of the Lamb who was slain" break the sense of the original text, in which "the beginning of the world" is related to the inscribing of names in the Book of Life. Ford notes that v. 8 is cumbersome, that these words may have been a gloss, and that they do not appear in the parallel 17:8. These words, if omitted, would grammatically improve the sense of the text (Ford:213).

4. Rv 14:12b-13 — The words at the end of verse 12, "and the faith in Jesus" are another appositive phrase appended to a complete thought. Verse 13, with its reference to the Spirit and to those who died in the Lord, is logically a sharp departure from the context. Allo considers these verses as out of place (Allo:219). Ford considers them a later addition (Ford:237). These words, then, appear in the text as a parenthetical Christian message on the blessedness of the Christian martyrs.

5. Rv 16:15 — This verse begins with "Behold I come like a thief," and continues with a sharp warning about being prepared for the coming judgment. This verse introduces a sudden break in thought, with a change of the verb to the first person singular. The verse is homiletic, and is expressive of the same expectation of the imminent *parousia* noted in the introduction and conclusion of Revelation.

Ford states that this verse, because it seriously interrupts the sequence of thought before and after, may be an interpolation (Ford:263).

6. Rv 17:6 — The words "and from the blood of the martyrs of Jesus" are appended as a duplicative final phrase

to a parallel thought. Charles states that these words give a
Christian character to an originally Jewish source, and adds
that the saints may refer to those who fell in the war of A.D.
66-70 (Charles:II, 66). Ford suspects that this may be an
interpolation, and underscores here the particular Christian
use of the word "martyr" (Ford:279).

7. Rv 18:13 — The final item on the cargo list, "and the
souls of men," changes the case of nouns on this part of the
list and presents the aspect of homiletic, Christian addition.

8. Rv 18:20 — the words "and the apostles" are found
as a part of the series that includes heaven, holy ones and
prophets. This Christian reference could be eliminated
without affecting the sense of the passage.

9. Rv 19:9b-10 — These words of the second saying are
out of sequence, and seem to be an interpolation from 22:6,
8-9. Charles notes the problems connected with these words
and their inappropriateness in this place (Charles:II, 128).
Ford states that these words may be a redactor's interpolation (Ford:311). Their Christian background is evident:
they mention Jesus twice.

10. Rv 19:13 — The clause "and his name is called the
Word of God" contradicts the previous statement that no
one but the Rider knows the name (v. 12). The elimination
of this clause would not only affect the sense of the passage,
but would improve the sense.

11. Rv 20:4 — The words "and the souls of those slain
by the sword for the witness of Jesus and for the Word of
God" are an intrusion into the logic and grammar of the
sentence. Without these Christian words the sentence would
be more clear.

12. Rv 20:6 — There the words "and of the Christ"
(Messiah?) stand as an appositive, with a possible Christian
meaning. These words could be eliminated from the text
without disturbing the grammar.

13. Rv 21:14 — This entire verse — a description of the wall of the heavenly Jerusalem, with 12 foundations bearing the names of the 12 apostles — has suspicious syntax. Ford notes that v. 14 seems to begin another structure without a main verb, so that it takes the appearance of something which has been added (Ford:333). Concerning the phrase "apostles of the Lamb," Ford says that this looks suspiciously like an interpolation.

14. Rv 22:7 — The words "and behold I come quickly" break the logical and grammatical sequence of the sentence. They are an interruption into the text, and express the theme which is major in the introduction (cf. 1:1; 1:3; 1:7) and will shortly be developed in the conclusion (cf. 22:12; 22:20).

These 14 passages have significant characteristics. They are Christian in spirit and vocabulary: they are in fact the only clearly Christian passages from 4:1 to 22:7 of Revelation. They could be eliminated without affecting the grammar of the text.

These few Christian texts, therefore, stand as glosses or parenthetical points on an original non-Christian text. They have not been woven into the fabric of the original document, but rather superimposed as patches on an old garment. These 14 glosses could fittingly be placed in parentheses, so as to make clear the way in which they were superimposed on the original text without disturbing or editing the original. A similar duplication in the expression "and of the Lamb" is to be found repeatedly towards the conclusion of Revelation (cf. 21:22, 23, 27; 22:1, 3). It can be argued that these are additions of a Christian editor, made to express belief in the divinity of Jesus Christ.

The Underlying Jewish Apocalypse

With these Christian interpolations removed, what kind of text remains? We find a carefully designed, disciplined Jewish apocalypse that in all characteristics is faithful to what we know of the Jewish apocalyptic traditions. Koch lists eight groups of motifs in apocalyptic summarized as: (1) an urgent expectation of the impending overthrow of all earthly conditions in the immediate future; (2) the end as a vast cosmic catastrophe; (3) the time of this world is divided into fixed, predetermined segments; (4) an army of angels and demons explains historical events and the end-time; (5) beyond the catastrophe a new salvation arises, paradisal in character, for the chosen remnant; (6) the transition from disaster to final redemption follows an act issuing from the throne of God; (7) a mediator with royal functions is frequently introduced to accomplish final redemption; (8) the catchword *glory* is used for the final state of affairs (Koch:28-33). Koch describes apocalyptic as not only a literary phenomenon, but as an attitude of mind (p. 33).

In his earlier study of Jewish apocalyptic, Russell lists the four main characteristics of that literature as (1) esoteric in character; (2) literary in form; (3) symbolic in language; (4) pseudonymous in authorship (Russell:107-139; Ford:26). Even more striking is the way in which the underlying Jewish text expresses every doctrine which Russel lists as the special message of that literature: (1) human history as systematically arranged and pre-determined under divine control; (2) angels and demons; (3) the imminent end of time and start of the new creation; (4) the messianic Kingdom; (5) the traditional Messiah; (6) the Son of Man; (7) life after death (see Russell:205-385).

The text is profoundly influenced by the *fons et origo* of

Jewish apocalypse: Daniel 7. From Daniel 7 it takes the traditions of visions, winds, the great sea, the beasts, animals, the one terrifying beast, thrones in heaven and myriads before God's glorious throne, record books in heaven, punishment of the beast, delayed punishment of others, the Son of Man coming on the clouds, victory of the beast against the saints until God favored the saints, persecution for 3½ years, and final, everlasting dominion of God's saints.

Some features of the Jewish text are solidly in the apocalyptic tradition: the warrior Messiah, the military hero, is met in the Psalms of Solomon, 17:24-32 (considering Pss. Sol. as an apocalypse). The description of the Messiah as various animals is frequent, and the analogy of the Lamb for the Messiah is also met in Testaments of the XII Patriarchs. The concept of a new creation after the End of history is common to this literature. II Enoch 33:1-2 describes a rest of 1000 years — a millennium — after history ends. The new Jerusalem, coming down from God out of heaven as a counterpart of the earthly Jerusalem, is also common to this literature — 2 Bar 4:3; 32:2-4; 2 Esd 7:26; 8:52-53; 10:44-59; 13:36.

Jewish apocalyptic is characterized by a dependence on the texts and words of Sacred Books. It has been estimated that of the 404 verses in Revelation, 278 were composed with OT material. Ford notes in Revelation 4-22 over 400 allusions to the OT (Ford:27). The books that most influenced Revelation are those associated with the apocalyptic tradition: Ezekiel, Isaiah, Zechariah and especially Daniel.

The message of this apocalypse, true to the tradition, is one of hope and consolation in times of distress. It is a message of highest hope, delivered in a time of lowest despair. The Jewish people have suffered through a terrible ordeal, the "great tribulation" (7:14). They have endured famine (6:6). They have lost the war (13:7), even their Temple (13:6). There has been a great loss of life (6:9-10). This crushing humiliation has been inflicted by the gentiles (11:2), and in particular by Rome (13:17). Worship of the Roman Emperor, and pressures on Jews to collaborate with the Emperor-worshiping Romans, have been major problems for the Jews (13:15-17; 20:4). In this respect, Tertullian states: "The entire religion of Roman camp life consists of venerating standards, swearing by standards, placing standards before all the gods" (*Apology* 16:8). The killing of the Jews is not yet ended (6:11).

In such circumstances of crushed hopelessness comes the Revelation. Its message reflects the domination of Rome, the recent slaughter of Jews, the importance of not worshiping the Emperor— all circumstances of the Roman-Jewish War.

The Seer (see Russell:117) is granted a vision of heaven, with God on his throne (a vision influenced by similar scenes in Isaiah, Ezekiel and Daniel). The Seer is told what will happen "after these things" — i.e., after the disastrous defeat by the Romans and destruction of Jerusalem and the Temple (Ch. 4). The scroll of history, with seven seals, is introduced, as well as the Messiah. The Messiah, slain in war, still lives, will do battle again, and will unroll history's scroll (Ch. 5). The first six stages are described, with most of them evoking memories of the recent war and with an influence of Ezekiel on the narrative (Ch. 6). Then comes a description of those with God in heaven, including a new group — those who came from the "great tribulation," whose bloody clothes are now shining white (Ch 7). Then the ultimate seventh seal is opened. The half-hour silence in heaven (8:1) is the time of composition of this document. But the ultimate Revelation is now delayed until seven trumpet blasts are sounded, each announcing in crescendo one future cosmic disaster after another (Ch. 8).

The 5th and 6th trumpets show an influence of Joel. There are hints of the Roman army, signaling its moves and attacks by trumpet signals, of protection of those faithful to God and not to the Romans, and of the Parthian horsemen (Ch. 9). Then all of heaven is described in terms similar to those of Ezekiel and Jeremiah, as awaiting the 7th trumpet (Ch. 10). Before the 7th trumpet comes a specific incident — the killing of two leaders, exposure of their corpses, and return to life (cf. Ezekiel 37). This reflects accurately the killing in A.D. 68 of the two high priests, Ananus and Joshua, and the horror of the people at seeing from the walls the two naked corpses which had worn the sacred vestments. Josephus thinks that the fall of the nation dated from that day (Josephus, *War* 4:238-70, 316, 324-5). But now the 7th trumpet sounds: God is taking charge of history; the Revelation is this (Ch. 11).

Now the instrument of God's design, the Messiah, is described. A midrash on Eve and her Messianic descendant, at odds with the devil (Gn 3:15-16) is used to describe the recent War, as seen now by Jews in the desert. The Messiah will return to battle the dragon (Rome) with its naval forces (Ch. 12). The Danielic beast is further described, with Nero *Redivivus* and Eastern allies, still trying to tempt Jews to accept Roman occupation (Ch. 13). Then comes the proclamation of the great revelation: the Messiah will return, lead a select force, and conquer Rome and all who follow the Romans (Ch. 14). However, the final Revelation is delayed for a further seven bowls of God's wrath, presented in Deuteronomic style (Ch. 15). There are plagues, cosmic versions of the Exodus plagues, with a reference to the Parthians, leading to the grand finale of history: the collapse of Rome, end of gentile power, and God's judgment on

Rome (Ch. 16). Rome, with its hills and emperors and allies, is graphically pictured as the Great Harlot, unfaithful to God (Ch. 17). Hatred against Rome, Rome's domination, opulence, persecution, occupation and crushing of the Jewish nation is expressed (Ch. 18). Then is described the apocalyptic final battle, with destruction of Rome, the allied Kings, the gentiles, the tribunes — all who fought against Judea in the war of 66-70 A.D. (Ch. 19). Then comes an apocalyptic vision of peace — a millennium of happiness, reward in heaven for the Jews who did not join the Romans, and the last judgment (Ch. 20). A new, glistening, perfect Jerusalem comes down from heaven, replacing the destroyed city, with God, the Messiah and the saints dwelling there in peace (Ch. 21). There in the new Jerusalem will Ezekiel's themes be realized — but only for those who have God's name and not Caesar's on their foreheads (Ch. 22:1-7).

The original language of the Jewish apocalypse was presumably Aramaic. Torrey makes a detailed case for Aramaic and not Hebrew (Torrey:27). He is highly critical of Charles' theory that the Seer thought in Hebrew and wrote in Greek (Torrey:28). Turner, after noting the linguistic differences between Chapters 1-3 and 4-21 (Turner:IV, 146; Ford:43-46) concludes that there are more Hebraisms in the book than Aramaisms and that the original language was Hebrew rather than Aramaic (Turner:150-158). The literal translation of the original text into Greek explains why the Greek is so strangely, artificially semitic.

The biblical base of this text has already been noted. For the apocalyptic exegete, the Scriptures carry God's revelation not only in their totality but in their every part. Therefore every word and phrase is of utmost importance and has its part to play in God's disclosure for the future. For this reason, one inherent characteristic of apocalyptic writing is adaptation of previous texts. This way of handling biblical texts shows a belief that God's Word is living and holds a message for the future, even if prophecy has fallen silent.

The time of composition of the Jewish work can be estimated from several indications. The people have come through a "great tribulation" (7:14) in which some were killed (6:9). The temple is in heaven (13:6). Jerusalem will be replaced from heaven (21:2).

There are several specific references — to famine (6:6), to a false prophet (19:20), to unburied bodies of two leaders (11:8), to horsemen from the East (9:16-19). These call for a greater degree of interpretation. All these can without forcing be understood of the 66-70 A.D. Roman-Jewish War. The struggle, it is noted, is not completely ended (6:11).

The text was written after Nero had died (13:3-18), at a time when a short-lived emperor had reigned, or had begun a reign destined to be short-lived (17:10), and at a time when the story and expectation of Nero *Redivivus* (10:8) were current in the Near East.

Suetonius described the strange post-mortem popularity of Nero, in Rome and in the Near East. Friends of Nero, he said, kept his memory alive in Rome for some years, pretending he was still alive and would soon return to confound his enemies. That popularity of the dead Nero in Parthia was illustrated by the request of King Vologaesus of Parthia to the Roman Senate for special honor to Nero's memory. Suetonius also noted that 20 years later — presumably 20 years after Nero's death in 68 A.D. — an imposter claiming to be Nero was supported by the Parthians (Suetonius, *The Twelve Caesars,* Nero, 57). Tacitus tells of an earlier imposter who in 69 A.D., shortly after Nero's death, upset Greece and Asia (Tacitus, *The Histories,* II, 8).

It is difficult to be precise, as the voluminous discussion on the dating of Revelation illustrates. The work is so studied and elaborate that it must have taken years to develop, whether by an individual or by a school of apocalyptic writers. The short-lived Emperor might be Titus (79-81 A.D.), so that the Jewish document was completed perhaps in the early years of Domitian — say in the early 80's.

In both date and message this apocalyptic work has certain similarities to both 2 Esdras and 2 Baruch.

The way in which Revelation is divided expresses the interpretation of the Book. Following this interpretation, the entire Book of Revelation is to be divided as:

A. The Christian introduction and Letters to 7 Churches (Chs. 1-3).

B. The Jewish Apocalypse:

    1. The Vision in heaven and Promise of God's Revelation (Chs. 4-5)
    2. Progressive Developments leading to the Revelation:

        a) the 7 seals (Chs. 6-7)
        aa) the 7 trumpets (Chs. 8-11)
        b) the Messiah is born and taken to heaven, and the people are persecuted (Chs. 12-14)
        c) the seven bowls (Chs. 15-16:17a)
        d) the Revelation:

            a) Rome collapses (16:17b-Ch. 18)
            b) the Apocalyptic battle that destroys all enemies (Ch. 19)
            c) the millennium and the Last Judgment (Ch. 20)
            d) eternal happiness with God (Chs. 21-22:7)

The message delivered by the Jewish Apocalypse is one of powerful encouragement. Though the Jews lost the Roman-Jewish War, the story is not all ended. Very soon God will enter the picture. The Messiah, already born, will be captain of a supernatural army. Rome and all Roman power and glory will in a short time be annihilated. The enemies of the Jews will be punished. Those killed in the War are now in heaven with God. Those on earth will be rewarded in eternity if they do not collaborate with the Romans but stay faithful to God's cause. After the final judgment they will be citizens of the heavenly Jerusalem, happy forever with God because of their fidelity.

The Christian Additions

The introduction, conclusion and glosses within the Jewish document express the expectation that the Parousia would come swiftly. That expectation is strong in both the introduction and conclusion (1:3; 3:11; 22:20). Such an expectation is of course consonant with other NT writings (1 Th, 2 Th, Heb) and of the spirit of the Christian Church during the last half of the First Century.

An expectation of the Parousia is the salient Christian doctrine expressed by the Christian redactor. Reaction to persecution is reflected in the Christian text (1:9). However, this is a reference to the trials, endurance and exile of John. John only shares his distress and endurance with his Christian readers. The letters to the seven Churches give no clear picture of a contemporary persecution of Christians: even 2:10 is a reference to further sufferings. This helps us understand why the tradition of a persecution of Christians by Diocletian — the traditional explanatory background of Revelation — have never been satisfactorily explained from historical records. The Letters to the Seven Churches express the problems of seven churches troubled not by Roman persecution but by the world, the flesh and the devil. The savage persecutions in Revelation are, generally speaking, persecutions of Jews and not of Christians.

The Christian editing was done at a time when there were difficulties with Judaizers (2:9; 3:9), and when the initial fervor of some had cooled considerably (2:4) or had increased (2:19). The major problem was that of a slackening of faith.

Presuming that the Jewish document was written in the early 80's, the Christian introduction, glosses and conclusion could have been composed at any time after that when the churches of Asia Minor were maturing in their troubles, were at peace, and could look back to the Apostle John and his suffering under persecution. The date must be at a time when there was still an expectation of the imminent return of Jesus. The Christian text, therefore, could have been written as early as the latter part of Domitian's reign, in the later 80's or early 90's, or very early in the 2nd century.

The Christian author was probably a convert from Judaism, competent in Aramaic (more than in Greek), thoroughly familiar with the Law and the Prophets and the Messianic allusions of the Old Testament, savoring those biblical texts of dramatic expression. He knew well the Christian life of the seven churches — so well that he could speak in detail of their life. With such talent and pastoral interest, he probably had risen in the Christian community of the area. If we only knew the names of the bishops of Ephesus — the "angels" of that church — around the turn of the 1st century, his name might be on that list.

He wrote, following the apocalyptic as well as the early Christian tradition, under the name of a famous figure. According to tradition, until about the end of the 1st century the great Christian authority in Asia Minor was the apostle John (D'Aragon:469). In those early Christian decades, the Jewish tradition of pseudepigraphy (as well as of apocalyptic) was being carried on. Such was the primitive Christian approach until the middle of the 2nd century, so that any writing presented under the author's actual name is the exception rather than the rule.

A reconstruction of the development of this text starts with a Jewish apocalyptic work similar to and contemporary with 2 Esdras and 2 Baruch, appearing in Jewish circles in the early 80's. Its message was typically Jewish apocalyptic: here is enormous hope in hopeless times when the nation had been ravaged. Soon God will take over human events; soon Rome will collapse; soon the faithful People of God will see the vindication of all their fidelity.

But at that very time the Jewish apocalyptic tradition was being discredited. And at that time the tradition and the writings of Jewish apocalyptic were being appropriated by Christians (Russell:17, 34). Such was this text. It was more appealing to a Christian mind than most Jewish apocalyptics. It expressed fiercely a hatred of Rome and of the deified Roman Emperors. It spoke of what would happen soon. It spoke of Jerusalem (where the Lord was crucified), of a final judgment, of an eternal blessedness with God. But most impressively, it spoke of a Messiah slain but yet living — a beautiful concept in relationship to Jesus the Messiah, slain yet risen.

There were indeed problems in the Jewish text. It was very political; its hatred of Rome was un-Christian; its Messiah was predominantly a Warrior; its Millennium was not a Christian belief. But it was a beautiful, biblically based work. So the Christian editor kept it as written, translated it into Greek, added only a few Christian glosses, developed an introduction and conclusion that showed a parallel appreciation of the Old Testament and also of the Jewish text itself (cf. 1:13; 3:12; 22:18-19) and circulated to the seven churches this salutary teaching and this warning to prepare for the Parousia.

The literary origins of this intra-Testamental book are

of considerable help in interpreting its various sections and teachings. And yet Christians who believe in biblical inspiration must stand firmly in their own tradition as they read this as a New Testament book. Any study of the literary origins of this book is in the last analysis not adequate. We must read this as a New Testament book, as inspired in its final form, as a book of the Church, as useful for liturgy and devotion, as carrying a meaning beyond its literary analysis. Its message of preparation for the Lord's imminent coming, of hope in God in spite of this world's idols and persecutions, of commitment to Jesus the risen Messiah, remains as a Christian given, as perennial Christian doctrine.

To look upon the Book of Revelation as a prophecy of events later than the First Century A.D. is to mistake its literary form.

Revelation did not foresee human history beyond the near future, when Rome would collapse. History did not develop at all in the way that this apocalyptic work predicted. Yet the apocalyptic mentality is, as usual, still flourishing among the People of God.

The lesson for the follower of Christ is that Jesus is the Messiah, that God remains Master of history, that our human expectations, predictions and horizons are limited, and that in Jesus, slain yet risen, we hold firm hope and courage in the face of this word's challenges and Caesars. This is a perennial, needed lesson for all generations of the Lord's followers until our Lord comes again.

FOOTNOTES

Allo, E.B. 1933. *Saint Jean L'Apocalypse,* 3rd. ed. (Paris: Gabalda).
Charles, R.H. 1970. *The Revelation of St. John* (Edinburgh: Clark).
Collins, A.Y. 1977. "The Political Perspective of the Revelation to John." *JBL* 96:241-256.

D'Aragon, J.L. 1968. "The Apocalypse." *Jerome Biblical Commentary.* ed. R.E. Brown et al. (Englewood Cliffs, NY: Prentice Hall).

Fiorenza, E.S. 1977. "Composition and Structure of the Revelation of John." *CBQ* 39:344-366.

Ford, J.M. 1975. *Revelation,* Vol. 38 of Anchor Bible (New York: Doubleday).

Koch, K. 1970. *The Rediscovery of Apocalyptic,* (Naperville, IL: Allenson).

Russell, D.S. 1964. *The Method and Message of Jewish Apocalyptic* (Philadelphia: Westminster).

Torrey, C. 1958. *The Apocalypse of John* (New Haven: Yale University Press).

Tumer, N. 1976. *A Grammar of New Testament Greek,* Vol. 4 *Style.* (Edinburgh: Clark).

THE FUTURE
OF BIBLICAL STUDIES

Introduction

MIRIAM WARD, R.S.M.
Trinity College
Burlington, VT 05401

In the articles collected for this commemorative volume, we have seen some of the major issues addressed in the field of biblical studies, and from various perspectives on the "hermeneutical circle." Underlying all of the essays is one common assumption: the Bible is a collection of faith documents — written by people of faith and for people of faith. Despite the different approaches and disagreements in nuances, the discerning reader will find much to encourage ecumenical dialogue.

I share some of the apprehension of those who see a crisis-situation in the area of biblical studies, especially in its seeming inability to speak to the fundamentalistic tendencies of our time, and in the dangers of the arbitrariness of some new methodologies. However, I am convinced — in regard to fundamentalism — that a biblical scholarship that challenges the faithful will have more enduring appeal, and that the current biblical fundamentalism based upon erroneous presuppositions, will bankrupt in time. As regards the second point, perhaps in no other field do scholars face the internal constraints on unfounded speculation or arbitrariness in methodology as in biblical studies. Given the vitality evident in *The Society of Biblical Literature* and *The Catholic Biblical Association,* and *Studiorum Novi Testamenti Societas,* among other organizations, judgment by one's colleagues is assured.

To address the subject of the future of biblical studies, Pheme Perkins, Professor of New Testament at Boston College, has written "Biblical Studies: Looking Toward the Future," specifically for this volume.

A true "Renaissance Woman" describes Pheme Perkins. Her writings and lectures reflect her sound liberal arts education that has made St. John's College famous. Since earning her M.A. and Ph.D. degrees from Harvard University in 1971, she has rapidly gained recognition as a leading commentator on the Gnostic writings, and as an incisive New Testament scholar. Her scholarly writings are complemented by application of biblical exegesis to spirituality. At the same time her interest in bridging the gap of which we have spoken a number of times in our introductions to the section of this volume, is shown in her numerous adult education classes on biblical topics. In addition, Pheme Perkins has been open to the world of modern technology and has mastered the computer and placed it in the service of conveying the Good News to the modern world.

In the article that follows Professor Perkins pulls together many of the threads that run through this volume: hermeneutics, archaeology, the Bible and the Community of Faith. After examining the positive and negative elements of the varied research current in our time, she concludes with a reminder that the Bible and the believing community go hand in hand, bringing us full circle from the point made by Bishop Krister Stendahl: the Bible can never be considered simply as a collection of great works of literature, but it is constitutive of and for faith. To the biblical scholar falls the exciting challenge of interpreting for each age the "living and active word of God" (cf. Heb 4:12)

Biblical Studies: Looking Toward The Future

PHEME PERKINS
Boston College
Chestnut Hill, MA 02167

A "Field Encompassing" Discipline

As one reads through the studies in this volume, one can see that much of the vitality of biblical studies has come from its interaction with other fields of study. Since the Bible itself is preserved as a written text, all of the methods of studying texts and language have their contribution to make. Since the events, nations and persons referred to in the biblical narrative belong to the world of "historical human experience" not to prehistory or to a time of mythical origins, the methods of archaeology and ancient history have their place in the field. Since the story concerns human persons and communities with their needs and intentions, the social sciences of anthropology, sociology and psychology have their claim to our attention. Since the Bible is not merely a religious or historical artifact but the foundation of the lived faith of millions of people, the religious and theological questions of our time make their demands on biblical scholarship.

This wealth of approaches reflects the explosion of what it means to understand human texts, persons and societies in our time. Interaction with the broad questions raised about how to understand our human story in the various fields of study has won biblical studies a place in many departments of the modern university. It demands that biblical scholars master methods and insights from fields that were not traditionally allied with Scripture study when it was conceived as an adjunct to dogmatic theology, ethics and homiletics in the seminary curriculum. For the future, that task may be even greater. It would hardly be healthy for the growth of our discipline to attempt to insulate biblical studies in a world of its own. The fragmentation, specialization and weakened breadth of much high school and undergraduate education makes it even more difficult to prepare graduate students for research in a discipline which must encompass many fields.

Whatever the difficulties of such a multidisciplinary approach, it will shape our future. It also contributes strength to the enterprise. The dialogue between biblical scholarship and other fields can provide a common concern that may serve to bridge the gap between disciplines. It can provide a point of dialogue with persons whose intellectual formation has been entirely within those fields about the historical, human and religious issues that emerge in biblical study. For those who are fearful that the Bible will lose its place as "scripture" in this multidisciplinary world, such dialogue, it may be argued, can and should take the place of the older forms of apologetics.

This possibility can only be realized within the horizon of a discipline of biblical studies that resists the temptations of relevance by reductionism. The Bible is not taken as "raw material" for anthropological, sociological or psychological analyses.[1] That would reduce the "meaning" of the Bible to its illustration of principles or theories within the particular fields. It would also run the risk of fracturing biblical studies into a multiplicity of sub-specialties, which no longer sought to or were no longer able to share results of their individual investigations with each other. The danger of such a future is already evident in the baffling mathematical formalisms that are presented to the exegetical community by the emerging schools of structuralist interpretation of the Bible.[2] For the present, at least, many biblical scholars wait to see if such analysis provides an illuminating perspective on the biblical texts and the questions of understanding that can be said to be common to a number of approaches before accepting structuralism in the exegetical "tool box." Though not formulated with any philosophical rigor, this hesitation represents a question about the boundaries of biblical studies. Of course any method that humans devise for the analysis and manipulation of texts can be applied to the Bible. The question, which yet remains to be debated in a sustained way, is whether every method yields meaningful insights into what the Bible is about. It may not be possible to make such judgments *a priori*. Methods of analysis emerging from other fields must be tried, and their results subject to general discussion and analysis.

Bible as Classic: Literary Methods

Recent years have seen a groundswell of literary critical approaches to the Bible. Often such studies castigate the more traditional approaches of source analysis, form criticism and tradition history for fragmenting the Bible. The older approaches, they charge, do not analyze the Bible at all but some other text or version that has been created as the product of scholarly investigation. The traditional methods are not really interested in the text but in a reconstruction of its genesis as an indication of historical development of the religion of Israel or of the early Christian community.[3] Even tradition history or redaction criticism, which claims to concern itself with the final composition, is preoccupied with the question of *theological motive* for the final text. It is not concerned with the integrity of the text as a whole. The change to literary analyses is explicitly defended by reference to contemporary theorists who analyze the dynamics of reader response, narrative world, narrator and implied audience in literature. The Bible, such approaches insist, is more like the narrative of literature than it is like the narrative that makes up the discipline of history.[4]

Enthusiasm for literary approaches to the Bible may also be fueled by the very success of the more traditional methods of historical critical exegesis and archaeology represented in this volume. In order to participate in that type of analysis, a person must invest years of study in Ancient Near Eastern and classical languages, history and culture. For persons without such training and access to scholarly resources to keep up with the developments in the field, it is necessary to invest some time in reading and attending biblical institutes such as the one whose anniversary we celebrate in order to retain a "current understanding" of the historical critical approach to the Bible. Even one's colleagues in the other theological disciplines like systematics and ethics, whose work is often affected by changes in consensus among exegetes, find the task of keeping reasonably current in the areas of biblical studies that relate to their work daunting. On the whole, we may have done better as a scholarly community in institutes such as this one for the more general public than in making exegetical and archaeological results available for the specifically theological community.

In contrast to the specialized knowledge required in

historical critical exegesis, the entry requirements for literary analysis of the Bible may seem quite modest. (Of course, we are not including the formalisms of the structuralist analyses in this category.) Much of the theoretical discussion which literary critics attach to their endeavor does not intrude into the presentation of the text. Most persons with some college English find the concepts of character, plot, narrator and point of view, dramatic irony and audience response easily understandable. The functions of symbol and metaphor they find more difficult to understand just as the majority of college English students find the units on poetry the most difficult. The prosaic, practical modes of concrete reference that make up our everyday English are, as Northrup Frye has insisted,[5] quite removed from the perception of reality through metaphor and correspondences so typical of the biblical world.

The literary critic might observe that the apparent simplicity of the method lies in its lack of a common technical language except in some schools of criticism. Good literary analysis still requires the experience of a wide range of literary works and expression. Some exegetes reject literary theories which apply categories of genre and aesthetic performance based on the modern development of literature in the past two hundred years to texts from antiquity. Such objections are beginning to be addressed by a species of literary analysis that has been developing within biblical studies, *rhetorical criticism*. Like the broader disciplines of literary criticism, rhetorical criticism insists upon taking the text as given, after whatever text-critical work is required. It seeks the internal shapes and patterns of the language in the text as a key to its structure. Unlike literary criticism, rhetorical criticism works with the text in its original language and must do so because it is concerned with the level of words, phrases and sounds as well as with broader parallels in metaphor, image and content.

Rhetorical criticism also seeks to pursue the question of genre and the artistic construction of texts in writings contemporary with the biblical material. George Kennedy has recently extended his knowledge of the history of rhetoric to analyzing the various speeches and passages of the New Testament as a person from the first or second century might have done.[6] In some instances, the rhetorical structure of the text has been distorted in modern translations. Such analysis may require that we reconsider the paragraphing of modern texts as well as their translation. In other instances disjunctions that were considered clear indications of redactional work or careless composition can be shown to belong to the rhetorical structure of a biblical passage. Rhetorical criticism is already an established tool of many exegetes and should form an expected part of any interpretation of a biblical passage.

Within the context of aesthetic and literary appreciation of the Bible, some theologians have attempted to retrieve the special demand for attention made by the Bible by speaking of it as a "religious classic."[7] The classic works of a tradition shape its culture and consciousness in a special way. Not everything that is literature enjoys the same claim for our attention and study as the "classics." Religious classics reveal the "boundary situations" of human persons in confrontation with the ultimate realities of life. That existential dimension requires that the reader engage the questions they raise at a greater depth than one might do with a literary work whose function is to entertain or even to present an illuminating insight into a slice of human life. Some critics have observed that such treatments of the Bible atribute to it a transforming power that belongs in the theological category of salvation. Such descriptions appear to be a secular translation of the Reformation concept of "inner witness of the Spirit."[8]

Bible and the Community of Faith

The development of biblical studies has led the discipline well beyond the church community. This development is nowhere more striking than in archaeology. Originally conceived as a handmaid to exegesis and biblical theology, archaeology now has its own rationale, "to illuminate the process of social and cultural change as revealed in the material remains of society."[9] Contact with new world archaeology has led excavators of biblical sites to employ new methods and ask new questions. One no longer seeks the significance of a site simply in terms of the broad sweep of Ancient Near Eastern political history. Instead, what the remains tell us about the broad spectrum of human habitation and culture is at stake. Anthropology, sociology, ethnology, geology, zoology, economics, and quantitative analysis are critical for the field archaeologist. Universities now have departments of archaeology in which those working on biblical sites and those working on prehistoric or new world archaeology are involved in training the next generation of archaeologists. Some archaeologists predict that we will see a new alignment within that discipline. Field archaeologists trained in the new methods will excavate the sites and publish those results. The application of these results to our understanding of the Bible will be the task of scholars trained in biblical studies to interpret archaeological reports. However, this new generation of "biblical archaeologists" will not be responsible for mounting excavations in the field.[10]

Church schools and seminaries no longer have the economic resources or personnel required for a modern, scientific expedition. Large, cooperative efforts are necessary and the task of "proving the Bible" will have less and less of a role in the selection of archaeological projects. The militant fundamentalism of Christians in both Protestant and Catholic churches takes such developments as evidence that the growth of biblical criticism has undermined the authority of the Bible in the community of faith. The churches should purge their houses of historical critical exegesis before it is too late and return to a literalistic reading of the Bible dictated by the dogmas of true Christian faith. Only the most iconoclastic of biblical scholars would like to see a future in which biblical studies as an academic discipline becomes polarized against a "Bible reading" church or, worse, a church which abandons Bible study for a rigid dogmatism that lacks the liberating breadth and depth of what we have learned to find in the Bible.

One antidote to the apparent wedge between the Bible and the community of faith may be found within the methods of biblical criticism. The biblical writings emerge from, are shaped by and in turn shape the community. Form critics sought the oral and pre-literary shape of the biblical materials in the cult and the common life of the people. The contributions of anthropology to our understanding of oral traditions, culture and the complex elements in the transition to literacy all have much to contribute to this dimension of biblical studies. Jonathan Z. Smith has used anthropological understanding to suggest new elements in the relationship between lists, canon and community.[11]

Tradition criticism asks how the biblical community reapplied both its own traditions and those it appropriated from the wisdom of the surrounding culture. This method assumes that even those biblical authors who might be considered creative individuals are reflecting the themes and memories that were important to the community as a whole. Sociological, political and cultic influences contribute to the emergence and reinterpretation of the biblical traditions. Scholars seek to discover the roles that the various themes of the Bible play as they are brought into new contexts in the life of the community. If particular traditions can be linked to specific geographic areas, then the archaeological study of the area may contribute to understanding the traditions derived from that area.[12]

Tradition history seeks to illuminate the growth of the community of faith in the concrete interaction of tradition and changing experience. Some advocates of literary criticism reject the historical orientation and the postulates about texts as a reflection of the community characteristic of this method. Tradition history views the Bible as "historical memory" accompanied by those interpretations through which the community found meaning in its experiences.[13] Paul Ricoeur's study of the character of historical narrative, while limited to contemporary disputes about the nature of historical investigation,[14] may contribute philosophical resources to a much needed articulation of the character of biblical narrative and its relationship to history.

A newer form of criticism, *canon criticism,* also seeks to forge new links between biblical interpretation and the religious community. This movement recognizes the multivalency of the meaning of the biblical traditions. It draws upon the results of tradition history in acknowledging that the traditions were repeatedly appropriated to illuminate, clarify and explain the concrete experiences of the community. Unlike much tradition history, however, canonical criticism focuses on the fact that the story is "God's story." It is not simply the reflection of what human beings thought about God at various times.[15] Rather than look only to the earlier or earliest reconstructed stages of the tradition as the basis for the meaning of the text, the final shape that the community gave to its traditions in the canon must also be considered in determining the meaning of the tradition. For Christians the meaning of the Hebrew Scriptures is not completed until one sees them as part of a canon which reaches its culmination in the New Testament. Within that context it is the foundation of the faith of the believing community.

Some of the critics of historical critical study of the Bible, even as it now includes the various social sciences and rhetorical criticism within its agenda, proclaim that it separates the believer from the transforming power of the text. What counts, they argue, is personal and social transformation in our time. This cry may be heard as much from the liberal "left," which looks to liberation theologies to provide the ideological underpinnings of social and political change as from the fundamentalist right, which advocates a personal piety of Bible reading. One's private experience of a personal relationship to Jesus is the foundation of salvation. The atemporal approaches of literary criticism may also be turned to such private and personal ends.

Not only is historical criticism charged with substituting a "new narrative" in place of the Bible, its practitioners are often in sharp disagreement over the appropriate reconstruction of the story. Ricoeur's study suggests that the proper telling of the historical story is, indeed, unlike the self-authenticating patterns of narrative. The historian places the issue of explanation and appropriate conceptualization outside the mere recital of the story. Historical understanding demands a separation between the individual and what he or she seeks to understand through the medium of its discipline. It is not sufficient to "tell the story." The story told must also be authenticated. However difficult the question of objectivity, it grounds important expectations of our discipline. One can presume that "facts" so-established will interlock with one another. Unlike the succession of purely imaginative works, one may also expect that there is an interactive relationship between one period and the next. Thus, it is possible to expect that various investigations can complement and mutually correct one another.

The processes by which the traditions were adopted as canon show that the community of faith understood that the past illuminates a present which is always new. Historical critical study of the Bible does not seek to reconstruct any stage in the story as though it provided a normative blueprint for discipleship today. But it can provide telling analogies to the ongoing problems of the community of faith precisely because it insists on finding meaning by locating the biblical material in the concreteness of human community.

The distancing demanded by historical-critical study is also necessary for the vitality of the community of faith in another way. It requires that we disengage ourselves from elements of our past that are unworthy of Christian faith like antisemitism or subordination and exclusion of some members of the human community. It may require that we criticize ourselves as a community and that we become conscious of the imperfect and developing faith in our own history with just as much energy as we devote to reconstruction of the biblical story. The danger with the flight from the multifaceted disciplines of historical critical study is that we will become locked in the cultural biases of our very limited present. For that reason, Leander Keck goes so far as to suggest that the survival of historical critical method and the continued existence of the Bible as the canon of a faith community go hand in hand.[16] These reflections suggest that our future is not to be forged among the academic disciplines of the modern university in any simple fashion, since the future of the Bible and that of the believing community go hand in hand.

FOOTNOTES

1. Examples of the use of sociological and anthropological methods to understand the New Testament can be found in H.C. Kee, *Christian Origins in Sociological Perspective*, (Philadelphia: Westminster, 1980); B.J. Malina, *The New Testament World: Insights from Cultural Anthropology*, (Atlanta: John Knox, 1981), and G. Theissen, *Sociology of Early Palestinian Christianity*, (Philadelphia: Fortress, 1978).
2. For an introduction to structuralism as an exegetical method see R.E. Collins, *Introduction to the New Testament*, (Garden City, NY: Doubleday, 1983), pp. 231-71.
3. See R.A. Culpepper, *Anatomy of the Fourth Gospel, A Study in Literary Design*, (Philadelphia: Fortress, 1983), pp. 4 ff.
4. See N. Petersen, *Literary Criticism for New Testament Critics*, (Philadelphia: Fortress, 1978), pp. 15-39.
5. N. Frye, *The Great Code: The Bible and Literature*, (New York: Harcourt, Brace, Jovanovich, 1982), pp. 3-30.
6. G.A. Kennedy, *New Testament Interpretation Through Rhetorical Criticism*, (Chapel Hill: University of North Carolina, 1984).
7. See D.A. Tracy, *The Analogical Imagination*, (New York: Crossroad, 1981), pp. 154-229.
8. L. Keck, "Will the Historical-Critical Method Survive? Some Observations," in *Orientation by Disorientation. Studies in Literary Criticism and Biblical Literary Criticism Presented in Honor of William A. Beardslee*, (ed. R.A. Spencer; Pittsburgh Theological Monograph Series #35; Pittsburgh: Pickwick Press, 1980), pp. 121 ff.
9. See L.J. Hoppe, *What Are They Saying About Biblical Archaeology?*, (Ramsey, NJ: Paulist, 1984), p. 9.
10. Hoppe, *Biblical Archaeology*, pp. 92-95.
11. J.Z. Smith, *Imagining Religion. From Babylon to Jonestown*, (Chicago: University of Chicago, 1982), pp. 36-52.
12. W.E. Rast, *Tradition History and the Old Testament*, (Philadelphia: Fortress, 1972), pp. 19-27.
13. Rast, *Tradition History*, pp. 30 ff.
14. P. Ricoeur, *Time and Narrative* (Volume One), (Chicago: University of Chicago, 1984).
15. J.A. Sanders, *Canon and Community: A Guide to Canonical Criticism*, (Philadelphia: Fortress, 1984), pp. 26-30.

16. Ricoeur, *Time,* pp. 175-77; Keck ("Historical-Critical Method", p. 123) insists that the various methods employed in historical criticism are tools of inquiry that have been developed so that learning can take place in a disciplined way and that the results of the various methods will be complementary.
17. Keck, "Historical-Critical Method," pp. 123 ff.

99